PROFESSIONAL PSYCHOLOGY
IN LONG TERM CARE

A Comprehensive Guide

PROFESSIONAL PSYCHOLOGY IN LONG TERM CARE

A Comprehensive Guide

Edited By

VICTOR MOLINARI, Ph.D.

A Hatherleigh CE book
HATHERLEIGH PRESS
New York

Hatherleigh Press
5-22 46th Avenue, Suite 200
Long Island City, NY 11101
1-800-367-2550

DISCLAIMER
This book does not give medical advice.
Always consult your physician and other professionals.
The names of people who contributed anecdotal material have been changed.

The ideas and suggestions contained in this book are not intended
as a substitute for consulting with a physician or other professional.
All matters regarding your health require medical supervision.

All Hatherleigh Press titles are available for special promotions and premiums.
For more information, please contact the manager of our Special Sales department at
1-800-367-2550.

Designed by Dede Cummings Designs
Printed in Canada on acid-free paper
10 9 8 7 6 5 4 3 2 1

ACKNOWLEDGMENTS

I WOULD LIKE TO ACKNOWLEDGE, all the members of the psychologists in *Long Term Care* whose practice, teaching, and research over the years has infused the clinical and scientific spirit of this book.

—*Victor Molinari, Ph.D. , Editor*

CONTENTS

CONTRIBUTING AUTHORS

CAMERON J. CAMP, Ph.D.
Dr. Camp is Senior Research Scientist, Myers Research Institute, Menorah Park Center for the Aging, Beachwood, OH.

JOSEPH M. CASCIANI, Ph.D.
Dr. Casciani is President, Senior Psychology Services, Inc., San Diego, CA.

ROYDA CROSE, Ph.D.
Dr. Crose is Associate Director and Associate Professor, Fisher Institute for Wellness and Coordination, Center for Gerontology, Ball State University, Muncie, IN.

JAMES A. D'ANDREA, Ph.D., AND ERIN CASSIDY, Ph.D.
Dr. D'Andrea is a Health Science Specialist, Veterans Affairs Palo Alto Health Care System and Stanford University School of Medicine, Palo Alto, CA.

Dr. Cassidy is a Postdoctoral Fellow, Stanford University School of Medicine, Department of Psychiatry, Stanford, CA.

MICHAEL DUFFY, Ph.D.
Dr. Duffy is Professor and Immediate Past Director of Training, Doctoral Program in Counseling Psychology, Texas A&M University, College Station, TX.

JANE E. FISHER, Ph.D., COLLEEN W. HARSIN, AND JACOB E. HAYDEN
Dr. Fisher is Associate Professor and Director of Clinical Training, Department of Psychology, University of Nevada, Reno.

Ms. Harsin is a graduate student, Department of Psychology, University of Nevada, Reno.

Mr. Hayden is a graduate student, Department of Psychology, University of Nevada, Reno.

MICHELE J. KAREL, Ph.D, SAMANTHA SMITH, Ph.D., AND SUZANN M. OGLAND-HAND, Ph.D.

Dr. Karel is Staff Psychologist, Veterans Affairs Medical Center, Brockton/West Roxbury, MA, and Instructor of Psychology, Department of Psychiatry, Harvard Medical Center, Brockton, MA.

Dr. Smith was Staff Psychologist, Veterans Affairs Medical Center, Brockton/West Roxbury, MA.

Dr. Ogland-Hand is Clinical Geropsychologist at Pine Rest Christian Mental Health Services, Grand Rapids, MI.

ROBERT KASTENBAUM, Ph.D.

Dr. Kastenbaum is Professor, Department of Communication, Arizona State University, Tempe, AZ.

NANETTE A. KRAMER, Ph.D., AND MICHAEL C. SMITH, Ph.D.

Dr. Kramer is Adjunct Associate Professor, Department of Counseling and Clinical Psychology, Teachers College, Columbia University, New York, NY.

Dr. Smith is Director of Psychology, Peninsula Hospital Center, Far Rockaway, NY.

MORGAN L. LEVY, M.D., AND HEATHER UNCAPHER, Ph.D.

Dr. Department of Psychiatry and Behavioral Sciences at Wake Forest University School of Medicine, Winston-Salem, NC.

Dr. Uncapher, Department of Psychiatry and Behavioral Sciences at Wake Forest University School of Medicine, Winston-Salem, NC.

PETER A. LICHTENBERG, Ph.D., ABPP, AND SUSAN E. MACNEILL, Ph.D.

Dr. Lichtenberg is Associate Professor of Physical Medicine and Rehabilitation, Wayne State University, School of Medicine, Detroit, MI.

Dr. MacNeill is Assistant Professor of Physical Medicine and Rehabilitation, Wayne State University School of Medicine, Detroit, MI.

REBECCA G. LOGSDON, Ph.D.

Dr. Logsdon is Associate Professor at the Department of Psychiatry and Behavioral Sciences, University of Washington, Seattle.

JENNIFER MOYE, Ph.D.

Dr. Moye is a Staff Psychologist, Veterans Affairs Medical Center, Brockton/West Roxbury, MA, and an Instructor in Psychology in the Department of Psychiatry, Harvard Medical School, Boston, MA.

MARGARET P. NORRIS, Ph.D.

Dr. Norris is Associate Professor Department of Psychology Texas A & M University, College Station, TX.

SUZANN M. OGLAND-HAND, Ph.D.,
AND ANTONETTE M. ZEISS, Ph.D.

Dr. Ogland-Hand is Clinical Geropsychologist at Pine Rest Christian Mental Health Services, Grand Rapids, MI.

Dr. Zeiss is Director of Training, Veteran's Affairs Palo Alto Health Care System, Palo Alto, CA.

HERNANDO PONCE-BURGOS, M.D.,
AND MARK EDWIN KUNIK, M.D.

Dr. Ponce-Burgos is Medical Director, Geriatric Psychiatry Unit, Pendleton Memorial Methodist Hospital; Clinical Instructor in Psychiatry Louisiana State University Medical Center New Orleans, Louisiana.

Dr. Kunik is Medical Director, Geriatric Psychiatry Service, VA Medical Center; Assistant Professor of Psychiatry Baylor College of Medicine Houston, Texas.

SARA HONN QUALLS, Ph.D.

Dr. Qualls is Associate Professor and Chair of Psychology and Director of the Center on Aging, University of Colorado at Colorado Springs.

ERLENE ROSOWSKY, PsyD.

Dr. Rosowsky is Assistant Clinical Professor in Psychology in the Department of Psychiatry, Harvard Medical School, Cambridge, MA, and President of Needham Psychotherapy Associates.

HOLLY RUCKDESCHEL, Ph.D.

Dr. Ruckdeschel is Director of Clinical Psychology, Philadelphia Geriatric Center, Philadelphia, PA.

PREFACE

O N MARCH 20, 1999, President Clinton signed the Nursing Home Resident Protection Act which will provide protection for nursing home residents who rely on Medicare to pay for their care. This Act will prohibit nursing homes from evicting residents who rely on Medicaid to pay for their stay in nursing homes. It is estimated that there are literally hundreds of thousands of such residents in this country. While many nursing home residents initially pay for their care in nursing homes, many of them eventually turn to Medicaid as their own funds begin to evaporate. Nursing home care currently averages around $40,000 per year. In addition, the President proposes an expenditure of $309 million for nursing home enforcement for the fiscal year 2000 budget, an increase of 31% over last year's level. If this legislation passes, nursing homes will be required to conduct criminal background checks for their employees, establish a national register of nursing home workers who have been convicted of abusing residents, and employ more workers in nursing homes to assist residents during busy mealtimes.

The current administration asserts that it is really vital that nursing home residents receive high quality care. To that end, there have been efforts to increase monitoring of nursing homes to make sure they are in compliance with current regulations. In addition, there have been efforts to insist that states place special emphasis on dealing with nursing homes that repeatedly violate health and safety standards. The inspection process will be improved to ensure the good health, safety, and nutrition of nursing home residents. Thus, states are now directed to investigate residents' complaints within 10 days and there is a current campaign to educate the public concerning the risks of dehydration and malnutrition and preventing abuse and neglect. Higher monetary penalties will be imposed on those facilities that violate regulatory standards.

When I was President of the American Psychological Association in 1997, I chose aging as the theme of my presidency. This was the first time that aging had been the primary focus in the 105 year history of the Association. During my presidency, I established a work group to prepare a brochure on "What the Practitioner Should Know About Working With Older Adults." A companion leaflet titled "Older Adults' Health and Age-Related Changes: Reality Versus Myth" was designed for the non-professional reader. That year we also were successful in securing approval from the Council of Representatives of the American Psychological Association for "Guidelines for the Evaluation of Dementia and Age-Related Cognitive Decline." In addition, for the first time ever, the American Psychological Association has a standing Committee on Aging.

Elsewhere, interest in aging is also evident. The Boston Museum of Science is planning an exhibit on the "Secrets of Aging" for the year 2000 which, coincidentally will also be the International Year of the Older Person.

All this is simply prelude to this book on *Professional Psychology in Long Term Care* edited by my friend Victor Molinari. He has assembled a stellar cast of contributors to focus on the most important issues for professional psychology. The book covers such topics as assessment, intervention and treatment, quality of life, ethical issues, training of professionals, basic psychopharmacology, public policy, culture and gender and clinical research.

Since we have an active training program for future geropsychologists as part of our doctoral program in clinical psychology at Michigan State University, I was particularly interested in the chapters on assessment, research, and intervention. I fully agree with the authors of the chapter on neuropsychological assessment in geriatric long term care facilities that the knowledge of geriatric neuropsychology is crucial to the practice of geropsychology in long term facilities. Knowing about the various aspects of dementia and knowing how to assess patients in long term settings is a vital task in providing the best care for our patients. With regard to intervention, we need to know about working with families of nursing home residents and we need to provide appropriate intervention not only for dementia patients, but also for patients with personality disorders. I also found the chapter on counseling the dying patient relevant and appropriate even though there has been an increase in hospice care which permits some patients to die in their own homes or that of family members.

I was particularly interested in the chapter on what the future holds for clinical research in long term care settings, since our students had been involved in such research several years ago. I liked the focus placed on ways in which clinical research can positively impact and improve the quality of long term care and the focus on the social psychological aspects of the care giving system. The chapter briefly describes the creation of a series of videotapes designed to hold the attention of impaired patients for brief periods of time in order to provide their caregivers a brief respite. It should be noted that this was not designed as a replacement for caregivers but as an overall attempt at providing appropriate services.

I was also pleased to see a chapter on basic psychopharmacology in the nursing home. Since long term care facilities usually place significant focus on pharmacological treatment, non-medical health providers need some knowledge and understanding about these treatments. I appreciate the authors maxim of "start low and go slow" when it comes to prescribing medications to older adults.

Let me comment briefly on the topic of ethics in long term care. It was good to see a chapter on this topic included in this volume. The author appropriately focuses on issues of consent, confidentiality, and competence and presents a strategy that acknowledges ethical issues and ethical principles.

Even though this book focuses on long term care, I cannot resist talking about prevention. I have advocated the concept of mood and memory checkups for older adults for several years now. I think it is as important to check on mood and memory periodically as it is to obtain regular physical checkups. While some argue that memory problems in able people are not really severe and are quite common, I counter that if that were the case, we would not need to have our vision or hearing checked until very late in life or until we were almost blind or deaf, since these problems are also quite common and are often not very severe.

Finally I just want to say how supportive I am of the focus in this volume on issues of aging and on long term care.

Norm Abeles, Ph.D.
Past President, American Psychological Association,
Professor of Psychology, Michigan State University,
East Lansing, MI.

INTRODUCTION

L ONG TERM CARE (LTC) has been defined as "a range of services that address the health, personal care, and social needs of individuals who lack some capacity of self-care" (Stone, Cafferata, & Sangl, 1987). As we shall see throughout this book, this definition should now be broadened to include psychological needs. Psychologists working in LTC settings face unparalleled opportunities and daunting challenges. Demographic trends indicate that the need for LTC will continue to grow rapidly for the foreseeable future. Almost 13% of the population of the United States is 65 years old or older (U.S. Bureau of the Census, 1996). It is estimated that there are 7 million older adults in need of LTC, a number that will double by 2030 (Stone, Cafferata, & Segal, 1987), and that more than half of the LTC population is over 65 (NAA, 1997). LTC settings include nursing homes, personal care homes, rehabilitation centers, day centers, and outreach teams providing in-home services.

At any one time, it is estimated that 5% of older adults reside in nursing homes; their average stay at nursing homes is approximately 5 years (Smyer, 1988). At age 65, the lifetime probability of spending time in a nursing home is 39%, while at age 85 (old–old age group), it is estimated to be 49%. With advances in medicine leading to a growing old–old population, the demand for nursing homes will almost certainly increase (NAA, 1997). Nursing home residents frequently have multiple problems including severe medical disabilities, impaired cognition, reduced social support, and significant psychological difficulties.

Despite legislation aimed at curbing the institutionalization of mentally ill patients, nursing homes remain a major destination for older adults with chronic psychiatric difficulties. Many older deinstitutionalized patients have merely been trans-institutionalized into nursing homes (Babigian & Lehman, 1987). The majority of nursing home residents have prior diagnosable psychiatric conditions (Carstensen & Fisher, 1991; Meeks et al., 1990; Rovner et al., 1986) and significant behavior problems (Zimmer, Watson, & Treat, 1984; Swearer et al., 1988), including 25%–50% who are physically restrained (Evans & Strumph, 1989; Farnsworth, 1977). Almost 20% of the admissions to geropsychiatric inpatient units are residents of nursing homes with behavioral disturbances (Kunik et al., 1996), and 35% of geropsychiatric inpatients are discharged to nursing homes (Ponce et al., 1997). Psychologists working in acute geropsychiatric settings must regularly address issues in the assessment, management, and discharge planning of LTC patients (Molinari, 1994).

When older adults are no longer able to function independently because of physical limitations, cognitive impairment, and/or emotional problems, but are not in need of the total care that nursing homes provide, they may be referred to personal care or board-and-care homes. This commonly occurs when individuals lack family support systems or their support systems are overstrained. Such residences offer some structured supervision for their residents, but still allow them a degree of independence. However, these sites may not be monitored closely enough by staff who are poorly versed in addressing the emotional needs of their residents. Psychologists may have the opportunity to assist in train-

ing personal care residence proprietors and in providing psychological assessment and treatment of their residents, who often have
few significant others to rely on for support.

Psychologists are also becoming increasingly involved in rehabilitation settings (Lichtenberg, 1998). Many older adults undergo-
ing rehabilitation for medical or neurological conditions require
neuropsychological assessment of their ability to maintain independent functioning. Psychological counseling may be provided to
improve compliance with medication regimens, encourage health-
related behaviors, and assist with readjustment of individuals' self-
concept. There is an evolving need for psychologists to be trained
in addressing the emotional sequelae of older adults' acute and
chronic medical problems.

In addition to the need to supply mental health services in
both total and partial care institutions, there is also a growing demand for LTC in traditional and nontraditional community settings. One report suggests that as many as 10% of adults over 65
have Alzheimer's Disease and that this number rises to 47% for
those over the age of 85 (Evans et al., 1989). Most of the care for
these patients is administered at home by family members
(Horowitz, 1985); access to a caregiver makes it much less likely
that an individual will be institutionalized. Among individuals with
LTC needs, about half of those without family support are in institutions, as compared with only 7% of those with a family caregiver
(NAA, 1997). Most of this informal family caregiving is provided
by women, frequently aging wives who may spend on average 4
hours a day, 7 days a week with their impaired husbands (NAA,
1997). Home health care has therefore become a burgeoning industry, but in-home agencies all too often do not offer psycholog-
ically-based interventions, in part because of continued federal and
state reimbursement biases against community care.

Caring for relatives with LTC needs takes a chronic psychological, medical, social, vocational, and financial toll on caregivers
(Haley et al., 1987). Overburdening of caregivers is a common
cause of elder abuse (Pillemer & Finkelhor, 1988) and a frequent

precipitant of admission to nursing homes (Lieberman & Kramer, 1991). Specialized geropsychiatric outpatient clinics or dementia evaluation centers frequently offer counseling services to demented patients and their family caregivers. Professionally led support groups for severely strained caregivers can reduce their burden (Molinari et al., 1994) and encourage them to consider in-home, day center, and institutional respite options. Psychologists are now joining treatment teams in day centers, where they can advise on programmatic considerations, train staff, counsel family caregivers, and assist demented patients in adjusting to the new environment (Molinari, 1993). They are also serving increasingly as part of the outreach team to perform in-home assessments of psychological or behavioral problems of homebound patients and may provide individual or family treatment as well.

Although relatively few psychologists currently report that they devote a significant amount of their time working with older adults (Taylor & Hartmann-Stein, 1995), federal legislation has finally created reimbursement incentives for psychological intervention in some LTC settings. The Omnibus Budget Reconciliation Act (OBRA) has allowed Medicare to directly reimburse qualified mental health services provided by clinical psychologists. Across the country, increasing numbers of psychologists are forming or joining small companies that contract with the proprietors of nursing homes to do psychological assessment and treatment of their residents. With these opportunities has come the obligation to render quality services. Standards of practice for psychologists in LTC settings have recently been developed (Lichtenberg, 1997), and it is now the profession's responsibility to develop the appropriate LTC training.

Unfortunately, most graduate schools do not furnish the requisite coursework or experiences necessary to perform optimally in LTC settings. Despite some expansion at the graduate and internship levels (APA, 1994, 1997), there are still not enough programs that offer major rotations in geropsychology, let alone experiences at LTC sites. Although the number of clinical geropsychology fellowship programs has been increasing, the current demand for geropsychological services is outstripping the available LTC training opportunities. In addition, the APA interdivisional task force's otherwise excellent document on the training of geropsychologists (APA, Draft Report, 1996) offers few guidelines on the core curriculum that should be required in LTC training.

Other than the informal network of Psychologists in Long Term Care who publish a quarterly newsletter and meet annually at the American Psychological Association and Gerontological Society of America conventions, there are no major forums for the dissemination of information relevant to psychologists working in LTC sites. Despite burgeoning research on psychological services in LTC, few resource books exist to guide the practitioner. The available sources include Brink (1990), which addresses general issues related to mental health in nursing homes; Hussian (1981) and Lundervold and Lewin (1992), which focus on treatment of long term institutionalized older patients from a behavioral perspective; and Lichtenberg (1994, 1998), which emphasize care of geriatric patients in rehabilitation settings.

The need for a book devoted entirely to the provision of psychological services in LTC is clear. *Professional Psychology in Long Term Care* is primarily written for psychologists who wish to familiarize themselves with state-of-the-art clinical practice in LTC settings. Throughout this book, strong emphasis will be placed on the need for the clinician to make accommodations for the unique aspects of older adults in LTC. Ageist stereotypes will be confronted, while cultural/ethnic variability will be extolled as both a virtue and a challenge to the creativity of professional psychologists working in this frontier area. Although this volume is geared to the nongeropsychologist, even specialists in this area will learn from the distilled expertise of the authors in LTC psychological treatment.

The first section of *Professional Psychology in Long Term Care*, which deals with psychological assessment of long term care patients, includes chapters on personality assessment, neuropsychological assessment, and medical assessment. The second section addresses psychological interventions with LTC patients; it contains chapters on individual therapy, family therapy, group therapy, interventions with disruptive patients with personality disorder, behavior therapy with dementia patients, counseling dying patients, interventions with nursing home staff, interdisciplinary teamwork and psychiatric/pharmacological interventions. The final section, which addresses professional issues in the management of LTC patients, comprises chapters on private practice consultation, ethical issues, training of psychologists, public policy, clinical research, cultural and gender issues, and enhancing patients' quality of life.

Professional practice regarding delivery of psychological services in LTC settings is still in an early stage. The psychotherapeutic interventions that benefit community-living older adults and their caregivers (Smyer, Zarit, & Qualls, 1990) may also be shown effective for the chronically impaired. However, mental-health researchers still need to study quality assurance and program efficacy in LTC settings. It is time for psychologists to become a major force in the development, provision, and evaluation of LTC mental health services. Meeting this challenge will require harnessing professional psychologists' general clinical and research expertise; introducing specialized training at the undergraduate, graduate, internship, and postdoctoral levels; developing creative nontraditional strategies for addressing the needs of multiproblem older patients; and maintaining perseverance born of the desire to assist society's most vulnerable citizens. It is my hope that the readings in *Professional Psychology in Long Term Care* will assist psychologists in defining and understanding their role in this growing field.

In this first section of *Professional Psychology in Long Term Care*, assessment is the major focus. Comprehensive evaluation of mental health problems is the cornerstone of appropriate psychological treatment. Assessment of older adults, particularly the frail elderly who comprise most of the residents of long term care (LTC) facilities, is generally much more complex than assessment of other age groups because of the greater prevalence of cognitive difficulties and acute medical problems in older adults. These factors affect the clinical presentation of psychiatric symptomatology and complicate the relationship between Axis I psychopathology and aberrant Axis II personality characteristics. Biopsychosocial assessment must inform interdisciplinary treatment.

In the first chapter, Drs. D'Andrea and Cassidy discuss general issues in the psychological assessment of older adults in LTC settings. They outline the goals of psychological assessment, the adjustments needed for valid evaluation in geriatric populations, the most common instruments employed, relevant diagnostic issues and pitfalls, and multicultural aspects of assessment in LTC facilities. Their discussion provides a valuable backdrop for the understanding of all geropsychiatric patients.

In the second chapter, Drs. Lichtenberg and MacNeil consider neuropsychological assessment. They review the common clinical syndromes encountered and emphasize aspects of neuropsychological assessment specific to the LTC patient. They also describe four brief neuropsychological batteries that psychologists working in LTC facilities will find useful.

In the third chapter, Drs. Ponce-Burgos and Kunik provide a wealth of information about the various medications, abuse of substances, medical conditions, and neurological disorders that can alter mental status in the older adult and that need to be considered in any in-depth assessment of a LTC patient.

In the second section of *Professional Psychology in Long Term Care*, the focus is on treatment. Given the variety of psychological, neuropsychiatric, medical, and social problems prevalent in long term care (LTC) settings, it is imperative that psychologists remain flexible in their therapeutic approach. The psychological techniques described by these authors, who are all experienced clinicians, are not mutually exclusive, and frequently the techniques must be used together for optimal efficacy. The authors express optimism about the potential effectiveness of these techniques in

LTC settings, noting that they could be used much more widely in such settings than they currently are.

Dr. Michael Duffy, who is currently editing a book on counseling interventions with older adults, discusses basic principles of individual therapy. He cautions therapists to avoid stereotypical countertransferential reactions that infantilize older patients and disrupt the therapeutic alliance, with self-fulfilling negative results. He exhorts psychologists to respect the psychological complexity of older adults and become aware of the unique opportunities that nursing home settings offer for natural and intimate therapeutic relationships.

Dr. Sara Honn Qualls provides advice on working with families in LTC settings culled from years of consulting experience. She emphasizes a frequently neglected aspect of elder care: the integral role that families often play in the lives of nursing home residents. Psychologists should seek to understand the historical and current relationships between patients and their families and the effect of these relationships on patients' psychological health. Dr. Qualls also discusses the importance of maintaining an ongoing dialogue between nursing home administration and families, and describes how psychologists may intervene systemically to further this collaboration.

Dr. Holly Ruckdeschel discusses the challenges of conducting group therapy in LTC. She outlines some of the common themes that emerge during group sessions, including adjusting to institutional life, grieving losses, coping with disability, and dealing with interpersonal conflicts. Given the diverse psychological difficulties that LTC patients face, the psychologist must be familiar with a variety of group approaches, including reminiscence groups, psychoeducational groups, support groups, and psychotherapy groups. The therapist needs both skill and creativity to manage the sensory difficulties and fluctuating participation of frail group members.

Dr. Rebecca Logsden discusses enhancing the quality of life of LTC residents. Presenting some of her own cutting-edge research in this area, she describes two instruments she has developed to gauge quality of life in patients with dementia. As she emphasizes, psychologists in LTC facilities should not only be concerned with those who have emotional problems but work to improve the quality of life of healthy residents as well.

The next three chapters address treatment issues for specific populations of LTC residents.

Dr. Erlene Rosowsky, who is currently editing a book on personality disorders (PDs) in older adults, discusses principles of intervention for LTC residents with these disorders. Her research suggests that PDs may frequently be unrecognized in geriatric contexts because of biases inherent in diagnosis by the *Diagnostic and Statistical Manual of Mental Disorders*. Her interpersonal approach to those with PD is based on awareness of countertransference feelings and of the ways in which these reactions may serve to further understand (and thereby generate novel treatment options). Her intervention model of assessment involves identifying the nature of the distress, any resistance to change, opportunities for positive change, and possible levels of intervention. She offers case examples of individuals with various PDs illustrating the practical implementation of this model through a coordinated approach that includes disruptive patients, nursing staff, and administrators.

Drs. Fisher, Harsin, and Hadden discuss behavioral interventions for dementia patients, and identify topographical and functional components of behavioral assessment. They persuasively argue that detailed understanding of the antecedents and consequences of disruptive behavior can guide effective interventions for such common problems as aggression, wandering, disruptive vocalization, and deficits in ADLs.

Dr. Robert Kastenbaum, internationally known for his work with dying patients, discusses the goals of counseling the dying institutionalized person and the factors that affect counseling strategies, including the therapist's vulnerability, the dying client's life course, the dynamics of the dying process, and the LTC setting. He eschews a "cookbook" stage approach to counseling dying patients in favor of a style informed by the values of both therapist and client.

Drs. Kramer and Smith then tackle the labor-intensive but rewarding task of training nursing assistants to care for LTC residents. As they emphasize, nursing assistants provide the bulk of the care in nursing homes but remain a great untapped resource. The authors provide background information about nursing assistants and their role, followed by detailed descriptions of the resources currently available for training nursing assistants. The authors urge psychologists to view these assistants as potential allies in the ongoing struggle to provide good mental health care, a practical and refreshing viewpoint.

Drs. Ogland-Hand and Zeiss discuss a long-neglected area of health care delivery: how to function as a psychologist within an interdisciplinary framework. These authors note the functions of different professionals in the LTC environment, the types of teams encountered, and how these teams are organized and sustained. Given the biopsychosocial nature of the mental health problems of older adults, and the particularly fragile nature of the nursing home population, it is incumbent upon a psychologist in LTC to be an integral part of the health team and to be able to understand and facilitate the development of effective team dynamics.

Drs. Levy and Uncapher address psychopharmacological treatment in LTC. They discuss the major psychiatric syndromes that occur, and the specific psychotropic agents that help to alleviate psychiatric symptoms. Depression, anxiety, psychosis, agitation, apathy, disinhibition, aberrant motor behavior, insomnia, appetite disturbances, and cognitive impairment may all be treated without unnecessary side-effects if physicians adhere to the basic psychopharmacological principles outlined by these authors.

In the last section of *Professional Psychology in Long Term Care*, we turn our attention to professional issues. Dr. Joe Casciani, who has served as the chief psychologist for a professional group that provides mental health care to long term care (LTC) residents, describes the nuts and bolts of setting up a psychology service. He outlines the steps to be taken to provide state-of-the-art care in LTC, the perils to be avoided, and the personal-fiscal rewards that can be attained. He recommends that psychologists clarify their roles to the nursing home administration and actively participate in multidisciplinary treatment teams.

In her thought-provoking chapter, Dr. Jennifer Moye describes ethical principles that psychologists may use as a basis for addressing common ethical issues in LTC and developing and promoting ethically defensible response strategies. Her model of ethical practice in a given situation involves identification of the relevant ethical issues (e.g., consent, confidentiality, and/or competency) and (sometimes competing) principles (e.g., beneficence versus respect for autonomy); clarification of the situation for all the parties (including patient, family, staff, and administration); and resolution of ethical dilemmas through open negotiation with all involved parties.

Drs. Karel, Smith, and Ogland-Hand offer guidelines for the training of psychologists in LTC settings, which is long overdue. These authors discuss system and reimbursement issues influencing training, describe common themes of supervisory sessions, and document available resources helpful in LTC training. Though setting up a training program demands time commitment and creativity, rewards include observation of the personal and professional growth of supervisors, and the opportunity for supervisors to participate in a cutting-edge subspecialty.

Dr. Royda Crose, the author of *Why Women Live Longer Than Men ...And What Men Can Learn From Them,* turns her attention to gender and cultural factors that affect the psychological care of LTC residents. She offers a review of the literature on the impact of culture and gender on mental health in long term care, noting that far more research needs to be done. As she explains, gender and cultural issues are reflected in patient and staff struggles for control; in such relational matters as isolation, sexual activity, and staff countertransference reactions; and in the responses of residents to the stress of institutional living. Like the other authors, Dr. Crose emphasizes that older adults are the most varied age group, and providing them proper assessment and treatment requires avoiding stereotypes and viewing each person within his or her unique sociohistorical life course.

Dr. Cameron Camp, a leading applied geropsychology researcher, describes his ongoing program of teaching demented patients practical memory strategies, a fine demonstration of the interface between research and clinical practice. Given the ever-expanding nursing home population in an era of quality control and cost consciousness, it is imperative that the efficacy of psychological interventions be empirically verified. As Dr. Camp exemplifies, there are unique opportunities in LTC awaiting applied researchers with an entrepreneurial spirit.

Finally, Dr. Margaret Norris, chairperson of APA's Clinical Geropsychology Public Policy Committee, furnishes important information on national health care regulations and finances. This chapter supplies a contextual backdrop for all psychologists who are employed in LTC settings. As Dr. Norris points out, recent legislation has dramatically promoted an increase in the quantity of psychological services at LTC sites, and it is now necessary for our profession to promote standards that assure optimal quality as well.

Victor Molinari, PH.D.
Director of Geropsychology, Veteran's
Affairs Medical Center, Houston, Texas

REFERENCES

American Psychological Association, Division 12, Section 2, (1997). *Directory of predoctoral internships with clinical geropsychology training opportunities and postdoctoral clinical geropsychology fellowships.* Washington, DC: American Psychological Association.

American Psychological Association, Division 20 (1994). *A guide to doctoral study in the psychology of adult development and aging including clinical psychology postdoctoral opportunities.* Washington, DC: American Psychological Association.

American Psychological Association, Division 20 & Division 12, Section 2. (1996). *Draft report #4 of the APA interdivisional task force on qualifications for practice in clinical and applied geropsychology.* Washington, DC: American Psychological Association.

Babigian, H. M., & Lehman, A. F. (1987). Functional psychoses in late life: Epidemiological patterns from the Monroe County Psychiatric Register. In N. E. Miller & G. D. Cohen (Eds.), *Schizophrenia in old age* (pp. 9–12). New York: Guilford.

Brink, T. L. (Ed.). (1990). Mental health in the nursing home. New York: Haworth Press.

Carstensen, L. L., & Fisher, J. E. (1991?). Treatment implications for psychological and behavioral problems of the elderly in nursing homes. In P. Wisocki (Ed.), *Handbook of clinical behavior therapy with the elderly client.* New York: Plenum Press.

Crose, R. (1997). *Why women live longer than men — and what men can learn from them.* San Francisco: Jossey-Bass.

Duffy, M. (Ed.). (in press). *Handbook of counseling and psychotherapy with older adults.* New York: John Wiley & Sons, Inc.

Evans, D. A., Funkenstein, H., Albert, M., et al. (1989). Prevalence of Alzheimer's Disease in a community population of older persons: Higher than previously reported. *Journal of the American Medical Association, 262,* 2551–2556.

Evans, K. L., & Strumph, N. E. (1989). Tying down the elderly: A review of the literature on physical restraint. *Journal of the American Geriatrics Society, 37,* 65–74.

Farnsworth, E. L. (1977). Nursing homes use caution when they use restraint. *Modern Nursing home, 30,* 4.

Haley, W. E., Levine, E. G., Brown, S., Berry, J., & Hughes, G. (1987). Psychological, social, and health consequences of caring for a relative with senile dementia. *Journal of the American Geriatrics Society, 35,* 405–411.

Horowitz, A. (1985). Family caregiving to the frail elderly. In C. Eisdorfer (Ed.), *Annual review of gerontology and geriatrics* (Vol. 5). New York: Springer-Verlag.

Hussian, R. A. (1981). *Geriatric psychology: A behavioral perspective.* New York: Van Norstrand Reinhold.

Kunik, M. E., Ponce, H., Molinari, V., et al. (1996). The benefits of psychiatric hospitalization for older nursing home residents. *Journal of the American Geriatrics Society, 44,* 1062–1065.

Lichtenberg, P. (1994). *A guide to psychological practice in LTC settings.* New York: Haworth Press.

Lichtenberg, P. (1998). *Mental health practice in geriatric health care settings.* Haworth Press: New York.

Lichtenberg, P., Smith, M., & Frazier, D., et al. (1996) Standards of practice for psychologists in long term care settings. *The Gerontologist 38*(1), 122–129.

Lieberman, M. A., & Kramer, J. H. (1991). Factors affecting decisions to institutionalize demented elderly. *The Gerontologist, 31*, 371–374.

Lundervold, D. A., & Lewin, L. M. (1992). *Behavior analysis and therapy in nursing homes.* Springfield, IL: Charles C. Thomas.

Meeks, S., Carstensen, L. L., Stafford, P. B., et al. (1990). Mental health needs of the chronically mentally ill elderly. *Psychology and Aging, 5,* 163–171.

Molinari, V. (1993). Psychological consultation to an Alzheimer Disease Day Center. *Psychologists in Long Term Care Newsletter, 7,* Winter, 6–8.

Molinari, V. (1994). The inpatient geropsychologist's role in LTC planning. *Psychologists in Long Term Care Newsletter, 8,* Winter, 8–9.

Molinari, V., Nelson, N., Shekelle, S., & Crothers, M. (1994). Family support groups of the Alzheimer's Association: An analysis of attendees and nonattendees. *Journal of Applied Gerontology, 13,* 86–98.

National Academy on Aging. (1997, September). Facts on long term care. *Gerontology News.* (Fact Sheet).

Pillemer, K., & Finkelhor, D. (1988). The prevalence of elder abuse: A random sample survey. *The Gerontologist, 28,* 51–56.

Psychological services in long term care: "Standards for practice," (Chair, R. Crose). Symposium presented at the *American Psychological Association Meeting,* Toronto, August 1996.

Rosowsky, E., Abrams, R. C., & Zweig, R. A. (1999). Personality disorders in older adults: Emerging issues in diagnosis and treatment. Hillsdale, New Jersey: Lawrence Erlbaum.

Rovner, B. W., Kafonek, S., Filip, L., Lucas, M. J., & Folstein, M. F. (1986). Prevalence of mental illness in a community nursing home. *American Journal of Psychiatry, 143,* 1446–1449.

Smyer, M. A. (1988). The nursing home community. In M. A. Smyer, M. D., Cohn, & D. Brannon (Eds.), *Mental health consultation in nursing homes* (pp. 1–24). New York: New York University Press.

Smyer, M., Zarit, S., & Qualls, S. H. (1990). Psychological interventions with the aging individual. In J. Birren & K. W. Schaie (Eds.), *Handbook of the psychology of aging* (3rd ed., pp. 375–403). New York: Academic Press.

Stone, R., Cafferata, G. L., & Sangl, J. (1987). Caregivers of the frail elderly: A national profile. *The Gerontologist, 27,* 616–626.

Swearer, J. M., Drachman, D. A., O'Donnell, B. F., & Mitchell, A. L. (1988). Troublesome and disruptive behaviors in dementia: Relationships to diagnosis and disease severity. *Journal of the American Geriatrics Society, 36*, 784–790.

Taylor, G. P., & Hartman-Stein, P. (1995). Providing psychological services to older adults: Opportunities for psychologists to sail beyond the sunset. *The Clinical Psychologist, 48*, Spring, 5–11.

U. S. Bureau of the Census (1996). *65th in the United States.* (Current population report, special studies, pp. 23–190). Washington, DC: U. S. Government Printing Office.

Zimmer, J. G., Watson, N. G., & Treat, A. (1984). Behavioral problems among patients in nursing home facilities. *American Journal of Public Health, 76*, 1118–1121.

1

Assessment of Psychopathology

JAMES A. D'ANDREA, PH.D.,

and ERIN CASSIDY, PH.D.

This work was supported in part by grants T32 MH19104 and MH40041 from the National Institute of Mental Health. This work was completed while both authors were at the Older Adult and Family Research Center at the Veterans Affairs Palo Health Care System.

The authors wish to acknowledge the invaluable assistance received from Dolores Gallagher-Thompson, PH.D., ABPP, who provided consultation throughout the preparation of this manuscript.

Abstract

WHETHER OUT of interest, demand, or necessity, psychologists are being called upon increasingly to contribute to the care of residents in long term care facilities. This chapter will serve as an initial guide for practitioners who wish to learn more about opportunities existing in this environment, including professional roles, the nature of this type of work, and how to provide useful information to an interdisciplinary treatment team. Suggestions, with regard to conducting psychological assessments of individual residents, including important methods and areas of concentration, are discussed along with the handling common referral questions. In addition, frequently seen cognitive and affective disorders, such as delirium, dementia, and depression are described to further facilitate the prompt recognition of these disorders to aid in treatment planning. To assist in this task, a sampling of useful measurement instruments for cognitive, functional, affective, and personality arenas are briefly reported. Finally, suggested readings, for those looking for a more in depth review of a particular area, are provided at the end of the chapter.

Introduction

As Americans age, there will be an increasing need for clinicians who are proficient in assessing older adults who reside in long term care (LTC) facilities. The number institutionalized elderly was projected to increase from 5.6 million in 1990 to 7.3 million in 2010 (Zedlewski et al., 1990). Mental health professionals will increasingly be called upon to assess a range of problems affecting the elderly, including changes in cognitive function, personality, mood, behavior, and the capacity to make decisions independently. Institutional staff will use these assessments to determine how to address such problems and improve the quality of life for the older persons under their care.

Preparing to Conduct an Assessment

Gathering Background Information:

The first step in addressing the psychological, social, and behavioral problems of older adults is gathering the appropriate background information.

In doing so, it is important to examine stereotypes that may influence how family members, institutional staff, and even mental health professionals perceive, interact with, and treat older patients. Clinicians must be cognizant of such assumptions and myths, which could undermine their work. **Anderson** (1990) **advises allowing older patients an adequate amount of time to respond to**

questions, without presuming cognitive decline or assuming that these individuals are incapable of changing.

History/Baseline Functioning

Clinicians gathering historical information should talk with family members and past caregivers as well as elicit information directly from patients. It is helpful not only to inquire about the history of the presenting problem or issue, but also to ask about the patient's educational level, current and previous family relationships, contact with mental health professionals, medical problems, and other issues.

Health Status

As patients get older, it becomes increasingly important to assess their medical status. Elderly patients are much more likely to have physical ailments than younger patients, and those ailments are likely to be more complicated. Such medical conditions often have a direct impact on their emotions and behavior. **It is important not only to get a clear picture of patients' current physical health, but to reassess the situation periodically, taking into consideration the environmental influences and constraints that might affect their ability to set therapy goals and participate in specific interventions** (Ham & Sloane, 1992). It is also necessary to evaluate each patient's cognitive status and functional level. Those with compromised cognitive skills will need to be assessed differently than those with intact cognitive skills, and different recommendations may need to be made.

Life Situation

Clinicians should also look at the current life situation of older individuals. Are they living at home? Do they live alone or with a partner? Are they working or retired? In addition, clinicians should inquire about patients' goals. This is where the interplay between diagnostic relevance and functional ability enters the clinical picture. In other words, do their expectations match well with what they are likely to achieve as a result of treatment? At times, modifying initial goals or changing the patients' expectations can help cultivate the motivation needed for therapeutic progress. Once this initial information is gathered, the clinician can more clearly formulate the goals of the assessment in terms of what each patient wants and what each patient is capable of achieving.

Special Considerations in Assessing Older Adults:

Clinicians must take into account the older adult's particular characteristics and needs when preparing to make an assessment. These differences can affect many aspects of the assessment process, including establishing a rapport, deciding whether to use touch, choosing a certain manner of speaking, and deciding whether to approach patients in additional ways, such as through written materials and printed symbols.

Rapport

To develop a rapport with patients, the clinician must elicit pertinent information from them and provide them with information they need, as well as display empathy. In each case, clinicians must choose a course of action that will facilitate the best use of the time spent with the patient (Othmer & Othmer, 1994). It may be helpful to approach older adults more formally than other patients, with a full introduction and explanation of what you do and why you need to talk with them. Use their title and surname initially and ask how they prefer to be addressed.

Touch

Using touch appropriately is another crucial aspect of developing a rapport with the individual. Handshakes and other forms of touch can be used to show respect and support. As in any situation, do what feels most comfortable for you and the patient, being careful to respect the patient's personal space.

Speech

It is helpful to speak to the older adult in a lower pitch while enunciating your words clearly; it is not helpful to raise the volume of your voice. **Studies have shown that the use of patronizing speech, which is louder and has an exaggerated intonation, may be interpreted as less respectful by some nursing home residents** (Ryan, et al., 1991). It is important to get to know each individual and adjust your communication style accordingly.

Written Information

Clinicians using written instruments should have copies with enlarged print available. If the patient has difficulty understanding verbal communication, don't assume that the difficulty is due to cognitive limitations. Try eliciting information in alternative ways, such as by writing your questions down. "Communication boards," which have enlarged letters and symbols representing common activities and needs, may be used with nonspeaking older persons who might have trouble writing the information.

Evaluating Referral Questions:

In preparing to conduct an assessment, it is important to begin by reviewing the nature of the referral question, identifying the person who will receive the feedback, explaining how to formulate feedback in a useful way and how to follow up in the future, if necessary. **The referral question is central to guiding the subsequent assessment;** it will tell you what the goal of the assessment is going to be. Separating the *who, what, why,* and *where* of the referral question will facilitate preparation for the assessment.

Who?

Knowing *who* is making the request will help you to determine what type of information is being sought, what it is

likely to be used for, and what "language" to use in writing the results. For example, if another mental health professional has requested the assessment, the writing style can be professional in tone. If, on the other hand, the family or the extended care staff in a residential facility has requested the assessment, then the language should be free of professional jargon and state conclusions and future recommendations clearly in terms that family members or staff can understand.

What?

The *what* of the referral question will help you determine the topics you need to gather the most information about. For example, if the charge nurse in an extended care facility has referred a patient who is disruptive during group activities for assessment, then you will probably focus more on a behavioral assessment than on the appropriateness of the patient's future discharge plans. In contrast, a request to assess the level and severity of depression may require the use of questionnaires, a detailed interview, and a description of the observations reported by family or staff. Older adults have complicated medical, psychological, and social interactions, so the key to solving a problem may not be clear initially.

Why?

Clarifying *why* the assessment referral was made is important in determining who actually has the problem, whom it is affecting, and what an assessment will do for all those involved. Is the motivating factor for the referral a desire to increase the quality of life for the patient or LTC resident, or for the staff's convenience?

Where?

Determining *where* the assessment will take place is also important. Clinicians who conduct assessments in an LTC

setting can tap many resources, including the patient's self-report, the clinical interview, a review of the patient's chart, and interviews with staff members and the patient's caregivers and family members. Of course, if the LTC resident can provide information about his or her situation and displays no cognitive impairments or only minimal ones, then he or she should be interviewed thoroughly. Assessments may also take place in the patient's home or in a regular office setting. Wherever the assessment occurs, the clinician must provide comfortable conditions, such as a table surface on which to write, good lighting, and sufficiently low noise levels to allow effective communication. They must also consider in advance whether to include family members, prepare to explain confidentiality rules and limitations, and ensure that the client's needs for privacy will be met.

Accessing the Resources of the Multi/Interdisciplinary Team:

The multidisciplinary team, comprised of the professionals and other individuals involved in a patient's care may be an excellent source of assessment information. A care team in a residential setting may, for instance, include a physician, a nurse, an aide, a social worker, a pharmacist, and (unfortunately more rarely) a psychologist. Important information about a patient's condition can sometimes also be elicited from security or housekeeping staff, even though they are not involved in direct patient care. The various team members may both provide information and support and serve as catalysts for change throughout the assessment process. For example, in the case of a patient who was angry and agitated, it would be counterproductive to formulate a behavior modification plan for the staff to implement if the true cause of the behavior problem was a recent change in medication. If, however, the clinician spoke with the pharmacist or psychiatric nurse to clarify this matter ahead of time, the assessment report and subsequent treatment recommendations would be far more effective.

Using Referral Questions to Guide the Assessment Process

LTC patients are often referred because of problem behaviors that disrupt activities in their institution and/or place other individuals at risk for physical or emotional harm. For instance, Ms. G may yell at staff members when they attempt to direct her to the dining room at mealtimes. In this case, the referral question might be: What can be done to stop her from yelling?

Another example is Mr. M, a patient with dementia who frequently wanders throughout the nursing home when he is nervous or depressed. Attempts to get him to return to an activity or to his room often result in his becoming verbally abusive. In this case, the referral question might ask whether these behavior problems are due to serious untreated depression.

Determining the Role of the Observed Behavior:

The first step in an assessment involves gathering information from the referring party and from others who have encountered the individual. Valuable resources are nurses aides (who often have the most contact with patients), nursing notes (which document patient behaviors over time and thus may reveal a pattern), and sometimes other residents who are alert and aware of their surroundings. **Whenever possible, the evaluator should also attempt to observe the behavior that is considered problematic.** In observing the patient first hand and paying attention to what happens before, during, and after the target behavior or emotional outburst, the evaluator should ask the following questions:

- **At what time of day does the behavior occur?**
- **What is going on around the patient when the behavior occurs?**
- **Who is around at the time of and just before the behavior in question?**
- **What happens immediately after the behavior is exhibited?**

Such questions will help the practitioner determine the role of the observed behavior. In other words, **is the patient using the behavior to avoid doing something unpleasant, to get positive or negative reinforcement, or to ensure that he or she will be removed from an averse situation?** Adverse behaviors can be triggered by something as simple as overstimulation of a patient with dementia or as complicated as a toxic drug reaction. For example, if we examine the case of Ms. G, we might learn (after carefully observing her) that she only acts out during mealtimes when in the dining room; she is then immediately escorted to the quiet atmosphere of her room, where she finishes her meal. In other words, the resident may find the noisy environment of the dining room averse, and she has found that disruptive behavior results in her being removed from it. This is a need that many residents could communicate directly; however, because of brain damage or other limitations, some residents rely on more primitive means of influencing their environment. Once the role of a patient's behavior is determined, the clinician can formulate an appropriate intervention to decrease or eliminate any behavior that is potentially harmful. By contrast, Mr. M needs a more traditional assessment for depression, including differential assessment of depression versus dementia, which is described in detail below.

The Need for Follow-Up:

The need for follow-up is determined, in part, by the relationship between the mental health practitioner conducting the assessment and the referral source. If the referring agency is a nursing home with which the practitioner is fairly constantly involved, then it may be both convenient and helpful for that professional to remain accessible and involved. By giving feedback on the results of the assessment, along with suggestions for intervention, the clinician increases the likelihood that the assessment information will be used to improve the patient's quality of life. **Follow-up is especially important in cases involving a detailed and complex psychological assessment.** The patients often benefit from repeated testing and examination over time to monitor any change in their functional level. This follow-up work also allows the practitioner to confirm or replicate diagnostic findings or modify these findings as needed.

The "Four Ds": Delirium, Dementia, Depression, and Delusional States

Psychologists are likely to be consulted in LTC settings when patients exhibit dramatic changes in their mental status, more gradual declines in cognitive function, depressed mood, and/or other delusional or psychotic behavior. Each of these problems entails a different assessment procedure.

Delirium:

Delirium is an acute shift in mental status that often leads to confusion and disorientation. Schogt and Myran (1992) describe it as a "wandering of the mind" in which "people seem to be in a world of their own, often unable to tell whether it is night or day, what meal they have just had, and sometimes even where they are." *The Diagnostic and Statistical Manual of Mental Disorders*, fourth edition (*DSM-IV*) (American Psychiatric Association, 1994), specifies that a delirious patient must exhibit impaired attention, deterioration in cognitive thinking, and rapid onset with fluctuating course.

Although delirium and dementia may initially appear to be similar, there are significant differences between them (Gintner, 1995). First, impaired attention does not need to be present in dementia. Second, delirium develops rapidly and has a fluctuating course, whereas in dementia, symptoms are relatively stable and develop over time. Third, delirium may have a reversible cause, while the progressive dementias do not. A wide variety of medical conditions may cause delirium, including medication reactions, substance abuse, hypoxia, infections (e.g., urinary tract infections), metabolic imbalances (including those caused during dialysis), and poor nutritional status.

To assess delirium, it is important to obtain a thorough history to document the course of symptom development and to assist in identifying a reversible cause. Often more than one mental status assessment (such as the Mini-Mental State Exam [MMSE], described below) needs to be performed to document fluctuations in sensorium. A useful method for diagnosing delirium when symptoms are present involves asking a series of 10 simple questions with obvious answers (e.g., What color is my shirt? Is it sunny or cloudy? What is your name?). If the patient is unable to answer these questions or gives wrong answers because of impaired attention, a delirium may be present and an immediate referral to the primary medical care provider is imperative.

Dementia and Changes in Personality:

Dementia is the acquired loss of intellectual ability. It affects multiple skill areas, including memory, reasoning ability, calculation, language, visuospatial skills, motor skills, and personality (Cummings & Benson, 1983). Although the central feature of dementia is impaired short-term memory, impairments in other modalities must also be observed. If memory alone is affected, then an amnestic disorder may be diagnosed. Similarly, in the absence of cognitive impairment, problems that result from personality alone may lead to a personality disorder diagnosis.

Personality changes in dementia vary according to the stage of the illness (Abrams, 1996). However, **no evidence exists for the popular belief that the personality changes that occur with dementia result in exacerbated premorbid personality styles** (Petry et al., 1988). The most common changes in the early stages of dementia include an increase in passivity (such as a loss of interest in hobbies and activities), a loss of spontaneity, and general disengagement (Rubin et al., 1987). Patients frequently report feeling that they are "losing their mind" or have changed in a negative way. When patients are assessed and dementia is diagnosed, they may react to the diagnosis with anxiety and depression about future loss of cognitive function. If the depression is left untreated, it can, in turn, exacerbate the symptoms of the disorder. Caregivers often observe uncharacteristic behaviors and subtle personality changes in their loved ones, which they may find difficult to understand.

As the illness progresses, agitated and self-centered behaviors and a sense of indifference develop (Rubin et al., 1987). During this phase, unpredictable behaviors resulting from emotional impairments tend to be interpreted as willful attempts to frustrate the caregiver, and a great deal of stress in the relationship between caregiver and care recipient often ensues.

In the final stages of dementia, patients appear to lose much of their identity and tend to have difficulty articulating their emotional states. Caregivers report that their loved ones appear to be "shells" of the persons that they once knew and feel resigned to providing basic custodial care. Caregivers also report feeling bereaved over the loss of their loved one's personality.

Depression:

After dementia, depression is the second most common ailment in LTC residents. Studies have found that 15% to 50% of residents have depression (Curlik et al., 1991). **Ironically, depression is also probably the most overlooked disorder in older adults, who tend to have multiple physical illnesses and social and economic problems that they and their health care providers may conclude are the causes of symptoms of depression.**

The DSM-IV describes three types of depression, which vary in duration of symptoms, severity of depressed mood, and onset of stressors. A diagnosis of the most severe form, major depression, requires the presence of depressed mood that causes impaired social and occupational functioning without other factors, such as physical causes or grieving for a recent loss, being involved. A diagnosis of dysthymia is made when the symptoms are less severe but are present for at least 2 years. Adjustment disorder with depressed mood is diagnosed when symptoms are attributable to a psychosocial stressor (e.g., nursing home placement) and remit within 6 months of the stressor's onset, except when the stressor has chronic effects (such as chronic disability).

Diagnosing depression in LTC residents is complicated primarily by medical problems and somatic complaints related to aging (Hartz & Splain, 1997). With regard to medical problems, depression can be caused or exacerbated by a variety of conditions, including metabolic disturbances (diabetes mellitus, hypothyroidism), viral infections (hepatitis, HIV infection, or pneumonia), tumors (of the lung, pancreas, and central nervous system), neurological disorders (Parkinson's disease, stroke, epilepsy, head injury, cerebrovascular disease, or Huntington's disease), and substance abuse. In addition, some medical conditions can predispose patients to develop depression by causing changes in brain structure and chemistry. **This is especially true for patients with a stroke, head injury, or Alzheimer's disease, who may show signs of emotional lability called** *pseudobulbar effects* (Strub & Black, 1989).

Depression can be an understandable reaction to loss of function that is associated with an illness. For example, patients in the early stages of Alzheimer's disease often become depressed when they consider the progressive nature of the illness and loss of independence. Depression can also aggravate an existing medical condition. Persons who have had a stroke may be unwilling to cooperate with therapists during rehabilitation because of lethargy caused by depression and changes in appetite or sleep problems. In addition, a belief that rehabilitation will not result in a return to baseline functional ability may lead to a sense of hopelessness and reduce the motivation of these patients to comply with their treatment programs.

Somatic complaints related to aging may also make depression difficult to diagnose because so many LTC residents are disabled. The challenge facing clinicians is to determine whether unintentional weight loss, sleep disturbance, and fatigue are the result of normal aging, a medical condition, or depressed mood. One study found that fatigue and sleep disturbance in LTC residents were more likely to be related to depression than poor appetite. However, poor appetite may also be a secondary symptom of conditions such as cancer or swallowing disorders or a side effect of medications (Morley & Kraenzle, 1994). Recent studies have also found an association between depression, poor outcomes, and personality disorder (Abrams, 1996; Monfort, 1995; Thompson, Gallagher, & Czirr, 1988). These findings underscore the need to assess patients for depression whenever physical causes are ruled out as a possible cause for the presenting complaints.

Risk Factors for Depression

Besides medical illness, situations such as caregiving for a demented relative or experiencing the common losses of later life often cause depression in older adults. It may be possible to change some of these situations and not others, but all should be addressed as part of a comprehensive assessment.

Caregiving

Providing ongoing in-home care to a cognitively or physically disabled individual is very stressful. Caregivers often experience feelings of anger, anxiety, guilt, and depression because of the emotional and physical demands of this role. **Caregivers of patients in the later stages of dementia, when symptoms are more severe, and of those recently placed in a nursing home are at higher risk for developing depression** (Lichtenberg & Barth, 1990). Social factors can also contribute to the overall level of stress and burden faced by caregivers. Stress among caregivers is often associated with social isolation and lack of family support. Moreover, spouses who become caregivers after a long and difficult marital relationship often have strong feelings of unresolved anger and are likely to become resentful when forced to assume the caregiver role.

Loss

Old age predisposes individuals to a variety of other losses, such as diminished ability to work, decreased social contact, and declining health. According to cognitive-behavioral theories of depression, these losses are associated with a decrease in reinforcement and consequently lead to depression (Teri & Lewinshon, 1986). However, the precise relationship among specific types of loss, aging, and depression is unclear. For example, retirement usually does not precipitate depression, but when it does, depression may be related to a decline in health status, income, or other social factors (Pahkala, 1990).

Bereavement

By virtue of their age, older adults are more likely to experience the loss of spouses and close friends than younger adults. The majority of bereaved elders are able to cope well with grief in spite of their diminished financial and social resources. **Although wide variability has been observed, depressive symptoms associated with bereavement usually remit within 6 months. When depressive symptoms persist longer than a year, a *DSM-IV* diagnosis of major depression is made.** In these situations, bereavement becomes complicated by persistent symptoms of worthlessness (e.g., the feeling that "life will never be the same"), suicidal preoccupation (e.g., a willingness to "join" the deceased person), excessive guilt (e.g., guilt about having placed the loved one in a nursing home), hallucinatory experiences, and psychomotor retardation.

For caregivers, grieving the loss of a loved one can begin before the loved one's actual death. While caring for a loved one with dementia, caregivers often experience a sense of gradual loss as they witness the care recipient's gradual loss of identity as the dementia progresses. The grieving process often resolves itself with the death of the care recipient, and caregivers may then express a sense of relief.

Delusional States:

Suspiciousness and paranoia may also be observed in patients within LTC settings. The paranoia occurs without clouded consciousness and ranges from suspiciousness to paranoid delusions. In European literature, the term *paraphrenia* has been used to refer to the onset of disordered thought in elderly patients. Predisposing factors for paranoid states include social isolation, sensory impairment, and decreased control over finances and living circumstances (Christison & Blazer, 1988). Paranoia can also develop during the course of a mood disorder, especially in individuals with organic mental disorders; the relationship between paranoid states and schizophrenia is currently the subject of debate.

Paranoid beliefs by patients with cognitive impairments may result from reactions to a new LTC environment that appears distorted and confused. Moreover, the elderly experience relatively high rates of sensory loss, which makes them prone to misinterpreting everyday events and thus developing paranoid ideation. Therefore, deficits in visual acuity and hearing must first be ruled out when assessing any paranoid reaction in cognitively impaired elders with no premorbid history of paranoid personality or delusional disorder. If sensory deficits are suspected, symptoms are usually ameliorated by providing patients with hearing aids or glasses and ensuring that these devices are used properly. Despite these impairments, patient reports that sound suspicious may still have some basis in reality.

In our experience, the likelihood of the practitioner being incorporated into a patient's delusional belief system is minimized by establishing a trusting therapeutic relationship. Once a good relationship is established, the clinician can reassure the patient and decrease preoccupation with delusions by presenting evidence disconfirming the delusions in a nonjudgmental manner.

Although paranoid ideation can take many forms, a common theme in LTC patients is money. In older adults, money can represent independence or become a source of anxiety, particularly when the older person's mental faculties are failing. As the ability of patients to manage their finances deteriorates, family members may become increasingly protective and take responsibility for managing their assets. Paranoid beliefs involving money usually take the form of the patient accusing close family members of withdrawing money from bank accounts without authorization or staff stealing petty cash and valuables from their personal belongings. **Socioeconomic status cannot be used to predict who will develop these beliefs.** Whenever a dependent elder alleges fiduciary abuse, adequate documentation and appropriate follow-up with the involved parties should be performed. Of course, investigations into actual fraud should be pursued if warranted to protect the patient's welfare.

Paranoia may also focus on personal effects such as sweaters, glasses, and hearing aids, which can be easily misplaced in institutional settings by memory-impaired patients. As a compensatory strategy, patients with mild to moderate memory loss will hide items in a "safe place" to ensure that they are not accidentally lost. However, such hiding places tend to aggravate the problem of losing things, since the "safe places" are usually not where the patient would naturally keep these items. More severely impaired patients may not recollect handling the items in question. Misplacing or losing items or forgetting where they are hidden can lead memory-impaired patients to make accusations of theft. This may be especially true among patients who had suspicious personality tendencies earlier in life.

Assessment Measures for the Elderly

Development of assessment measures that are appropriate for the elderly continues to receive attention (see National Center for Cost Containment, Department of Veterans Affairs, 1996, for a comprehensive list of assessment measures for older adult populations). Although many tests that are currently used in LTC settings were originally developed for and "normed" on younger populations, more tests that are specifically for older adults are being created. Selected cognitive, functional, and personality measures appropriate for use in LTC settings are described below.

Cognitive Measures:

Mini-Mental State Exam

The MMSE is a widely used and easily administered cognitive screening measure of cognitive impairment (Folstein, et al.,

1975). It assesses orientation, attention, immediate and short-term verbal memory for simple words, basic language, and construction. Many LTC facilities and home health agencies routinely administer the MMSE to monitor cognitive status at various time intervals or when a change in mental status is observed. Because of its widespread use and familiarity, the MMSE can be administered and interpreted by a variety of care providers.

However, clinicians using the MMSE must keep several interpretive issues in mind. The first concerns the test's sensitivity to impairment. **Although the MMSE has been used to diagnose dementia, performance is highly correlated with age and educational history. False positives are obtained when it is used in the diagnosis of patients with limited education and advanced age.** Second, low scores on the MMSE should not be equated with deficits in functional ability, as patients often develop compensatory methods of coping with environmental demands. Third, the test is not appropriate for all patients. For instance, patients with very poor hearing, low vision, speech deficits, or English as a second language will score below their actual level of cognitive ability. Finally, patients in LTC often fluctuate in their cognitive ability, making repeated testing necessary to obtain a baseline measure of functioning.

Cognistat

This test, formerly known as the Neurobehavioral Cognitive Status Examination, is gaining popularity in LTC settings where it is beginning metric properties to show promise as a reliable cognitive function screen in older adults (Engelhart et al., 1994). Like the MMSE, the Cognistat tests abilities across a variety of cognitive domains, including alertness, orientation, attention, language, memory, calculation, visuoconstruction, and reasoning. However, it also addresses verbal fluency, immediate figural memory, and verbal registration. Test items are presented in order of difficulty, with screening test items providing a baseline score for each domain being assessed.

In addition to being more comprehensive than the MMSE, the Cognistat provides normative data for young, geriatric, and neurosurgical populations (Kiernan, Mueller, Langston, & Van Dyke, 1987). Test scores also produce a profile across assessed cognitive domains rather than a single summary score. This allows the clinician to match a specific patient's performance profile with actuarial profiles and descriptions listed in the manual of cognitive deficits caused by a variety of etiologies. The Cognistat strikes a good balance between the amount of time required to administer it (20 to 30 minutes) and the amount of data it provides.

Mattis Dementia Rating Scale

The Mattis Dementia Rating Scale (DRS) is a comprehensive test of cognitive function in older adults suspected of having dementia. It describes cognitive function in terms of attention, initiation/perseveration, construction, conceptualization, and memory. Sensitivity of the DRS to dementia has been established through cutoff scores derived from a standardization sample of Alzheimer's patients (Vitaliano et al., 1984). In addition, the DRS assesses a broader range of functions and provides more clinically relevant information than most tests that have been normed specifically with older adults. The length of time required to administer the DRS (45 minutes) is its primary limitation for use in assessing severely impaired patients.

Functional Measures:

Independent Living Scale

The Independent Living Scale (ILS), formerly known as the Community Competence Scale, is a relatively comprehensive test of functioning, similar in format and scoring to the Wechsler intelligence scales. It measures performance of a set of daily activities that are judged to be important by clinical professionals from various disciplines involved in working with older patients. The ILS has five scales (memory/orientation, managing money, managing home and transportation, health and safety, and social adjustment) and consists of 68 items that are presented to the patient in order of difficulty. Norms are provided for adults aged 65 years and older. Its primary strength is its reliability, which is due to its use in assessing the patient's functional ability directly rather than relying on the self-report of patients or their caregivers.

Hopkins Competency Assessment Test

The Hopkins Competency Assessment Test (HCAT) was developed to assess the patient's ability to understand and give informed consent for medical procedures and to create advance directives (Englehart, 1992). The test can be presented as a self-report measure to hearing-impaired patients or administered verbally by the examiner to patients with poor visual acuity. The HCAT consists of a brief description of informed consent for medical procedures, which is followed by 10 questions about the concept of informed consent. The description is written at three different grade levels (4th, 8th, and 13th grades) to accommodate those with various reading achievement levels. Although it has been reported that the HCAT reliably discriminates between decisionally incapacitated elderly and those who are competent to give informed consent, it has been criticized for measuring reading comprehension rather than knowledge of informed consent per se. Therefore, the HCAT should not be relied upon to assess the patient's ability to give informed consent.

Affective Measures:

Beck Depression Inventory

Most clinicians are familiar with the Beck Depression Inventory (BDI) as a quick, reliable, and valid measure of depression. A self-report measure, it consists of 21 symptom items presented in semantic differential form with cut-off scores indicating the level of severity of depression. Although the BDI is a sensitive and reliable measure of depression in older adults (Gallagher, 1986), some evidence suggests that the Geriatric Depression Scale (GDS) has better psychometric qualities for assessing mood in this population (Pachana, Thompson, & Gallagher-Thompson, 1994).

Geriatric Depression Scale

A widely used self-report measure of depressive symptomatology, the Geriatric Depression Scale (GDS), is the test of choice for use with medically ill elders, for several reasons. First, it correlates highly with the BDI, the most popular self-report measure of depression. (Yesavage et al., 1983). Secondly, it is face valid and easily comprehended by patients, and its "yes/no" format facilitates its administration. Third, and perhaps most important, the GDS is not confounded with somatic complaints, which are commonly found in both depressed and medical populations. Most GDS questions assess behavioral, affective, and cognitive aspects of depression rather than vegetative complaints, because a greater number of the elderly tend to suffer from physical ailments, regardless of psychiatric status. Finally, a 15-item short form of the GDS is available when a rapid screen for depression is required.

Despite its advantages and popularity, the GDS should not be used alone to diagnose depression, especially with patients who have dementia. Studies have shown mixed agreement between GDS-based diagnoses of depression and assessments based on clinical interviews (Lichtenberg, 1994). Therefore, the clinician should combine the GDS results with impressions of staff and family members to arrive at a comprehensive understanding of the patient's mood status. In addition, the GDS, unlike the BDI, does not specifically address suicidal tendencies. Clinicians need to know that suicide rates are highest for elderly men and that an assessment of suicidal ideation should follow administration of the GDS.

Personality Measures:

Neuroticism, Extroversion, Openness

The Neuroticism, Extroversion, Openness (NEO) tests are relatively quick and reliable measures of personality that have been standardized for elderly populations. McRae and Costa (1985) used the NEO tests in their studies of personality across the lifespan to validate the "Big Five" personality factors: neuroticism, extroversion, openness, agreeableness, and conscientiousness. These five factors were identified by Costa and McRae (1989) in their taxonomy of normal personality traits. Two versions of the NEO exist: the Neuroticism, Extroversion, Openness—Personality Inventory (NEO-PI) and the Neuroticism, Extroversion, Openness—Five Factor Inventory (NEO-FFI). The decision to use one test instead of the other will depend upon the purpose for the assessment (Hooker, et al., 1994; Strauss, et al., 1993).

The more comprehensive NEO-PI consists of 240 items that are presented on a five-point Likert scale and takes approximately 45 minutes to complete. Self-administered and observer-administered parallel forms of the test have been published. Scoring results in a personality profile consisting of T-scores for each personality factor, along with 30 facet scales. Validity scales and subtle items are obtained to assist in its interpretation. The NEO-PI has been translated into 12 languages, allowing it to be used with patients from different ethnic backgrounds.

The NEO-FFI is a shorter version of the NEO-PI. It consists of only 60 test items and takes 15 minutes to complete. Unlike the NEO-PI, the NEO-FFI does not measure facets of the five personality domains. The NEO-PI is useful for making personality assessments when time is a limiting factor and a global description of personality is sufficient.

Minnesota Multiphasic Personality Inventory—II

The Minnesota Multiphasic Personality Inventory—II (MMPI-II) is among the best known measures of psychological function, but its utility in LTC settings is limited due to its length. The MMPI-II has more than 500 questions, which most institutionalized older persons will not have the mental or physical endurance to complete it on their own, despite its simple yes/no format. Patients with poor eyesight, low educational attainment, and low motivation may also encounter difficulty in answering questions. In some circumstances, its administration by the clinician can increase the likelihood of the patient completing the test. A shortened form of the MMPI (the Mini–Mult) also exists, but its validity for older adults has not been examined as extensively as for the full MMPI (Lawton et al., 1980). Research using the MMPI across the lifespan has revealed that older adults tend to score higher than younger adults on the Depression, Hypochondriasis, and Hysteria scales and lower on "acting out" scales, such as Psychopathic Deviance and Mania (Lawton, Whelihan, Belsky, 1980).

Conclusion

In this article, we have attempted to highlight a number of issues that should be considered when conducting psychological assessments of frail elderly individuals, including the need to clarify the referral question; consider the sensory, medical, and cognitive status of person (in order to select an appropriate assessment instrument); and to observe the behavior in order to help select targets for intervention. We have also reviewed the "Four Ds"—delirium, dementia, depression, and delusional states—which represent the most common mental health problems that are likely to be found in older adults, and discussed a select group of measures that are appropriate for use with frail elders, particularly those in LTC settings. However, a key point that was not addressed is the role of ethnicity in helping the clinician understand mental health problems of older adults—particularly members of an ethnic minority group. The term *ethnicity* refers to the cultural background, language preferences, immigration history, family structure and values, and set of health beliefs and practices that strongly influence how the older adult sees the world (Yeo & Gallagher-Thompson, 1996). Ethnicity often has a very strong influence on the entire assessment process, from the selection of therapeutic measures to the interpretation of findings (see Espino, 1995, and Yeo & Gallagher-Thompson, 1996, for review of this topic as it applies to the four major ethnic groups recognized by the U.S. Census Bureau). Specific information on African-American elders can be found in Baker (1995), Hispanic American elders are discussed in Pousada (1995), Asian/Pacific Islanders in Lum (1995), and Native American elders in Rousseau (1995). The reader is referred to all of these sources to develop a basic understanding of the issues involved, as well as for guidance regarding currently available valid and reliable assessment instruments for each group.

References

Abrams, R. C. (1996). Assessing personality in chronic care settings. *Journal of Mental Health and Aging, 2,* 231–242.

American Psychiatric Association. (1994). *Diagnostic and statistical manual of mental disorders (4th ed.)* (DSM-IV). Washington, DC: American Psychiatric Association.

Anderson, E. G. (1990). How not to talk with elderly patients. *Geriatrics, 45,* 84–85.

Baker, F. M. (1995). Mental health issues in elderly African Americans. In D. V. Espino (Ed.), *Clinics in geriatric medicine: Ethnogeriatrics* (pp. 1–14). Philadelphia: W. B. Saunders.

Christison, C., & Blazer, D. (1988). Clinical assessment of psychiatric symptoms. In M. S. Albert & M. B. Moss (Eds.), *Geriatric neuropsychology* (pp. 82–99). New York: Guilford Press.

Cummings, J. L., & Benson, D. F. (1983). *Dementia: A clinical approach.* Woburn, MA: Butterworth Publishers.

Curlik, S. M., Frazier, D., & Katz, J. R. (1991). Psychiatric aspects of long term care. In J. Sadavoy, L. Lazarus, & L. Jarvik (Eds.), *Comprehensive review of geriatric psychiatry* (pp. 547–564). Washington, DC: American Psychiatric Press.

Engelhart, C., Eisenstein, N., & Meininger, J. (1994). Psychometric properties of the NCSE. *The Clinical Neuropsychologist, 8*, 405–415.

Englehart, J. (1992). The Hopkins Competency Assessment Test: A brief method for evaluating patients' capacity to give informed consent. *Hospital and Community Psychiatry, 43*, 132–136.

Espino, D. V. (1995). *Clinics in geriatric medicine: Ethnogeriatrics* (Vol. 11). Philadelphia: W. B. Saunders.

Folstein, M. F., Folstein, S. E., & McHugh, P. R. (1975). Mini-Mental State: A practical method for grading the cognitive state of patients for the clinician. *Journal of Psychiatric Research, 12*, 189–198.

Gallagher, D. (1986). The Beck Depression Inventory and older adults: Review of its development and utility. *Clinical Gerontologist, 5*, 149–163.

Gallagher-Thompson, D., Hanley-Peterson, P., & Thompson, L. W. (1990). Maintenance of gains versus relapse following brief psychotherapy for depression. *Journal of Consulting and Clinical Psychology, 58*, 371–374.

Gintner, G. G. (1995). Differential diagnosis in older adults: Dementia, depression, and delirium. *Journal of Counseling and Development, 73*, 346–351.

Ham, R. J., & Sloane, P. D. (1992). *Primary care geriatrics: A case-based approach* (2nd ed.). Chicago: Mosby/Year-Book.

Hartz, G. W., & Splain, D. M. (1997). Psychosocial intervention in long term care: An advanced guide. New York: Haworth Press.

Hooker, K., Frazier, L. D., & Monahan, D. J. (1994). Personality and coping among caregivers of spouses with dementia. *Gerontologist, 34*, 386–392.

Jarvik, L. F., Mintz, J., Steuer, J., & Gerner, R. (1982). Treating geriatric depression: A 26 week iterim analysis. *Journal of the American Geriatrics Society, 30*, 713–717.

Kiernan, R. J., Mueller, J., Langston, J. W., & Van Dyke, C. (1987). The neurobehavioral cognitive status examination: A brief approach, to cognitive assessment. *Annals of Internal Medicine, 107*, 481–485.

Lawton, M. P., Whelihan, W. M., & Belsky, J. K. (1980). Personality tests and their uses with older adults. In J. E. Birren & R. B. Sloane (Eds.),

Handbook of mental health and aging (pp. 874–892). Englewood Cliffs, NJ: Prentice-Hall.

Lichtenberg, P. (1994). *A guide to psychological practice in geriatric long term care.* New York: Haworth Press.

Lichtenberg, P., & Barth, J. (1990). Depression in elderly caregivers: A longitudinal study to test Lewinsohn's model of depression. *Medical Psychotherapy: An International Journal, 3,* 147–156.

Lum, O. M. (1995). Health status of Asian and Pacific Islanders. In D. V. Espino (Ed.), *Clinics in geriatric medicine: Ethnogeriatrics* (pp. 53–68). Philadelphia: W. B. Saunders.

McRae, R. R., & Costa, P. T. (1985). *Emerging lives, enduring dispositions: Personality in adulthood.* Boston: Little, Brown.

Monfort, J.-C. (1995). The difficult elderly patient: Curable hostile depression or personality disorder? *International Psychogeriatrics* 7(Suppl).

Morley, J. E., & Kraenzle, D. (1994). Causes of weight loss in a community nursing home. *Journal of the American Geriatrics Society, 42,* 583–585.

National Center for Cost Containment, Department of Veterans Affairs. (1996, February). *Geropsychology assessment resource guide,* 1996 revision (PB96-144365). Milwaukee, WI. National Center for Cost Containment.

Othmer, E., & Othmer, S. C. (1994). *The clinical interview using DSM-IV.* Washington, DC: American Psychiatric Press.

Pachana, N., Thompson, L. W., & Gallagher-Thompson, D. (1994). Measurement of depression. In M. P. Lawton & J. Teresi (Eds.), *Annual review of gerontology and geriatrics* (Vol. 14, pp. 234–256). New York: Springer Press.

Pahkala, D. (1990). Social and environmental factors and atypical depression in old age. *International Journal of Geriatric Psychiatry, 5,* 99–113.

Petry, S., Cummings, J. L., Hill, M. A., & Shapira, J. (1988). Personality alterations in dementia of the Alzheimer type. *Archives of Neurology, 45,* 1187–1190.

Pousada, L. (1995). Hispanic-American elders: Implications for healthcare providers. In D. V. Espino (Ed.), *Clinics in geriatric medicine: Ethnogeriatrics* (pp. 39–52). Philadelphia: W. B. Saunders.

Rouseau, P. (1995). Native-American elders: Health care status. In D.V. Espino (Ed.), *Clinics in geriatric medicine: Ethnogeriatrics* (pp. 1–14). Philadelphia: W. B. Saunders.

Rubin, E. H., Morris, J. C., & Berg, L. (1987). The progression of personality changes in senile dementia of the Alzheimer's type. *Journal of the American Geriatrics Society, 35,* 721–725.

Ryan, E. B., Bourhis, R. Y., & Knops, U. (1991). Evaluative perceptions of patronizing speech addressed to elders. *Psychology and Aging, 6*(3), 442–449.

Schogt, B., & Myran, D. (1992). Delirium. In D. K. et al., (Eds.), *Practical psychiatry in the nursing home* (pp. 63–85). Seattle, WA: Hogrefe & Huber.

Strauss, M. E., Pasupathi, M., & Chatterjee, A. (1993). Concordance between observers in descriptions of personality change in Alzheimer's disease. *Psychology and Aging, 8,* 475–480.

Strub, R. L., & Black, F. W. (1989). *Neurobehavioral disorders: A clinical approach.* Philadelphia: F. A. Davis.

Teri, L., & Lewinshon, P. M. (1986). *Gerontological assessment and treatment: Selected topics.* New York: Springer.

Thompson, L. W., Gallagher, D., & Czirr, R. (1988). Personality disorder and outcome in the treatment of late life depression. *Journal of Geriatric Psychiatry, 21,* 133–146.

Vitaliano, P. P., Breen, A. R., Russo, J., Albert, M., Vitiello, M., & Prinz, P. N. (1984). The clinical utility of the Dementia Rating Scale for assessing Alzheimer's patients. *Journal of Chronic Disabilities, 37,* 743–753.

Yeo, G., & Gallagher-Thompson, D. (1996). *Ethnicity and the dementias.* Bristol, PA: Taylor & Francis.

Yesavage, J. A., Brink, T. L., Rose, L. R., & Aday, M. (1983). Development and validation of a geriatric depression screening scale: A preliminary report. *Journal of Psychiatric Research, 17,* 37–49.

Zedlewski, S. O., Barnes, R. O., Burt, M. R., McBride, T. D., & Meyer, J. A. (1990). *The needs of the elderly in the 21st century.* Washington, DC: Urban Institute Press.

Recommended Readings

Birkett, D. P. (1991). *Psychiatry in the nursing home: Assessment, evaluation, and intervention.* New York: Haworth Press.

Dejowski, E. F. (1990). *Protecting judgment-impaired adults: Issues, interventions and policies.* New York: Haworth Press.

Gallo, J. J., Reichel, W., & Andersen, L. (1988). *Handbook of geriatric assessment.* Maryland: Aspen Publishers.

Ham, R. J., & Sloane, P. D. (1992). *Primary care geriatrics: A case-based approach* (2nd ed.). Chicago: Mosby Year-Book.

Hartz, G. W. (1997). *Psychological interventions in long term care: An advanced guide.* New York: Haworth Press.

Kane, R. A., & Kane, R. L. (1981). *Assessing the elderly: A practical guide to measurement.* Lexington, MA: Lexington Books.

Kane, R. L., Ouslander, J. G., & Abrass, I. B. (1994). *Essentials of clinical geriatrics* (3rd ed.). San Francisco: McGraw-Hill.

Lichtenberg, P. A. (1994). *A guide to psychological practice in geriatric long term care.* New York: Haworth Press.

Wehry, S. (1997). Mental health needs of the homebound elderly. In P. W. Brickner, F. R. Kellogg, A. J., Lechich, R. Lipsman, & L. K. Scharer (Eds.), *Geriatric home health care: The collaboration of physicians, nurses, and social workers* (pp. 147–174). New York: Springer Publishing.

2

Neuropsychological Assessment in Geriatric Facilities

PETER A. LICHTENBERG, PH.D., ABPP, *and* SUSAN E. MACNEILL, PH.D.

Abstract

THE PRACTICE of geropsychology in long term care (LTC) facilities requires knowledge of geriatric neuropsychology. In many LTC facilities, geropsychologists will be asked to conduct assessments and provide interventions for persons with dementia. The purpose of this chapter is to familiarize the geropsychologist with (1) the most common forms of dementia and delirium in order to be able to assist in diagnostic assessment and treatment planning, and (2) assessment batteries that are well suited to patients in LTC. Alzheimer's disease, vascular dementia, and subcortical dementia represent the most commonly seen dementias in older adults. This chapter describes the general presentation of these disorders both at onset and throughout the progression of the disease. Delirium is also common among older adults in LTC facilities. The diagnostic features of this syndrome and its major etiologies are presented.

In the remainder of the chapter, the authors discuss the assessment process. Areas of assessment covered in cognitive testing are reviewed, as are questions that guide the process of test interpretation. Finally, four commonly used brief test batteries for assessing cognition in long term care are described.

Introduction

Most elderly patients in long term care (LTC) suffer from some degree of cognitive impairment. Because of this, neuropsychological assessment—the study of brain-behavior relationships can be an extremely useful component of long term care. Clinical neuropsychology is the application of brain-behavior knowledge to patient care. As a subspecialty of clinical psychology, the field of clinical neuropsychology has expanded rapidly since the early 1970s. Supervised instruction and clinical practice are prerequisites for neuropsychological assessments in the nursing home. This chapter will first review clinical syndromes that impact cognition and are frequently seen in geriatric LTC and then address aspects of the neuropsychological assessment that are specific to the elderly LTC patient.

Common Clinical Syndromes

"Is the patient demented?" This is the most common question asked of psychologists working in LTC settings. *The Diagnostic and Statistical Manual of Mental Disorders,* fourth edition (DSM-IV) (American Psychiatric Association, 1994), defines dementia as a decline in memory and at least one other cognitive domain that interferes with a patient's social and/or occupational skills. The major types of dementia commonly found in frail older adults include Alzheimer's disease, vascular dementia, and subcortical dementias.

Alzheimer's Disease:

The most common cause of dementia is Alzheimer's disease, and prevalence studies have shown that increased age

is the greatest risk factor for the development of Alzheimer's disease. The percentage of older adults with Alzheimer's disease jumps from 3% among those aged 65 to 74 years to 18% among those aged 75 to 84 years, and increases to 35% to 45% among those over 85. Other documented risk factors include low education, genetics, family history, and exposure to glues, fertilizers, or pesticides at work (Evans, Funkenstein, Albert, Scherr et al., 1989).

Symptoms of Alzheimer's disease can be broken up into neuropsychological deficits, behavioral symptoms, and emotional symptoms. **The onset of neuropsychological deficits associated with dementia is slow and insidious, with the hallmark cognitive deficit found in memory function.** Language problems may be subtle in earlier stages; they may include word-finding difficulties and impoverished speech, as well as deficits in abstract reasoning. **There is strong evidence for the use of neuropsychological test findings to identify these early signs of dementia.** Behavioral symptoms that are present in earlier stages of dementia include periods of confusion, getting lost in familiar surroundings, and forgetfulness. Apathy is the most common early emotional symptom of the disease. Consequently, Alzheimer's victims often cut themselves off from family and friends. At other times, they may have outbursts as well as depressive syndromes. Rarely seen in the early stages of dementia are symptoms of decreased strength or gait disturbance.

As the disease progresses, neuropsychological deficits—including aphasia, apraxia, and agnosia—become more pronounced. *Aphasia* refers to a true language disturbance. During the course of Alzheimer's disease, expressive language is severely reduced and comprehension becomes impaired. *Apraxia* involves the inability to perform planned motor movements. A substantial number of Alzheimer's patients, for example, cannot get dressed due to an apraxia. *Agnosia* refers to a lack of recognition of people and objects.

The progressive behavioral symptoms of Alzheimer's disease are the most troublesome for caregivers, including

the family and LTC staff. The increased need of Alzheimer's patients for supervision and their inability to perform daily living activities makes their care time consuming and intense. Patients often develop night waking patterns, whereby they are up at late hours and catnap during the day. **Common behavioral problems that lead to the placement of Alzheimer patients in LTC facilities include incontinence, physical violence, and dangerous behaviors, such as wandering or cooking without supervision.** Late-onset emotional symptoms may also be difficult for family members. Suspiciousness toward the caregiver and actual hiding of objects are common in up to a fifth of patients.

Providers who are responsible for diagnosing Alzheimer's disease need to be knowledgeable about the clinical criteria of the disorder. **A clinical work-up should include a physician's examination, an electroencephalograph** (EEG), **and neuroimaging** (via computerized axial tomography [CT] or magnetic resonance imaging [MRI]). **The EEG and neuroimaging scans will show normal structures; neuropsychological testing will confirm dementia.** These clinical criteria, which were established in 1984, have led to dramatic improvement in the accuracy of diagnosis. Since the establishment of such criteria, the accuracy of diagnoses of Alzheimer's disease has increased from 72% to 90% (Blacker, Albert, Bassett, Rodney, et al., 1994).

Vascular Dementia:

The second most common form of dementia in older adults is vascular dementia. Risk factors for vascular dementia are similar to those identified for stroke; they include hypertension, heart disease, diabetes mellitus, smoking, gender (a higher risk in men), and, most significantly, age. **Persons more than 75 years of age are five to nine times more likely to have a stroke than those in their early 50s** (Tatemichi, 1990). Lacunar infarcts, or small strokes in the subcortical areas of the brain, are the most common cause of vascular dementia. **Studies have shown that cognitive impairment is most closely related to the number of small strokes or lacunes present and to the ex-**

tent of ventricular enlargement due to brain atrophy. Neither the location of lacunes nor the size of the infarct has been related to cognitive deficits. Other causes of vascular dementia include large cortical strokes and infarction resulting from hypoxic–ischemic processes, as seen in severe hypotensive episodes. Gait disturbance is very common in early vascular dementia. In one study of mildly demented individuals, for example, 57% had severe gait disturbances and 32% had moderate disturbances.

The typical course of vascular dementia involves an abrupt onset of cognitive and neurological symptoms and a stepwise progression of additional symptoms. Unlike the slow, insidious nature of Alzheimer's disease, the symptoms of vascular dementia often appear suddenly, which is not surprising as stroke is a rather unexpected, striking event. In addition, whereas Alzheimer's disease is progressive, deficits associated with vascular dementia may "plateau," with no discernible cognitive decline in symptoms seen until a new neurological event occurs (a reminder that the best predictor of a stroke is a previous stroke). Cognitive deficits associated with vascular dementia are heterogeneous, varying with the site and extent of vascular events. Behavioral symptoms of early vascular dementia include slowed reaction time and lower-extremity gait disturbance. Vascular dementia does not differ significantly from other forms of dementia in its emotional symptoms, which may include depression, flat affect, irritability, or apathy.

Several groups have established clinical criteria for the diagnosis of vascular dementia. Although they vary, the essential criteria include a dementia and clinical and neuroradiological evidence of stroke and are supported by the aforementioned risk factors as well as the presence of transient ischemic attacks, gait disturbances, and being male. Another useful tool for assessing the vascular components of dementia is the Hachinski Ischemia Scale, which was originally constructed to differentiate between Alzheimer's disease and vascular dementia. This scale assesses the presence of stroke through time of onset, risk factors, and course of illness. **It is now recognized that vascular disease and Alzheimer's disease can and often do coexist; no tool, in-**

cluding neuroradiological imaging, has been effective in distinguishing between them. In one recent study, for example, magnetic resonance imaging scans were able to differentiate between patients with and without dementia in 90% of cases, but they performed only at chance level when attempting to differentiate between patients with vascular dementia vs. Alzheimer's disease (Jobst, Hindley, King, & Smith, 1994).

Subcortical Dementia:

A final group of dementias that are commonly seen in older adults are the subcortical dementias, so-called because they primarily affect the subcortical parts of the brain. Diseases such as Parkinson's disease, Huntington's disease, and subcortical stroke account for many of the subcortical dementias.

Early neuropsychological symptoms of subcortical dementias include slowed information processing and retrieval and complex attention deficits; language function is typically intact. **Because information is processed extremely slowly, it becomes critical to pace instructions so that they can be followed.** Assessment of memory will typically indicate retrieval deficits in patients with subcortical dementia. Memory can be broken up into aspects of encoding, storage, and retrieval, as described below. Despite intact encoding and information storage abilities, patients with subcortical dementia cannot retrieve or access their memories. Because of slowed processing and increased inefficiency, complex attention deficits are also commonly seen in individuals with subcortical dementia. Common emotional symptoms include depression and constriction of affect.

There are literally hundreds of etiologies for dementias. In addition to the major ones described above, common causes include hydrocephalus, infectious disease, head trauma, tumor, alcohol abuse, toxins, and medications. Most dementias are progressive and get worse with time; however, some are reversible. Pseudodementia, a descriptive but not diagnostic term, was once thought to be highly prevalent in frail elders. It was widely believed that a great proportion of seemingly demented individuals had a cognitive disturbance because of undetected depression, and once the depression was treated, the cognitive disturbance would disappear. The experience of Alzheimer's centers across the country has not supported this optimistic view (Linn, Wolf, Bachman, Knuefel, et al., 1995). **Typically, dementia and depression coexist, but treating the depression does not eliminate the dementia, although it can lead to functional improvement.**

A new line of longitudinal research on reversible dementia due to depression has helped clarify the presence of late-life depression. **Patients with severe depression whose cognition improves when their depression is treated are almost five times more likely to develop a full-blown dementia within the following 3 to 5 years than hospitalized depressed patients without coexisting cognitive deficits.**

Delirium:

Clinicians may also be asked to determine if a patient is suffering from delirium. This critical question surfaces frequently in geriatric LTC settings because delirium has serious implications if it remains undetected and untreated. **The DSM-IV defines delirium as a disturbance of consciousness accompanied by a change in cognition, with a presentation that develops over a short period and fluctuates throughout the day.** Assessment should focus on several key aspects of delirium:

- **Delirium is characterized by abrupt onset as the result of changes in medical conditions** (e.g., urinary tract infections or medication toxicity).
- **Perceptual disturbances, such as visual illusions or difficulty discriminating between dreams and reality, are common symptoms of delirium.**
- **Hallucinations can and do occur, and they can be auditory, visual, or tactile.**
- **Delusions may be present and, if so, are new and poorly organized.**

- Psychomotor symptoms of agitation and/or combative-ness are relatively common for patients with delirium.
- The patient's sleep-wake cycle is frequently disturbed, which results in lethargy, decreased alertness, or sleep disruption.

The causes of delirium are numerous. In LTC settings, the most common causes are infections (e.g., urinary tract infections or pneumonia), medications, heart disease, or new strokes. **Delirium is four times more common in individuals with dementia than in those who do not have a dementia** (LaRue, 1993). The effects of delirium are not always transient. Sadly, half of the patients do not recover their full functional capacity after a delirious episode, and delirium leaves them susceptible to loss of activity-of-daily-living (ADL) skills and even a shortened lifespan. Thus, it is critical to detect delirium early and refer persons suspected of having delirium to physicians for the necessary medical work-up to determine cause and treatment.

General Aspects of Neuropsychological Assessment

Armed with knowledge about the different types of dementia, the psychologist in a LTC facility will be able to conduct a cognitive assessment that evaluates the five areas of cognition: attention, language, memory, visuospatial skills, and mental flexibility.

Attention is often viewed as the basic building block of cognition. When a patient is unable to attend, it is often because of delirium (discussed later) or a late-stage dementia. Attention can be broken down into several distinct abilities. *Focused attention* involves the ability to orient to an important stimulus, (e.g., listening to words). Selective attention refers to the ability to block out extraneous stimuli. *Sustained attention* refers to continued concentration. Attention skills are clearly relevant to basic self-care tasks in LTC facilities. Often, improved self-care and participation can be achieved by teaching nursing assistants to help the patient attend better or alter the extraneous environment to eliminate distractions.

Assessment also focuses on language, the basic means of communication. Dementia often affects the patient's expressive abilities, (i.e., the patient's ability to produce words). Many patients with left-hemisphere strokes, for example, speak fewer words and those that are spoken are often incomprehensible. Speech output is also reduced with Alzheimer's disease, and words are often empty of meaning. *Receptive language* refers to the ability to comprehend language. Some stroke patients have a poor comprehension of words; their speech output is fluent but makes no sense because they are unable to understand the conversation. *Receptive aphasia* is often a later symptom in patients with Alzheimer's disease; it may not be present at all during the early stages. Additional language skills include confrontational naming and repetition. A reduced ability to name common objects can be a hallmark symptom of the early stages of Alzheimer's disease. Repetition, one of the most basic aspects of language, is one of the last to be lost.

Memory is the third area of cognitive function explored in a geriatric neuropsychological evaluation. Research has repeatedly demonstrated that memory dysfunction is the best means of distinguishing between older persons with dementia and those without dementia. Memory dysfunction is also highly correlated with poor adherence to medications, decreased safety, and poor financial management. It is useful to think of memory in terms of its components: encoding, storage, and retrieval. *Encoding* is how new information is acquired or incorporated into memory. For example, does new information enter into memory after the individual attends to it? *Storage* refers to the transition of newly acquired information to the knowledge base. Finally, *retrieval* is the active process of accessing the specific memory by searching through memory storage. In Alzheimer's disease, memory is disrupted at the encoding stage; thus, new information never gets stored. In contrast, memory is disrupted at the retrieval stage in subcortical dementias. That is, the information is stored but not readily accessible through active retrieval.

Two testing paradigms can be adopted to distinguish between storage and retrieval deficits. First, clinicians may use a word-list learning task that emphasizes recall (which involves encoding, storage, and retrieval processes) and recognition (which taps into encoding and storage but bypasses retrieval). Examples of such a task include the Rey Auditory Verbal Learning Test and the California Verbal Learning Test. Second, clinicians may turn to a selective reminding paradigm, as is used in the Fuld Object Memory Evaluation. Because patients are reminded only of missed words on each trial, this test measures both storage and retrieval, and allows the clinician to examine the consistency of responses.

The evaluation should also assess visuospatial skills, i.e., motor and perceptual abilities that do not readily lend themselves to verbalization, including tasks such as dressing, bathing, and driving. Almost no test is purely without language, and thus tests of visuospatial functioning should never be considered language free. **Nevertheless, an examination of visuospatial abilities may reveal unique strengths or deficits that impact daily self-care or participation in leisure activities.** Wide ranges of visuospatial tasks are available, including copying of figures, block design, and perceptual organizational tasks (as assessed, for example, by the Hooper Visual Organization Test).

Mental flexibility, abstract reasoning, and executive skills are all associated with the fifth area of cognitive function, which involves the ability to solve more complex problems. Interestingly, tests of mental flexibility do not correlate highly with one another; these tasks thus tap into different aspects of cognitive function. Trails B, for example, evaluates complex visuomotor tracking, whereas the Controlled Oral Word Association Test measures initiation and maintenance of verbal output. **The ability to view problems from different perspectives and to solve problems that are presented in an unclear way are clearly very relevant to the higher-order activities of daily living, including managing one's own finances and making decisions.**

Interpreting the Nueropsychological Test Data:

Three questions can help guide the clinician in interpreting cognitive performance on neuropsychological tests: Is there evidence of cerebral impairment? Which areas of cognition are most affected? How can test results be used to make recommendations?

Is There Evidence of Cerebral Impairment?:

The search for the answer this question can be an exercise fraught with misinterpretation and resulting in an inappropriate assessment and misinterpretation. **Psychometric testing, which is rooted in quantitative data, is the best way to detect dementia, and psychologists who are proficient in geriatric neuropsychology are best qualified to perform these assessments.** A psychometric test relies on standardized administration and scoring to evaluate general cognition or a specific area of cognition. The Mini-Mental State Exam (MMSE) and the Mattis Dementia Rating Scale represent general approaches to the assessment of cognitive impairment. Specific procedures for test administration are provided along with specific scoring criteria. Tests such as the Fuld Object Memory Exam and the Boston Naming Test focus more narrowly on assessment of memory and particular aspects of language; they also have standardized procedures and scoring rules.

It is essential that neuropsychological tests be administered correctly, with scores calculated accurately and used only in conjunction with normative data. Cognitive assessments, like most medical tests, use a deficit model to assess cognition. Thus, a patient's MMSE score is compared with the scores of older adults without dementia. **Test scores are affected by a number of variables that have nothing to do with experiencing a dementia.** Scores for normal, healthy older adults are affected by factors such as educational and cultural background (particularly familiarity with standard English) and age.

Psychologists with training and experience in the neuropsychology of older adults are uniquely qualified to interpret cognitive test scores. Psychologists understand the assessment process and the importance of following standardized procedures. The field of geriatric neuropsychology has produced the best normative data available, and psychologists who are trained in this area are best equipped to apply these data properly. **Failure to identify normative data, including data for persons of comparable age and education, can lead to faulty test interpretation and result in serious under- or overestimation of cognitive abilities.** When evaluating the performance of urban older adults on the *Boston Naming Test,* for example, the use of improper norms can result in misclassification of 80% of normal performances (Lichtenberg, 1998). This error can be explained through differences in education. Urban older adults typically have less than a high school education, whereas other subjects included in frequently used normative data had an average of 15 years of education; this results in significant differences between urban older patients and the normative group.

The need for current and appropriate norms cannot be overemphasized. There are a number of sources of up-to-date norms. The Veterans Affairs Center for Cost Containment published the *Geropsychology Assessment Resource Guide* in 1994 and revised it in 1996 (National Center for Cost Containment, 1996). Journals such as *Clinical Neuropsychologist* and the *Archives of Clinical Neuropsychology* have also published many articles and special issues containing normative data on older adults. Spreen and Strauss (1991) is a compendium of tests and norms.

What Areas of Cognition Are Most Affected?

Clinicians should next profile cognitive strengths and weaknesses to determine which areas of cognition are most affected (i.e., which areas are dysfunctional and which remain strong). **It is essential to determine how the individual can best learn new information or retain what he or she already knows; this will be helpful to assist staff members who work with the patient, develop treatment plans, and/or implement behavioral management programs.**

How May Test Results Lead to Practical Recommendations?:

The final challenge in test interpretation is to develop practical recommendations based on test results. To do so, the clinician must address issues such as competency, drive, ADL skills, placement and supervision needs, and treatment planning on the unit. How can the patient's strengths best be adapted for leisure activities? How are cognitive deficits related to behavioral disturbances, and how can these be ameliorated? The case study at the end of the article outlines the test results and interpretation for one patient.

Test Batteries

Given the limited capacities of patients in long term care and recent changes in health care coverage, test batteries in LTC settings must be relatively brief. Outlined below are four brief batteries that can be used in LTC settings.

The Washington University Battery:

One of the first brief test batteries constructed to document the cognitive effects of dementia, The Washington University Battery was designed as part of a longitudinal study of Alzheimer's disease (Storandt, Botwinick, & Danziger, 1986). The authors utilized portions of the Wechsler Adult Intelligence Scale (WAIS), the Wechsler Memory Scale, the Benton Visual Retention Test, the Boston Naming Test, Trail Making Part A from the Halstead Reitan Battery, the Bender Gestalt Test, and the Crossing Off Test in their 90- to 120-minute test battery. The initial sample test included 43 individuals with mild Alzheimer's disease and 43 control subjects enrolled in the Washington University Memory and Aging Project. The subjects were matched by age (mean: 71 years) and on education (mean: 12.5 years). Follow-up data, collected for 2.5 years, was obtained for 22 of the Alzheimer's subjects and 39 of the control subjects. There were noteworthy findings in both the cross-sectional and the longitudinal data. **Almost all the tests differentiated the groups initially, including the tests hypothesized to be resistant to the effects of cerebral deterioration** (the

Information and Comprehension subtests of the WAIS). The Logical Memory subtest of the Wechsler Memory Scale was the most powerful in initially distinguishing between Alzheimer and control subjects. The only measure that was not useful in distinguishing the groups initially was the Digit Span forward subtest of the WAIS. Analysis of the longitudinal data from this study indicated that overall, the Alzheimer's subjects deteriorated during the follow-up period, whereas there was no change in the normal controls (Eslinger, Damasio, Benton, & Van Allen, 1985).

The Iowa Battery:

A comprehensive neuropsychological assessment of 60- to 88-year-old adults with and without dementia led to the development of a 30- to 45-minute battery capable of identifying dementia. The original test battery consisted of eight tests: four memory tests, one auditory attention task, one verbal fluency task, and two visuospatial tasks. The sample consisted of 53 normal control subjects and 53 dementia subjects matched for age, education, and sex. The means and standard deviations for all tests were significantly higher for the normal subjects than for the subjects with dementia. Certain tests, however, were far better than others in detecting dementia. For example, whereas tests for orientation alone detected dementia in 57% of the subjects with dementia, facial recognition detected only 32%.

Stepwise linear discriminate function analyses were used to determine the most effective and parsimonious group of tests to detect dementia. **Three tests–the Temporal Orientation Test, the Controlled Oral Word Association test, and the Benton Visual Retention test–together allowed clinicians to classify 85% of cases accurately.** The authors then cross-validated their findings using a new sample of 53 normal individuals and 53 individuals with dementia. **The overall correct classification in this sample was 89%, which provided strong support for the original findings.**

The Consortium to Establish a Registry for Alzheimer's Disease Battery:

In 1989, the 16 Alzheimer centers associated with the National Institutes of Health (NIH) worked together to produce the Consortium to Establish a Registry for Alzheimer's Disease (CERAD) neuropsychological battery (Morris et al., 1989). The aim of the project was to produce a brief, 30- to 40-minute test battery that would characterize the primary manifestations of Alzheimer's disease. Tests were thus chosen to evaluate aspects of memory, language, and praxis. They included a verbal fluency test (animal naming), the 15-item Boston Naming test, the full MMSE, a word-list memory task created by the authors, four line drawings, and a word-list recognition task created by the authors. The authors described the results from 350 subjects with Alzheimer's disease and 275 control subjects. Test-retest reliability correlations during a 1-month period ranged from .52 to .78. The tests readily distinguished normal controls from Alzheimer's patients. The authors interpreted these data as providing solid support for the CERAD battery as a useful measure for evaluating patients with dementia.

The next investigation of the utility of the CERAD battery used 196 subjects matched for sex, age, and education. The subjects were each placed into one of four groups: a control group, a group with mild dementia, a moderate dementia, or severe dementia. The average age of the subjects was 71, and the average education level was 14 years. Stepwise linear discriminant function analysis was used to determine how accurately the CERAD battery classified subjects. **Ninety-six percent of subjects in the normal controls and the moderate and severe dementia groups were classified accurately, and 86% of subjects in the mild group were classified accurately** (Morris, Heyman, Mohs, & Hughes, 1989). The best predictor was the delayed recall score from the word list. Retention dropped from 86% for the normal controls to 36% for the mildly impaired group and 16% for the moderately and severely impaired group. The worst predictors were the recognition memory score and the number of intrusion errors on the word-list recall and recognition tasks. The authors concluded that the CERAD battery may facilitate the early detection of dementia.

The Normative Studies Research Project Battery:

The Normative Studies Research Project test battery takes 75 minutes to 2 hours to administer (Lichtenberg, 1998). Memory testing is emphasized; language, visuospatial skills, executive functioning, and reading skills are also tested. A sample of 237 patients received the following tests: the Dementia Rating Scale, the Boston Naming Test, the Hooper Visual Organization Test, the Visual Form Discrimination Test, and the Logical Memory I and II tests. Of the 237 patients tested, 74 were cognitively intact and fully independent in ADL abilities, 89 were cognitively impaired and had deficiencies in at least 3 ADLs, and the remaining 73 patients were either cognitively intact with ADL deficiencies or cognitively impaired with few ADL limitations.

Logistic regression analysis was performed to determine the clinical utility of the test battery in distinguishing patients with no cognitive impairment from those with mild impairment. Because of the high degree of relationship between tests, only the Dementia Rating Scale (DRS) was used. **The DRS was a significant predictor of intact and impaired cognition (Chi square=36.03, P < .01), with an overall accuracy of 75%.** Sensitivity was 77%, and specificity was 74%. The DRS had a positive predictive power of 72% and a negative predictive power of 79%; that is, the DRS was relatively better at identifying patients without cognitive impairment than patients with cognitive impairment. **The data clearly indicate the usefulness of the Normative Studies Research Project test battery for older urban medical patients, because it is relatively accurate in discriminating between patients without cognitive impairment and those with impairment in this group.**

Summary of the Batteries:

Across a heterogeneous group of participants, brief batteries proved accurate in their detection of dementia. The studies summarized above provide clear guidance for the use of brief cognitive test batteries in working with older adults. **Data on distinguishing elderly patients with dementia from those without dementia point to the importance of emphasizing memory assessment in the cognitive evaluation.** Indeed, memory function was a key test in each of the brief batteries reviewed. However, tasks of attention, language, visuospatial functioning, and executive ability, as well as general tests of cognitive function, were all clinically useful in the identification of dementia. Reading tests, by contrast, are relatively poor at discriminating between individuals with dementia vs. those without dementia but can be used to make a crude estimate of premorbid intellectual functioning. **The data on brief batteries show that cognitive assessment of older adults can be completed in a timely, cost-effective fashion without sacrificing diagnostic accuracy.**

Conclusion

Clinical neuropsychology plays a unique and important role in geriatric LTC settings. Among the most common syndromes encountered in such settings are those affecting cognitive abilities, including various forms of dementia and delirium. Consequently, understanding the patterns of these syndromes, as well as normal aspects of aging, is critical when working with this population. Because of their specialized training in the behavioral aspects of both neurological disorders and assessment, clinical psychologists with training in neuropsychology are best qualified to determine the presence and extent of cognitive deficits in elderly patients. When treating the elderly patient, having a clear understanding of geriatric clinical syndromes is essential, but it is not sufficient. Geriatric neuropsychologists must also remain aware of normal aging processes and use appropriate normative data when interpreting neuropsychological results. Particularly helpful in this arena are several recently developed brief batteries that are appropriate for assessing dementia in elderly patients.

Case Study

Mr. W was a 76-year-old retired factory worker who entered the hospital because of chest pain 3 weeks before his neuropsychological evaluation in a long term rehabilitation unit. It was determined that he had suffered a heart attack. Other medical problems included hypertension, non-insulin-dependent diabetes mellitus, and a coronary bypass surgery 3 years earlier. Before this hospitalization, Mr. W lived with his wife. He had been independent, with all of his ADLs, and was driving; at the time of this hospitalization, he was confused and exhibiting poor memory. He completed 12 years of education. His neuropsychological test scores were as follows:

Wide Range Achievement Test—Revised

Reading (scaled score)	85
Dementia Rating Scale-Total	18
Attention	36
Initiation/Perseveration	30
Construction	5
Conceptualization	34
Memory	13
Multi-Lingual Aphasia Examination (MAE) Aural Comprehension	18
Boston Naming Test	37
Logical Memory	111
Logical Memory	110
Fuld Storage	26
Fuld Retrieval	18
Fuld Repeated Retrieval	9
Fuld Ineffective Reminders	20
Visual Form Discrimination	21
Hooper Visual Organization Test	18.5
Controlled Oral Word	20
Geriatric Depression Scale	2

On all indices of memory (Logical Memory and the Fuld), Mr. W scored significantly below the normative data. In the Logical Memory II subtest, for example, the percent retained was 0; in the Fuld storage, he scored several standard deviations below the mean. These low scores on memory tests were in sharp contrast to his reading score, which was in the average range.

Mr. W displayed many strengths, particularly in the areas of language (including naming), visuoperceptual, and visuo-organizational skills. Weaknesses were notable in both memory and mental flexibility tasks. At this point, it was useful to integrate these findings with Mr. W's history to facilitate diagnosis. The onset of Mr. W's cognitive deficits had been rather sudden, occurring immediately after the apparent heart attack. Thus, his test results were probably not due to pre-existing, progressive dementia. The pattern of results, plus the history of a heart attack and sudden onset of severe memory dysfunction were also entirely consistent with a hypoxic episode, which could damage the hippocampus. Damage to the hippocampal regions that are particularly susceptible to hypoxia, can cause the type of severe memory deficits seen here (Albert & Knoefel, 1994).

The test results had profound implications for Mr. W's lifestyle. Given his cognitive deficits, he might not be able to drive, manage his own medications, cook without supervision, or manage household finances. Assessment of these skills in his occupational therapy tests proved that he needed help in all these tasks. His wife would have to assume the role of 24-hour caregiver; it was also recommended that she petition the court for guardianship.

References

Albert, M. L., & Knoefel, J. E. (1994). *Clinical Neurology of Aging.* New York: Oxford University Press.

Blacker, D., Albert, M. S., & Bassett, S. S., Rodney, C. P., et al. (1994). Reliability and validity of NINCDS-ADRDA criteria for Alzheimer's Disease. *Archives of Neurology, 51,* 1198–1204.

Eslinger, P. J., Damasio, A. R., Benton, A. L., & Van Allen, M. (1985). Neuropsychological detection of abnormal mental decline in older persons. *Journal of the American Medical Association,* 253, 670–674.

Evans, D., Funkenstein, H. H., Albert, M. S., & Scherr, P. A., et al. (1989). Prevalence of Alzheimer's Disease in a community population of older persons. *Journal of the American Medical Association, 262,* 2551–2556.

Jobst, K. A., Hindley, N. J., King, E. A., & Smith, A. D. (1994). The diagnosis of Alzheimer's Disease: a question of image? *Journal of Clinical Psychiatry, 155,* 22–31.

LaRue, A. (1993). *Aging and Neuropsychological Assessment.* New York: Plenum Press.

Lichtenberg, P. A. (1998). *Mental Health Practice in Geriatric Health Care Settings.* Binghamton, New York: Haworth.

Lichtenberg, P. A. Manning, C. A., Vangel, S. J., & Ross, T. P. (1995). Normative and ecological validity data in older urban medical patients: A program of neuropsychological research. *Advances in Medical Psychotherapy, 8,* 121–136.

Linn, R. T., Wolf, P. A., Bachman, D. L. Knuefel, J. E. et al. (1995). The preclinical phase of probable Alzheimer's Disease. *Archives of Neurology, 52,* 485–490.

Morris, J. C., Heyman, A., Mohs, R. C., Hughes, J. P. (1989). Consortium to establish a registry for Alzheimer's Disease (CERAD). Neurology, 44, 1427–1432.

National Center for Cost Containment. *Geropsychology Assessment Resource Guide* (1996). Department of Veteran Affairs: Milwaukee, WI.

Spreen, O, & Strauss, E. (1991). *A Compendium of Neuropsychological Tests.* New York: Oxford University Press.

Storandt, M., Botwinick, J. & Danziger, W. L. (1986). Longitudinal changes: Patients with mild SDAT and matched healthy controls. In L. W. Poon (Ed.) *Handbook for Clinical Memory Assessment for Older Adults* (pp. 277–284). Washington, DC: American Psychological Association.

Tatemichi, T. K. (1990). How acute brain failure becomes chronic. *Neurology, 40,* 1652–1659.

3

Conducting a Medical and Psychiatric Assessment

HERNANDO PONCE-BURGOS, M.D.,
and MARK EDWIN KUNIK, M.D.

Abstract

THIS CHAPTER will present prevalence rates of psychiatric disorders in long term care (LTC). It will then discuss the major psychiatric conditions: psychosis, depression, delirium, anxiety, and neurologic illnesses with psychiatric symptoms. General principles of psychiatric assessment in LTC settings suggest the importance of staff education regarding humane, individualized care and the need to be alert for the manifestation of psychiatric problems and side effects of medications. A biopsychosocial approach to assessment and treatment is necessary for optimal psychiatric care of LTC residents.

Introduction

Optimal treatment of elders with mental disorders requires an awareness of the psychophysiological aspects of old age. It has been estimated that approximately 15% of the older population needs mental health services. Older people suffer from the same types of psychiatric disorders as persons of other ages, but particularly from dementia, mood disorders, and delusional disorders. The goals for the treatment of all elderly persons, both at home and in long term care (LTC) settings, should be to help patients recover from or reduce symptomatology and disability due to their psychiatric illnesses, to minimize the adverse effects of treatment, and to establish appropriate living situations that are tailored to the needs of the individual patient.

Several studies have shown a high prevalence of psychiatric disorders among nursing home residents (Chandler & Chandler, 1988; Merriam et al., 1988; Rovner et al., 1986; Snowdown, 1993). When psychiatric disorders are directly assessed, the estimated prevalence among nursing home residents generally exceeds 50%. According to the 1984 National Nursing Home Survey Pretest, however, only 2% of residents were receiving help from a mental health specialist (Burns et al., 1988). Dementia, sleep disorders, adjustment disorders, psychosis, anxiety, and depression are typical diagnoses. Nursing homes may address common behavioral disturbances such as agitation and social withdrawal (Everit et al., 1991), which frequently accompany these disorders, with behavioral therapy, psychotropic medications, restraining or protective devices, emotional support for patients and their families, and regular care planning meetings by staff members. However, poor access to outpatient geropsychiatric services, staff shortages, and inadequate nursing home design may impede the use or success of such treatment measures (Chandler & Chandler, 1988), and psychiatric hospitalization often ensues.

During the past few decades, several studies have proposed models for delivering better psychosocial care in the LTC setting (Brody, 1977; Bienenfeld & Wheeler, 1989; Grossberg et al., 1990;

Sakauye & Camp, 1992; Santmyer & Roca, 1991; Taube et al., 1984). These models share the goals of involving mental health professionals in the residents' daily care, improving the diagnosis of mental disorders, directing psychiatric treatment to patients with mental illnesses, and providing active consultation for emergency situations in the nursing home.

Psychosis

As the population ages, the number of older persons experiencing psychotic symptoms for the first time continues to grow. **Approximately 4% of older persons** (those 65 years of age or older) **living in the community** (Christenson & Blazer, 1984)**, 17% of outpatients seen at geriatric psychiatry clinics, and 21% of those newly admitted to nursing homes have psychotic symptoms.** This underscores the need for psychiatric consultants in the LTC setting. Staff members should understand the risk factors and common medical/psychiatric causes of psychotic symptoms in the elderly patient. The principal risk factor in the elderly is pre-existing cognitive impairment. Several medical disorders and medication-induced disorders can also produce delirium with psychosis in elderly patients (Tables 1 and 2).

Individuals who have sensory impairments (visual or auditory), **especially those that occur abruptly, have a higher risk for developing psychotic symptoms. Social isolation, poor social support, male gender, and emotional trauma in early life may also predispose individuals to late-life psychosis.** Psychiatric causes of psychotic symptoms include late-onset (age 45 or later) schizophrenia, affective disorders (e.g., depression and bipolar illness), dementia, delirium, and late-life delusional disorder.

Depression

The most common "noncognitive" psychiatric disorder in the elderly is depression, which is also the most common reversible psychopathology in the nursing home setting. Depression in LTC

Table 1
Medical Disorders Associated With Psychosis

AIDS	Parkinson's disease
Cushing's disease	Sleep deprivation
Hypoglycemia/Hyperglycemia	Electrolyte imbalance
Hypothyroidism/Hyperthyroidism	Vitamin B-12 and folate deficiency

---

Table 2
Medications That Can Produce Psychosis in the Elderly

Alcohol (through intoxication/withdrawal)
Analgesics/Anti-inflammatory agents (e.g., indomethacin, aspirin)
Corticosteroids (e.g., prednisone)
Antiarrythmics (e.g., digitalis, quinidine, procainamide)
Cardiac agents (e.g., propranolol)
Anticholinergic/Antihistaminic agents (e.g., diphenhydramine, hydroxyzine)
Antineoplastic agents
Histamine-H2 blockers (e.g., cimetidine)
Anticonvulsant agents (e.g., phenytoin, primidone, carbamazepine)
Antiparkinsonian agents (e.g., L-dopa/carbidopa, amantadine, bromocriptine)
Benzodiazepine (through paradoxical reaction/withdrawal)
Stimulants (e.g., methylphenidate, amphetamine, thyroid hormone replacement, ephedrine)
Tricyclic antidepressants (amitriptyline, imipramine, doxepin)

settings often goes unrecognized and may even be dismissed as normal. (A common misconception is that the elderly do not need as much sleep as they did in earlier years or that "it would be normal to be depressed if you had no family and lived in a nursing home.") In fact, depression is not a part of normal aging and most often occurs in the context of multiple physical and psychosocial problems (Katz, 1996). The symptoms can be variable and vague (with somatic complaints and anxiety common), and depression can manifest as agitated behavior or withdrawal. Depression occurs in both cognitively intact patients and those with dementia, and its incidence increases with age.

The prevalence of major depression in the general population of noninstitutionalized elderly is low (from 1.8% to 2.9%); in nursing homes, it is 6%. Late-life depression causes dysfunction (withdrawal, apathy, decreased energy, decreased appetite with poor nutrition) and excess disability in the medically ill patient. It also increases the risk of premature death (including suicide). Approximately 40% of elderly patients with depression will become chronically depressed if they remain untreated, and in 30% to 40% of cases, depressive symptoms will recur within a year after recovery. **The severity of the concomitant medical illnesses is often the most powerful predictor of depressive symptoms.** Many medical illnesses and medications have been associated with depression (Tables 3 and 4). Individuals who commit suicide after age 55 are likely to have suffered from major depression, substance abuse, or other risk factors. About 20% of all suicides are committed by persons 65 years of age or older; the suicide rate for men aged more than 80 years was 70 per 100,000 in 1992, whereas the suicide rate in the general population was 12.5 per 100,000 in 1988.

It may be difficult to distinguish between dementia and depression, particularly in patients with mild dementia or moderate to severe depression. Approximately 25% to 40% of elderly patients with dementia also have mild to severe depressive symptoms that require treatment; 80% of them can be treated effectively using combined pharmacotherapy and psychotherapy. **Pseudodementia refers to the cognitive impairment associated with depression in the elderly and occurs in 10% to 15% of cases.** Cognitive deficits in the areas of information processing and executive skills have been shown to improve with antidepressant treatment.

There is clear evidence that elderly patients respond to antidepressant medications, even in cases with severe medical comorbidi-

Table 3
Medical Conditions Associated With Depression

Hypertension	Cerebrovascular accidents
Coronary bypass surgery	Myocardial infarct
Hyperparathyroidism	Hypothyroidism
Autoimmune diseases	Chronic pain syndromes
Rheumathoid arthritis	Dementia (Alzheimer's, Renal dialysis, vascular
Amyotrophic lateral sclerosis	Multiple sclerosis
Brain tumors	Sexual dysfunction
Chronic obstructive pulmonary disease	Hypercortisolism
Congestive heart failure	Parkinson's disease
Diabetes mellitus	Cushing's disease
AIDS	Electrolyte imbalance
Sleep deprivation	Hypothyroidism/Hyperthyroidism
Hypoglycemia/Hyperglycemia	
Vitamin B-12 and folate deficiency	

Table 4
Medications That Can Cause Depression

Methyldopa	Reserpine
Thiazide diuretics	Propranolol
Benzodiazepines	Anti-inflammatory agents
Antineoplastic agents	Cimetidine
Clonidine	Neuroleptics
Guanethidine	Progesterone

ties and advanced age. Positive outcome is as high as 75% to 80% with adequate medication and psychotherapy (Reynolds et al., 1995). Improving recognition and treatment of late-life depression in LTC settings could markedly reduce excess disability and improve quality of life for the elderly patient.

Delirium

A delirium is a disturbance characterized by changes in conscious-

Table 5
Medical Conditions Associated With Depression

Systemic infections
(e.g., viral encephalitis, meningitis, syphilis)

Metabolic disorders
(e.g., hypoxia, hypercarbia, shock)

Fluid or electrolyte imbalance

Hepatic or renal disease
(e.g., hepatic encephalopathy, renal insufficiency)

Vitamin deficiencies
(e.g., B-12, niacin, thiamine, hypovitaminosis)

Trauma
(e.g., postoperative states, heat stroke, burns, head injury)

Hypertensive encephalopathy

Endocrinologic disorders
(e.g., hyperadrenal/hypoadrenal cortisolism, hypoglycemia/hyperglycemia)

Heavy metal toxicity
(e.g., lead, mercury, manganese)

Central nervous system diseases
abscess, normal pressure hydrocephalus, cerebrovascular accidents, tumors)

Inflammatory conditions
(e.g., vasculitis)

Focal lesions of the right parietal lobe and inferomedial surface of the occipital lobe

ness and cognition that develops over a short period of time (hours to days) and tends to fluctuate during the course of the day. Delirium has various etiologies: it may arise from a medical condition (Table 5), be substance induced (Tables 6 and 7), have multiple etiologies, or have unknown etiology. The essential feature of delirium is a change in cognition that is not explained by a pre-existing or evolving dementia. The symptoms may resolve in a few hours or may persist for weeks, particularly in patients with dementia. If the

Table 6
Substances Reported to Induce Delirium

Alcohol	Fuel or paint
Amphetamines and related	Opioids
substances	Phencyclidine and
Cannabis	related substances
Cocaine	Sedatives
Hallucinogens	Hypnotics
Inhalants	Anxiolytics

underlying etiologic factor is corrected or self-limited, the recovery is likely to be complete.

The change in the level of consciousness is manifested by decreased awareness of the environment. Patients are unable to focus, maintain, or shift attention. They might perseverate with an answer to a previous question and get easily distracted by irrelevant external stimuli. Sometimes it is very difficult for the clinician to engage the person in conversation or to assess the person for changes in cognitive function. The accompanying change in cognition includes memory impairment (mainly recent memory), disorientation (temporal and/or spatial), or language disturbance (dysnomia or dysgraphia). Delirious patients may also develop perceptual disturbances (misinterpretations, illusions, or hallucinations).

Table 7
Medications Reported to Cause Delirium

Anesthetics	Antimicrobials
Analgesics	Antiparkinsonian
Antiasthmatic agents	drugs
Anticonvulsants	Corticosteroids
Antihistamines	Gastrointestinal
Antihypertensive	medications
medications	Muscle relaxants
	Anticholinergic
	agents

Psychiatric manifestations of delirium include disturbances in the sleep-wake cycle (daytime sleepiness, nighttime agitation, difficulty falling asleep or maintaining sleep, and reversal of the night-day sleep-wake cycle); psychomotor agitation (picking at the bedclothes, trying to get out of bed, calling out, screaming, cursing, muttering, moaning, repeated nonpurposeful vocalizations), or retardation (lethargy); and emotional disturbances (anxiety, fear, depression, irritability, delusions, anger, euphoria, and apathy), which are associated with rapid and unpredictable shifts from one emotional state to another.

The prevalence of delirium in individuals more than 65 years of age who are hospitalized for a general medical condition is approximately 10% at the time of admission. Another 10% to 15% develop delirium while in the hospital.

Anxiety

Anxiety disorders have a peak age of onset in early adulthood, and their incidence and prevalence tend to decline with age. Most cases of anxiety disorder in late life are chronic and consist of generalized anxiety and agoraphobia. Late-life generalized anxiety is usually associated with depressive illness (Flint, 1997). Anxiety in the elderly is often unrecognized and inadequately treated, with benzodiazepines overused in such treatment and behavioral approaches underused. Several factors complicate recognition and treatment, including concomitant illness, overlap of cognitive disorders, cohort effects, ageism (age-related prejudice), and comorbid depression. In addition, anxious older patients will often present with somatic complaints rather than complain of "nervousness" (Table 8).

According to the National Ambulatory Medical Care Survey, 11% of all primary care patient visits were for anxiety. In a national survey of family practitioners (Orleans et al., 1995), physicians rated anxiety as the most common psychiatric problem seen in their practices. This may explain why approximately 80% of benzodiazepines are prescribed by nonpsychiatric primary care physi-

Table 8
Somatic Complaints in Patients With Anxiety

Tremors, shakiness	Numbing
Body aches and pains	Nausea, vomiting
Fatigue	Frequent urination
Restlessness	Sweating
Palpitations	Facial flushing
Dizziness	Insomnia
Faintness	Shortness of breath

cians. Total anxiety rates range from 0.7% to 18.6%. A recent study by Priegerson et al. (1996) attempted to distinguish the symptoms of anxiety from those of depression and grief in elders whose spouses had recently died. They found that anxiety symptoms among widowed elders appeared to be distinct from the symptoms of depression and grief and that the baseline severity of both types of anxiety predicted severity of depression. These findings suggest the need for more specific identification and treatment of anxiety, depression, and grief symptoms in the context of late-life spousal bereavement. In LTC settings, anxiety can occur due to unfamiliar surroundings.

This disorder is characterized by persistent fears of recurrent, unexpected panic attacks. Individuals with panic disorder often anticipate a bad outcome from a mild physical symptom or medication side effect (e.g., thinking that a headache indicates a brain tumor or an impending stroke). Such individuals are less tolerant of medication side effects and generally need continued reassurance to take medication. If this disorder is not treated appropriately or is misdiagnosed, the belief in an undetected life-threatening illness may lead to both chronic debilitating anxiety and excessive visits to health care facilities. This pattern is usually emotionally and financially disruptive.

Major depression occurs frequently in individuals with panic disorder (at rates of 50% to 65%). In approximately one third of individuals with both disorders, the depression precedes the onset of panic disorder. Persons with panic disorder with superimposed major depression, substance abuse, and personality disorders are reportedly at increased risk for suicide ideation and suicide attempts (Henriksson et al., 1996). The key to effective treatment, which may strongly affect an individual's quality of life, is early recognition of the condition. Deciding when to refer LTC patients and to whom is often difficult, because the symptoms can be confused with those of medical conditions (Table 9). Early referral to a psychiatrist or psychologist can be cost effective in the long run.

A panic attack involves a sudden onset of intense apprehension, fearfulness, or terror, which is often associated with feelings of impending doom. Other symptoms include shortness of breath, palpitations, chest pain, choking sensations, and a fear of "going crazy" or losing control. Transient tachycardia and moderate elevation of systolic blood pressure may occur during some panic attacks. Some studies have suggested that mitral valve prolapse and thyroid disease are more common among individuals with panic disorder.

Phobia is the most common anxiety disorder in the general population. Occurring twice as frequently in females as in males, it is the most common psychiatric disorder next to cognitive impairment in persons 65 years of age or older, with a prevalence estimated at 10%. Depression is experienced by up to 39% of the elderly with phobic symptoms. Phobic disorders are characterized by significant anxiety provoked by exposure to a specific feared object or situation and often leads to avoidance behavior. They may take the form of simple phobia, agoraphobia, or social phobia. The clinician, however, should keep in mind that many of the fears of elderly persons are real (for example, an older person may become homebound because of fears of being robbed, particularly if he or she lives in a high-crime area).

Table 9
Medical Conditions Associated With
Geriatric Anxiety

Drug reactions:

Stimulants, antidepressants, caffeine, tobacco, nonsteroidal anti-inflammatory drugs, over-the-counter hypnotics, alcohol/barbiturate/benzidiazepine withdrawal

Endocrine disorders:

Hyperthyroidism, hyperparathyroidism, hypoglycemia, pheocromocytoma

Cerebral event:

Cerebrovascular accidents, transient ischemic attacks

Neurologic disorders:

Parkinson's disease, epilepsy, dementias, chronic pain

Infectious disorders:

Influenza, hepatitis, encephalitis, pneumonia

Cardiac disorders:

Congestive heart failure, myocardial infarction, pulmonary embolism

Metabolic disorders:

Dehydration, electrolyte imbalance, fecal impaction

Neurologic Illnesses With Psychiatric Symptoms

Dementia:

This syndrome involves a persistent compromise of mental function that affects memory and produces deficits in language, visuospatial function, calculation, and/or executive functions (abstraction, judgment, planning, and sequencing) **or changes in personality** (apathy, indifference, or disinhibition). The syndrome must be sufficiently severe to interfere with social or occupational function and must not occur exclusively during a state of delirium. It is not associated with an altered level of consciousness. It is most common in the elderly, but it is not an invariable accompaniment of normal aging. **The course of dementia is determined by its etiology** (Table 11): **degenerative disorders are progressive, whereas reversible dementias may remit with appropriate treatment.** Five percent of older persons in the United States (approximately 1 million individuals) have significant dementia and are unable to take care of themselves; 10% have mild to moderate dementia. Approximately 60% of nursing home residents carry a diagnosis of dementia, and about 1% of those more than 65 years of age develop dementia each year. Even after a careful diagnostic workup (Table 10), only 10% of dementias are reversible. Psychological factors influence the degree and severity of the dementia; for example, greater premorbid intelligence and education is associated with increased ability to compensate for cognitive deficits.

There are two major types of dementia: Alzheimer's and vascular. Alzheimer's dementia is a progressive disorder characterized by severe loss of intellectual functioning. It is the fourth leading cause of death among elderly people and is more common in women than in men. The cause remains unknown, but genetic and environmental factors are presumed to play a role. The prevalence is 3% among individuals aged 65 to 74 years, 19% among individuals aged 75 to 84 years, and approximately 47% amount individuals aged 85 years or older.

Table 10
Diagnostic Work-Up of Dementing Disorders

- Good psychiatric and medical history, including mode of onset, duration, specific cognitive and behavioral changes, toxic exposures, substance use, head trauma, medications, and nutrition

- Physical examination, including a good neurological exam

- Laboratory tests: complete blood count, sedimentation rate, liver function, thyroid function, electrolytes, vitamins B-12 and folate, rapid plasma reagent, heavy metal screen, drug screen, and serum protein electrophoresis

- Neuroimaging studies (magnetic resonance imaging or computerized axial tomography scan of brain)

- Other tests (electroencephalogram, lumbar puncture)

- Neuropsychological testing

Table 11
Causes of Dementia

- Alzheimer's disease (most common cause of dementia, accounting for 50%–65% of cases)

- Vascular dementia (second most common cause of dementia, accounting for 20% of cases)

- Infections (e.g., syphilis, chronic meningitis, AIDS)

- Neoplastic disorders (e.g., meningioma, glioma, metastatic disease)

- Myelinoclastic disorders (e.g., multiple sclerosis, adrenoleukodystrophy)

- Traumatic conditions (e.g., posttraumatic encephalopathy, subdural hematoma)

- Inflammatory conditions (e.g., lupus, temporal arteritis, sarcoidosis)

- Toxic conditions (e.g., alcohol-related conditions, polysubstance abuse, heavy metal poisoning)

- Metabolic disorders (e.g., heart failure, anemia, deficiency states, porphyria)

- Hydrocephalic dementias (e.g., normal pressure hydrocephalus, intraventricular tumors)

Vascular dementia is diagnosed when cerebral injury from vascular disease leads to multiple cognitive impairments. It can be the result of an accumulation of cerebral infarctions (multi-infarct dementia) or chronic ischemia. It is more common in men, the risk factors are multiple (Table 12), and the usual age of onset is approximately 60. Most patients survive 6 to 8 years after diagnosis and die of cardiovascular disease or stroke. Its clinical presentation depends on the location of cerebral injury. Onset is abrupt and coincides with cerebrovascular insult, with the dementia generally following a stepwise progression and a fluctuating course. There are usually focal neurologic signs, and the cognitive deficits display a patchy profile. Among the behavioral manifestations of dementing disorders (Table 13), agitation is often the factor that determines placement in a LTC facility.

Table 12
Risk Factors for Vascular Dementia

Hypertension	Alcohol abuse
Smoking	Hyperlipidemia
Diabetes mellitus	

Table 13
Behavioral Manifestations of Dementia

Sleep disturbances	Aggression
Delusions	Anxiety
Hallucinations	Apathy
Agitation	Social isolation
Wandering	Appetite disturbances
Combativeness	Depression

Parkinson's Disease:

The primary manifestations of Parkinson's disease include tremor, rigidity, bradykinesia, and unsteady gait. Psychiatric symptoms may be related to the disease process itself or develop secondary to pharmacological treatment. The prevalence of psychiatric symptoms as a result of antiparkinsonian agents has ranged from 5% to 81% (Giroti et al., 1988). Psychosis is a frequent complication of Parkinson's disease, with a reported prevalence of up to 22% (Friedman & Sienkiewics, 1991), which climbs as high as 60% in the later stages of the disease. Psychotic symptoms include confusion, hallucinations (more often visual than auditory), paranoia, delirium, and agitation. The risk for developing psychiatric symptoms increases with multiple or high doses of antiparkinsonian medications, cognitive impairment (with symptoms occurring in up to 48% of patients without cognitive decline and up to 81% of patients with pre-existing dementia), comorbid psychiatric disorder, and advanced stages of the illness. Depressive symptoms can be found in up to 45% of patients with Parkinson's disease.

General Principles of Medical and Psychiatric Assessment in Long Term Care

The Importance of Staff Education:

Psychopharmacologic treatment in institutional environments is often insufficient when patients are negatively affected by their caregivers and the environment. In these situations, geriatric psychiatrists typically provide caregiver education and support by meeting with families, answering their questions, and referring them to support groups or agencies.

The problem of meeting the needs of staff in LTC is initially paradoxical. We commonly assume that LTC facilities have professional caregivers who have some expertise in dealing with mental illnesses. Yet inappropriate medication use is common and frequently based on outdated algorithms. Sometimes the behavior of residents will not improve even with expert treatment, because erroneous staff beliefs lead to inappropriate responses to the disruptive behavior and promote continued behavioral disturbance. In these cases, intervening at the level of staff behavior and training will improve the patients' quality of life.

To meet the training needs of LTC facilities, geriatric psychiatrists should develop a routine education service that includes (but is not limited to) in-service training, treatment team meetings, and around-the-clock telephone coverage. In-services regarding mental health and treatment should involve all staff members (including dietetic, laundry, and maintenance personnel, since they have frequent patient contact). Topics may include management of aggressive and agitated behaviors, depression, dementia, delirium, psychotropic medications and their common side effects, stress management, and sleep disorders. Although didactic in-services are clearly needed, clinicians should also apply this information directly, through treatment team meetings, proactive telephone calls, and inquiries with the staff about patients' behavior (e.g., during bathing and toileting).

Psychiatric Educational Principles

Sakauye and Camp (1992) proposed seven guiding principles for delivering psychiatric care within the nursing home setting:

1. *Make the patient human.* Teach the staff to see nursing home residents not as clinical entities but as people. Use case conferences to present patients' life histories, residences, work histories, interests, and habits, which may all help to make nursing home residents real individuals to the staff.

2. *Assume that no behavior is random.* In a low verbal population, assume that pathological behavior is an attempt by the patient to communicate something.

3. *Look for the existence of depression or psychosis.* Psychotropic medications are often very effective in treating major psychiatric disorders. In the elderly without dementia, spontaneous recovery from depression or psychosis, by contrast, almost never occurs.

4. *Reduce multiple medications and medication doses.* Elderly patients often respond to lower doses of psychotropic medications and are at higher risk for drug interactions.

5. *Create a home-like environment.* Such an environment depends more on how individuals interact (with less hierarchical relations between patients and staff) than on the home's physical structure.

6. *Provide appropriate activities.* Patients should be able to participate in a range of activity programs. Teas might be better than bingo for encouraging social interaction.

7. *Remember that learning still occurs.* Patients with advanced dementia may be capable of learning new information or responding to positive reinforcement.

Guidelines for Psychiatric Consultation

If a patient is identified as having a possible psychiatric symptom (e.g., acute change in cognitive status, psychosis, depression, anxiety, or behavioral disturbances), referral to a psychiatrist should be made as early as possible. This is particularly essential if the patient suffers from active hallucinations, threatens suicide or homicide, refuses medical treatment, is violent or combative, or if severe depression, anxiety, or anorexia are present. It is important to clarify the reason for the psychiatric consult in order for the psychiatrist to identify the target symptoms and best determine the treatment. Careful review of the medical records is essential to rule out underlying medical problems that may be contributing to the psychiatric symptoms and to make a referral to the proper medical specialty, if warranted. Assessment of the psychosocial elements in the patient's environment will also affect treatment choice. Continued symptom monitoring is crucial to recognition of treatment nonresponse. If this is addressed at an early stage, the mental health team may be able to find alternative or adjunctive treatments, ultimately improving the patient's quality of life. Psychopharmacological assessment and treatment must be integrated within a biopsychosocial model for optimal care of the LTC patients.

References

Bienenfeld, F., & Wheeler, B. G. (1989). Psychiatric services to nursing homes: A liaison model. *Hospital and Community Psychiatry, 40,* 793–794.

Brody, E. M. (1977). *long term care of older people: A practical guide.* New York: Human Sciences.

Burns, B. J., Larson, D. B., Goldstrom, I. D., (1988). Mental disorder among nursing home patients: Preliminary findings from the National Nursing Home Survey pretest. *International Journal of Geriatric Psychiatry, 3,* 27–35.

Chandler, J. D., & Chandler, J. E. (1988). The prevalence of neuropsychiatric disorders in a nursing home population. *Journal of Geriatric Psychiatry and Neurology, 1,* 71–76.

Christenson, R., & Blazer, D. (1984). Epidemiology of persecutory ideation in an elderly population in the community. *American Journal of Psychiatry, 141,* 1088–1091.

Everit, D. E., Fields, D. R., & Soumerai, S. S., (1991). Resident behavior and staff distress in the nursing home. *Journal of the American Geriatric Society, 39,* 792–798.

Flint, A. J. (1997). Epidemiology and comorbidity of anxiety disorders in later life: Implications for treatment. *Clinical Neuroscience, 4,* 31–36.

Friedman, A., & Sienkiewics, J. (1991). Psychotic complications of long–term levodopa treatment in Parkinson's disease. *Acta Neurologica Scandinavica, 84,* 111–113.

Giroti, F., Soliveri, P., Carella, F., (1988). Dementia and cognitive impairment in Parkinson's disease. *Journal of Neurology Neurosurgery and Psychiatry, 51,* 1498–1502.

Grossberg, G. T., Rakhshanda, H., Szwabo, P. A., (1990). Psychiatric problems in the nursing home. *Journal of American Geriatrics Society, 38,* 907–917.

Henriksson, M. M., Isometsa, E. T., Kouppasalmi, K. I., Panic disorder in completed suicide. *Journal of Clinical Psychiatry, 57,* 275–281.

Katz, I. R. (1996). On the inseparability of mental and physical health in aged persons. *American Journal of Geriatric Psychiatry, 4,* 1–16.

Merriam, A. E., Aronson, M. K., Gaston, P., (1988). The psychiatric symptoms of Alzheimer's disease. *Journal of the American Geriatric Society, 36,* 7–12.

Orleans, C. T., George, L. K., & Houpt, J. L. (1985). How primary physicians treat psychiatric disorders: A national survey of family practitioners. *Archives of General Psychiatry, 42,* 52–57.

Prigerson, H. G., Shear, M. K., Newsom, J. T., (1996). Anxiety among widowed elders: Is it distinct from depression and grief? *Anxiety, 2,* 1–12.

Reynolds, C. F., Frank, E., Perel, J. M., (1995). Maintenance therapies for late-life recurrent major depression: Research and review circa 1995. *International Psychogeriatrics, 7,* 27–39.

Rovner, B. W., Kafonek, S. D., Filipp, L., (1986). The prevalence of mental illness in a community nursing home. *American Journal of Psychiatry, 143,* 1446–1449.

Sakauye, K. M., & Camp, C. J. (1992). Introducing psychiatric care into nursing homes. The Gerontologist, *32,* 849–852.

Santmyer, K. S., & Roca, R. P. (1991). Geropsychiatry in long term care: A nurse-centered approach. *Journal of the American Geriatric Society, 39,* 156–159.

Smyer, M. A., Brannon, D., & Cohn, M. (1992). Improving nursing home care through training and job redesign. *The Gerontologist, 32,* 327–333.

Snowdon, J. (1993). Mental health in nursing homes: Perspectives on the use of medications. *Drugs and Aging, 3,* 122.

Taube, C. A., Burns, B. J., & Kessler, L. (1984). Patients of psychiatrists and psychologists in office practice, 1980. *American Psycholgist, 39,* 1435–1447.

4

Individual Therapy in Long Term Care

MICHAEL DUFFY, PH.D., ABPP

Abstract

THIS CHAPTER gives a close-up view of the process of providing psychotherapy for older adults in a nursing home. It emphasizes the need, above all, to establish an intense therapeutic relationship which will serve as the basis and principal vehicle for all other interventions. The chapter details key elements of this relationship, including developing therapeutic "posture," psychological "engagement," and appreciation of psychological complexity of older clients. Using case material, this chapter pinpoints several aspects of the psychotherapeutic process, such as psychological pace, confidentiality, and time limits, in terms of working with late-life anxiety depression and cognitive confusion.

Upon completing this chapter, readers will:

1. Understand the practical environment of long term care settings, limitations and opportunities in utilization, time limits, and confidentiality.
2. Understand the impact of the therapeutic relationship in facilitative conditions for therapeutic effectiveness and corrective therapeutic experience for problems.

3. Understand the role of specific techniques in alleviating symptoms of anxiety, depression, and cognitive disorientation.

Introduction

Little emphasis has been placed on the processes of psychotherapy with older adults. Even less research has been done on psychotherapy in long term care (LTC) settings, even though the nursing home has become a major setting for psychotherapeutic services. Contemporary older persons are infrequently self-referred for psychotherapy; instead, the nursing home—on behalf of nursing staff, physicians, or family members—has become a frequent source of referral for counseling and psychotherapy for older residents. The involvement of psychologists in the Medicare program and Medicare's current policy of reimbursing for psychological services has also directed practice toward LTC.

This chapter will paint a portrait of the practice of individual psychotherapy in such settings, which include assisted care residential settings and skilled and intermediate care nursing homes. It is based on the author's own experience in providing and supervising psychotherapeutic services in nursing homes during the past 19 years, as well as a review of the limited available clinical and research literature (Duffy, 1992b; Duffy & Morales, 1997). This chapter addresses therapeutic "posture" for working with older adults, the practical process of therapy for nursing home residents, and the clinical issues that arise when working with older adults in LTC. It also presents a typical case that illustrates many of the issues, dynamics, and strategies involved in providing psychotherapy to LTC patients.

Therapeutic Posture

Therapeutic Relationship:

Much of the research on psychotherapy that has been conducted during the last 10 years illustrates that theoretical approaches in psychotherapy are less responsible for outcome effectiveness than the common elements of psychotherapeutic process (Bergin & Garfield, 1994). These are probably present in the actual practice of therapies derived from a variety of theoretical approaches. Thus, the type and intensity of the therapeutic relationship seems to be a pivotal force for generating and supporting change in older clients. The therapeutic alliance that develops between therapist and client is frequently not discussed overtly with the patient but is, rather, implicitly enhanced by various aspects of the therapeutic process. There are some stereotypical notions of late life that could be used to argue against the relevance of developing an intense sustained therapeutic relationship with older adults; it is implicitly assumed that there is a decline of psychological intactness over time that militates against the possibility of developing an intense psychotherapeutic relationship. There is, however, no evidence that this applies globally; certainly the clinical experience of the author and others does not support such thinking (Knight, 1986; Duffy, 1992a). **It is, in fact, essential to take the time to develop an intensive relationship with older clients and not restrict therapeutic interventions to purely technical approaches that involve little time and attention.** At the broadest and most relevant level, psychotherapy with older adults is very similar to psychotherapy with younger adults.

Most of the mistakes that are made when providing psychotherapy for older adults are due to a stereotypical delimiting of the capacity, interest, and psychological complexity of late life. A particularly extreme example of this tendency is the "infantalizing" or "parentifying" of the older client. In the first case, which is seen very often in nursing homes, is the tendency to talk to older adults as if they were children. **The opposite mistake is to transferentially treat all older adults as if they were psychologically similar to our own parents or grandparents.** This leads therapists to diminish their own psychological power in the relationship and, therefore, deprive the client of effective therapy. In fact, whenever we (old or young) ask for help, we are in a position of need, which the helper should recognize. So, for example, when an

87-year-old woman comes to a 30-year-old therapist for help, the chronological ages are psychologically reversed, so that the therapist may assume an adult and/or even parental role with the older person, as necessary. An overly "respectful" attitude toward an older client will deprive that person of our best therapeutic efforts and restrain us from even gentle direct confrontation when it is needed.

Psychological "Engagement":

Psychological engagement, or connectedness between therapist and client, is particularly important in the hustle-and-bustle world of the nursing home. Health care professionals are notorious for their "pleasant but distant" style of interacting with patients. Although there are certainly examples of unpleasant and uncaring caregiving, most health professionals, including nurses and psychologists have a positive but clinically detached relationship with patients. In a world that is characterized by chronic illness and death, it is not surprising that such an attitude toward patients would be common. However, this approach is antithetical to the development of an effective and intense therapeutic relationship, in which the degree and quality of psychological engagement with the client are critical for therapeutic progress. Amid the activity and confusion of the nursing home or retirement community, it is particularly crucial that therapists enhance their listening and attending skills, as if entering a "cocoon" with the older client, blocking out distractions and avoiding the temptation to be pleasantly deferential and distant while maintaining an omnipresent smile. As in all significant human relationships, clients in therapy recognize the verbal and nonverbal signs of psychological "distance" when they experience it. **The power of the therapeutic moment will be diminished if the therapist does not fully engage with the client during the therapeutic encounter** (Duffy, 1988). Such engagement is also the very ingredient that enlivens the therapeutic encounter and ensures that we do not become bored or burnt out.

Psychological Complexity:

As we age, we do not become psychologically less complex or diminished in the variety and "color" of our psychological selves. There is, however, a stereotypical view of psychotherapy with older adults being less interesting than younger clients. Many therapists approach psychotherapy with older adults with an attitude of forbearance, not expecting the rich, complex, and often very troubled lives that older clients live. The general physical and neurological slowing process that characterizes persons in their later years may, understandably, convey the impression that they are less vulnerable psychologically and have diminished inner lives. However, a person who, for example, was abused as a child is no less affected by that experience late in life than in midlife. We need to listen with the same interest, concern, and curiosity to the unfolding stories that older clients tell of their long, multifaceted lives. Personality problems and styles are no less challenging and fascinating in an 80-year-old than they are in a 20-year-old, although, of course, we recognize that time and human experience alters these patterns and sometimes made the individual more resilient.

The following case study presents a good example of psychological complexity. Several aspects of this case will be discussed in later sections.

Case Study:

Ms. L, an 87-year-old woman who lived in the assisted living section of a retirement community, was referred for psychotherapy. The referral came from her family through a local psychologist. Ms. L was in the midst of a very agitated depression with some cognitive disorientation and surrounded by a family and professional staff who were also feeling highly anxious and immobilized. During the first session, I focused intensively on "soothing" the client and teaching her anxiety management strategies. She was much calmer during the next session and ready to tell me her story. Ms. L, who grew up in a traditional family in the northeastern United States and continued to live in that area after getting married, reported having an emo-

tional and sometimes psychologically abusive relationship with her husband. After about 11 years of marriage and the birth of their third child, her husband was committed for inpatient psychiatric care with a provisional diagnosis of schizophreniform disorder. She and her husband subsequently were divorced. She then moved to the southwest with her children, aged 10, 6, and 2. As a single mother, she seems to have felt very vulnerable psychologically during the following years; however, she recounted a long term supportive relationship with psychiatrists that appears to have been a very positive experience and helped her overcome her deep-seated sense of vulnerability. Her presenting problems of agitated depression and some accompanying cognitive confusion began shortly after her admission to the retirement community. She had recently moved from a city in which she lived in close proximity to her youngest child, a daughter, to the city where her two sons lived. With the exception of her youngest son, with whom she had a close relationship, her children felt a mixture of anxiety and anger at her "manipulative" and "hypochochondriacal" behavior.

Subsequent therapeutic strategies involved an intensive interpersonal approach to the depression along with the anxiety management strategies and some cognitive restructuring interventions. The therapist also met with the two sons and their wives and helped them understand and relate better to Ms. L in her agitated condition. During this meeting, the family members reported a long term pattern of psychosomatic-like symptoms in Ms. L, which seemed to have engendered an impatient and distrusting attitude, especially in her daughters-in-law. During the first 4 weeks of therapy, the therapist met with Ms. L two times a week. The frequency was then reduced to once a week for the next ten weeks, with each session lasting 1 hour; thereafter, the depressive and agitated symptoms declined considerably. At this point, another meeting was held with the family, during which the anger of the older son and both daughters-in-law was again evident and suggested a need for further inquiry into the dynamics of this extended family. The daughters-in-law seemed reluctant to accept any development and reduction of symptoms in their mother-in-law and felt that it was only a matter of time until her "real" personality re-emerged. The therapist avoided reacting to or contesting this portrayal, attempting instead to help the family understand more empathetically the interpersonal dynamics of psychosomatic eliciting behavior (Kell & Mueller, 1966). Later, and as if on cue, Ms. L had a severe case of diarrhea that family members interpreted as "only hypochondriacal." In fact, this was probably partly a medical event (nurses had to assure the family that diarrhea really did occur!), but it was also typical of a lifetime psychosomatic pattern of anxiety-driven gastrointestinal distress in which the symptoms themselves threw Ms. L into a vicious circle of self-defeating anxiety about her own well-being and recovery. It became obvious that this psychosomatic anxiety pattern, rather than the initial depression, was the dominant aspect of her personality and coping style. The therapist subsequently utilized anxiety management and imagery as well as intensive relaxation techniques, and Ms. L responded well, eventually having considerable success. The therapist also attempted to teach Ms. L preventive self-management strategies so that she could de-catastrophize her symptomatic anxiety-related pattern in future moments of stress. Throughout all of these phases of treatment, the therapeutic alliance with Ms. L seemed to be both the basis for her trust and response to therapy and the experiential "stage" on which her problems could be dramatized, encountered, and confronted. She was encouraged to reminisce, by free association, about unresolved issues involving her early childhood, her seemingly passive-dependent relationship with her own parents, and her troubled marriage, including the hospitalization of her husband and the subsequent divorce.

During this latter phase of therapy, the medical team played a critical role. As expected, the diarrhea had a significant physically debilitating effect (including dehydration), and Ms. L was on the verge of requiring hospitalization. The nursing home staff, in consultation with the therapist, was responsive to the psychological aspects of her medical condition. The physician, who had discontinued all medication at an earlier point, fearful of the narcotic effect, was eventually willing to recommend a mild tranquilizer to assist in settling the gastrointestinal tract irritation and discomfort. This was given as needed and, in conjunction with the anxiety management and the therapeutic relationship, seemed to be successful. After Ms. L's medical condition stabilized, she was able to walk again and was more motivated and socially active in the life of the retirement community. She seemed comfortable with a periodic session with the therapist and the assurance that therapy was available as needed.

The Structure of Psychotherapy

Psychological Pace:

In LTC settings, the amount of space and time, the setting, and privacy provide both difficulties and potential opportunities for enhancing the psychotherapeutic process. Every clinician that enters a nursing home for the first time probably goes through a period of adaptation. This ranges from the first reaction, often of horror, to chronic and disabling illness to discomfort with the sights and smells, to impatience with the unusually slow pace of the residents, which is in sharp contrast with the rather hectic pace of the staff and health care professionals. This slowed pace of life among older adults certainly provides psychotherapists with a challenge but also represents an opportunity. Entering the clients' psychological world requires slowing down the often hectic pace of our own professional and interior lives, which is often a blessing. It is the author's experience that the therapist's entire physical and psychological system is slower after completing a psychotherapy session with an older person in a nursing home. In "joining" them, the therapist enters a sphere that is less hectic, more interior, and more relaxed.

Privacy:

One of the difficulties of LTC settings is the lack of private space in which to conduct psychotherapy. Even when such space is available (as in a single occupancy room or a meditation room), it is not unusual to be interrupted by other residents who are simply interested in or curious about the proceedings or, alternatively, are cognitively confused and wandering throughout the facility. It does not help to be reactive at moments like these and to insist on conditions that are unlikely to exist in any institutional setting. **It is better to accept the complexity of the situation and even to incorporate the interruptions into the therapeutic process** (e.g., by moving from a dyadic to a group interaction), thus attending to the well-being of both the client and the inter-loper. Such opportunities occasionally provide a means of teaching interpersonal skills or encouraging friendship between residents who otherwise may not have had any contact, as often happens in institutional settings. For professionals working in nursing homes, where space is at a premium because of the need for direct reim-bursement on all available beds, it is not unusual to use spaces such as chapels, libraries, administrative offices, and empty rooms. In the case of Ms. L, meetings were initially held in her independent liv-ing private room. Later, when she shared a nursing home room, they took place in an administrative office; they were moved to her own room after her roommate's death (which was itself traumatic). The author has even conducted therapy and supervision with pa-tients who were sitting under hair dryers in the beauty salon! In such settings, it is a challenge to focus entirely on the client and completely enter that person's world.

However, the complexity of providing psychotherapy for nurs-ing home residents results in a relatively naturalistic view of the process of psychotherapy, which may have distinct advantages. Af-ter all, nursing homes are not hospitals and are certainly not viewed by residents as psychiatric or mental health settings. Residents therefore approach the therapist with a fairly informal and natural attitude, welcoming the therapist into their lives as if into their own home. Although good psychological boundaries obviously need to be maintained, such informality can enhance the intensity of the therapeutic relationship and speed the process of therapy.

Confidentiality:

Obviously, maintaining appropriate confidentiality for clients is something of a challenge under these conditions, especially con-sidering the recent strengthening of professional ethics on confi-dentiality. Until a few years ago, professionals involved in the same case were free to discuss clinical and diagnostic issues; today, such discussions are usually conducted only with written consent and on a "need to know" basis. Although there are legitimate reasons for such developments, current professional behavior is often influenced significantly by therapist liability in ways that may be at odds with patients' well-being. It is clearly in the clients' interest to maintain privacy during psychotherapy. However, in some circumstances, psychotherapy in nursing homes (indeed, these may pertain to general psychotherapy settings) may engender different perspectives on the ethics of confidentiality. For example, if a therapist becomes aware of certain personality dynamics, family dynamics, or eliciting behavior that affects a resident, how ethical can it be not to convey such understandings to other members of the health care staff, such as nurses' and nurses aides, whose actions might directly violate the resident's needs. In the case of Ms. L, her psychosomatic eliciting pattern almost always produced resistance and impatience on the part of health care professionals who spent much time convincing her that she was not ill and psychologically "pushing her away." How ethical can it be not to instruct the professional staff in the critical but counterintuitive dynamics of hypochondriacal behavior? Ironically, to be effective, the staff must entertain a welcoming stance with such patients. The result of this counterintuitive behavior is, in fact, to limit the need to use physical disorders to express distress and elicit attention. This example emphasizes the need to rethink the ethics of confidentiality in LTC. We have already made such adjustments for minors when their well-being dictates that their parents be kept informed.

Time Limits:

Pervasive myths also surround the issue of time limits when providing psychotherapy for older adults. It is often said that psychotherapy sessions with older adults need to be relatively short due to their limited attention span and physical disabilities. **However, if the therapist establishes a significant psychological connection with the client, then the element of time fades into the background.** This is perhaps true of all meaningful human relationships; when we are mutually engaged in a manner that stimulates our interest, curiosity, and fascination, then time ceases to be a factor. Even in cases of chronic medical illness and physical fatigue, clients may be energized rather than fatigued by an engaging therapy session. At the same time, it may be true that as we age, we become more discriminating about human interactions and more willing to express dissatisfaction when relevant (although it sometimes comes as a surprise to new trainees to find residents rejecting their offer of counseling and telling them to go away and not bother them). The point is that when we are interesting and engaging, others will want to listen to and converse with us—whatever their age.

Another factor may influence the preference for shorter psychotherapy sessions with older adults: reimbursement patterns established by the Health Care Financing Administration (HCFA) for psychotherapy. It can be financially advantageous for health care companies and individual geropsychologists working in nursing homes to use multiple short sessions (25 minutes) rather than full-length sessions (50 minutes). The HFCA has begun to monitor this practice, suspecting that the use of multiple short sessions with multiple clients has more to do with financial benefit than client need. If therapists in nursing homes do establish significant relationships with their clients, they may offset the potential danger of such exploitation and abuse.

Issues and Related Interventions

The Therapeutic Alliance and Corrective Experiences:

As mentioned earlier, the so-called *therapeutic alliance* (Bordin, 1976) must be given a central role in psychotherapy interventions for older adults. An intense psychotherapeutic relationship with an older person provides a stage on which major psychological issues in that person's life may be reexperienced. In many cases, psychotherapeutic change is about redoing or correcting psychological strategies that were developed earlier in life to cope with life's vicissitudes. Persons entering therapy often have reached a point in their lives when formerly effective adaptive coping styles (e.g., avoiding an abusive family situation through denial and disassociation) have become redundant and counterproductive in contemporary relationships. Ms. L, for example, had developed an interactive style that involved psychosomatic signaling as a means of gaining empathy from significant others. Initially, family members and caregivers responded to her medical needs with sympathy; only later did they (predictably) begin to feel angry with and manipulated by her. However, in the course of the therapeutic relationship the therapist was able, counterintuitively, to allow Ms. L to obtain what she needed without using psychosomatic symptoms and was able to show her how to ask for emotional support and closeness directly. The next phase of the therapy, of course, is to transfer this new experience of relationship to family members and other health care providers so that she could learn to express her emotional needs directly and avoid pushing people away through misguided eliciting behaviors.

Late-Life Anxiety:

In Ms. L's case, while agitated depression was the presenting symptom in the initial phase of therapy, the most pervasive and prevailing symptom in her life pattern was anxiety. Anxiety in older adults is an interesting and challenging problem. Generally, as the sense of self strengthens across the life span, anxiety diminishes. However, in Ms. L's case, continuing insecurity led to a lifelong pattern of anxiety that manifested itself in various ways, including gastrointestinal distress, cognitive confusion, and insecurity in interpersonal relationships. Addressing her anxiety meant dealing aggressively with the symptom patterns of anxiety through the use of relaxation, breathing prescription, and imagery while also attending to the impoverished sense of self that was the basis of her generalized anxiety. Symptomatically, anxiety in its various forms—such as gastrointestinal distress, agoraphobia, and compulsive behavior—can look very different, but dynamically they may be quite similar. It is thus important to work at both ends of the anxiety spectrum, dealing aggressively with each anxiety symptom and also (perhaps parsimoniously) dealing with the more generalized sustaining sense of anxiety drawn from the insecure self (Kohut, 1977).

Depression and Interpersonal Therapy:

Dealing with depression may be a relatively straightforward matter. The interpersonal therapy approach (Frank et al., 1993), which uses an intensive therapeutic relationship and stimulation of the interpersonal world of the client, may be helped by cognitive strategies, such as thought stopping and cognitive restructuring, as well as the use of guided physical activity. **When the etiology of depression is viewed as a loss of the sense of self, an intensive relationship in itself can be rapidly healing.** Regardless of the verbal or theoretical content of the psychotherapy sessions, the "soothing" effects of the relationship (over 10 to 12 weeks of therapy for a moderate depression) appear to be critical for the resolution of the depression. This explains the research findings of no difference in outcome for cognitive vs. relational forms of therapy; the underlying therapeutic relationship may be the critical component in both cases.

Life Review and Reminiscence:

The use of reminiscence as a means of therapeutic life review (Butler, 1968) has become a standard LTC therapeutic technique. Although reminiscence is often restricted to narrative and factual remembering, the most powerful use of the strategy is to focus on inner life experiences and their meaning and evaluation. In this context, the boundary between past and present becomes blurred. **As older persons begin to review and evaluate their life experiences, they encounter issues that are located chronologically in the past but experientially in the *psychological present*.** In therapy with Ms. L, life review reminiscence was woven in and out of most of the sessions as she dealt with and reconstructed elements of her life that felt unfinished and full of pain. Thus she traversed elements of early childhood that involved what seems to have been a somewhat symbiotic relationship with her parents, a troubled marital relationship and many years as a parent, during which she felt psychologically very weak but in fact did a relatively good job of parenting.

Unfinished Business:

Many professionals who work with older adults consider the issues of aging—retiring, losing friends, dying, etc.—to be among the primary therapeutic themes. In my experience, this has not been the case. It is persons in their early and middle years who have concerns about aging and death. Generally, older persons have resolved these issues quite well and are, instead, troubled by unresolved issues and events of their *earlier* lives. As life comes to its conclusion, opportunities for completion, closure, and resolution in important relationships dry up, and there is an increasing sense of urgency to complete unfinished business from earlier life. In a world that paid little attention to mental health and well-being, there were few opportunities to deal with these unfinished emotional domains; psychotherapy provides an opportunity to do so. While some have suggested that psychotherapy is redundant for older adults because it is "too late to make a difference," frequently the reverse seems to be true. Our lives are scattered with words that were never said, with love never expressed, and with forgiveness never asked, and late life becomes the opportunity to set this right.

Family Issues:

It is in this context that individual therapy with older adults in nursing homes often becomes family therapy. It may indeed be strategically more useful to spend several hours in family therapy healing unfinished relationships than endless hours in individual therapy dealing with symptomatic resolution of an unyielding depression. Many depressions in nursing homes are reactive by nature, and it is often useful to work on the source of the stress or hopelessness. Intergenerational family therapy is almost always helpful in the nursing home. It is critical that the therapist become aware of the family environment and system of the resident and be willing to reach out to the family, both as a means of accurate diagnosis as well as effective therapy. In many cases, contact with family will be through strategic phone calls and prescriptions for therapeutic family interventions (Duffy, 1987). In Ms. L's case, with her nearly desperate and frustrated daughters-in-law, the suggestion was made to respect their own limits of tolerance, to decide on reasonable and small increments of caregiving and visiting, and then to give that amount willingly without anger (using the example of caring for our own children, where giving is based on *choosing to* rather than *feeling like* helping).

Cognitive Confusion:

Finally, it is important to discuss cognitive confusion and the impact that this has on the therapeutic process. Traditional behaviorist treatments are most helpful in situations of serious cognitive confusion and deterioration. When an older person is in the middle to late stages of a dementia such as Alzheimer's disease, a verbal approach to therapy is insufficient. It is often much more compassionate to help a person maintain functional abilities as long as possible through conditioning methods that focus on eating, toilet, and wandering behaviors. In cases of serious cognitive decline, several useful behavior therapy approaches are available for dealing with and maintaining activities of daily living (Hussian, 1988). **However, there is a tendency to assume that psychotherapy becomes redundant when a person is no longer capable of logical language or discourse.** This assumption has led to the suggestion that Medicare reimbursements for psychotherapy should be disallowed in cases of dementia; this completely fails to acknowledge the continuing presence of emotional life after the loss of logical thought and language. It is this continuing emotional life, for example, that accounts for the presence of comorbid depression in Alzheimer's patients; it is even signaled in the emotion of embarrassment that is so often present in the early and middle phases of dementia. In other words, patients are aware of their cognitive confusion and may experience great distress at this decline. Depression is also a meaningful symptom of the sense of emotional abandonment that Alzheimer's patients feel when family members and even professional staff withdraw from them because of their cognitive and language deficits. We seem to assume that when we can no longer communicate verbally with one another, no relationship exists, let alone one that needs to be continually nourished. This actually flies in the face of our continuing life experience. How many of us really believe that intimacy and emotional exchange occur solely through the words we exchange? In many cases, intimate relationships exist in silence, in the comfort of human touch and close proximity. Psychotherapy itself exists, not in the words we use, but in the presence that those words convey. It is not simply the verbal exchange that characterizes the therapeutic alliance but rather the intention, meaning, comfort, and power of the therapist's psychological presence. Working with older patients with dementia tests the capacity of the therapist and family members to find nonverbal means of being present with older persons. Therapists, having mastered this capacity for being psychologically present without relying on narrative and linguistic means, can in turn teach family members to find comfort and peace in their relationship with their demented relative.

Conclusion

Providing individual psychotherapy in LTC involves opportunities as well as limitations. Although the available literature in this area is scant, psychotherapy in nursing homes is an increasing domain of psychological practice because of the rapid increase in the size of the old-old population. Psychotherapy with older and younger adults in fact has many more similarities than differences. The constraints of working in nursing homes fosters the development of a more naturalistic and intimate psychotherapeutic environment, which enhances the therapeutic relationship. At the same time, the psychological stress generated in such environments suggests that a full range of psychological techniques and treatments are needed.

References

Bergin, A. E. & Garfield, S. L. (1994). *Handbook of psychotherapy and behavior change.* New York: John Wiley & Sons.

Bordin, E. S. (1976). The generalizability of the psychoanalytic concept of the working alliance. *Psychotherapy: Theory, Research and Practice, 16,* 252–260.

Butler, R. N. (1968). The life review: An interpretation of reminiscence in the aged. In B. Neugarten (Ed.), *Middle age and aging.* Chicago: University of Chicago Press.

Duffy, M. (1987). The techniques and contexts of multigenerational therapy. *Clinical Gerontologist, 5,* 347–362.

Duffy, M. (1988). Avoiding clinical attachment in working with the elderly in nursing homes. *Clinical Gerontologist, 7,* 58–60.

Duffy, M. (1992a). Challenges in geriatric psychotherapy. *Individual Psychology, 48,* 432–440.

Duffy, M. (1992b). A multimethod model for practicum and clinical supervision in nursing homes. *Counselor Education and Supervision, 32,* 61–69.

Duffy, M., & Morales, P. (1997). Supervision of psychotherapy with older patients. In C. E. Watkins Jr. (Ed.), *Handbook of psychotherapy supervision.* New York: John Wiley & Sons.

Frank, E., Frank, N., Cornes, et al. (1993). Interpersonal psychotherapy in the treatment of late-life depression. In M. Weissman and G. L. Klerman (Eds.), *New applications of interpersonal psychotherapy.* Washington, DC: American Psychiatric Press.

Hussian, R. A. (1988). Modification of behaviors in dementia via stimulus manipulation. *Clinical Gerontologist, 8,* 37–43.

Kell, B. L. & Mueller, W. J. (1966). *Impact and change: A study of counseling relationships.* New York: Appleton-Century-Crofts.

Knight, B. (1986). *Psychotherapy with older adults.* Beverly Hills, CA: Sage Publications.

Kohut, H. (1977). *The restoration of the self.* New York: International Universities Press.

5

Working With Families in Nursing Homes

Sara Honn Qualls, Ph.D.

Abstract

FAMILIES ARE an integral part of life in nursing homes. These facilities vary, however, in the roles and expectations they create for families through their policies and climate. Psychologists working within nursing homes need to be familiar with the regulatory, funding, and organizational structures that shape decisions about care. Similarly, psychologists need to know the families' preinstitutionalization caregiving history in order to understand their concerns about the nursing home care. Families may have trouble dealing with the institution for many reasons, including confusion about the system, incongruent role expectations, long-standing conflicts, caregiver stress, and the many ethical dilemmas that they may face. Psychologists can influence family well-being by ensuring that accurate assessments of the resident's decision-making capacity are made, that families are involved in preventive activities that offer education and support, and that family interventions engage families and staff collaboratively in problem solving. Upon completion of this chapter, psychologists should be able to:

- Identify major participants in the nursing home industry who influence care decisions.
- Describe common family conflicts that arise in nursing homes.
- Describe the role of assessment in addressing family conflicts.
- Discuss preventive interventions that are likely to reduce the number and intensity of family conflicts.
- Discuss strategies for intervening with families in ways that will enhance their relationship with the nursing home residents and staff.

Introduction

How can psychologists help the families of residents in long term-care (LTC)? What special skills do psychologists bring to the LTC setting? This chapter addresses these questions by framing the roles of psychologists and families within the larger systems that govern LTC, by reviewing the challenges faced by families interacting with these systems, and by examining specific interventions that psychologists can use to assist these families. A nursing home might request a psychologist's assistance in each of the following cases:

- **A resident's wife is driving staff members crazy by criticizing everything they do to care for her husband.**
- **A resident's children are embroiled in an ongoing argument about do-not-resuscitate orders.**
- **The children of a resident are distressed with staff because the resident is unable to feed himself.**
- **The daughter of a resident, who visits her mother daily, leaves the facility in tears when her mother chastises her for not visiting in recent weeks.**

Psychologists, Families, and the Larger Systems

Psychologists who work with residents in LTC settings and their families are embedded in a complex set of political, legal, economic, regulatory, professional, and cultural systems. Many factors directly or indirectly affect residents' well-being (including their mental well-being, the traditional concern of psychologists). **A hierarchy of legislators, regulatory agencies, and nursing home survey teams controls funding for nursing homes, laws that protect residents' rights, and standards for mental health services.** The organization of nursing homes themselves is typically hierarchical, with the residents at the bottom, in the least powerful role as recipients of services. This hierarchy is influenced directly by health care providers, corporate offices, the labor pool, and families, who are also at the bottom of the hierarchy. The staff has its own internal hierarchy (e.g., the least powerful staff members are the nursing assistants, who provide the bulk of intimate care).

Although official relationships are usually structured hierarchically, the complex interrelationships among systems are not fully captured by the hierarchical model. Consider that families vote for the legislators who enact LTC legislation, pay taxes to fund the salaries of the regulatory agency staff members who write implementation rules, and often pay directly for the services provided by health providers and nursing home administrators. Furthermore, residents are, of course, members of these families, not just a separate group subject to their influence. Finally, note the additional relationships and paths of influence among health care providers, including psychologists, and corporate offices and families.

Psychologists may be called upon to address family problems that involve conflicts among these complex, overlapping systems. For example, a family member who complains because his mother couldn't get her breakfast at 10:30—when she would prefer to eat it—has raised a complex issue. Meeting the family member's demand would probably put the facility in conflict with regulations set by state health departments, as well as practices the facility itself has established to enable the entire range of residents' needs to be met; cost-control issues might also limit the ability of staff to plan individualized eating schedules. In such cases, family displeasure with particular staff members might be more appropriately targeted at an entire LTC system that offers institutionalized rather than individualized care. **Psychologists need an intimate understanding of the inner workings of the particular facilities in which they work, but they also need to know the larger regulatory, legislative, and funding contexts in which care is provided** (Smyer, 1989).

The Family's Journey Into Long Term Care Facilities

It is now well documented that families are continuously and substantially involved in the lives of older adults (Shanas, 1979), including those who live in nursing homes (York & Calsyn, 1977). The facility's view of its role with regard to residents and their families may determine whether the families work well with nursing homes. **As one gerontologist claims, "Good nursing home care is a continuation of family life, not the end of it"** (Cohn, 1985, p. 169). For families, the personal history of the nursing home resident is richly embedded in a family context. For staff, however, the family connection may be much less clear.

Although facilities vary in their use of family-friendly policies and informal interactional styles that encourage family involvement (Grau & Wellin, 1992), they generally recognize that families affect the delivery of services. In some facilities, families are seen as complicating factors that make the basic work of providing care more difficult. Other facilities view families as a valuable untapped resource for staff encouragement, resident care and socialization, and institutional support. Some even view family care as an integral part of their institutional role. **In other words, facilities**

may view families as obstacles, exploitable resources, or care recipients, among other things.

The path culminating in the placement of an older person in a nursing home is often difficult for family members, who may find that caring for their frail elder becomes an "unexpected career"(Aneshensel et al., 1995).The family usually provides a considerable amount of instrumental, hands-on care at home for months or years prior to nursing home placement. For many families, the decision to make the placement implies failure: failure to maintain a commitment to provide the care directly, failure to live up to their own expectations as a loving family, or failure to keep their loved one as healthy and happy as he or she "deserves" to be. Following admission to the nursing home, some families cope with the stress of placement by withdrawing, while others engage excessively in caring for the resident within the institution. Regardless, the transition, which involves handing direct control over daily care decisions to the institution while retaining other roles, is fraught with anxiety and rarely brings out the most creative, productive behavior.

Sources of Difficulties for Families in Nursing Homes

Systemic Confusion:

The complexities of nursing home systems often leave families feeling confused, frustrated, and helpless.Who makes up all of the regulations that the staff claims keeps them from doing what the family member wants them to do? Why can't care be more individualized? What happened to the woman who was bathing the resident yesterday; why isn't she providing that care today? Which administrator is responsible for getting something done about this specific concern? **The size and complexity of the facility** (and the nursing home industry) **may undermine a family's sense of competence about ensuring that their loved one receives proper care. In such cases, efforts to build a collaborative relationship between the family and the institution are likely to pay off** (Montgomery, 1983; Stewart, 1984).

Incongruent Role Expectations:

Residential care institutions send contradictory messages that often make it difficult for staff to know how to respond. **The name "nursing home" itself is an oxymoron. The medical model of care is in direct contradiction to what we create in a home.** The subtexts of many interactions reflect this paradoxical idea. Staff members are told to be professional and treat residents in a loving personal way. Members are also told to be personal, yet use rubber gloves (Smyer et al., 1985). Families may respond to this ambivalence by demanding that staff be both professional and personal, a true impossibility.

Families and staff often report receiving mixed messages from each other. The staff may encourage family involvement but offer no roles or mechanisms for their participation. Or staff members may ask the family to be involved, but then make the family feel they are in the way. Conversely, families may want the staff to treat their relative as if he or she were a member of the family but complain if the strictest controls are not maintained over nutrition or choice of clothing. These mixed messages stem, at least in part, from the self-contradictory effort to make a medical institution a "home."

The role expectations that families have for themselves and for the nursing home staff may, in addition, not be congruent with those of the administration, residents, and staff members. Although data on staff and family expectations show considerable similarities in expectations, there are also notable areas of disagreement (Bowers, 1988; Moulton, 1993; Schwartz & Vogel, 1990). Staff and families agree that safety, security, and physical health are primarily staff responsibilities. They also agree that families are responsible for special services, as well as for maintaining their relatives' hopes, dignity, and family connectedness and for helping their relatives retain choice over care decisions in that environment. Families express more of a desire to assist with personal care and activities, however, than staff expect. Families also have high expectations regarding the staff's ability to preserve the residents' dignity during routine instrumental tasks, such as bathing or dressing: expectations that are often not met. Staff, on the other hand, want stronger family involvement in end-of-life decision making than residents desire, again sending families a mixed message (Wolf-Klein et al., 1992).

Long-Standing Family Conflict:

Family problems in LTC may also frequently be rooted in ongoing family difficulties. Many families send a member to a nursing home after decades of conflicted relationships. **The behavior seen by staff and administration may be consistent with the family's lifelong patterns of internal or external interactions.** Sibling conflicts, verbal abuse, and withdrawn or withholding behavior can all be exhibited during any stage of the life cycle, including the final, dependent stages of an older adult's life. With the nursing home as an available arena, family conflicts can end up with the staff used as scapegoats or with some staff members being treated as if they were perfect while others are "scapegoated." The staff can easily become embroiled in conflict with each other as a result of the family's distorted perceptions.

Ethical Dilemmas:

Finally, the inherent difficulties of caring for very frail older adults who are experiencing multiple illnesses may be a challenge for families. The multiple problems experienced by residents of nursing homes often generate confusion among priorities. Balancing the need for aggressive rehabilitative treatment of individuals with acute illnesses and conditions (e.g., a urinary tract infection or a broken hip) against the need for long term interventions for chronic problems (e.g., muscle weakness, chronic diseases, and depression) requires sophisticated planning and ethical reasoning. Although many residents participate actively in planning their own care, the majority of residents in nursing homes face some degree of cognitive impairment that limits their ability to make decisions on their own. The everyday ethics (Kane & Caplan, 1990) of nursing home care are quite complex, requiring sophisticated consideration of the ethical principles such as beneficence and autonomy that must be balanced. Even with the most careful reasoning, decision making may be neither easy nor comfortable (Collopy, 1995).

Specific Family Problems That May Generate a Psychological Referral

Decision-Making Dilemmas:

High and Rowles (1995) describe the "progressive surrogacy" which characterizes the slow shift in responsibility for care decisions from the resident to others. Families and staff often share the surrogate role, with one or the other taking control of a particular set of decisions. For example, the hair care of a particular resident may involve the staff in determining the best position for hair washing, even though the family chooses the hair style and shampoo. On the other hand, families may leave all of those hair care decisions to staff, though some may become incensed that staff members are not retaining the hair style the resident has had for several decades. It is easy to imagine how such simple decisions can lead families to identify the staff as a problem (and vice versa). Both sets of participants can claim unique expertise. **Usually, the staff has a heightened awareness of immediate care needs in an institutional setting. Families, by contrast, are most knowledgeable about the preferences of the resident and may be able to think holistically and comprehensively about his or her life.**

Dramatic end-of-life decisions represent a minority of the care decisions made for LTC residents, but they often provoke exceptional anxiety among family, staff, administrator, and health professionals. Such decisions may, for example, involve determining whether to use a feeding tube for a severely demented person or whether to treat the resident with congestive heart failure aggressively. State law provides a clear protocol for who can make such decisions if the resident is deemed incompetent to do so, but that does not disengage other care providers from having a strong opinion. Occasionally, families and staff strongly disagree about such decisions and have difficulty acknowledging the legitimacy of the other's opinions; this may lead not only to hurt feelings but to disruptions in the quality of care.

Case Vignette:

Two adult children of a resident have repeatedly been asked by the staff to help with decisions regarding their mother's medical treatment. The children agree that they do not wish to prolong their mother's life with medical interventions. Staff members became concerned that the children viewed these decisions as precluding palliative care. The resident recently developed another urinary tract infection which is probably quite painful, although she cannot communicate about it. The children are very hesitant to permit antibiotic treatment. The staff became angry with them for "not caring" about their mother.

Rehabilitation decisions involve the longer-term issue of the aggressiveness with which maximum autonomy should be pursued. Although rehabilitation questions are often not controversial, they can generate interfamilial conflict or family-staff conflict over priorities in maintaining the quality of a resident's life. Whereas a resident's wife may maintain that physical therapy is too painful for her husband, their daughter may argue that not pushing him to walk again will kill him indirectly by limiting him to an unacceptable quality of life. A physician may consider a resident's risk of choking to be so great that the resident must use a thickener, but the resident's daughter may support her mother's refusal of the thickener because her mother detests the taste of the thickened water.

Conflicts over everyday care decisions are likely to be the most common and the most intense (e.g., should a resident be required to wear poorly fitting teeth that cannot be fixed because of gum disease?). One child may insist that without the teeth, his father's dignity will be compromised; another child may consider it cruel and not particularly dignifying to see his father struggle to keep the ill-fitting teeth in his mouth. When a resident lacks control over decisions about daily routines such as bathing, dressing, eating, ambulation, smoking, and visits, the potential for conflict among surrogate decision makers is enhanced.

Case Vignette:

A woman and her husband of 62 years had never lived apart during their marriage until he was placed in a nursing home last year. Now, she comes to help with his feeding, take home his laundry, and entertain him for hours on end. Despite his dementia, he is able to play simple card games with her, look at picture books, and enjoy a television program while holding her hand. Lately, his resistance to bathing and dressing has been intense, a noted contrast to his lifelong pattern of fastidiousness. His wife agrees with the staff that they should simply reduce the frequency of bathing and dress him only in clothes that are very simple to put on. The couple's son and daughter-in-law also visit at least twice a week, however, and are very critical of the staff for not keeping their father looking "like himself."

The case illustrates a common dilemma: how to prioritize between comfort and personal identity.

Families' Criticizing Staff:

Case Vignette:

The daughter of a resident visits her mother daily, often staying for several hours. The staff dreads being assigned to the resident because they know they will not complete a single task without being corrected by the daughter. The administrator and director of Nursing also know the daughter very well, because she frequently asks them to reassign staff members so that her mother will receive care from the staff she prefers. Following her visits, the resident is often agitated and hard to calm down.

Families criticize the nursing home staff for many reasons, and the tension that results from that criticism is only rarely useful.

Certainly, criticized staff members are often, indeed, performing below acceptable standards. The challenge of maintaining an adequate labor pool in nursing homes is legendary. Families are perfectly correct in considering their role to include that of advocate and overseer (Collier, Prawitz, & Lawrence, 1994). **However, families may also criticize the staff for a myriad of reasons that stem from their own anxiety about the nursing home experience, which may lead to hypervigilance over the staff. Regardless of the motive, family criticism of the staff usually leads to an adversarial relationship that does not contribute to a sense of home.**

Caregiver stress is likely to require some outlet, and the staff is a perfect target. **Guilt over the decision to place a loved one in an institutional setting may provoke a caregiver to demand exceptional services that are unrealistic to expect.** One administrator offered the example of a daughter who insisted that her mother's spinach salad never again be served with cold dressing; only heated dressing was acceptable. Of course, this daughter may simply have had inappropriate expectations, but it is the intensity of the affect in such cases that makes the conflict difficult for staff to manage on their own. Especially vulnerable are those staff members who provide intimate care in the privacy of the resident's own room. Their mistakes may only be seen by family members, and their defense against accusations of inferior care usually pits their word against that of the family member.

Caregiver Depression:

Psychologists may be called upon to work with family members whose well-being is threatened by the stresses and strains of their role as caregiver to a nursing home resident. Staff are often quite affectionate toward family members, especially those who show devotion to their loved one. When the devotion takes a toll that appears to threaten the well-being of the family member, as in the following case, staff will often seek assistance for the family member.

Case Vignette:

A daughter's visits with her mother, a nursing home resident, are not very satisfying because the mother can no longer speak or recognize her daughter. The staff is worried about the daughter, who insists on visiting for an hour each evening, despite significant work and family demands. In recent weeks, three different staff members have mentioned to the social worker their concern that the daughter is becoming depressed.

A daughter who is experiencing intensive role overload in balancing the competing demands of a three- or four-generation family with work and home responsibilities may be referred to a psychologist for assistance. Staff members may also refer a spouse caregiver whose children criticize or fail to support her. **In such cases, the nursing home's role extends beyond that of providing services to its residents to include care for the community of persons involved in the facility.** Occasionally, an administrator may also refer a staff member whose family concerns are compromising his or her mental health or work quality.

Psychologists' Roles in Long Term Care Facilities

Psychologists can play many roles within LTC facilities. They may assess the mental health and decision-making capability of residents; intervene with residents and staff on the residents' behalf; consult with management on staff development, education, and personnel issues; consult with families; attend care conferences; provide staff in-services; and even represent various parties in court. Any of these roles may bring them in contact with families and potentially allow them to assist families. For example, they may alleviate a family conflict over a particular care decision for a resident by showing the family neuropsychological test data indicating the resident's functional cognitive status. In this case, a traditional assessment is the main tool for family intervention.

For psychologists, the nursing home is distinguished from other settings by the length of time that residents live there and the declining health that most residents are likely to experience during their stay. Because residents live in facilities for months or years, the quality of their lives is determined by the quality of care and the institutional climate. **Psychologists who are asked to address the residents' mental health must therefore gain a long term perspective by examining institutional policies and practices that affect the residents' well-being.** For example, meal preparation and presentation, dining room rules about seating arrangements, bathing schedules, and staff rotations all may affect the residents' quality of life. Psychologists do not have the luxury of entering the facility to perform an hour of psychotherapy or 2 hours of testing with the presumption that this will be the full extent of their involvement with a given resident.

Psychologists working in LTC settings must also be cognizant of the downward trajectory of health and well-being for most residents. Except for rehabilitation-oriented, subacute care facilities, nursing homes generally admit patients when they are extraordinarily frail and facing a terminal decline over a period of days, months, or years. Whereas residential facilities for younger persons (e.g., child or adult psychiatric facilities) are expected to care for residents who stay only long enough for their psychological functioning to be stabilized, nursing homes are expected to care for permanent residents. Most residents have some form of dementing illness that will render them fully incompetent to provide any self-care. The psychologist's role is often to minimize the loss of function or maximize control over the functions that remain rather than fully rehabilitate all functions to the point of complete autonomy.

The extent to which the psychologist is integrated into the facility will determine the specific tasks that he or she is assigned. Psychologists who serve as consultants on an on-call basis may be perceived by all parties within the facility as neutral advocates for a resident. These psychologists are most likely to be called on to assess functional capacity or intervene with circumscribed disorders such as depression. Psychologists who are hired within a facility or have a contractual arrangement with the facility are more likely to be perceived as representatives of the facility. These psychologists may be asked to contribute to the evaluation of the effectiveness of staffing patterns, policies, and procedures and to help the administration persuade families to participate in care in ways that are congruent with the facility's expectations. Psychologists who are hired by the family may be viewed with caution by the facility if it presumes that the psychologist is primarily loyal to the family. Whom the psychologist represents will have a direct impact on the psychologist's degree of leverage over administrative policies (e.g., who can attend patient care conferences), procedures (e.g., how laundry is handled), and climate (e.g., family-staff interactions). The first step for psychologists in any family intervention is to make their role clear to all involved.

Recommended Strategies for Intervening With Family Problems

Assessment:

Psychologists must first verify the thoroughness and accuracy of assessment data regarding the resident's physical and psychological condition and social skills (Lichtenberg, 1994). Without accurate information, conflicts among staff, residents, and families can escalate needlessly. **Given the frequency of compromised decision-making capacity among nursing home residents, it is particularly essential to have accurate data regarding cognitive function.** Competency for self-determination must be based on data. Interestingly, most of the signals indicating that surrogate decision making will be necessary are informal and are handled informally (High & Rowles, 1995).

The strategy for assessing a resident's ability to make any specific decision must be appropriate for that particular decision. A staff member's hunch about what a resident can do is not a good basis for determining what the resident may or may not decide to do. Informal data are highly unreliable and do not meet the standards of care expected of psychologists (Lichtenberg, 1997). However, a score on an intelligence test or a memory test that is not linked to the demands of the specific decision in question is not an appropriate guideline either (Grisso, 1986). In the absence of full legal guardianship, surrogate decisions must be made only when it is clearly demonstrated that the individual cannot make those specific decisions competently. Accurate data provided by a qualified professional will be helpful in resolving much of the conflict that arises among family members and between families and staff.

Preventive Interventions:

Psychologists need to be active players in many domains of the facility. If possible, they should attend patient care conferences (PCCs), where both problem-finding and problem-solving occurs. Staff members may describe a situation that is easily recognizable by the psychologist as indicative of a mental disorder or a shift in the level of cognitive function. By themselves, staff members might never have recognized the problem (or sought assistance) until it reached a crisis stage, which is often made evident by upset family members. Intrafamily and family-staff conflicts may also be brought up in PCCs, and the psychologist may be able to suggest useful approaches to these problems. Once the psychologist has made his or her presence felt at PCCs, it might be possible to encourage more routine family involvement in the process of resident care review. One challenge, of course, is that attendance at PCCs is not reimbursable under Medicare, so the psychologist must find alternative funding arrangements (e.g., a contract with the facility) or else consider it part of his or her investment in marketing.

When working with facility administration, psychologists should ask some broad questions about family interactions within the system. Cohn (1985) offers a set of questions to guide such an exploration; I offer the following four sets. **One of the sets of questions, based on Cohn's, is based on data on family in-**

volvement and actual family behaviors. For example: When are families in the building, and where do they spend their time? With whom do they interact? What do they do? What information about the facility are families missing simply because of the times and places at which they view the activities of the facility?

A second set of questions is based on the desire for family involvement. What kinds of family involvement make sense in this facility? What helps families assume appropriate roles that are meaningful to them? Is family input desired? What kind of relationship between families and staff seems desirable? Many facilities offer support groups for families to enhance family input as well as provide support (Brubaker & Scheifer, 1987; Cox & Ephross, 1989). Other facilities encourage family involvement in community support groups that address the specific diseases of their loved one (e.g., groups sponsored by the Alzheimer's Association) or in more general groups (Safford, 1980; Steuer, 1982.) **The educational function of support groups improves the relationship between the family member and resident** (Dziegielewski, 1991) **and helps reduce stress for the caregivers.**

A third set of questions is based on the mechanisms through which a resident's family may have a voice in the resident's care. Exactly how do families communicate their concerns? Does everyone have equal access to that mechanism? Does the mechanism provide a voice for family members before the problems reach crisis level? To address these concerns, many facilities develop a resident council and a family council (Palmer, 1991). These councils are organized and run by the residents or families themselves, with staff invited only when needed.

A fourth set of questions focuses on possible means of enhancing staff-family collaboration in providing care. What would promote respectful attitudes? What might engage families and staff in shared or parallel tasks? Activities that involve staff members' families along with residents and their families in social events, facility fund-raisers, and holiday events may help foster more personal connections between families, staff, and residents.

Finally, the psychologists may help administrators identify the facility's roles in promoting family well-being. What supportive services should be offered? How might the facility promote success in caregiving? **It is important to note that there is no single best answer to any of these questions.** Each facility will develop its own culture, and the answers depend on this culture. For example, **options for promoting mutual respect will be very different when the members and residents have similar backgrounds than when they have significantly different ethnic, racial, or social class backgrounds** (Grau & Wellin, 1992).

Assessing Leverage:

A psychologist addressing intrafamilial conflict should determine the importance of the issue being debated to the resident's well-being. If it is of major importance, then the psychologist may have considerable backing within the facility to demand a family meeting with all involved parties in attendance. If it is of minor consequence, the psychologist will have less leverage.

Family Education:

Psychologists should take the time to be sure that all family members understand the problem. The caregiving intervention model of Zarit and colleagues (1985) emphasizes the value of family education in dealing with families of demented persons. This principle extends to other conditions as well. **Ensure that all family members are equally informed about the diagnosis, the consequences of the diseases or disorders, the prognosis, and strategies for managing the attendant difficulties.** One benefit of family education is that it often undermines the basis for attributing malintent to other family members.

Promoting Insight into Family Development Patterns:

When education does not solve the family problem, psychologists should consider making a more in-depth evaluation of the family's history. Cohn (1985) offers a guideline for family evaluation in nursing home consultations that explores the family's developmental history, its history of dealing with aging members, its values and expectations about caring for relatives at the end of life, the family relationship history, and the family caregiving history with regard to this particular resident. Drawing upon the work of Herr and Weakland (1979) and Zarit and colleagues (1985), Cohn (1985, pp. 180-181) recommends the following principles for conducting family interviews:

- Model open communication skills.
- Be genuine and open, but not overinvolved.
- Recognize that the messages that are sent are not necessarily the messages that are received.
- Observe family leadership and participation patterns.
- Agree to disagree, and acknowledge the family members' rights to see things differently.
- Explore family history straightforwardly.
- Make small, concrete, realistic, behaviorally described suggestions that can represent goals.
- Mutually identify the events that trigger "the problem" and seek means to circumvent those precipitants.
- Mutually find rewards for changed behaviors.

The detailed assessment of family history, combined with a behavioral assessment of the problem, sets the stage for the psychologist to accomplish two goals. **First, an effective interview in which the family examines its past and the context of the current problem will reduce the rate of blaming and personality attributions for the problem.** The detailed behavioral analysis reduces the temptation to target a personality characteristic that is viewed as immutable in favor of a specific description of a problem behavior that is potentially fixable. It will usually allow the family to view the problem as a normal consequence of a lack of knowledge, poor communication, or unsuccessful attempts to solve the problem by reasonable, although not useful, means. If the interview is done well, family members may respond with reduced anxiety and less of a need to defend themselves against feelings of incompetence or failure.

Second, a solid behavioral description of the problem and the small steps that should be taken to improve it allows the psychologist to engage staff and families in collaborative problem solving. Instead of blaming one another, family members and/or staff can focus on what they want to accomplish (Herr & Weakland, 1979; Zarit & Zarit, 1991). Presenting the tasks in small steps allows the family and staff to see the possibility of success, thereby encouraging them to invest more commitment and energy. The psychologist needs to anticipate barriers to implementing the plan and new problems with the plan. **Families and staff should think of any intervention as an experiment that can only succeed: if it works, so much the better; if not, they will have learned something that will help them redesign the plan.** Follow-through is therefore critical. **A method for monitoring the effects of the plan needs to be put in place, with responsibility for following up clearly assigned.**

The Chronically Conflicted:

Chronically unhappy families need to be offered choices that will enhance their sense of control and competence in meeting the needs of their loved ones, including the choice of selecting another facility. Psychologists may occasionally reach the point at which a recommendation to change facilities will relieve all parties involved.

Conclusion

Families are key players in the nursing home environment and an integral part of the lives of nursing home residents. Psychologists can often be helpful to LTC facilities because their ability to analyze conflicts may facilitate the empowerment of families as well as residents and institutions. The work of psychologists in nursing homes differs from their work in other settings primarily because of the nature of the institutional environment, the high rate of cognitive impairment in nursing home residents, and the high rates of serious chronic illnesses. Psychologists must have strong assessment skills (including the ability to assess decision-making capacity as well as analyze problems within both family and institutional systems. Traditional intervention tools are useful with families and residents, but familiarity with the regulatory and funding environments of nursing homes is critical, as it allows psychologists to identify their sources of leverage and constraint in changing policies and procedures.

References

Aneshensel, C. S., Pearlin, L. I., Mullan, J. T., Zarit, S. H., & Whitlatch, C. J. (1995). *Profiles in caregiving: The unexpected career.* San Diego, CA: Academic Press.

Bowers, B. J. (1988). Family perceptions of care in a nursing home. *The Gerontologist, 28,* 361–368.

Brubaker, E., & Schiefer, A. W. (1987). Groups with families of elderly long term care residents: Building social support networks. *Journal of Gerontological Social Work, 10* (1–2) 167–175.

Collopy, B. J. (1995). Power, paternalism, and the ambiguities of autonomy. In L. M. Gamroth, J. Semradek, & E. M. Tornquist (Eds.). *Enhancing autonomy in long term care: Concepts and strategies* (p. 314). New York: Springer.

Cohn, M. (1985). Consultation strategies with families. In M. Smyer, M. Cohn, & D. Brannon (Eds.), *Mental health consultation in nursing homes.* New York: New York University Press.

Collier, M. W., Prawitz, A. D., & Lawrence, F. C. (1994). Families as monitors of quality of care in nursing homes. *Psychological Reports, 75,* 1242.

Cox, C., & Ephross, P. H. (1989). Group work with families of nursing home residents: Its socialization and therapeutic functions. *Journal of Gerontological Social Work, 13,* 61–73.

Dziegielewski, S. F. (1991). Social group work with the family members of elderly nursing home residents with dementia: A controlled evaluation. *Research on Social Work Practice, 1*, 358–370.

Grau, L., & Wellin, E. (1992). The organizational cultures of nursing homes: Influences on responses to external regulatory controls. *Qualitative Health Research, 2*, 42–60.

Grisso, T. (1986). *Evaluating competencies: Forensic assessments and instruments.* New York: Plenum Publishing.

Herr, J. J., & Weakland, J. H. (1979). *Counseling elders and their families.* New York: Springer.

High, D. M., & Rowles, G. D. (1995). Nursing home residents, families, and decision making: Toward an understanding of progressive surrogacy. *Journal of Aging Studies, 9*, 101–117.

Kane, R. A., & Caplan, A. L. (Eds). (1990). Everyday ethics: *Resolving dilemmas in nursing home life.* New York: Springer Publishing.

Lichtenberg, P. A. (1994). *A guide to psychological practice in geriatric long term care.* New York: Haworth Press.

Lichtenberg, P. A., Smith M., Frazer, D., Molinari, V., Rosowsky, E., Crose, R. et al. (1997). Standards for psychological services in long term care facilities. *The Gerontologist, 38*, 122–127.

Montgomery, R. J. V. (1983). Staff-family relations and institutional care policies. *Journal of Gerontological Social Work, 6*, 25–37.

Moulton, H. J. (1993). Linkages between nursing homes and families: A literature review. *Physical and Occupational Therapy in Geriatrics, 11*, 112.

Palmer, D. S. (1991). Co-leading a family council in a long term care facility. *Journal of Gerontological Social Work, 16*, 121–134.

Safford, F. (1980). A program for families of the mentally impaired elderly. *The Gerontologist, 20*, 656–660.

Schwartz, A. N., & Vogel, M. E. (1990). Nursing home staff and residents' families role expectations. *The Gerontologist, 30*, 49–53.

Shanas, E. (1979). Social myth as hypothesis: The case of the family relations of old people. *The Gerontologist, 19*, 39.

Smyer, M. A. (1989). Nursing homes as a setting for psychological practice: Public policy perspectives. *American Psychologist, 44*, 1307–1314.

Steuer, J. L. (1982). Family support groups within a research project on dementia. *Clinical Gerontologist, 1*, 87–95.

Stewart, R. P. (1984). Building an alliance between the family and the institution. *Social Work, 29*, 386–390.

Wolf-Klein, G. P., Wagner, C. S., & Silverstone, F. A. (1992). The do-not-resuscitate order in a nursing home: Patient's choice or staff's decision. *New York State Journal of Medicine, 92*, 131–134.

York, J. L., & Calsyn, R. J. (1977). Family involvement in nursing homes. *The Gerontologist, 17*, 500–505.

Zarit, J. M., & Zarit, S. H. (1991). Behavioral programs for families of dependent elderly. In P. Wisocki (Ed.) *Handbook of clinical behavior therapy with the elderly client.* New York: Plenum Publishing.

Zarit, S., H., Orr, N. K., & Zarit, J. M. (1985). *The hidden victims of Alzheimer's disease.* New York: New York University Press.

6

Group Psychotherapy in the Nursing Home

HOLLY RUCKDESCHEL, PH.D.

Abstract

MENTAL HEALTH clinicians increasingly provide much needed psychological services to individuals residing in nursing homes. Conducting group psychotherapy in the nursing home setting enables the clinician to treat a greater number of individuals in need of psychological services using fewer resources. Group therapy is also well suited to the nursing home population because it addresses the social isolation commonly experienced by the residents. This chapter provides an overview of the process and issues involved in conducting group therapy in a nursing home setting. Mental health issues of particular relevance to the elderly nursing home population are identified, including adjustment to institutional life, losses, coping with illness and death, and interpersonal conflicts. Effective treatment in the group setting is enhanced by the cohesiveness that is achieved in the group. Techniques for developing cohesion in the group are discussed. Three types of groups that can address the mental health needs of nursing home residents include psychoeducational, support, and psychotherapy groups. Each type of group is defined and specific examples offered, including discussions of membership, format, and appropriate goals. The systemic and patient-related challenges inherent in conducting groups in the nursing home setting are examined and potential solutions are offered.

Introduction

In a review of recent studies, Streim and Katz (1996) reported that prevalence rates for psychiatric disorders among nursing home residents range from 80% to 94%, with the prevalence of depression specifically ranging from 15% to 50%. Mental health professionals can provide valuable services for nursing home residents with such disorders, including evaluation, assessment, and treatment. **Group therapy is a treatment modality that is especially well suited for nursing homes because it allows more individuals to receive treatment using fewer resources and because a group approach facilitates the discussion of issues of loss and social isolation which are of particular concern to the resident population** (Hartford, 1980; Leszcz, 1987; Moran & Gatz, 1987; Toseland, 1995; Weiss, 1994).

This chapter provides an overview of the process and issues involved in conducting group therapy in a nursing home setting. It is assumed that practitioners planning to offer such services have been educated and trained in the theory and techniques of group psychotherapy. This article discusses the practical application of these skills and knowledge to the nursing home population.

It is important for the therapist working with this population to have a basic knowledge of both the normal and pathological aspects of the aging process. In addition, the therapist should develop a clear sense of the nursing home environment and learn who the primary care team members are and how they function. Effectively treating the nursing home resident often requires communicating and working with staff members who may be able to provide information about how the patient functions outside the group and offer suggestions for treatment interventions by staff members.

Common Themes With the Nursing Home Population

In conducting group psychotherapy in the nursing home, the therapist is likely to encounter certain recurrent concerns. **Adjusting to institutional life is often a focus of the group, especially if there are group members who are new to the facility.** Sharing a room with a stranger, having to eat at prescribed mealtimes, not being able to take a shower whenever one desires, and/or having to wait 20 minutes to receive medication are examples of the day-to-day lifestyle changes that can make a person feel "institutionalized." **Residents often feel that they are treated "like a number" or seen by others in terms of their medical illnesses and physical care demands.** Internal conflicts regarding dependency often arise, with an ensuing struggle to maintain a sense of personal control and dignity while accepting the need for assistance in basic tasks of daily living.

In contrast, the group can provide the opportunity for the resident to be viewed as and responded to as a whole person, taking into account the full range of lifetime experiences that have made the person who he or she is. Involvement in the group produces a feeling of being known and offers a setting in which residents can achieve success rather than failure.

A primary issue for older persons, both in and outside the nursing home, is coping with loss. There are many losses associated with old age that involve multiple areas of a person's life. The nursing home resident may face the loss of (a) **relationships** (with a spouse, family member, and/or friends) **because of death or relocation;** (b) **physical function** (vision, hearing, muscle strength, ability to walk, continence) **as a result of the normal aging process or disease;** (c) **privacy;** (d) **his or her home and/or personal possessions;** (e) **roles** (in the workplace, the community, and/or the family); (f) **cognitive function** (through either decrements related to normal aging or dementing processes); (g) **independence; and** (h) **autonomy. Participating in a group can help the nursing home resi-**

dent mourn, adapt to, and sometimes compensate for these losses.

Coping with illness and death is more likely to be an issue for groups in nursing homes than for therapy groups in other settings (with the exception of groups whose members have been diagnosed with terminal illnesses). Illness can result in absence from the group, but it also can be a focus of group discussion. The group members may share their feelings about their own and each others' declining health, confronting their fears, expressing concern, and offering support for one another. For some, the group may be the only place they feel comfortable dealing with such issues openly. When a member of the group dies, the therapy group provides an excellent opportunity to process the loss. **As group members remember the deceased member and express their feelings of appreciation and loss, they may be reassured that they too will be missed and acknowledged upon their passing.** Clinicians conducting therapy groups in the nursing home must be able to deal effectively with their own issues regarding death and dying to facilitate the process of working through grief in the group.

Addressing concerns related to loss and death can lead to the emergence of existential issues. Residents may have trouble coming to terms with their lives and successfully working through Erikson's (1982) developmental stage of integrity versus despair. In the face of multiple losses, many residents struggle with a continuing search for meaning in life. Group therapy can provide the opportunity to explore and work towards resolution of these issues.

Interpersonal conflicts make up another issue that is commonly dealt with in group therapy. A patient may have difficulties getting along with a roommate, unresolved issues with family members, or problems communicating effectively with nursing staff to have his or her needs met. The group can provide feedback to the individual regarding his or her interpersonal style and offer suggestions for improving social relationships.

Promoting Cohesion:

In psychotherapy groups involving almost any population, fluctuation in group membership and lack of effective leadership can hinder the development of group cohesion. The therapist must promote cohesion in the group to generate a sense of belonging and acceptance and to optimize the potential for emotional intimacy among the group members. There are a variety of ways a therapist can facilitate the development of cohesiveness in the group.

Having closed group membership is one way to foster a sense of cohesiveness. Consistent membership enhances the capacity to develop trust among group members and promotes a sense of belonging. Open group membership and wide variability in who attends from week to week inhibit the development of a sense of group identity and make it difficult to build on content or process from past sessions, which can hinder group progress. Meeting regularly at the same time, day, and place each week can also promote a sense of stability. Being able to count on the group reassures the members and reinforces the message that they are worthy of the therapist's attention and caring.

Periodically restating the reason the group is meeting further instills a sense of its purpose and function, particularly among nursing home residents for whom memory deficits and lack of familiarity with psychological interventions may cloud their understanding of group therapy. The therapist can begin each session with a "setting the stage" statement that clarifies the norms, intended structure, and process of the group. If a new patient joins the group, a member, rather than the therapist, may be asked to explain why the group meets and what they do in the course of each session. It may also be necessary to remind the group of its purpose when diversions occur. For example, the focus of the group may linger on complaints about day-to-day institutional problems (e.g., unappetizing food) without any productive or purposeful outcome except providing an opportunity to ventilate. The therapist might want to remind the group that other channels exist for addressing those concerns and reiterate the intentions and goals for the therapy group.

The capacity for cohesion in the group is enhanced when every member of the group feels respected, cared

for, and valued. The therapist must ensure that everyone has the opportunity to speak; those who don't participate spontaneously should be addressed directly to demonstrate that their thoughts and feelings are important to the group. A "round robin" approach is one way to guarantee that every member will be attended to in the course of the session; in this approach, the therapist begins the session by going around the room and giving each member a chance to state what is on his or her mind, with others free to respond.

Group members who are absent from the session should also be addressed. The therapist can explain why the absent members could not attend (e.g., because of a conflicting appointment or not feeling well). Acknowledgement of missing group members helps to preserve a sense of intactness and sends the message that one is noticed and missed when unable to attend the group.

Group members should be encouraged to address each other and not communicate only through their interactions with the therapist. For example, after hearing about one member's traumatic experience, another member may turn to the therapist and state that she understands what it is like to go through such an experience, as she has had similar troubles. The therapist can gently stop her and suggest that she tell the first member directly, encouraging a personal interchange through which a relationship can develop.

Types of Groups

Most nursing homes offer group programs for their residents to provide socialization and recreational opportunities. These groups are usually run by activity therapists or nursing staff, and they are generally open to all interested or able residents. They may be centered around an activity, such as making decorations for an upcoming holiday, or a topic area, such as a discussion of current events. This type of group is useful for meeting some of the residents' basic psychosocial needs for cognitive and social stimulation, and it can contribute to the residents' overall quality of life in the nursing home.

The groups directed by mental health clinicians offer something different. They are targeted to a specific membership, usually those experiencing emotional distress, having difficulty coping or adjusting, or subject to psychological factors that affect their physical health and ability to function. Appropriate candidates for such groups are identified through clinical evaluation of mood, behavior, and cognitive status. When informed of the purpose and goals of the group, nursing home staff, who are most familiar with the residents, may be very helpful in referring residents who might benefit from the group. **The clinician must make it clear to the staff and residents that the group he or she offers is oriented toward treatment as opposed to leisure or recreation.** Given this distinction, group therapy can be further differentiated into several types, depending on the treatment goals and targeted patients.

Psychoeducational Groups:

A psychoeducational group is usually focused on a particular problem or issue for which increased knowledge is of potential therapeutic benefit. **A key component of the group is the dissemination of information that may help patients better understand, cope with, and/or treat the condition or situation they are experiencing.** Teaching a particular skill to assist in coping, such as relaxation techniques or assertiveness training, may also be an objective of the group.

This type of group is commonly offered in the community, but it can also be appropriate in a nursing home. For example, a psychoeducational group could address nursing home residents who have been diagnosed with diabetes. Goals for this group might include promoting compliance with dietary restrictions, increasing levels of exercise, and improving their ability to cope with the potential loss of function associated with diabetes (such as blindness or amputation). Patients in this group will need to be sufficiently cognitively intact to remember and make use of the material from the session. Ability to benefit from such a group usually depends on introspection or self-disclosure by the participants.

Typically, psychoeducational groups are structured, time limited, and have an open membership. Obviously, individuals will benefit most by participating in all of the scheduled sessions, but the integrity of the group will not be compromised by fluctuating member attendance. Psychoeducational groups may also address other diseases, such as Parkinson's disease or osteoarthritis, or deal with an aspect of health promotion, such as diet, exercise, stress reduction, or smoking cessation. Memory enhancement groups that teach strategies for compensating for declining memory may also be offered. **Clinicians who lead psychoeduational groups that address medical concerns must have adequate knowledge of the diseases or conditions being addressed and should consult regularly with professional medical staff.**

Example of a Psychoeducational Group

Many nursing homes are implementing restorative care programs aimed at improving residents' abilities to perform daily living activities and promoting high levels of independence. For example, a restorative care program for one resident might involve performing exercises to increase leg strength so that a walker could be used instead of a wheelchair. These programs are usually implemented by the nursing staff, often with the guidance of a physical therapist. **It might be difficult to motivate residents with depression to take part in restorative care programs; however, a restorative care psychoeducational group for such residents could give them the support and encouragement they needed to participate fully in such programs.** In this type of group, the leader might (a) emphasize the benefits of restorative care programs, (b) challenge the obstacles that patients perceive and identify, (c) mobilize group members to provide peer support, and (d) monitor progress towards goals and provide ongoing encouragement.

Support Groups:

Like psychoeducational groups, support group members are

brought together on the basis of a common theme, but with less of a focus on education and more emphasis on sharing among group members. The purpose of many support groups is to improve the ability of participants to cope with stressful life events or transitions (Toseland, 1995). Support groups appropriate for a nursing home setting may, for example, deal with a chronic illness, the death of a spouse, or adjusting to institutional living. In addition to serving nursing home residents, support groups may also serve their families' needs. **The goals of support groups are usually to provide an outlet for emotional expression, to share coping skills, and to promote a sense that individuals are not alone in dealing with the identified issue.**

The role of the therapist in this type of group is less directive and more facilitative. Instead of the group leader offering strategies or techniques for improved coping, the members of the group are encouraged to share their own experiences. Willingness to self-disclose and to interact with other members of the group is vital for the success of such groups. An important function of the group therapist is to promote group cohesion so that the members feel safe and connected with one another. A support group can be time limited or ongoing. Group membership can be open or closed as well, but a closed group with consistent attendance will provide a safe, trusting environment conducive to optimal interpersonal sharing.

Example of a Support Group

The resident populations of most nursing homes usually include a small number of married couples living in the same facility. **The spouses may differ in their physical and cognitive status and in their reasons for needing nursing home placement.** For example, the wife may be nonambulatory because of the progression of Parkinson's disease; her husband may have moderate dementia and need structure and supervision. **In such cases, the nondemented spouse often struggles with the changes in the relationship as the demented spouse becomes more impaired and less able and available to meet the social, emo-**

tional, and physical needs of the nondemented spouse. A support group targeting married residents with demented spouses could address the concerns and issues presented in this situation.

Such a support group would primarily aim to improve the members' ability to cope with having a spouse with dementia. It is likely that members would be experiencing feelings of loss, frustration, and even guilt about having "negative" feelings such as anger or resentment towards their spouse. The group could provide a place to express these feelings with others who would understand and not judge them. Because of differing care needs, many couples may not reside in the same room or on the same unit. Group members might offer each other suggestions for making the most of the time spent with their spouses, such as joining the spouse when an activity or party was taking place on the unit, which would provide a meaningful shared experience. **As a facilitator of this group, the therapist would promote a supportive environment for the members to** (a) **express feelings** (anger, sadness, disappointment, helplessness) **about the changes in themselves, their spouses, and the marital relationship;** (b) **meet some of the social and emotional needs that are no longer met through the spouse by means of relationships developed with other group members;** (c) **share coping strategies for dealing with difficult behaviors exhibited by the demented spouse; and** (d) **find a satisfactory balance between time and energy that is devoted to the spouse and that which is invested in each member's own continuing quality of life.**

Psychotherapy Groups:

Whereas the defining concept behind psychoeducational or support groups is a common issue or shared interest in a topic, psychotherapy groups are intended to provide treatment for psychological symptoms and emotional distress. The other types of groups do address psychological and emotional needs, but they are not necessarily designed to provide treatment for identifiable, diagnosable psychiatric disorders or symptoms. Thorough clinical assessments, treatment plans, and ongoing progress notes are written and maintained for individuals in a psychotherapy group to assist the therapist in monitoring the effectiveness of the group in meeting individually established treatment goals. The goals of psychotherapy groups include symptom relief, behavior change, and personal growth and development (Capuzzi, et al., 1990; Toseland, 1995). **Although a patient need not have a psychiatric disorder to benefit from being in a psychotherapy group, mental health clinicians should be cautioned that payment from third-party payers for group therapy** (and other forms of psychotherapy) **is often contingent on the presence of a treatable, diagnosable psychiatric disorder.** For example, a therapist who is providing service for an individual who is experiencing feelings of loneliness and sadness related to being separated from family members but otherwise not meeting the criteria for any diagnosis in the *Diagnostic and Statistical Manual of Mental Disorders, fourth edition* (DSM-IV) (American Psychiatric Association 1994) may not be reimbursed for the service.

As in other settings, a psychotherapy group in a nursing home can be ongoing and long term or time limited. A long term model offers the advantage of providing a sense of constancy and stability for the group members, who are otherwise faced with cumulative losses and changes in both themselves and their environments over which they usually have no control. The group may be perceived as one of the few safe, nurturing, and reliable experiences available in their lives. Psychotherapy groups are generally run as closed-membership groups to promote optimal trust and cohesion, as a high degree of self-disclosure is usually necessary for the group's success. The degree of structure and the extent to which the therapist has a more directive or facilitative role will depend on the theoretical orientation of the group leader.

Group psychotherapy, like individual therapy, can utilize a variety of theoretical approaches in the nursing home setting. A behaviorally-oriented psychotherapy group might address issues related to social isolation through social skills training and role-modeling techniques. A group psychotherapy format using a cognitive approach might involve group members in identifying and challenging negative cognitions regarding aging and assisting each other with the development of more positive cognitive schemas. A dynamically-oriented psychotherapy group might work on improving interpersonal relationships and increasing self-understanding through the exploration of transferential interactions among the group members.

Clinicians must be flexible in their approach to group psychotherapy with the nursing home population. For example, whereas contact among group members outside group time is often strongly discouraged in traditional psychodynamic group therapy, the communal setting of the nursing home would make this restriction nearly impossible; in fact, it might be undesirable to do so if the goals of the group include increasing social connectedness. Modifications in technique might also include but would not be limited to providing more structure and eliminating the requirement to do "homework" in cognitive-behaviorally oriented groups due to members' sensory and motor difficulties.

Example of a Psychotherapy Group

A psychotherapy group with an interpersonal approach could be used to treat depression in cognitively intact residents. Members of the group would be selected on the basis of having been diagnosed with a depressive disorder, such as major depression, dysthymic disorder, adjustment disorder with depressed features, or depression not otherwise specified. **A primary goal of the group would be to decrease the feelings of loneliness and depersonalization that can occur in response to both depression and institutional living.** Active participation in the group could facilitate the development of meaningful relationships between group members, decreasing isolation, compensating for interpersonal losses, and improving members' self-esteem.

A group format conducive to active participation would involve "checking in" with each member in the first part of the session. In the course of this "round robin," issues or themes would emerge that could become the focus of a discussion during the rest of the group session. For example, after one member shared a negative experience she had with a roommate, others might also relate roommate stories at their turn. When everyone had made his or her initial update, the therapist could return the focus of the group to the issue of coping with difficult roommates. Members could share their feelings, experiences, and coping strategies with each other. This format would provide some degree of structure, but it would also allow the flexibility to address salient issues raised by group members themselves, as opposed to following a predetermined agenda with specific content and objectives.

In a group with members who are highly cognitively intact, group members would have the opportunity to obtain insight through their interactions with each other. This would require that the level of trust and cohesion in the group permit the sharing of feelings and reactions not only to the content being discussed but also to one another as individuals. Group members could learn how their behavior affected those around them and receive ongoing feedback and support in their efforts to change or better understand themselves and others. **In this psychotherapy group, the members might** (a) **discuss and receive support from each other regarding issues of relevance to their condition** (e.g. losses, peer conflicts, dependency); (b) **develop significant relationships with others, allowing for the experience of emotional intimacy;** (c) **express different aspects of themselves by taking on various roles** (e.g., helper, nurturer, intellectual, humorist); (d) **have the opportunity to test new behaviors, such as appropriate ways of expressing needs, that would improve coping skills and increase life satisfaction.**

Reminiscence Groups:

Reminiscence and life review techniques based on the work of Butler (1963) are widely used in therapy groups in nursing home settings (Capuzzi, et al., 1990). Some groups are formed for the explicit purpose of reminiscing; other groups use reminiscing as one of several interventions to meet their goals. Reminiscence allows the individual to make a connection with meaningful past experiences to identify his or her strengths and successes and to rework unresolved conflicts. Additionally, reminiscing in the group setting can enhance cohesion by illuminating common experiences shared by the group members.

Groups with Dementia Patients:

Cognitively intact nursing home residents are not the only individuals capable of benefiting from group intervention (Akerlund & Norberg, 1986; Fernie & Fernie, 1990, Gilewski, 1986). Prospective group members need to be screened to assess their levels of cognition. The Mini-Mental State Exam (Folstein et al., 1975) and the clinical interview may provide the therapist with a preliminary indication of whether the resident is sufficiently cognitively intact to participate in and benefit from the group experience. Therapy groups can be modified specifically to address the needs of residents in the mild to moderate stages of dementia, assuming they are verbal, can maintain attention, and have sufficient memory capacity for some carryover from session to session. In such cases, the therapist might take on a more directive role and provide a higher degree of structure. Individuals with widely different levels of cognitive impairment should not be placed in the same group, as their needs and abilities may differ significantly (Fernie & Fernie, 1990; MacLennan et al., 1988; Weiss, 1994).

Challenges in Running Therapy Groups

Institution-Related Challenges:

Administrative Support

Running therapy groups in institutional settings such as nursing homes involves distinctive challenges. Unlike psychiatric hospitals, where there is administrative support, the expectation of therapeutic groups, and designated space for conducting them, the nursing home setting can make the development of a group therapy program problematic. **It is crucial to obtain administrative sup-**

port at the highest level possible to ensure the cooperation of all staff members who may be necessary for the success of the group (Abramson & Mendis, 1990).

Finding a Space for the Group

A primary issue that must be addressed involves deciding where to hold the group. The obvious spaces available for group therapy may be dining rooms, lounges, or activity rooms, all of which have competing uses and offer limited privacy. Even if a dining room is not in use for dining at the time you would like to use it for group, it may be the spot of choice for a particular set of residents to congregate. **The therapist must be respectful of the habits and needs of the residents and attempt to schedule the group at a time that is least interruptive of the usual nursing home activities and routines.** Intrusions while the group is in session are often unavoidable. Sometimes a nurse will interrupt to give a medication, or a confused resident may enter the room and need to be redirected.

If the therapist has the support of the administration, he or she may request to use staff conference areas as an alternative to patient areas. It is necessary to have a room that is large enough to accommodate at least four to six patients, some or all of whom may be in wheelchairs. **It is also important that there be sufficient privacy for the group members to express themselves without fear of being overheard.**

Assistance From Staff

The assistance and cooperation of the nursing staff is also important for getting patients to the group. It is helpful for the staff to remind the residents who attend that the group will be held on that day so that a resident does not forget and leave the unit. Additionally, transporting residents to and from the group room can be very time consuming if the therapist is the only one doing it. The therapist's needs for assistance should be discussed with the head nurse to ensure that requests are appropriate and staff compliance is feasible.

Patient-Related Challenges:

Sensory Deficits

Group therapy in a nursing home setting also presents challenges related to the frailty of the long term care population. Group members often have significant sensory deficits that can make it very difficult to run the group. **If a patient has visual problems, it is helpful if the group members identify themselves when they speak until the visually impaired member is able to recognize their voices.** Having group members sit in the same formation during each session may also enhance recognition.

Hearing impairment can be frustrating for both the impaired individual and the rest of the group. A quiet room that reduces extraneous noise is optimal. Personal amplifying devices with headphones may be helpful for some people. Using a microphone is also an option, but this often enables people outside the room to hear what is being said in the group and thus can compromise confidentiality. The most successful approach for the therapist may involve sitting next to the hearing-impaired individual and paraphrasing the content of conversation periodically, specifying who said what. Limiting the group size to four or five members and seating them in a tight circle so that they can see each other's faces has also been recommended (Speer & O'Sullivan, 1994). **Modifying the group format to accommodate the hearing-impaired members may seem cumbersome, and indeed repeating in a clear, deliberate manner at regular intervals can be tiring. However, the alternative of limiting the group to only those who can hear well excludes those most at risk of feeling socially isolated.**

Fluctuating Membership Resulting From Absences

Another patient-related difficulty that clinicians should anticipate when conducting groups in the nursing home setting involves frequent absences of group members. **Even the most highly motivated members of a group may have difficulty attending**

regularly because of conflicting medical appointments, physical therapy sessions, acute illness, or simply "a bad day" resulting from exacerbated symptoms of a chronic illness. Sometimes a patient who initially defers because of fatigue or pain can be encouraged to attend and will benefit from the stimulation and distraction from somatic concerns.

In some cases, the facility may be offering a popular activity at the same time the therapy group is held. For example, a patient may be torn between attending the monthly birthday party and the therapy group. It is advisable to consult the facility activity schedule and plan to hold the group at a time that does not regularly conflict with a desirable activity. Sometimes the recreation therapy staff may be able to schedule activity groups suitable for a more impaired population at the same time that the psychotherapy group is held, thereby reducing the likelihood of competing interests.

Patients may also be absent from the group because they are receiving visitors at the time the group is meeting. Visits from family and friends are generally extremely important to nursing home residents and are likely to take precedence over attending the group. Once invested in the group, a patient might ask visitors to come at other times, but many patients will not want to risk discouraging their visitors. It is important for the group therapist to respect what is valuable to each individual and be flexible in attendance policies for the group to avoid alienating motivated members who are caught between conflicting loyalties.

Conclusion

Although conducting group therapy in the nursing home setting involves unique challenges, it also has an enormous potential to enhance the lives of residents. This chapter has attempted to familiarize the reader with the basic issues and practical considerations that confront the mental health clinician working in the nursing home. Building on an assumed foundation of group theory and practice, this overview has addressed treatment issues relevant to the nursing home elderly, the types of therapy groups that can be offered, and the challenges associated with the practice of group therapy in this setting. With this basic understanding, the mental health clinician is prepared for further exploration of this growing practice opportunity.

References

Abramson, T. A., & Mendis, K. P. (1990). The organizational logistics of running a dementia group in a skilled nursing facility. In T. L. Brink (Ed.), *Mental health in the nursing home* (pp. 111–122). New York: Haworth Press.

Akerlund, B. M., & Norberg, A. (1986, March/April). Group psychotherapy with demented patients. *Geriatric Nursing, 83*–84.

American Association of Retired Persons. (1995). *A profile of older Americans* [Brochure]. Washington, DC: Author.

American Psychiatric Association. (1994). *Diagnostic and statistical manual of mental disorders* (4th ed.). Washington, DC: Author.

Butler, R. (1963). The life review: An interpretation of reminiscence in the aged. *Psychiatry, 26*, 65–76.

Capuzzi, D., Gross, D., & Friel, S. (1990, winter). Group work with elders. *Generations,* 43–48.

Erikson, E. H. (1982). *The life cycle completed.* New York: W.W. Norton.

Fernie, B., & Fernie, G. (1990). Organizing group programs for cognitively impaired elderly residents of nursing homes. In T. L. Brink (Ed.), *Mental health in the nursing home* (pp. 123–134). New York: Haworth Press.

Folstein, M., Folstein, S., & McHugh, P. (1975). Mini-Mental State: A practical method for grading the cognitive state of patients for the clinician. *Journal of Psychiatric Research, 12*, 189–198.

Gilewski, M. J. (1986). Group therapy with cognitively impaired older adults. In T. L. Brink (Ed.), *Clinical gerontology: A guide to assessment and intervention* (pp. 281–295). New York: Haworth Press.

Hartford, M. E. (1980). The use of group methods for work with the aged. In J. E. Birren & R. B. Sloane (Eds.), *Handbook of mental health and aging.* Englewood Cliffs, NJ: Prentice-Hall.

Leszcz, M. (1987). Group psychotherapy with the elderly. In J. Sadavoy & M. Leszcz (Eds.), *Treating the elderly with psychotherapy: The scope for change in later life* (pp. 325–349). Madison, CT: International Universities Press, Inc.

MacLennan, B. W., Saul, S., & Weiner, M. B. (1988). Group psychotherapies for the elderly. *American Group Psychotherapy Association Monograph Series, 5,* 1–290.

Moran, J. A., & Gatz, M. (1987). Group therapies for nursing home adults: An evaluation of two treatment approaches. *The Gerontologist, 27,* (5) 588–591.

Speer, D. C., & O'Sullivan, M. J. (1994). Group therapy in nursing homes and hearing deficit. *Clinical Gerontologist, 14*(4), 68–70.

Streim, J. E., & Katz, I. R. (1996). Clinical psychiatry in the nursing home. In E. W. Busse & D. G. Blazer (Eds.), *Textbook of geriatric psychiatry* (2nd ed.) (pp. 413–432). Washington, DC: American Psychiatric Press.

Toseland, R. W. (1995). *Group work with the elderly and family caregivers.* New York: Springer Publishing.

Weiss, J. C. (1994, March 19). Group therapy with older adults in long term care settings: Research and clinical cautions and recommendations. *The Journal for Specialists in Group Work,* (1), pp. 22–29.

7

Enhancing Quality of Life in Long Term Care

REBECCA G. LOGSDON, PH.D.

Preparation of this lesson was supported by grants from the Alzheimer's Association (FSA95009), the National Institute on Aging (AG1084504), and the South Tacoma Eagles. The author would like to acknowledge the contributions of Nolana Newton, who assisted with the analysis of nursing home pleasant event data, and Maureen Dolan Valentine, who assisted with the vignettes. The vignettes provided in this chapter are based on actual events, but have been modified to protect the identities of people described and for illustrative purposes.

Abstract

MAXIMIZING QUALITY of life (QOL) is an important goal in the care of older adults, particularly when physical or cognitive changes limit their ability to care for themselves independently. Research indicates that it is possible to assess the QOL of individuals in long term care (LTC) by asking them to rate their own QOL, by directly observing their affective states, and/or by having knowledgeable proxies provide an assessment of residents who may be unable to communicate their own ratings. A number of common factors have been identified by residents from different types of facilities who have participated in research on QOL in LT LTC settings. **A friendly, cheerful, and compassionate direct care staff is the most necessary ingredient, according to residents.** The availability of enjoyable and meaningful activities, family involvement in the resident's care, and the ability to make decisions and choices and function as independently as possible are the other ingredients that residents describe as essential to life quality.

The first objective of this chapter is to provide a definition of quality of life that can be used in LTC settings with chronically ill older adults at varied functional levels. The second objective is to review QOL assessment tools that have been used or show potential for use in LTC settings and to describe the types of residents with whom they are most appropriate and effective.

The chapter also describes research on how residents, families, and LTC staff conceptualize QOL and what factors they identify as most important to QOL in the LTC setting.

Finally, strategies are suggested to enhance QOL for LTC residents and accompanied by illustrative vignettes.

Thus, this chapter provides a review of relevant research literature, along with practical ideas for psychologists and other health care professionals working in LTD settings.

Introduction

Maximizing quality of life is the guiding principle and primary goal of long term care (LTC) for chronically ill older adults. Whitehouse and Rabins (1992) describe quality of life (QOL) as "not an isolated concept to be included as one of many measurements of the benefits of our care, but rather the central goal of our professional activity, driving the organization of both our clinical and our research efforts" (p. 136). Yet little objective information is available on how to assess and improve QOL in LTC settings.

QOL is an elusive concept that has been defined in a variety of ways, depending on the context in which it is used and the conceptual orientation of the investigator (c.f. McSweeny & Creer, 1995). From a bioethical view, QOL has been defined as the set of essential conditions beyond mere survival that individuals need in order to have experiences that provide them with meaning and joy (Post & Whitehouse, 1995; Roy, 1992). From a medical standpoint,

QOL includes appropriate physical, social, and role opportunities; mental heath; and perception of health (Cella, 1992; Wilson and Cleary, 1995). In a review of the state of the art of QOL research in frail older adults, Birren and Dieckmann (1991) recommended that QOL be considered a multidimensional construct that includes social, environmental, health, spiritual, and emotional states. Lawton (1983, 1991) provides a theoretical framework for QOL in older adults that includes four domains of importance: behavioral competence (the ability to behave in adaptive and socially appropriate ways), objective environment (everything external to the individual, including both physical and interpersonal factors), psychological well-being (mental health and emotional status), and the individual's subjective perception of and satisfaction with his or her overall QOL. A report from the Institute of Medicine (1986) echoed these views specifically for individuals in nursing homes, describing a good QOL for nursing home residents as consisting of a sense of well-being, satisfaction with life, and self-esteem obtained through the care received, the accomplishment of desired goals, and the ability to exercise a satisfactory degree of control over one's life. Despite their differences, all these definitions recognize the importance of the individual's personal sense of satisfaction with various areas of life, as well as their physical comfort, emotional well being, and interpersonal connections.

Residents of LTC facilities are subject to a complex mixture of disabling conditions, including physical and mental illnesses (Rovner & Katz, 1993). Cognitive impairment is present in more than two-thirds of LTC patients and is often the primary cause of placement in a facility (Institute of Medicine, 1986). There is little doubt that these conditions affect residents' QOL in profound ways. As physical, cognitive, and functional abilities are lost, individuals become unable to engage in many of the activities that once gave them a sense of purpose or pleasure (Logsdon & Teri, 1997; Teri & Logsdon, 1991). Behavior and social skills may also deteriorate, precipitating interpersonal conflict that causes the individual to become socially isolated (Pearson, et al., 1989; Reisberg, et al., 1987). This, in turn, impacts the emotional state Logs-don & Teri, 1997; Teri, et al., 1994). For individuals in need, LTC environments can be a positive force for improving QOL (Cohn & Sugar, 1991), but they can also foster conditions in which life quality deteriorates even further (Siv, 1987; U.S. Congress, Office of Technology Assessment, 1987). **In this chapter, QOL in LTC settings will be defined as the optimization of health, day-to-day activities, mood, and life satisfaction, regardless of illness state.** Three important questions about enhancing QOL in long term care will be addressed in this chapter:

1. How may QOL be assessed in LTC settings?
2. How do residents, family members, and LTC staff conceptualize quality of life, and what specific factors impact the QOL of residents?
3. What strategies can be used to enhance QOL for LTC residents?

Assessment of Quality of Life in Long Term Care

Assessing QOL in LTC settings is not a simple task, because residents often experience cognitive or other difficulties that impair their ability to communicate in ways that are easily understood and measured. Prior reports have reviewed a variety of different measures for assessing the QOL of nursing home residents (Albert, 1997; Arnold, 1991; Wieland, et al., 1995). These will not be revisited in this chapter, but several newer measures or approaches will be described. To be most useful, an assessment of QOL in LTC settings should include both objective and subjective assessments, encompass multiple perspectives about the individual's QOL, and evaluate all four conceptual domains of QOL (health, mood, function, and life satisfaction). In addition, it should include general items that are important among older adults, along with additional items specific to the unique circumstances of LTC, and exclude items that are irrelevant to individuals living in LTC facilities. No single measure has been developed and validated that meets all these requirements. Nonetheless, investigators have identified several useful strategies for evaluating the QOL in LTC settings, which highlight areas in which positive changes may improve the QOL for residents.

Positive and Negative Affect:

Lawton and colleagues (Lawton, et al., 1992; Lawton, et al., 1996) have assessed QOL in LTC settings by examining positive and negative affect among residents. Two versions of affect rating scales have been validated: a self-report version for individuals who are able to report their own positive and negative feeling states, and an observational version that provides objective criteria for directly assessing resident characteristics without relying on the resident's report (which often becomes unreliable or impossible to understand as individuals lose the ability to communicate verbally).

The self-report version consists of 10 items, of which 5 reflect positive affect (happiness, interest, energy level, contentment, and warmheartedness) and 5 reflect negative affect (sadness, annoyance, worry, irritation, and depression). The measure was administered to 486 cognitively intact individuals in LTC facilities using an interview format. Residents rated the degree to which each feeling currently applied to them on a scale of 1 (not at all) to 5 (very strongly). This measure had good validity in this setting; positive affect correlated negatively with measures of depression, anger, and tension and positively with vigor. The negative affect scale showed the opposite correlational pattern (Lawton, et al., 1996).

For individuals whose cognitive impairment precludes self-reporting of affective state, the observer-report version contains three items assessing positive affect (pleasure, interest, and contentment) and three items that assess negative affect (sadness, worry/anxiety, and anger), along with detailed descriptions of facial expression, body movement, and other observable cues. It was validated on a sample of 157 nursing home residents with dementia by research assistants who observed each subject 16 times for 10-minute periods during a 4-week period. The measure was found to be valid and reliable; a structured training program is currently being developed for future use (Van Haitsma, personal communication, May 1, 1997). In the future, this approach may be useful in facilities that train the nursing staff to conduct behavioral observations of residents who are unable to communicate verbally.

Participation in Pleasant Events and Activity:

Engagement in pleasant activities despite significant physical or cognitive impairment provides another piece of behavioral evidence of positive QOL (Logsdon & Teri, 1997). An instrument developed for use with Alzheimer's disease patients, the Pleasant Events Schedule Alzheimer's Disease (PES-AD) (Logsdon & Teri, 1997; Teri & Logsdon, 1991), can help in evaluating participation in such activities. Two versions are available, a 53-item scale and a 20-item scale, each of which has been shown to have excellent internal consistency (α=.90 for the long version and α=.86 for the short version) and to correlate well with depression diagnosis (r=.40 and r=.43 respectively). **Although the PES-AD was developed and validated on individuals living in the community, it has also been used successfully in institutional settings, serving as a tool that facility, staff, and families can use together to identify the types of activities that residents will enjoy.** The short version of the PES-AD is shown in Figure 1. Items were selected to assess two primary domains: passive-active and social-nonsocial. For example, "listening to the sounds of nature" would be classified as a passive activity, while "exercising" would be considered an active activity. Similarly, "having coffee/tea with friends" is social; "watching television" is nonsocial. All items were selected to be within the capability of individuals with moderate degrees of dementia and thus are also appropriate for many LTC residents.

Figure 1
Pleasant Events Schedule–AD (short version)

Activity	Frequency in the past month			Enjoyed	
	Not at all	1-6 Times	7+ Times	Yes	No
1. Being outside					
2. Shopping, buying things					
3. Reading or listening to stories, reading					
magazines, newspapers					
4. Listening to music					
5. Watching TV					
6. Laughing					
7. Having meals with family or friends					
8. Making or eating snacks					
9. Helping around the house					
10. Being with family					

An additional version of the Pleasant Events Schedule is currently being developed specifically for LTC facilities. It overlaps with the short version of the PES-AD and includes additional items suggested by nursing home staff (adding up to 25 items, total). In pilot testing in six nursing home special care units, 33 staff members—including activity staff, nursing assistants, nursing supervisors (RN or LPN), and unit directors—completed the questionnaire about residents on their units. They rated the percent of residents who enjoyed each activity, as well as the frequency with which the activity was carried out on their units (not at all in the past month; one to six times in the past month; seven or more times in the past month). Tables 1 and 2 show (in order) the 10 most enjoyable activities and the 10 most frequent activities, according to these ratings. Listening to music was rated as the most

Figure 1 (cont.)
Pleasant Events Schedule–AD (short version)

Activity	Frequency in the past month			Enjoyed	
	Not at all	1-6 Times	7+ Times	Yes	No
11. Wearing favorite clothes					
12. Listening to the sounds of nature (bird songs, wind, surf)					
13. Getting/sending letters, cards					
14. Going on outings (to the park, a picnic, etc.					
15. Having coffee, tea, etc. with friend					
16. Being complimented					
17. Exercising (walking, dancing, etc.)					
18. Going for a ride in the car					
19. Grooming, Wearing makeup, shaving, having hair cut)					
20. Recalling and discussing past events					

© 1996 R.G. Logsdon & L. Teri, University of Washington, Seattle, WA.
(Administration instructions available upon request.)

enjoyable activity across all sites, and it was reported by every staff member at every site to have occurred seven or more times in the past month. Residents also reportedly enjoyed being complimented, engaging in grooming activities such as having their hair or makeup done, attending parties, having conversations with each other or with staff, eating snacks, entertaining visitors, watching children or animals, and low-intensity exercising (such as dancing or walking). **Staff who completed the measure reported that**

Table 1
Ten Activities Rated as Most Enjoyable to
Long Term Care Residents

Activity	Percent of respondents rating activity as "enjoyable"
Listening to music	94
Being complimented	88
Grooming (hair, makeup)	79
Birthday or holiday parties	76
Having conversations	76
Making and eating snacks	73
Visits from family or friends	73
Being with animals (live or stuffed)	73
Watching children play or perform	64
Exercising (dancing, walking, etc.)	64

Table 2
Ten Resident Activities Rated as Most Frequent by Long
Term Care Staff

Activity	Percent of respondents rating activity as "enjoyable"
Listening to music	100
Being complimented	94
Grooming (hair, makeup)	91
Exercising (dancing, walking, etc.)	91
Visits from family or friends	82
Conversations	79
Making and eating snacks	70
Attending religious services	67
Watching television or videos	67
Reading or listening to stories	61

it gave them new ideas about small, inexpensive activities that residents in their facilities might enjoy and reinforced the importance of carrying out enjoyable activities on a regular basis. A popular item with staff members was *theme days,* during which everyone would dress up (e.g., in Hawaiian or Western clothing or in funny hats) and the unit would have special menus for meals and special activities following the theme. Staff who tried theme days reported that they improved morale for both staff and residents and that residents requested more of them in the future. These data are based on a small sample and are preliminary, but they indicate the types of activities that LTC residents enjoy.

Proxy Assessment of QOL in Cognitively Impaired Individuals:

Albert and colleagues (1996) modified and combined the Affect Rating Scale and PES-AD to create an index of QOL for individuals with moderate cognitive impairment. Using the combined measures, family members and/or institutional caregivers were interviewed by telephone to obtain assessments of affect and activity level for individuals participating in a longitudinal investigation of dementia. Of the 130 participants in the investigation, 66% lived at home and the rest were in residential LTC facilities. Analysis of data from family and institutional caregivers showed good agreement regarding enjoyment and frequency of pleasant activities and regarding both positive and negative affect in subjects with dementia. Subjects were defined as having high QOL if both positive affect and frequency of pleasant activities were high. Twenty-three percent of subjects (4 of 43 who lived in nursing homes and 26 of 82 living in the community) met these criteria. Nursing home residents with high QOL and those with low QOL did not differ in cognitive or functional status, gender, age, or education. The only area of significant difference involved use of antipsychotic medication; no resident with high QOL was on such medication. For the community-residing subjects, a high QOL was associated with a higher cognitive and functional status. This approach to assessment of LTC residents integrates subjective (affect) and more objective (pleasant activity) aspects of QOL. **The results demonstrate that both family members and paid caregivers may provide valid and reliable proxy assessments of QOL for cognitively impaired individuals who cannot provide meaningful self-reports.**

Self-Report of Perceived Quality of Life:

Research with LTC residents currently lacks a subjective assessment measure of the resident's perception of his or her quality of life. Yet research with community-residing chronically ill older adults has identified subjective assessment as one of the most important aspects of QOL (Patrick, et al., 1988; Pearlman & Uhlmann, 1991), and two recent investigations provide evidence that cognitively impaired individuals may be more capable of providing self-reports of depressive symptoms or health status than was previously recognized. Parmelee and colleagues (1989) found that cognitively impaired subjects in a supervised residential setting were able to reliably rate their own depressive symptoms on the Geriatric Depression Scale (Yesavage et al., 1983) when adequate assistance was provided with reading and marking the test instrument. McHorney (1996) reported that a sample of 36 mildly to moderately cognitively impaired subjects were able to provide self-report information about their health status on the Medical Outcomes Study SF-36 Health Survey with reliability and validity comparable to that of cognitively intact older adult respondents. **This evidence supports the need to develop a self-report QOL measure for residents of LTC facilities.**

The Quality of Life-Alzheimer's Disease (QOL-AD) survey, developed by Logsdon and colleagues (1996), shows promise for use with older adults who are chronically ill and/or have mild to moderate dementia. This brief measure was designed to obtain a rating of the patient's QOL from both the patient and the caregiver. To maximize its usefulness with patients who have mild to moderate dementia, the QOL-AD uses simple and straightforward language and responses. The questions were reviewed by patients and caregivers, as well as experts in the field of geriatrics and gerontology, to maximize construct validity and encompass the QOL domains that are thought to be important in cognitively impaired older adults. For example, the measure includes assessments of the individual's relationships with friends and family, concerns about finances, physical condition, mood, and overall life quality. Caregivers complete this measure as a questionnaire about their patients' QOL, whereas patients complete it in the format of an interview about their own QOL. This measure, shown in Figure 2, consists of 13 items rated on a four-point scale, with 1 being poor and 4 being excellent. Total scores range from 13 to 52. It generally takes caregivers about 5 minutes to complete the measure about their patients; for patients, the interview takes about 10 to 15 minutes to administer. Detailed instructions for interviewer administration have been developed.

In a sample of 77 community-residing Alzheimer's disease patient-caregiver dyads, this measure has been found to have good internal reliability for both patient and caregiver reports (α=.88 and α=.87, respectively). Agreement between patient and caregiver ratings of the patient's QOL was adequate (r=.40), and correlations with other related constructs, including depression (r=.56) and pleasant activity level (r=.41), were significant. Preliminary results indicate that most non–aphasic residents whose Mini Mental State Exam scores (Folstein et al., 1975) are greater than 10 out of 30 are able to complete this measure reliably.

Each of these measures was developed specifically for cognitively impaired individuals and was designed to focus on aspects of QOL that are most salient for a population with chronic illnesses and/or dementia, whether living in the community or in a LTC setting. Additional research is needed to evaluate each measure's effectiveness, clinical utility, and sensitivity to spontaneous change over time and with treatment.

Interventions to Enhance Quality of Life

A number of factors have been proposed that may impact QOL for LTC residents, including the quality of care received, interpersonal

---

Figure 2
Quality of Life–AD (Participant Version)

1. Physical Health	Poor	Fair	Good	Excellent
2. Energy	Poor	Fair	Good	Excellent
3. Mood	Poor	Fair	Good	Excellent
4. Living situation	Poor	Fair	Good	Excellent
5. Memory	Poor	Fair	Good	Excellent
6. Family	Poor	Fair	Good	Excellent
7. Marriage	Poor	Fair	Good	Excellent
8. Friends	Poor	Fair	Good	Excellent
9. Self as a whole	Poor	Fair	Good	Excellent
10. Ability to do chores around the house	Poor	Fair	Good	Excellent
11. Ability to do things for fun	Poor	Fair	Good	Excellent
12. Money	Poor	Fair	Good	Excellent
13. Life as a whole	Poor	Fair	Good	Excellent

Comments:

_____

_____

© 1996 R.G. Logsdon, University of Washington, Seattle, WA.
(Administration instructions available upon request.)

---

relationships with staff, independence, ability to maintain personal belongings, the atmosphere (home-like or institutional), and autonomy in making choices about basic daily activities involving eating, sleeping, dressing, etc. Opportunities to engage in a variety of activities, privacy, and family involvement with the resident are also frequently cited as important for resident's positive QOL (Institute of Medicine, 1986). Empirical validation of these factors is rare, however, and there have been only a few attempts to identify the factors that are most relevant to individuals whose lives are being assessed or to refine further the meanings of these factors in practical terms.

Resident, Family, and Staff Conceptualizations of Quality of Life:

In an investigation of nursing home residents' perspectives on quality of care, Spalding and Frank (1985) conducted a series of discussions with 455 residents from more than 100 nursing homes in 15 different cities. The participants were cognitively intact and able to participate in three group discussion sessions held outside their own facilities; thus, they represent the least disabled of all nursing home residents. However, they do provide an inside perspective on what is important to QOL for individuals in long term care. These residents rated the availability of nurses' aides who were cheerful, friendly, and competent and who treated them with dignity and respect as the most important factor in the quality of their lives. Having a variety of daily activity programs, especially social activities (including activities on weekends), was rated as the second most important influence on QOL by these residents. Their other priorities included food and food service, including a choice of menus; autonomy about decisions regarding basic activities, such as when to arise and go to bed and when to eat; and individualization of services to meet their needs.

Cohn and Sugar (1991) also investigated how QOL for frail older people in five urban nursing homes was perceived and defined by the residents themselves (n=75); their family members (n=40); professional staff, including physicians, nurses, and social workers (n=46); and direct care staff, i.e., nurses' aides (n=46). Participants were asked open- and closed-ended questions about factors influencing the residents' QOL during hour-long, one-on-one interviews. The interviews were coded by independent raters according to content domains, including professional care, activities and entertainment, basic needs, institutional philosophy, physical environment, social-emotional environment, and resident functional abilities, autonomy, and morale.

The majority of residents (73%) reported that they felt their lives were "contented, comfortable, and meaningful," and 86% made positive comments about their QOL. As expected, perceptions of QOL differed among the groups. For residents, the most frequent comments about the meaning of QOL had to do with morale, focusing on their own responsibility for creating meaning in their lives (i.e., "Life is what you make it") and on social-emotional factors (being listened to by aides, having visitors, having someone to talk to, etc.). For family, staff, and aides, the most frequent comments concerned care issues (meals, activities, and access to medical care). In discussing specific aspects of care that contributed most to resident QOL, residents and aides most often cited pleasant and entertaining activities, whereas families and professional staff most often cited medical, nursing, and social services. All four groups described family contact as an important interpersonal factor in QOL. The greatest discrepancy in ratings among groups involved physical limitations and health problems, which residents rated as "not at all important" to their QOL, and family, staff, and aides all rated as "very important."

Residents and their families were also asked what the residents missed most about their prior homes. Residents reported missing social-emotional activities such as shopping with friends, entertaining, and going to meetings or on trips. Families, on the other hand, believed that the residents most missed aspects of the former physical environment, such as personal belongings, space, and food. **Both residents and family members noted the importance of autonomy issues, such as control over one's checkbook and ability to set one's schedule.**

Finally, all four groups were asked what they felt could be improved in their facility and what three things they would change if they could. All four groups agreed that "increasing the number of staff" to ensure continuity on weekends and holidays was a priority. Residents mentioned specific food-related recommendations, including having the residents choose menus and recipes; staff mentioned increasing space for residents to allow them privacy; families mentioned larger closets and more privacy for residents.

In summary, each group tended to perceive and define QOL differently. Aides' responses were most similar to those of residents, while staff and family also tended to agree with each other in most areas. **These findings emphasize the importance of including multiple points of view** (including those of residents) **in decision and policy making. Changes might easily be made in many of the areas mentioned by respondents at little or no cost** (e.g., menu planning)**; others should be considered as a priority when program or staffing changes are planned** (e.g., providing pleasant activities for residents). This investigation provides a wealth of information for future research, as well as practical suggestions for improving QOL in nursing home settings.

Finally, Nores (1997) surveyed 120 elderly women living in seven LTC facilities in Finland. Data were collected from both unstructured interviews and questionnaires. Factors that reportedly affected their QOL included being listened to and understood by staff, getting relief from pain and worry, receiving gentle and compassionate personal care, living in a pleasant and warm interpersonal environment with sufficient activity, and having a sense of autonomy and of being accepted as a person. These findings were consistent with those of other studies emphasizing the importance to residents of a friendly, compassionate, and competent direct care staff; enjoyable and meaningful activities; involvement with their families; and autonomy.

Strategies to Enhance Quality of Life in Long Term Care:

Enhancing QOL in long term care is not about meeting basic needs, although meeting such needs is a prerequisite for a good QOL. **Optimizing health, mood, functional levels, and life satisfaction, regardless of illness state, requires an ongoing, individualized assessment of residents and the physical and interpersonal environment in which they live.** Enhancing QOL requires a creative and flexible treatment plan for each resident. Often psychologists are called only when residents are exhibiting psychopathology, behavioral disturbances, or adjustment problems, or when the staff perceives families as problematic. **In reality, psychologists should be involved in the ongoing care of all residents, even those who are functioning according to expectations.** Psychologists can help to enhance QOL for all residents because of their training and experience in assessment, behavioral analysis, developmental issues, psychological adjustment, staff education, and team building among various helping disciplines.

Friendly, Cheerful, and Compassionate Direct Care Staff:

Direct care staff characteristics impact QOL in numerous ways, because residents depend on these individuals for assistance with many daily tasks, including intimate personal care, and nurses' aides are often the residents' primary source of interpersonal contact. Policy makers, consumer advocates, and nursing home administrators have emphasized the importance of ongoing staff training. Direct care staff—many of whom are minimally educated, young, and not psychologically sophisticated—must obtain the skills necessary to provide safe, appropriate, and compassionate care. Psychologists may be called upon to plan and/or conduct such training.

Residents stress the need for staff to be friendly and cheerful, characteristics that are difficult to achieve through education alone. Staff can be trained to bathe a resident safely; they cannot always be trained to change their demeanor toward residents. Because of this, priority must be given to interpersonal characteristics in the hiring of staff, with references checked, personal interviews conducted, and requirements for care discussed. The input of the psychologist can also be very useful in this area.

Once staff is in place, it is in the best interests of the staff members and residents to maintain a consistent staffing team, that is, have the same staff members work with the same residents every day. This allows staff members to get to know the residents as individuals, to meet and talk with family members who visit, and to identify successful and unsuccessful care strategies for each person. It is essential for residents, including those who apparently don't recognize their caregivers from one day to the next, to have caregivers who know them and their likes and dislikes. The following case illustrates this.

Case Vignette:

Mr. F had been "kicked out" of three nursing homes before he arrived at the state hospital dementia unit. He had a reputation for being assaultive, especially during personal care activities. Because of this, he was given psychotropic medication and assigned a male aide—a strong, burly former high school wrestler. Over the weeks, they developed a special rapport, which improved even more when the aide learned that Mr. F was a former high school football coach. The aide began calling the resident "Coach" and gave him a baseball cap that Mr. F wore constantly. After a month with no episodes of agitation, Mr. F's psychotropic medication was discontinued, but problems developed around mealtime when staff tried to get him into the dining room. Once again, Mr. F's aide came up with the solution—when it was time to eat, he went to the resident and said, "Come on, Coach, let's go down to the cafe' and get some lunch." Arm in arm they walked down the hall and into the dining room, where they "ordered" coffee and the blue plate special, after which Mr. F left a tip from the change he had in his pocket. When Mr. F was transferred back out to a new, less restrictive nursing home setting, staff were provided with his history, called him "Coach," dressed him in his baseball cap, and let him eat in the "cafe'." This final placement was successful, and Mr. F did not return to the state hospital.

Pleasant Activities and Events

Residents consistently report that activities, especially social activities, improve their QOL. In response to this finding, many facilities have an activity director and an activity calendar posted in a shared area. This is a good first step towards meeting the residents' needs for activities and recreation but by itself it does not enhance the residents' QOL. **In an investigation of community-residing individuals with moderate dementia, a positive correlation was found between the number of pleasant events experienced in the past month and both mood** (r=.77) **and overall quality of life** (r=.79) (Logsdon, 1996; Logsdon & Teri, 1997). **However, overall activity level was not associated with either mood or QOL—only pleasant/enjoyable activity correlated significantly with either one.** This finding has important implications in LTC settings which often emphasize planning and carrying out group activities. **There is little or no benefit in coercing individuals to participate in activities that they do not find enjoyable; only activities that are pleasant and meaningful to the individual are likely to reduce depressive symptoms and enhance quality of life.** Individualized assessments and plans for pleasant daily activities will be most effective in ensuring that the activity actually meets these goals. An assessment of activities a resident has enjoyed in the past may suggest the types of activities that may still be enjoyable. Sources of such information include the PES–AD (discussed earlier), interviews with the family, old scrapbooks or photo albums, and a discussion with the resident about prior hobbies and occupational interests.

Case Vignette:

Mrs. P was a tiny, very prim and proper lady who was always stylishly dressed and made up. Over the course of her stay in the facility, she became increasingly agitated in the late afternoon, a common phenomenon among nursing home residents referred to as "sundowning." Staff tried a number of strategies to calm Mrs. P during this time, including reassuring her, giving her extra attention, giving her a snack, and involving her in arts and crafts activities, but nothing worked very well. One day, volunteers were visiting from a local church, and they brought a tea set, tea sandwiches, and a tablecloth. They gathered a few of the more sedate residents for teatime, but did not approach Mrs. P because she was already becoming somewhat agitated. As they started serving tea, however, Mrs. P walked over to their table and joined them. They gave her a chair and a cup, and she sat down for a lovely social occasion, during which she chatted about the old days when she played the church organ. Teatime became a regular routine for Mrs. P and other residents, with an assortment of "china" cups and table linens that staff brought in or purchased from a thrift shop. The fact that the cups and linens were all different was a major topic of conversation during these times, with residents comparing patterns or talking about cups they had owned in the past.

Family Involvement

The individual's quality of life is intertwined with that of his or her family (Berardo & Berardo, 1992). Families are often very concerned about the ongoing care of their loved one, and their concern may be seen as threatening to the nursing staff. Understanding family issues and facilitating good communication between family and staff is important in long term care (Austrom & Hendrie, 1992). Family concerns often center around the adequacy of care and the timeliness and compassion with which residents' needs are attended to. Families also face the significant cost of ongoing care and the guilt associated with relegating care of their loved one to others. Family caregivers of older adults with dementia have been found to experience high levels of depressive symptoms, with 14% to 83% of caregivers experiencing significant depression (Drinka, et al., 1987; Gallagher, et al., 1989; Pearson, et al., 1993). Before placing their loved one in an LTC facility, families have usually been through an extended period of caregiving and may still feel isolated, depressed, angry, frustrated, and exhausted. **Involving family members in problem solving and ongoing care is often facilitated by identifying specific tasks they can perform and planning special social occasions to which they are invited.** (Having a group of volunteers to attend these occasions with residents whose families are not available is also very important.) Even severely demented residents will often "rise to the occasion."

Case Vignette:

A facility planned a festive holiday buffet dinner for high-functioning resi-

dents, with dainty plates and an assortment of delicious foods, but did not in-clude the dementia unit in the plans. As one administrator said, "these are residents who are constantly grabbing food off of other people's plates at din-ner; I can just imagine the potential for disaster here." The direct-care staff from the excluded unit protested and insisted that they also have the oppor-tunity to participate. As a compromise, they were provided with their own buffet on their unit, and they invited family members of their residents to at-tend. To everyone's surprise, latent social skills emerged in the residents, and they and their and family members alike had a wonderful time. The staff in-stituted a monthly buffet dinner on their unit as a result of this experience.

Family members also play a central role in personalizing care of their loved one. Their long term, intimate knowledge of the resi-dent is crucial in developing effective treatments for behavioral or psychological problems. When they are included as an integral part of the care team, family members benefit, residents benefit, and the staff benefits. The case of Mr. C illustrates this point.

Case Vignette:

Mr. C was a plumber, as was his father before him and his son after him. They owned a local business that Mr. C headed until he became disabled by a series of strokes which left him confused and partially paralyzed. Af-ter he was admitted to the nursing home, Mr. C suffered from severe de-pression, often remarking that he wished he had died when he had the stroke. Antidepressants helped him sleep but did little to improve his morale until his son brought in a box of plastic PVC pipes and joints, and asked him to help him plumb a freestanding sink. Mr. C's face lit up; he selected the appropriate pieces and worked on assembling them for his son to pick up the next day. When his son picked up the assembled pipes, he asked his father to put together a section for connecting a dishwasher to a garbage disposal. Each day, Mr. C's son brought in a project; Mr. C was also given the job of "inspecting" the pipes at the facility each day. Staff asked him questions about their own plumbing projects, such as "why are copper pipes so great?" Mr. C talked plumbing with anyone who would listen. This activity continued for many months until Mr. C had a massive

stroke and died. By working together, family and staff found the key to pro-
viding him a high QOL in his last days.

Autonomy

Residents identified autonomy as particularly important to their QOL. Deciding (within reason) when to go to bed at night, when to get up in the morning, when to eat, bathe, and get dressed—these are among the small daily decisions that are often taken away from LTC residents. In the Cohn and Sugar (1991) interview-based investigation of QOL, residents were asked to rank the importance of different autonomy issues. At the top of their list was access to a telephone (which is often restricted in LTC facilities); followed by access to a private place to be alone; availability of transportation; choice of roommates; having keepsakes; setting schedules; frequency of baths; and choice of food, location, and company for meals. For less independent residents, autonomy issues might involve the desire to choose where to sit, what music to listen to, what to wear, and the desire to have access to indoor and outdoor areas where they could wander freely and safely. Even residents who are unable to communicate their choices verbally often express clear preferences through their behavior, as illustrated by the following case:

Case Vignette:

Ms. B was quite demented by the time she moved into the LTC facility and needed assistance with dressing each morning. Her morning aide typically picked something out of the closet and asked her whether she wanted to wear it that day. Over the months, the aide noticed that Ms. B always chose items of clothing that were pink, no matter what the season or occasion. As Ms. B lost the ability to communicate her choices, the aide continued to choose pink items for her. One day, Ms. B was uncharacteristically agitated and tearful throughout the day. Staff wondered whether she was ill, had fallen, or was in pain. Then someone noticed Ms. B's clothing—she was very nicely dressed in a green pantsuit. The aide who usually dressed Ms. B was out ill that day, and a substitute from the temporary pool had been used to replace her. The substitute, a competent and caring aide, did not know about Ms. B's preference for pink, and Mrs. B made her wishes known in the only way she could—through her behavior. Once her clothing was changed and Ms. B was back in one of her pink outfits, her agitation and tearfulness ceased. Facility staff removed all non-pink clothing from her closet and posted a note about the resident's preference inside the closet door to avoid a repeat episode.

Conclusion

In the past, QOL in long term care might have been considered an oxymoron, because nursing homes were often thought of as warehouses for individuals who had no other alternatives for care. Now, however, the rapidly growing elderly population has increasingly varied residential options which offer a range of levels of care. **The best LTC programs have a variety of goals, including supporting and maximizing residents' day-to-day activities, providing recreational and therapeutic activities, and preventing or treating psychological and behavioral problems such as depression or agitation.** Along with program development comes the need to assess outcomes, from specific symptom amelioration to improvement in overall life satisfaction. For residents (who are increasingly considered consumers rather than patients) and their families, satisfaction with the resident's living situation and QOL has become particularly important. **Ultimately, LTD residents, regardless of disability, want what we all want: to be treated with kindness and respect; to engage in pleasant, meaningful activities; to have good relationships with our families and other people; and to make our own choices about the things that are important to us on a daily basis.** When residents lack some aspect of QOL, psychologists are in a position to identify the problem and provide interventions, remembering that the goal of all treatment is to optimize health, day-to-day activity, mood, and life satisfaction, regardless of illness state.

References

Albert, S. (in press). Assessing health-related quality of life in chronic care populations. *Mental Health and Aging.*

Albert, S. M., Castillo-Castaneda, C. D., Sano, M., Jacobs, et al. (1996). Quality of life in patients with Alzheimer's disease as reported by patient proxies. *Journal of the American Geriatrics Society, 44,* 1342–1347.

Arnold, S. B. (1991). The measurement of quality of life in the frail elderly. In J. E. Birren, J. E. Lubben, J. C. Rowe, & D. E. Deutchman (Eds.), *The concept and measurement of quality of life in the frail elderly* (pp. 50–73). San Diego, CA: Academic Press.

Austrom, M. G., & Hendrie, H. C. (1992). Quality of life: The family and Alzheimer's disease. *Journal of Palliative Care, 8,* 56–60.

Berardo, D. H., & Berardo, F. M. (1992). Quality of life across age and family stage. *Journal of Palliative Care, 8,* 52–55.

Biren, J. E. & Deutchman, D. E. (1991). Concepts and content of quality of life in the later years: An overview. In J. E. Birren, J. E. Lubben, J. C. Rowe, & D. C. Deutchman (Eds.), *The concept and measurement of quality of life in the frail elderly* (pp. 344–360). New York: Academic Press, Inc.

Cella, D. F. (1992). Quality of life: *The concept. Journal of Palliative Care,* 8, 8–13.

Cohn, J., & Sugar, J. A. (1991). Determinants of quality of life in institutions: Perceptions of frail older residents, staff, and families. In J. E. Birren, J. E. Lubben, J. C. Rowe, & D. E. Deutchman (Eds.), *The concept and measurement of quality of life in the frail elderly* (pp. 28–49). San Diego, CA: Academic Press.

Drinka, J. K., Smith, J. C., & Drinka, P. J. (1987). Correlates of depression and burden for informal caregivers of patients in a geriatrics referral clinic. *Journal of the American Geriatrics Society, 35,* 522–525.

Folstein, M. F., Folstein, S. E., & McHugh, P. R. (1975). Mini-Mental State: A practical method for grading the cognitive state of patients for the clinician. *Journal of Psychiatric Research, 12,* 221–231.

Gallagher, D., Rose, J., Rivera, P., Lovett, S., & Thompson, L. W. (1989). Prevalence of depression in family caregivers. *The Gerontologist, 29,* 449–456.

Institute of Medicine. (1986). *Improving the quality of care in nursing homes.* Washington, DC: National Academy Press.

Lawton, M. P. (1983). The dimensions of well-being. *Experimental Aging Research, 9,* 65–72.

Lawton, M. P. (1991). A multidimensional view of quality of life in frail elders. In J. E. Rirreu, J. E. Lubben, J. C. Rowe, and D. E. Deutchman (Eds.), *The concept and measurement of quality of life in the frail elderly.* New York: Academic Press, Inc.

Lawton, M. P. (1994). Quality of life in Alzheimer disease. *Alzheimer Disease and Associated Disorders, 8,* 138–150.

Lawton, M. P., Kleban, M. H., Dean, J., Rajagopal, D., & Parmalee, P. A. (1992). The factorial generality of brief positive and negative affect measures. *Journal of Gerontology: Psychological Sciences, 47,* 228–237.

Lawton, M. P., Van Haitsma, K., & Klapper, J. (1996). Observed affect in nursing home residents with Alzheimer's disease. *Journal of Gerontology: Psychological Sciences, 51,* 314.

Logsdon, R. G. (1996). Quality of life in Alzheimer's disease: Implications for research [Abstract]. *The Gerontologist, 36,* 278a.

Logsdon, R. G., & Teri, L. (1997). The Pleasant Events Schedule-AD: Psychometric properties and relationship to depression and cognition in Alzheimer's disease patients. *The Gerontologist, 37,* 40–45.

McHorney, C. A. (1996). Measuring and monitoring general health status in elderly persons: Practical and methodological issues in using the SF-36 Health Survey. *The Gerontologist, 36,* 571–583.

McSweeny, A. J. & Creer, T. L. (1995). Health-related quality of life assessment in medical care. *Disease-a-Month, 41,* 11–71.

Nores, T. H. (1997). What is most important for elders in institutional care in Finland? *Geriatric Nursing, 19,* 67–69.

Parmelee, P. A., Lawton, M. P., & Katz, I. R. (1989). Psychometric properties of the Geriatric Depression Scale among the institutionalized aged. *Psychological Assessment, 1,* 331–338.

Patrick, D. L., Danis, M., Southerland, L. I., & Honh, G. (1988). Quality of life following intensive care. *Journal of General Internal Medicine, 3,* 218–223.

Pearlman, R. A., & Uhlmann, R. F. (1991). Quality of life in elderly, chronically ill outpatients. *Journal of Gerontology: Medical Sciences, 46,* M31–M38.

Pearson, J., Teri, L., Reifler, B.V., & Raskind, M. (1989). Functional status and cognitive impairment in Alzheimer's disease patients with and without depression. *Journal of the American Geriatrics Society, 37,* 1117–1121.

Pearson, J. L., Teri, L., Wagner, A., Truax, P., & Logsdon, R. (1993). The relationship of problem behaviors in dementia patients to the depression and burden of caregiving spouses. *The American Journal of Alzheimer's Disease and Related Disorders & Research, 8,* 15–22.

Post, S. G., & Whitehouse, P. J. (1995). Fairhill Guidelines on ethics of the care of people with Alzheimer's disease: A clinical summary. *Journal of the American Geriatrics Society, 43,* 1423–1429.

Reisberg, B., Borenstein, J., Salob , S. P., et al. (1987). Behavioral symptoms in Alzheimer's disease: Phenomenology and treatment. *Journal of Clinical Psychiatry, 48,* (Suppl. 5), 915.

Rovner, B. W., & Katz, I. R. (1993). Psychiatric disorders in the nursing home: A selective review of studies related to clinical care. *International Journal of Geriatric Psychiatry, 8,* 75–87.

Roy, D. J. (1992). Measurement in the service of compassion. *Journal of Palliative Care, 8,* 3–4.

Siu, A. L. (1987). The quality of medical care received by older persons. *Journal of the American Geriatrics Society, 35,* 1084–1091.

Spalding, J., & Frank, B. W. (1985, July). Quality care from the residents' point of view. *American Health Care Association Journal, 37.*

Teri, L., & Logsdon, R. G. (1991). Identifying pleasant activities for Alzheimer's disease patients: The Pleasant Events Schedule-AD. *The Gerontologist, 31,* 124–127.

Teri, L., Logsdon, R. G., Wagner, A., & Uomoto, J. (1994). The caregiver role in behavioral treatment of depression in dementia patients. In E. Light, G. Niederehe, B. Lebowitz (Eds.), *Stress effects on family caregivers of Alzheimer's patients: Research and interventions* (pp. 185–204). New York: Springer Press.

U.S. Congress, Office of Technology Assessment. (1987). *Losing a Million*

Minds: Confronting the Tragedy of Alzheimer's Disease and Other Dementias. OTA-BA-325. Washington, D.C.: U.S. Government Printing Office.

Whitehouse, P. J. & Rabins, P. V. (1992). Quality of life and dementia. *Alzheimer's Disease and Associated Disorders, 6,* 135–137.

Wieland, D., Rubenstein, L. V., & Hirsch, S. H. (1995). Quality of life in nursing homes: An emerging focus of research and practice. In P. R. Katz, R. L. Kane, & M. D. Mezey (Eds.), *Quality care in geriatric settings* (pp. 149–195). New York: Springer.

Wilson, I. B., & Cleary, P. D. (1995). Linking clinical variables with health-related quality of life: A conceptual model of patient outcomes. *Journal of the American Medical Association, 273,* 59–65.

Yesavage, J. A., Brink, T. L., Rose, T. L., et al. (1983). Development and validation of a Geriatric Depression Screening Scale: A preliminary report. *Journal of Psychiatric Research, 17,* 37–49.

8

Interventions for Older Adults With Personality Disorders

ERLENE ROSOWSKY, PSY.D.

Abstract

This chapter presents an overview of Axis II conditions, including a brief history of Personality Disorders (PD) through *The Diagnostic and Statistical Manual of Mental Disorders* editions. It addresses in depth the presentation of Axis II disorders in the older adult, as well as difficulties in assessment and diagnoses specific to this population.

The major learning points are: (1) understanding what might be the age effects on PD in the older adult; (2) recognizing age-resistant core diagnostic criteria; (3) identifying the psychosocial, developmental referents that are central to the expression and recognition of PD in older adults; (4) understanding the dimensional model of personality traits (using Costa and McCrae's Five Factor Model as an example); (5) understanding the concept of "goodness of fit," and recognizing its utility as applied to older adults in specific contexts and under demanding condition; (6) identification of professional challenges in work with the older adult with PD, and the unique utilization of the countertransference; (7) recognition of the "difficult" (PD) older adult in the long term care setting.

Introduction

The Diagnostic and Statistical Manual of Mental Disorders, fourth edition (DSM-IV) (American Psychiatric Association, 1994) defines personality disorders (PDs) as pervasive, chronic, maladaptive personality styles that result in social and/or occupational impairment or in the subjective experience of distress. The premise is that PDs reflect extreme variants of normal personality traits; there is nothing pathological about the traits per se.

Since the inception of PDs as a diagnostic category in *DSM-I* (1952), the number of specific personality disorders listed in the *DSM* has decreased from 27 to 10. In *DSM-IIIR* (1987), however, PDs were grouped into three phenomenologically based clusters: (1) the *odd* and *eccentric* category, which includes paranoid, schizoid, and schizotypal disorders; (2) the *erratic* and *emotional* category, which encompasses antisocial, borderline, histrionic, and narcissistic disorders; and (3) the *anxious* and *fearful* category, which includes avoidant, dependent, and obsessive-compulsive disorders.

In addition, the category *not otherwise specified* (PD, NOS), formerly termed *mixed PD,* is now applied to personality patterns that meet the general criteria for a PD but not the criteria for a specific disorder and to cases meeting the criteria for a PD that is not included in the current *DMS* classification. When an individual meets the criteria for more than one diagnosis, each PD is identified.

Personality disorders are coded on Axis II. **An Axis II condition is more central than the adventitious disorders coded on Axis I. PDs represent an individual's persistent, ego-syntonic way of experiencing and engaging his or her world. The personality "feels like me" to the individual** (i.e., it is syntonic). **What is experienced as dystonic is usually the negating feedback experienced by others or difficulty in achieving academic, occupational, or social goals. In contrast, Axis I conditions, which involve isolated or episodic psychiatric events, are typically experienced as dystonic and are accompanied by an expectation of re-**

turning to a baseline functional status. A case could be made that Axis II therefore should be Axis I (as it is more central and defining of the person), and that Axis I (a disorder superimposed on the individual's character structure) should actually be Axis II.

The Axis II diagnosis is helpful in predicting the point of least resistance to treatment (and identifying likely points of greatest resistance). For example, the individual with a schizoid personality could be expected to resist closeness and the suggestion of intimacy and to terminate treatment, or at least not to comply with it. In the nursing home, this individual could be expected to respond better to clear written or verbal instructions about care regimens than to coaching and cajoling. While face-to-face and friendly urging might often be helpful, this particular personality would probably perceive this as threatening, unpleasant, and anxiety provoking.

A personality trait model may be useful in a clinical assessment because of its (a) predictive value as a measure of the probability of certain problems occurring, (b) interpretive value in clarifying behaviors that are maladaptive within the LTC context or in response to specific task demands, and (c) planning value in guiding the clinician to select appropriate treatment options and therapy interventions.

Axis II Personality Disorders and the Older Adult

The prevalence of PDs is estimated to be 6% to 13% for community-dwelling older adults, compared with 10% to 17% for younger adults (Sadavoy & Fogel, 1992). The prevalence rate for mental health care patients is much higher. It is estimated that 33% to 50% of psychogeriatric outpatients have a PD diagnosis (Zweig & Hinrichsen, 1992).

In spite of the prevalence and clinical and social significance of PDs, they frequently remain undiagnosed and thus are not considered in treatment planning. Clinical research in the area of PDs in the older adult has been scant. **Failure to diagnose PD in this population reflects a number of considerations, including** (a) **an unstated belief that PD is**

somehow (magically) **outgrown with advancing age,** (b) **dramatic age-related changes in the clinical picture that make a PD difficult to recognize, and** (c) **an assumption that, even if a PD is identified, it will not affect treatment and care because PDs cannot be cured.** Clinicians may be particularly unlikely to diagnose a PD, which is an Axis II, feeling it is not as important as a diagnosis on Axis I or Axis III. (General medical conditions that may relate to the mental disorder(s) diagnosed are coded on Axis III.)

Personality Disorders and the Institutional Setting

In any institution, patients with a severe PD affect the staff and other residents. They are, as a group, hard to manage, hard to contain, hard to live with, and hard to bear. Although there are no direct data, it is highly probable that individuals with a PD (with other variables held constant) are more likely to be institutionalized than individuals without a PD; thus, individuals with PDs may well be overrepresented in long term care (LTC) settings. Individuals with a PD often have (a) **fewer intimate relationships,** (b) **a history of unstable, conflictual relationships,** (c) poor anger **control,** (d) **a tendency toward impulsivity and acting-out behaviors,** (e) **a history of problems with potential caregivers, and/or** (f) **difficulty accepting help and dependence on the care of others.** These factors also have an impact on their new care providers within the institutional setting.

The Transition to a Long Term Care Setting:

Older adults in general, and the very old especially do not transplant well. There is always the likelihood of temporary regression and the risk of permanent reduction of function when they are moved from one setting to another. The severely character-disordered older adult is particularly likely to experience the transition to an LTC setting as negative and feel victimized, flooded by anxiety, and/or engulfed by rage. **A hallmark of character disorder is reliance on a small repertoire of primitive defenses that**

are used in response to a broad range of experiences, regardless of whether these experiences are adaptive or maladaptive. We can expect the individual with a character disorder to have considerable difficulty accommodating the new challenge presented by the transition, especially with the whole context of his or her life changing.

Residents with a PD can be expected to adjust less well, overall, than those without a PD, although there are no direct data on this. However, the stressors that surround the transition to a nursing home are likely to have an especially intense negative impact on the more primitive patient. Consider the following:

- For the *narcissistic character*, loss of control and increased dependency on others is experienced as shameful and wounding.
- For the *schizoid character*, the need to create and maintain new relationships in order to secure care is experienced as extremely uncomfortable; perhaps uncomfortable enough to avoid getting the care.
- For the *paranoid character*: the need to relinquish vigilance and trust caregivers may be an impossible task. This individual may experience great conflict in determining whether the new caregiver is a source of help or a source of harm.

There is evidence that individuals with a dependent character adjust well to the nursing home setting. However, they are also likely to melt into a dependency position and lose some functional abilities as the system allows them to become more and more dependent.

Countertransference and Personality Disorders:

Countertransference refers to the emotional responses evoked in a clinician by a patient. These responses have origins in the clinician's early object relationships (usually with parents). **Countertransference can be positive as well as negative.** Examples of positive countertransference include feelings of protectiveness, heightened self-esteem, specialness, and omnipotence. Examples of negative countertransference include feelings of rage, frustration, fear, and powerlessness.

Countertransference can also be expressed through fantasies about the patient. Positive countertransference fantasies about the patient might include fantasies of rescue, unique understanding, or perfect love. Negative countertransference fantasies might involve retaliation, escape, violence, or death. **Powerful countertransference reactions to the patient with a PD appear to be inherent to and descriptive of pathognomonic PD at all ages, and the strength of the countertransference is often an indicator of the degree of the patient's emotional distress.**

Countertransference and Clinical Work With Older Adults

Certain countertransference responses are highly consistent among individuals involved in clinical work with older adults in general. Clinicians may confront their own fears and worries about aging, and their responses may reflect unresolved conflicts with their parents as they watch them age and move toward death.

Realizing that no matter how good, smart, and caring we are, we cannot reverse the aging process, stop time, or stave off death, clinicians may themselves be narcissistically wounded, ashamed, and enraged.

Other typical responses include fear of being consumed by the expanding dependency of the patient and revulsion at and rejection of the sight and sounds of the frail, ill patient.

As therapy is a microcosm of the patient's universe, with the therapist as proxy for intimate others, it serves as an important window into the patient's phenomenology, particularly the care-provider-recipient relationship. Thus, therapy has a predictive quality that can be applied to other venues and relationships. The patient's probable response to an individual, situation, or intervention can be anticipated.

Specific Countertransference Issues in Long Term Care

Intense emotions may be evoked as the caregiving staff reflects society's bias against nursing home placement. These nursing home residents are, after all, someone's parents, someone's spouse, someone's sibling. One powerful, common personal staff response is overidentification with the patient and the patient's family; another common but contrasting response is denial of the resident's identity as a real person.

Other professional considerations that may affect the staff's responses include (a) the belief that work with the elderly in a nursing home is on the lowest rung of the professional ladder, (b) the experience of being an "anger magnet" for the displaced negative ambivalence of residents' families, (c) inadequate training in the psychosocial development and needs of older adults, and (d) relatively poor pay for very difficult, nonglamorous work (Genevay & Katz, 1990).

The Effect of Personality Disorders on Staff, Family, and Other Residents:

Staff

Personality disorders may prompt behavior by care providers that differs significantly from their usual way of providing care. Such responses may include excessive thinking about the patient, time spent with the patient, after-hours attention to the patient's needs or general care of the patient. The clinician may also try to defend the patient against a staff that is perceived as nonempathic or adversarial (splitting) or, conversely, deny or withhold usual care or attention because of negative feelings (from repugnance to hate) about the patient. In the latter case, the clinician may miss meetings or sessions, use poorly considered notes or treatment plans, and, overall, not put the usual attention and energy into the patient's care.

These responses may offer a clue to the patient's psychopathology and what he or she typically evokes in oth-

ers. For example, if an experienced clinician is provoked to punish a patient by being excessively critical and meeting increased dependency demands with increased withholding, this patient probably evokes similar sadistic responses and punishment from others as well. Grove, in his seminal article, "Taking Care of the Hateful Patient" (1978), distinguished among several types of patients who induce negative responses in caregivers:"Clingers evoke aversion[,] … [h]elp rejectors evoke depression [, and] … [s]elf-destructive deniers evoke feelings of malice."

The following case presents a patient who evoked negative, adversial responses and suggests how staff may respond in such a case:

Case Study:

Mr. R was a 76-year-old man who emigrated to the United States from Ireland at age 30. In the old country, he did day labor and got into many scrapes with the law. He was an outspoken critic of the treatment of workers and encouraged others to join him in acts of vandalism and other acts to send a message to the people in charge. With a change in government, the new officials regarded him as more than a minor nuisance and encouraged him to emigrate. He came to Boston and landed a job the next day doing physically demanding jobs for the only company he ever worked for in this country.

He was an alcoholic, probably by his late teens. His friends were "pub pals," with whom he had no contact other than drinking. He lived in an apartment that was located close to his job. He had no car, took no vacations, and had no friends other than the people with whom he drank and worked. Around age 70, while still working, he developed symptoms of Parkinson's disease and had a cerebral vascular accident (CVA) at age 71. After the hospitalization, he could not work and could not afford his apartment on his pension. He moved to a single-room occupancy (SRO) hotel in the same community. His one source of happiness was being near the ocean, and he would walk miles along the beach throughout the year. When he was unable to work, he spent more time drinking. There were several episodes of falling and boisterous behavior, so he was evicted from

*his SRO. He went back to the hospital to adjust his medications to re-
duce the number of falls. He was discharged to an LTC shelter far from
the ocean, where he roomed with 6 to 8 men and was required to participate in various socialization groups daily. After 3 weeks he bolted, went
on a drinking binge, walked along the beach, got beaten up by neighborhood thugs, and ended up in a hospital, bruised and homeless. His extremely autonomous, idiosyncratic, and isolating personality style was in
opposition to the traits that were valued by the system, namely compliance, conventional behavior, and an interpersonal public style. The clinical mental health consultant explained the case of Mr. R to the staff at
the rehabilitation hospital, and the implications for his treatment and discharge plan were discussed For example, knowing that the patient would
reject group activities, staff members were told not to interpret his rejection
as a personal failure and respond to it as such. Staff members were also
encouraged to support the patient's interacting with one other resident or
one staff member, using a salient common interest as an overt bond. Mr.
R's love of the ocean and beach could be pressed into service to forge a
critical level of interaction. His need for autonomy and control could be
addressed by allowing him to select from a menu of available activities
or even a choice of times for required activities, such as physical therapy
sessions. The staff was encouraged to consider other activities that
would both meet his need for autonomy and solitude and reinforce socia-
ble interactions.*

Family

**Placing a family member in a nursing home has a pro-
found effect on the family system. This may be especially
true when there is a history of intense negative ambivalence in the relationship with the patient. The patient
struggles to achieve an optimal distance from others, vac-
illating between closeness and separateness, with each
move to the opposite pole accompanied by internal discomfort and often the expression of hostility.** The move
into a nursing home, one's last home, usually heralds a unique
process of bereavement; it marks the death of family life as it once

was. Family members often feel that they have failed to care for the individual at home, which had been at least a covert expectation. Life with the personality-disordered adult has been an emotional roller-coaster, and family members may be relieved to be freed from the chore of caring for him or her; they may also feel an enormous amount of guilt because of these feelings. They may become hypercritical of the care the individual receives from the nursing home staff. Knowing first-hand that the individual is "difficult," they may hope he or she will not be treated by the staff in the way his or her personality can provoke, especially without the tempering effect in the caregivers of family love or filial or spousal responsibility. Conversely, if the care is too good, if the staff's relationship with the patient is less conflictual than the family's, it can exacerbate the family's sense of guilt over their own inability to continue to provide care or their rage about the patient's having made life so much harder for them than for the nursing home staff.

Other Residents

The benchmark of severe character disorder is the individual's problematic relationships with intimate others. In the nursing home, this may apply to both staff members, especially those providing direct care, and the patient's roommate(s). Cohabitation may be particularly difficult because of physical ills (such as severe respiratory or gastric problems), behaviors (for example, the screaming of a patient with dementia), or personality disorders. **Irritability, poor anger control, and extreme suspiciousness are characteristic of some PDs and contribute greatly to a negative roommate relationship.**

Using Knowledge of Personality Disorders to Guide Interventions

Why should clinicians bother with the assessment of PD? Such an assessment may lead the clinician to use counseling before introducing "help" to encourage patients to make their own determination that professional help would benefit them. This is important; since personality is typically experienced as egosyntonic, such counseling may help minimize resistance to care.

Clinicians may also focus on building the patients' skills: teaching them how help is secured, training them in appropriate behaviors, and helping them understand what the provider expects and what changes they do not have to make. What do they do in exchange for accepting help? This has special relevance to family caregiving dynamics, especially when there is a change in power and role position.

Clinicians should ensure ongoing monitoring of the patient's functional status and specify strict limits on the parameters of the help that is needed or provided. They should encourage patients to use more adaptive ways of getting attention and social approval and make certain that these efforts are reinforced by the system. **Alerting the patient care staff to specific personality dynamics can help neutralize the negative effects of a PD.**

An Intervention Model of Assessment:

In this model, the PD assessment is based on finding the answer to three questions:

1. **Where is the distress?** This allows the clinician to determine who is hurting in the institution: the system, the staff, a particular staff person, or a staff member performing a specific task.
2. **Where is the resistance?** This focuses on the factors that are maintaining the individual's resistance to making positive changes (i.e., developing more adaptive behavior).
3. **Where is the opportunity for a positive change with the least resistance?** Can certain staff behaviors could bring about desirable change, and can the family can be recruited to support a positive change or inhibit negative behavior? Is it the patient who needs to change? If so, how would this be most likely achieved: through modeling, talking about feelings, behavioral techniques, or cognitive restructuring?

Using Interventions at Different Levels:

Clinicians can examine the circumstances under which maladaptive behavior appears and those aspects of the patient's environment that allow "degrees of freedom" or movement away from such behavior. In so doing, the clinician may examine the situation in terms of the level of the (a) *role* in which the individual manifests the behavior—as patient, competent adult, dying individual, or resident advocate; (b) *task* that provokes the maladaptive response; (c) *context,* that is, the specific venue of the maladaptive response; and (d) *relationship* (involving the resident, the staff, and/or the family) in which the behavior occurs.

Therapy for Long Term Care Patients With Personality Disorder

Therapy for patients with PD in LTC settings is based on several premises:

1. **The background for any kind of therapy is what it means to the individual to be in a nursing home.** Does the individual experience the staff and other residents as a new family or community, as the failure of the individual's own family to be able to tolerate and care for him or her, or as a final stop before death?

2. **Any change in any part of the system will effect change in other parts of the system.** This change can be in affect, cognition, or behavior.

3. **The primary concern of residents is the ability of the system to meet their physical, psychological, and social needs.**

4. **The primary concern of the staff is to maintain a smooth and efficient routine.**

5. **The primary concern of the mental health clinician is to get feedback** (through observation, interview, history/report, and countertransference) **showing that interventions are reducing distress in the system and promoting healing and health in the patient.**

6. Identification of both the PD and the level of the intervention indicated can provide a useful template for suggesting and guiding a specific treatment plan.

Personality Disorder Clusters:

Cluster A: "Odd and Eccentric" Character

The dominant features of this character are distrust, detachment, restricted emotional expression, perceptual distortions, and peculiar behaviors. The following case presents an example of this character:

Case Study:

Mr. O an 81-year-old, was brought to the community hospital after being found on the floor, unconscious and lying in vomit and blood, by the postman, who had noticed that Mr. O had not picked up his mail for a few days. After being cleaned, hydrated, and stabilized and spending 2 days in intensive care, Mr. O was transferred to the general medical unit. When he regained consciousness, he would not interact with the staff and refused to eat the food they brought him, despite their best efforts at encouragement. The clergy came to visit, and still Mr. O would not cooperate in his care. Volunteers also visited him twice a day to keep his spirits up, as it was noted that he had no relatives to visit him. Despite these efforts and his medical stability, his attitude worsened. He would not eat or walk to the shower; he would speak only reluctantly and in short phrases. Staff members were beside themselves; his doctor was furious and at his wit's end. I was called as a mental health consultant, and the referring physician said, "If you want him, he's all yours."

By interviewing the physician, the social worker, and one family member, I learned the following about Mr. O's personal history. He was born in this small town, one of four children in a respectable, hard-working, middle-class family. He finished public school through high school, participating in what he would not identify as a trade curriculum. He had always been con-

sidered odd and was a true loner. He did not get into trouble but had run away on several occasions, always finding his way home, and telling his family that he had gone into the woods. He worked locally and marginally as a night guard for a factory and lived at home with his parents while his siblings got married and raised families. He did not need to interact with his parents (being out at night and sleeping during the day), and they apparently had great tolerance for their "peculiar" son. One day, however, he ran away into the woods and did not return. He was known to live in a shack in the woods of New Hampshire; his whereabouts were known by the local authorities and his family, but nobody bothered him. He was seen by the locals stocking up on food and liquor at intervals. His family sent him enough money to get by. He was notified when each of his parents died, at which point he was in his late fifties. He returned to live in his parents' home and tried to replicate his reclusive existence, with apparent success.

Mr. O had lived this way until about 8 years previously, when he was taken to the hospital after a fall. He was grossly malnourished and sent to a health facility for his fracture to heal; during his stay, he was admitted to the facility as a permanent resident. At a certain point, he ran away from the facility. He apparently did not come back to the town until over 2 years ago, when the neighbors noticed a light on in the house and other signs of occupancy. Once again, this peculiar old man was welcomed into the community by being generally ignored until he became very ill and was taken to the hospital under the care of the same doctor. This time, the hospital staff knew not to transfer him to a nursing home. Although they were willing to let him regain his health again and return home, where he could receive Meals on Wheels, he refused to cooperate with them or eat.

It wasn't difficult to make an Axis II diagnosis of a PD. I consulted and worked with the staff that was responsible for his care and aftercare plans. We talked about the meaning of his schizoid and schizotypal traits within the context of the hospital and the health care facility. We brainstormed to develop ways in which both his needs and the staff's needs could be met, deciding, for example, to draw his privacy curtain whenever his food was brought to him, and discourage volunteers or staff from encouraging him; there was no need for him to be watched by others while eating. Mr. O was also reassured that he would not be discharged to anywhere but home.

Being educated about the patient's character structure enabled the staff members to choose interventions that were most likely to be successful and to avoid highly charged, negative reactions to this disconnected, isolative, odd patient, who had made them feel worried, inadequate, and frustrated in their efforts to provide care.

Cluster B: The "Dramatic and Emotional" Character

The dominant features of this character are intense, roller–coaster relationships; affective lability; great need for feedback from others; excessive and inappropriate anger; and a tendency to elicit negative responses from caregivers. The following brief case example suggests ways of addressing the problems elicited by such a character:

Case Vignette:

Ms. P has a PD with dominant narcissistic and histrionic traits. The chief complaint of staff is her unwillingness to participate in any group activity. She has frustrated and angered her primary nurse an the activities director. The focus of the intervention is at the level of the staff, who will be trained and coached in ways to support her narcissism—the illusion of specialness and entitlement that prevents her from becoming a part of the group—in ways that will lead her to choose to become part of a group. They will likewise be shown how to provide her with the requisite attention to elicit positive behavior (i.e., behavior adaptive to the setting) as opposed to negative behavior such as refusing to participate in available activities.

Cluster C: The "Anxious and Fearful" Character

The dominant features of this character are timidity and insecurity, hypersensitivity to criticism, a tendency to anticipate rejection, indecisiveness, a tendency to be overly precise and cautious, and fretfulness. The following is a brief case example of such a character:

Case Vignette:

Mrs. Q is a nursing home patient with a dependent personality disorder. Every time her son visits, he ends up yelling at her and at the staff for "babying her" and "letting her get away with it." The intervention will be at the level of the family-patient and family-staff dyads. The legitimacy of the son's accusations will be explored and addressed, with attention given to intradyadic communication processes.

Conclusion

We may be heading toward a diagnostic classification that better addresses the manifestation of PDs in older adults than does the current diagnostic system. For older adults, it often appears more appropriate to diagnose a PD, NOS than a specific PD (Rosowsky & Dougherty, 1998). When the diagnostic net is cast too broadly, the utility of the diagnosis is diminished. Perhaps identifying PDs by clusters for older adults might be the best compromise between specificity and sensitivity.

We know that characterological difficulties can and generally do last a lifetime and are continually shaped and reinforced by the individual's interaction with the environment, which includes the individual's setting, relationships, roles, and requisite tasks (Koenig, et al., 1990). Given the chronicity of such disorders, we can use what we know are salient features of the disorder as well as typical behaviors to predict responses to determine the structure of clinical interventions and prevent certain behaviors from occurring. We can then progressively shape the interventions and responses of the patient and the system to their greater mutual satisfaction. The goal is to promote the expression of personality styles, rather than personality disorders, by the LTC resident.

References

American Psychiatric Association. (1952). *Diagnostic and statistical manual of mental disorders.* Washington, DC: Author.

American Psychiatric Association. (1987). *Diagnostic and statistical manual of mental disorders* (3rd ed., rev.). Washington, DC: Author.

American Psychiatric Association. (1994). *Diagnostic and statistical manual of mental disorders* (4th ed.). Washington, DC: Author

Genevay, B., & Katz, R. (Eds.) (1990). *Countertransference and older clients.* Newbury Park, CA: Sage Publications.

Grove, J. E. (1978). Taking care of the hateful patient. *New England Journal of Medicine, 2 98,* 16, 883–887.

Koenig, H., Siegler, I., & George, L. (1990). Religious coping and personality in later life. *International Journal of Geriatrics, 5,* 123–131.

Rosowsky, E., & Dougherty, L. M. (1998). Personality disorders and clinician responses. *Clinical Gerontologist, 18,* 4, 31–42.

Sadavoy, J., & Fogel, B. (1992). Personality disorders in old age. In J. E. Birren, R. B. Soane, & G. D. Cohen (Eds.), *Handbook of mental health and aging.* (2nd ed., pp. 433–4621). San Diego: Academia Press.

Zweig, R., & Hinrichsen, G. (1992). Impact of personality disorders on affective illness in older adults. Paper presented at GSA annual scientific meeting. Washington, D.C.

9

Behavioral Interventions for Patients With Dementia

JANE E. FISHER, PH.D.,

COLLEEN W. HARSIN, *and*

JACOB E. HAYDEN

Work on this paper was supported by Grant R29 AG11241 from the National Institute on Aging. Address correspondence to Jane E. Fisher, Department of Psychology/298, University of Nevada, Reno, NV 89557–0062; E-mail: fisher@equinox.unr.edu. This paper is dedicated to the memory of Richard Hussian.

Abstract

MENTAL HEALTH professionals working with dementia patients within long term care (LTC) facilities face significant challenges due to the continued behavioral degeneration experienced by their clients and the need to enlist the cooperation of staff in order to effect change. This chapter describes a functional analytic approach to the treatment of severe behavioral disturbances in dementia patients residing in LTC facilities. When their behavior is examined within a functional analytic framework (i.e., when considered in the context of declining competencies and increasingly challenging environmental demands) it often emerges as adaptive.

Behavioral interventions are designed to address the function of a behavior or the reason why it occurs. Advantages of behavioral approaches to assessment and intervention include their idiographic nature and an emphasis on positive control strategies. Idiographic approaches to treatment planning are desirable, given the significant variation in behavioral functions across patients and within patients over the course of a degenerative dementia. Positive control strategies that address the reason a behavior occurs may ultimately be the most ethical, given the increasingly limited ability of dementia patients to access reinforcement in their environments.

Introduction

Relocating to a nursing home presents significant challenges to individuals with dementia and to their family members. Typically, LTC is pursued as a last resort, usually after instrumental and emotional resources have been exhausted during efforts to maintain the individual with dementia at home. In spite of the fear of institutionalization that is reported by many older adults and the guilt experienced by family members when a loved one is admitted to a nursing home, LTC facilities provide a highly valuable service to older adults when the challenges presented by a home environment exceed their personal competencies. Well-designed LTC facilities provide environments that match a dementia patient's behavioral repertoire (i.e., they neither understimulate the patients nor exceed their personal competencies [Lawton, 1975]). Optimally, a LTC facility should permit "aging in place" by altering the environment and the challenges it presents to match the resident's competencies as they diminish over the course of the disease.

A behavioral conceptualization of the functional level of dementia patients is readily compatible with efforts to design environments that maximize the ability to develop adaptive skills and thus minimize the development of behavior problems. Behavioral interventions are based on an idiographic analysis of the relationship between the resident's personal characteristics (e.g., mental competence and health status) and his or her behavior (both adaptive and maladaptive) and the environmental conditions associated with the behavior (i.e., antecedent stimuli and consequences). Behavior assessment involves an analysis of the context in which a behavior occurs and provides information regarding the "reason" for its occurrence. Understanding the reason why a behavior occurs can lead to the selection of interventions that encourage the resident to develop adaptive behaviors, rather than interventions that focus on eliminating behaviors in an individual whose behavioral repertoire is already diminishing.

Within a behavioral conceptualization of dementia, it is assumed that the relationship between behavior and environmental stimuli will be altered over the course of a degenerative dementia such as Alzheimer's disease (AD), and the environment will require modification in order to continue to optimize a resident's functional level. It is also assumed that while cognitively impaired residents may exhibit behaviors that are, on the surface, similar (e.g., aggression, wandering, or disruptive vocalizations), the etiology of these behaviors may vary across individuals (Hussian, 1987) and, thus, may require an individualized approach to treatment planning.

In this chapter, issues associated with behavioral assessment and treatment planning for nursing home residents with dementia will be discussed. In addition to providing an overview of behavioral assessment methods and interventions, this chapter will discuss their application to prevalent problems experienced by individuals with dementia.

Behavioral Assessment

When designing interventions for dementia patients, the clinician should asses two aspects of behavior: (1) its topographical features, and (2) its functional context.

Topographical Assessment of Behavior Disturbances:

Topographical assessment focuses on the form or observable aspects of behavior. It is used to identify target behav-

iors, describe the intensity and frequency of behaviors, and evaluate the effects of treatments. Whereas a topographical assessment is an essential component of behavior assessment, it is insufficient for treatment planning as it does not address the relationship between the behavior and the environment in which it occurs. Understanding the context of behavior is critical for generating hypotheses regarding the purpose of the behavior.

Therapists working with dementia patients should assume that topographically similar behaviors may be elicited by different environmental factors in different individuals. It should also be assumed that the cause of similar behaviors within a single individual may have different causes over the course of a progressive dementia (Fisher & Swingen, 1997). A sampling of instruments that focus on behavioral topography are listed in Table 1.

Functional Assessment of Behavior Disturbances?

In contrast to the topographical assessment, the purpose of functional assessment is to describe, categorize, and verify the relationship between behavior and the environment (Carr et al., 1994). **The information that is necessary to make a functional assessment may be gathered through interviews, direct ob-**

Table 1

Topographical Assessment Instruments Relevant to Dementia Patients

Instrument	Primary Citation
Cohen-Mansfield Agitation Inventory (CMAI)	Cohen-Mansfield, J. (1986)
Pittsburgh Agitation Scale (PAS)	Rosen, et al. (1994)
Overt Aggression Scale (OAS)	Yudofsky, Silver, Jackson, & Endicott (1986)
Blessed Dementia Scale (BDS)	Erkinjuntti, Hokkanen &, Sulkava, Palos (1988)

servation, and empirical tests (Carr et al., 1994). A functional assessment differs from a topographical assessment in that it attempts to identify the factors that contribute to the maintenance of a particular behavior by examining the context within which that behavior occurs. By addressing etiology, a functional assessment can be used to link assessment with intervention in a logical manner.

Traditionally, it has been assumed that behavioral disturbances in dementia patients are a result of the disease process. A functional assessment is not based on that assumption, and considers environmental causes as well. The consideration of environmental factors has important implications for the types of interventions that may be selected to control behavioral disturbances in this population. Depending on the function of a particular behavior, an intervention can target the environment in three areas: environmental antecedents, environmental consequences, and setting events.

Agitated behaviors may be functionally related to environmental antecedents (events that precipitate the occurrence of a given behavior), including task demands (Fisher, 1995) or the presence of other people (Ryden, 1988). Environmental consequences may maintain agitated behaviors through two primary mechanisms: positive reinforcement, in which the occurrence is associated with favorable stimuli (e.g., caregiver attention); or negative reinforcement, in which the occurrence is associated with the removal of aversive stimuli, such as task demands (Fisher et al., 1997). Setting events are factors that affect the function of antecedent or consequent stimuli (Bijou & Baer, 1966). Setting events that may affect agitated behaviors in dementia patients include pain (Fisher et al., 1997), time of day (Cohen-Mansfield et al., 1989), and emotional state (Swearer et al., 1988).

Functional assessment instruments that are relevant to dementia patients with behavior problems include the Functional Analysis of Behavior Recording and Tracking Form (FAB) (Lundervold & Lewin, 1992), the Motivation Assessment Scale (MAS) (Durand and Crimmins, 1988), and the Behavior Environment Taxonomy of Agitation (BETA) (Fisher, 1995). The FAB is designed to assess the antecedents and consequences of verbal abuse and combativeness. Respondents record each instance of a problem behavior, along with the situations that immediately precede and follow that behavior. The MAS is a questionnaire that is used to identify variables that maintain self-injurious behavior. It can assist caregivers in specifying how a given behavior functions for an individual. The information provided by these functional assessment instruments addresses the etiology of the behavioral disturbances and is directly relevant to treatment planning.

The BETA (Fisher, 1995), a modification of the MAS, is a 16-item checklist that asks respondents to describe the likelihood of specific agitated behaviors occurring in any of four types of situations, which have been identified in the literature (Anderson, 1970; Colenda & Hamer, 1991; Hamel et al. 1991) and by caregivers (Fisher et al., 1994) as being associated with the occurrence of agitation in dementia patients and in other clinical populations, including developmentally disabled persons and psychiatric patients (Durand & Crimmins, 1988; Paul & Lentz, 1986). The situations described on the BETA include those that are used to gain (1) social attention, (2) escape from unpleasant situations, (3) increased

Table 2
Functional Assessment Instruments Relevant to Dementia Patients

Instrument	Primary Citation
Behavior Environment Taxonomy of Agitation (BETA)	Fisher, (1995)
Functional Analysis of Behavior Recording and Tracking Forms (FAB)	Lundervold & Lewin, (1992)
Motivation Assessment Scale (MAS)	Durrand & Crimmins, (1988)

sensory consequences, and (4) reduced sensory consequences. Caregivers rate the likelihood of occurrence of four examples of each of these situations on a 7-point Likert-type scale with a range of "0-never" to "6-always." Information obtained from the BETA can be used to generate hypotheses regarding the function a behavior serves for an individual patient.

The validity of the results of behavioral assessment should be evaluated by examining the effects of the associated intervention. Interventions provide empirical tests of hypotheses concerning the variables that influence behavior. For example, if staff attention is thought to be responsible for maintaining aggression for a resident, then manipulation of staff attentiveness should affect that resident's aggressive behavior.

Interventions

Behavioral interventions are designed to manipulate factors in the environment that have been hypothesized to contribute to the maintenance of a targeted behavior. Behavioral interventions are both part of and result from the functional assessment; as part of a continuing assessment process, they provide a basis by which assessment can be self-correcting. Hypotheses developed during the assessment process that do not lead to successful interventions will be systematically discarded in favor of new hypotheses that can then be tested.

Behavioral interventions alter the ways in which problem behaviors function for an individual. Interventions are developed and implemented idiographically and should be monitored closely over time. Behavior disturbances can be conceptualized as excesses or deficits. Examples of behavioral excesses include aggression, wandering, and disruptive vocalizations. Behavioral deficits associated with dementia include a decline in performance of physical activities of daily living (ADLs), such as eating, dressing, toileting, walking, bathing, or transferring.

Behavioral Excesses

Aggression:

Definitions of aggression in dementia patients have included references to the behavior's topographical features (e.g., verbal vs physical aggression) (Patel & Hope, 1993), purpose (e.g., "intent to harm") (Siann, 1985), and consequences (Patel & Hope, 1993). **Physical aggression includes such behaviors as spitting, grabbing, pushing, kicking, hitting, and throwing** (Patel & Hope, 1993). **Verbal aggression includes such behaviors as threats, cursing, and negative vocalizations** (Patel & Hope, 1993). Due to the inconsistency in definitions of aggression, it is difficult to make an accurate determination of the prevalence rates of aggressive behavior for dementia populations. It has been estimated that aggressive behavior occurs in approximately 20% to 65% of dementia patients (Becker et al., 1994; Burns et al., 1990; Swearer et al., 1988).

The consequences of physical aggression are extremely serious for both patients and caregiver. Caregivers experience the risk of physical injury and an increase in the stress of caregiving. Consequent to physically aggressive behaviors, patients risk the increased use of chemical and physical restraint (Moak & Fisher, 1990; Sloane et al., 1991).

Serious ethical problems can arise with the use of chemical and physical restraint for behavior problems in this population. **Specifically, restraint-based interventions further eliminate behaviors from an already impoverished behavioral repertoire; they do not address the possibility that these behaviors may serve an important function for the patient** (e.g., to communicate distress) (Fisher & Swingen, 1997). **Behavioral interventions can provide an alternative for managing aggressive behavior without further reducing a patient's repertoire.**

Behavioral interventions for aggression in other populations have focused largely on the manipulation of the consequences of that behavior and on the teaching of new skills (Carr, 1994; LaVigna & Donnellan, 1986). Examples of such behavioral interventions include "time-out," differential reinforcement of incompatible responses (DRI), and skills training. These interventions may not be appropriate for patients with dementia due to severe short-term memory loss and problems with the acquisition of new information in this population.

Fisher (1995) found that aggressive behavior typically serves as an escape function for cognitively impaired nursing home residents. Dementia patients were estimated to behave aggressively in order to terminate situations that they perceived as threatening. A study by Bridges-Parlet and colleagues (1994) found that the majority of instances of physically aggressive behavior were directed at staff during caregiving activities or during attempts by staff members to redirect the resident. These investigators concluded that aggressive behavior appears to be a defensive reaction to a perceived threat. This conclusion is consistent with that of Fisher (1995), who found that aggression typically serves to terminate an aversive situation or event.

If aggression functions as a form of escape for a given resident, then distraction may effectively decrease aggressive behavior in this population (Fisher & Swingen, 1997). Distracting a patient's attention from the stimuli that typically precipitate aggression may be an effective form of prevention. A distraction-based intervention has one advantage: it does not attempt to eliminate behavior, but instead alters the conditions that elicit the behavior. An example of such an intervention involves the presentation of reinforcing stimuli during caregiving interactions. In an ongoing intervention for aggression, dementia patients are oriented to a preferred stimulus (e.g., a videotape of babies playing, a live animal, or an attractively wrapped gift box) before caregiving begins. The patient is then continually reoriented to the stimulus throughout the caregiving activity.

Other interventions focus on setting events that alter the functions of environmental stimuli. One setting event that may be particularly important to the occurrence of aggression is anxiety. An association between anxiety and aggression in dementia populations was reported by Swearer and colleagues (1988). If anxiety contributes to aggressive behavior, then it may be an appropriate target for interventions. For example, a dementia patient may become anxious when approached by unfamiliar caregivers. This individual may then behave aggressively whenever unfamiliar caregivers make demands of him or her. An intervention involving the manipulation of setting events might consist of having all staff members who deal with this patient wear the same color uniform so as to make it easier for the patient to recognize them and thus make them less threatening.

Differential reinforcement of incompatible behavior (DRI) may be effective for controlling aggressive behaviors that are maintained through social or tangible consequences. For example, if aggression is associated with a need for attention of staff members, then staff members may intervene by providing attention to the patient contingent upon the presence of other behaviors that are incompatible with aggression, such as participation in grooming activities, appropriate handling of objects such as a stuffed animal or picture album, or participation in group recreation. Roseberger and MacClean (1983) used a DRI procedure to control aggressive behavior in a 79-year-old stroke patient. The intervention consisted of staff members greeting the resident and praising her for appropriate behavior, and brief periods of time-out following problem behaviors. The patient's aggressive behavior was reduced to zero in 3 weeks, and the effects were maintained after 5 months (Roseberger and MacClean, 1983).

Another reinforcement-based intervention for reducing aggression involves the presentation of noncontingent reinforcement (NCR) for nontarget behaviors (Hagopian, et al., 1994; Lalli, et al., 1997; Marcus & Vollmer, 1996). In recent years, NCR has emerged as one of the most widely adopted methods for reducing aberrant behavior in individuals with developmental disabilities. It has been applied successfully for the reduction of aggression in children with mental retardation (e.g., Lalli et al., 1997; Vollmer et al., 1997). As with other reinforcement based interventions, NCR has the advantage of not directly targeting the reduction of behavior in an already impoverished repertoire, but instead strengthening alternative behaviors. Reinforcement is provided over time and is not contingent upon the occurrence of specific behaviors. An example of this type of intervention is verbally soothing statements made throughout the caregiving activity instead of waiting until the patient is in obvious distress and/or verbal aggression has already occurred.

Wandering:

Generally, wandering is described as aimless, in that it does not appear purposeful (Burnside, 1980; Cohen-Mansfield, 1986). However, some researchers have described subtypes of wandering that have implications for functional analysis and intervention (Hussian, 1987; Martino-Salzman et al., 1991). **Rather than identifying wandering as aimless, Hussian** (1987) **described four subtypes of wanderers, each with a different etiology:**

1. *Akasthesiacs.* **Individuals whose wandering has a neuroleptic effect. These individuals wander frequently but show little evidence of self-stimulatory or exiting behavior.**
2. *Exit seekers.* **Individuals whose wandering appears to be primarily a search for an exit, as evidenced by attempts to open doors as well as by requests to leave or "go home."**
3. *Modelers.* **Individuals who wander only when in the presence of other wanderers.**
4. *Self-stimulators.* **Individuals who wander to produce sensory stimulation and possibly additional behaviors. These individuals often touch or rub objects as they pass by, including doorknobs.**

Wandering may thus be adaptive for some dementia patients, as it may provide stimulation or represent an effort to escape.

Prevalence estimates differ with the definition of wandering, the population sampled (e.g., nursing home vs. community residents), and methodology (e.g., observational research vs. report of caregivers), as well as interactions among these factors. For example, Teri and colleagues (1988) documented that an average of 26% of a sample of 127 geriatric outpatients exhibited wandering, with a range of 18% for dementia patients with mild cognitive impairment to 50% for dementia patients with severe cognitive impairment. Wandering has also been reported to be associated with the level of cognitive impairment, with more wandering occurring in individuals with greater cognitive impairment (Teri et al., 1988).

Within institutional settings, safety concerns are heightened for dementia patients who wander because of the increased risk of becoming lost and encountering dangerous situations. In addition, other residents in a facility may be disturbed by the dementia patient wandering into their rooms or interrupting activities. Health may also be a concern, as dementia patients may have increased nutritional requirements due to excessive caloric expenditure during wandering (Gray, 1989). **A dementia patient who wanders is likely to be restrained physically or pharmacologically** (Mitchell-Pederson et al., 1985; Roper et al., 1991). **While such interventions may be effective in the short term, they are not acceptable options for long term management of wandering. Pharmacological restraint** (typically by means of neuroleptics or anxiolytics) **and physical restraint** (typically by means of geri-chairs, belts, or special beds) **not only decrease the disruptive or problematic behavior but also decrease more positive adaptive behaviors.** Restraints have been associated with an increased likelihood of falls and muscle atrophy due to lack of use (Cohen-Mansfield, 1986; Mitchell-Pederson et al., 1985; Werner et al., 1989) while having minimal or no effect on the frequency of disruptive behaviors (Werner et al., 1989).

Assessment efforts should first focus on the topographical features of wandering, including its frequency and duration. They should then identify the antecedents and consequences of the behavior. Patterns of wandering may exist, indicating that the behavior may be under stimulus control; in other words, the behavior may occur in response to particular cues or circumstances in the environment (Hussian, 1987). For a given patient, the clinician might ask, "Is the wandering behavior reinforced by attention from staff, such as talking to the individual, escorting the individual back to his or her room, or providing activities for the individual?" For an individual with an increasingly limited behavioral repertoire, wandering may serve an important adaptive function, specifically seeking or avoiding stimulation.

A primary goal of assessment, then, is to identify the function(s) that wandering may serve for the dementia patient. Once the function has been identified, interventions can be implemented that promote alternative behaviors with a similar function but that are more easily tolerated by caregivers. Thus, the idiographic functional assessment of wandering behavior that identifies setting-events, antecedents, and consequences of the behavior guide the clinician in designing behavioral interventions. For example, wanderers seeking stimulation may access similar stimulating reinforcers by having social interactions with staff when seated in his or her room or in a lounge area.

Ambulation in safe areas may be encouraged by environmental features such as floor grids and locked doors to block access to unsafe areas. In general, the subtypes of wanderers already listed are likely to be amenable to different alterations in stimulus control. Rather than attempt to eliminate the behavior from the individual's limited repertoire, it may be more desirable to allow wandering in safe areas where supervision is available, particularly in light of the aforementioned adaptive functions of wandering. In a study of three individuals who exhibited wandering in an institutional setting, Hussian (1982) succeeded in pairing two different colors with two different consequences: one with positive consequences, the other with negative consequences. Once the individuals learned these pairings, cards with the color associated with positive consequences were placed in areas that were considered safe for ambulation and cards with the color associated with negative consequences were placed in areas where wandering was considered

192 PROFESSIONAL PSYCHOLOGY IN LONG TERM CARE

unsafe. This technique resulted in substantially less wandering in unsafe areas (Hussian, 1982). Wandering in and of itself is not the target behavior in such interventions; the specific target is wandering in unsafe or unsupervised areas. For example, for an individual who exhibits primarily exit-seeking patterns of wandering, repeated encounters with locked doors may result in a decline in exit-seeking behavior.

Disruptive Vocalizations

Disruptive vocalizations include but are not limited to screaming, crying, cursing, constant requests for attention, and making strange noises. The prevalence of these behaviors vary with the definition, population, and method employed in research studies. A study by Cariaga and colleagues (1991) found screaming to be the most common type of disruptive vocalization; abusive language and moaning were also reported as prevalent. In general, disruptive vocalization is a common problem among cognitively impaired elderly adults and is frequently carried out by residents who also exhibit other forms of behavior disturbance (Cariaga, et al., 1991). The most salient problem with these behaviors is the disruption of the care environment and agitation of other residents. Although disruptive vocalizations may seem random or purposeless to an observer, it is likely that they are specific and voluntary; thus, they are likely to be under stimulus control. The behaviors themselves may not be problematic for the individual exhibiting them; in fact, they may represent alternative means of communicating such conditions as hunger, pain, or the need for attention. Disruptive vocalizations may become a problem if they result in the individual being excluded from activities or contact with others. Alternatively, they may create a safety problem if other residents become aggressive in an attempt to quiet the vocalizing patient.

No medication has been found to be particularly effective in decreasing disruptive vocalizations without heavily sedating the patient, thus restricting the behav-

ioral repertoire in general (Cariaga et al., 1991). Limiting the individual's interactions with staff or other residents may make the behavior less noticeable to others but is not a desirable option. Isolation may further reduce access to sources of reinforcement and does not consider the potential function of the vocalization. Disruptive vocalizations should not be assumed to be a normal consequence of a progressive dementia.

The etiology of disruptive vocalizations may include pain, sensory deprivation, lack of stimulation, or excessive stimulation (Carlson et al., 1995; Gerdner & Buckwalter, 1994). An idiographic functional assessment to identify environmental (internal and external) factors that accompany the problem behavior may also identify treatable causes of the behavior. Sensory impairment, physical discomfort, or pain may be expressed by the dementia patient as moaning or screaming when the patient can no longer communicate verbally. Treatments appropriate for such conditions may substantially decrease the frequency and/or duration of disruptive vocalizations. For example, a hearing aid may decrease disruptive vocalizations by the individual whose hearing is impaired and, consequently, sensory deprived. Pain relief that is achieved by physical therapy or analgesics may decrease these behaviors in an individual who is experiencing pain. A functional assessment that focuses on the antecedents and consequences of disruptive vocalizations may indicate that an individual is more likely to produce disruptive vocalizations in an overstimulating situation. Preventive measures, such as placing the individual in a minimally stimulating environment is a possible, although not always feasible, option.

Other common behavioral interventions implemented for disruptive vocalizations include time-out from reinforcement and differential reinforcement of other behavior (DRO) schedules (e.g., Carlson et al., 1995; Hussian & Davis, 1985; Lundervold & Lewin, 1992). **Providing positive reinforcement** (such as attention or food) **when an individual is not exhibiting disruptive vocalizations is likely to increase other more socially ap-**

propriate behaviors, thereby decreasing disruptive vocalizations. Not attending to these vocalizations may also function as an effective time-out from reinforcement, as the individual learns that the behavior no longer has the effect of increased attention. Providing additional sources of sensory stimulation may also decrease disruptive vocalizations, if it has been determined that the disruptive vocalizations occur under conditions of low sensory stimulation (Cariaga et al., 1991). During a DRO procedure, the patient periodically receives the positive reinforcer when he or she is engaged in behavior other than the problem behavior. This method of reducing problem behavior is often preferred, because it does not involve the delivery of an aversive stimulus and ideally increases the amount of positive reinforcement received.

Deficits in Activities of Daily Living

Physical activities of daily living (ADLs) include eating, dressing, toileting, walking, bathing, and transferring. Behavioral deficits in this area include various gradations of disruption in self-feeding, grooming, or toileting skills. It is estimated that 22.7% of individuals more than 65 years of age and living in the community have difficulty with one or more of these activities, and 9.6% of them receive help with one or more of these activities (National Center for Health Statistics, 1987). It is difficult, if not impossible, to accurately estimate the prevalence of these behavior deficits in institutionalized care settings, because it is not always clear whether limitations are physical, cognitive, or shaped by environmental contingencies that do not support independent ADL behaviors (see Baltes & Zerbe, 1976 for a discussion of the functions of dependent behaviors within health care facilities).

Deficits in ADLs are significant reasons for the institutionalization of older adults, particularly when they are accompanied by agitated or aggressive behaviors that occur when caregiving is provided. The deficits may not be due to physical disability but may be due to other factors, such as cognitive decline or depression. Another closely related problem is the likely reinforcement of these deficits by an overworked caregiving staff which performs many of these activities as part of the nursing routine (Baltes & Zerbe, 1976). It is usually faster to assist the individual with dementia in eating, perhaps even to hand-feed the individual, than to wait for the individual to complete the task unassisted. Inadvertent promotion of dependent behavior is most evident during times of the day when most caregiving tasks are performed, such as morning routines and mealtimes. It may be necessary for caregivers to accomplish their tasks as efficiently as possible during these times. However, it is not likely that this type of assistance is beneficial in terms of maintaining an individual's functional abilities.

Caution should be exercised in the design of programs to promote independence in nursing home residents, as the caregiving context may provide important opportunities for social contact (Baltes & Zerbe, 1976). Physical limitations should be assessed, as the individual may no longer be physically able to complete ADL tasks. In conducting a functional assessment, the clinician should consider that there may be aspects of the environment that reinforce dependence through increased social interactions when the resident is assisted during eating, grooming, or toileting. Staff involvement in program implementation is of utmost importance. Providing contingencies for the staff to comply with program changes will increase adherence to behavioral intervention programs. Physical guidance may be necessary for all aspects of eating, grooming, and toileting, at least initially. Inappropriate behavior excesses, such as throwing utensils or grooming implements, may also occur during these activities. Behavior excesses are treated most effectively with time-out from reinforcement (e.g., removing attention). Praise or tangible reinforcers can be offered during successive attempts at engaging appropriately in the desired ADL activity. In general, positive reinforcement of the individual's attempts to engage appropriately in ADL behaviors is critical (Lundervold & Lewin, 1992).

Modifications of relevant aspects of the environment can greatly increase the likelihood of dementia patients maintaining some of their functional abilities (Charness & Bosman, 1995). For example, the handles of eating utensils or grooming tools can be made larger and or thicker so that they are easier to grasp. Dishes that are unbreakable and have nonslip outer surfaces and rims can greatly enhance the ability to eat with minimal or no assistance, as can the use of no-spill cups, straws, or drinkware that is easy to grasp and hold. Interventions that promote independent dressing (e.g., clothing with Velcro-fasteners, slip-on shoes, and shirts with zippers, snaps, or large buttons) can make dressing more manageable for the individual as well as caregivers. Further, it is recommended that clothing choices be kept to a minimum to prevent overstimulation. Toileting facilities can be, and often are, equipped with handrails. Non-skid floors are also helpful, as is the placement of necessary items within reach of the individual. Obstacles in the environment may also need to be moved to promote independent ADL behaviors Maximizing stimulus control for these behaviors may prove helpful. This can be achieved by conducting the activities in the same location and at the same times as often as possible. ADL skills are more likely to be maintained if they become routine for the individual.

Providing prompts to assist the individual in performing the desired behavior will be increasingly necessary over the course of a degenerative dementia. Specifically, assistance may begin with a verbal prompt and progress to physical assistance for a portion of the task and, finally (if necessary), to total guidance of the desired behavior (Lundervold & Lewin, 1992). Small steps and successive approximations of the desired behavior should be positively reinforced.

Conclusions

Currently, there are no treatment options available for preventing cognitive decline for the majority of individuals with dementia. It is clear that behavioral interventions hold promise for improving the quality of life of cognitively impaired older adults. Given the challenges that nursing staff confront within LTC settings, it should be noted that treatment programs that are based on a functional analysis of a behavior are initially more time consuming to implement than restraint-based interventions. In the long term, however, such interventions are likely to be more effective in reducing problem behaviors and preventing the development of behavioral disturbances. Behavioral interventions that promote adaptive behavior rather than further eliminating behaviors comprise a powerful and ethical option for maximizing the quality of life for dementia patients.

References

Baltes, M. M., & Zerbe, M. (1976). Independence training in the nursing home resident. *The Gerontologist, 16*, 428–432.

Becker, D., Hershkowitz, M., Maidler, N., Rabinowitz, M., & Floru, S. (1994). Psychopathology and cognitive decline in dementia. *Journal of Nervous and Mental Disease, 182*, 701–703.

Bijou, S. W., & Baer, D. M. (1966). Methods in child behavior and development. In W. K. Honig (Ed.), *Operant behavior: Areas of research and application*. New York: Appleton-Century-Crofts.

Bridges-Parlet, S., Knopman, D., & Thompson, T. (1994). A descriptive study of physically aggressive behavior in dementia by direct observation. *Journal of the American Geriatrics Society, 42*, 192–197.

Burns, A., Jacoby, R., & Levy, R. (1990). Psychiatric phenomena on Alzheimer's disease 4: Disorders of behavior. *British Journal of Psychiatry, 157*, 86–94.

Burnside, I. M. (1980). Wandering behavior. In I. M. Burnside, (Ed.), *Psychosocial nursing care of the aged*. New York: McGraw-Hill.

Cariaga, J., Burgio, L., Flynn, W., & Martin, D. (1991). A controlled study of disruptive vocalizations among geriatric residents in nursing homes. *Journal of the American Geriatrics Society, 39*, 501–507.

Carlson, D. L., Fleming, K. C., Smith, G. E., & Evans, J. M., (1995). Management of dementia-related behavioral disturbances: A nonpharmacologic approach. *Mayo Clinic Proceedings, 70*, 1108–1115.

Carr, E. G., Levin, L., McConnachie, G., Carlson, J. I., Kemp, D. C., & Smith, C. E. (1994). *Communication-based intervention for problem behavior:*

A user's guide for producing positive change. Baltimore: Paul H. Brooks Publishing Company.

Charness, N., & Bosman, E. A. (1995). Compensation through environmental compensation. In R. A. Dixon & L. Backman, (Eds.), *Compensating for psychological deficits and declines: Managing losses and promoting gains.* Mahwah, NJ: Lawrence Erlbaum Associates.

Cohen-Mansfield, J. (1986). Agitated behaviors in the elderly II. Preliminary results in the cognitively deteriorated. *Journal of the American Geriatrics Society, 34,* 722–727.

Cohen-Mansfield, J., Marx, M. S., & Rosenthal, A. S. (1989). A description of agitation in a nursing home. *Journal of Gerontology: Medical Sciences, 44,* M77-M84.

Covert, A. B., Rodrigues, T., Solomon, K., (1977). The use of mechanical and chemical restraints in nursing homes. *Journal of the American Geriatrics Society, 25,* 85–89.

Dawson, D., Hendershot, G., & Fulton, J. (1987, June 10). *Functional limitations of individuals age 65 and over.* (Advance Data, Vital and Health Statistics, No. 133) Hyattsville, MD: U.S. Public Health Service, National Center for Health Studies.

Durand, M. V. & Crimmins, D. B. (1988). Identifying the variables maintaining self-injurious behavior. *Journal of Autism and Developmental Disorders, 18,* 99–117.

Erkinjuntti, T., Hokkanen, L., Sulkava, R., & Palos, J. (1988). The Blessed Dementia Scale as a screening test for dementia. International *Journal of Geriatric Psychiatry, 3,* 65–74.

Fisher, J. E. (1995). *Agitation and adaption: Functional characteristics of the behavior of dementia patients.* Paper presented at the Annual Convention of the American Psychological Association, New York.

Fisher, J. E., & Carstensen, L. L. (1990). Behavior management in dementia. *Clinical Psychology Review, 10,* 611–629.

Fisher, J. E., & Swingen, D. N. (1997). Contextual factors in the assessment and management of aggression in dementia patients. *Cognitive and Behavioral Practice, 4,* 171–190.

Fisher, J. E., Swingen, D. N., & Harsin, C. M. (1998). Agitation and aggression. In B. Edelstein (Ed.), *Comprehensive clinical psychology*, 8. New York: Elsevier.

Gerdner, L. A., & Buckwalter, K. C. (1994, April). A nursing challenge: Assessment and management of agitation in Alzheimer's patients. *Journal of Gerontological Nursing*, 11–20.

Gray, G. E. (1989). Nutrition and dementia. *Journal of the American Dietetic Association, 89* (12), 1795–1802.

Hagopian, L. P., Fisher, W. W., Legacy, S. M. (1994). Schedule effect of noncontingent reinforcement of attention-maintained destructive behavior in identical quadruplets. *Journal of Applied Behavior Analysis, 27*, 317–325.

Hussian, R. A. (1982). Stimulus control in the modification of problematic behavior in elderly institutionalized patients. *International Journal of Behavior Geriatrics, 1*, 33–42.

Hussian, R. A. (1987). Wandering disorientation. In L. L. Carstensen & B. A. Edelstein (Eds.), *Handbook of clinical gerontology.* New York: Pergamon.

Hussian, R. A., & Davis, R. L. (1985). Responsive care: *Behavioral interventions with elderly persons.* Champaign, IL: Research Press.

Lalli, J. S., Casey, S. D., & Kates, K. (1997). Noncontingent reinforcement as treatment for severe problem behavior: Some procedural variations. *Journal of Applied Behavior Analysis, 30*, 127–137.

LaVigna, G. W. & Donnellan, A. M. (1986). *Alternatives to punishment: Solving behavior problems with non-aversive strategies.* New York: Irvington Publishers.

Lawton, M. P. (1975). Competence, environmental press and adaptation of older people. In P. G. Windley & G. Ernst (Eds.), *Theory development in environment and aging* (pp. 13–70). Washington, D.C.: American Psychological Association.

Lundervold, D. A., & Lewin, L. M. (1992). *Behavior analysis and therapy in nursing homes.* Springfield, IL: Charles C. Thomas.

Marcus, B. A., & Vollmer, T. R. (1993). Combining noncontingent reinforcement and differential reinforcement schedules as treatment for aberrant behavior. *Journal of Applied Behavior Analysis, 29*, 43–51.

Martino-Salzman, D., Blasch, B., Morris, R. D., & McNeal, L. W., (1991). Travel behavior of nursing home residents perceived as wanderers and nonwanderers. *The Gerontologist, 31 (5), 666–672.*

Mitchell-Pederson, L., Edmund, L., & Fingerote, E. (1985). Ontario Association of Homes for the Aged (OAHA) *Quarterly Journal of Long Term Care, 21,* (10), 23–27.

Patel, V. & Hope, T. (1993). Aggressive behavior in elderly people with dementia: A review. *International Journal of Geriatric Psychiatry, 8,* 457–472.

Roseberger, Z. & MacClean, J. (1983). Behavioral assessment and treatment of "organic" behaviors in an institutionalized geriatric patient. *International Journal of Behavioral Geriatrics, 1,* 33–46.

Rosen, J., Burgio, L., Kollar, M., Cain, M., Allison, M., Fogleman, M., Michael, M., & Zubendo, G. S. (1994). The Pittsburgh agitation scale (PAS): A user-friendly instrument for rating agitation in demented patients. *American Journal of Geriatric Psychiatry, 2* (1), 52–59.

Siann, G. (1985). *Accounting for aggression; Perspectives on aggression and violence.* Boston: Allen & Unwin.

Swearer, J. M., Drachman, D. A., O'Donnell, B. F., & Mitchell, A. L. (1988). Troublesome and disruptive behavior in dementia: Relationship to diagnosis and disease severity. *Journal of the American Geriatrics Society, 36,* 784–790.

Teri, L., Larson, E. B., & Reifler, B. V. (1988). Behavioral disturbance of the Alzheimer's type. *Journal of the American Geriatrics Society, 36,* 1–6.

Vollmer, T. R., Ringdahl, J. E., Roane, H. S., & Marcus, B.A. (1997). Negative side effects of noncontingent reinforcement. *Journal of Applied Behavior Analysis, 30,* 161–164.

Werner, P., Cohen-Mansfield, J., Braun, J., & Marx, M. S. (1989). Physical restraints and agitation in nursing home residents. *Journal of the American Geriatrics Society, 37,* 1122–1126.

Yudofsky, S. C., Silver, J. M., Jackson, W., & Endicott, J. (1986). The overt aggression scale for the objective rating of verbal and physical aggression. *American Journal of Psychiatry, 143,* 35–39.

10

Counseling the Elderly Dying Patient

ROBERT KASTENBAUM, PH.D.

Introduction

Elderly people who live in long-term care (LTC) facilities usually die there as well (Kahana, 1995). Others are transferred to LTC facilities after short-term hospital stays as they approach the end stage of their illness. The emergence of hospice care has provided a valuable alternative, enabling more people to end their lives in their own home or that of a family member (Saunders & Kastenbaum, 1997). There is also a recent trend toward reduced utilization of nursing homes in the United States (U.S. Public Health Service, 1995), as a comparison between the increasing population of elders and the number of those residing in LTC facilities indicates. Nevertheless, many a long life still ends in a congregate living facility.

How do these lives end? And how might psychologists be of service? To answer these questions it will be useful to consider several interrelated topics: (a) the goals of counseling the dying institutionalized person, (b) the role of the counselor/therapist, (c) the role of the client, (d) the dying process, (e) the situation, and (f) the intervention. The relationship among these topics will be developed as we proceed.

Setting the Goals

Textbook accounts of counseling and psychotherapy sometimes emphasize the early establishment of fixed goals. This person should have the behavioral outcome of returning to work; that person should be able to discuss relationship conflicts rather than acting out verbally and physically. This approach is attractive for its clarity and focus, and in some instances it is possible to establish the intervention goals at the outset and work steadily toward their achievement. There are other instances, however, in which early establishment of fixed goals can inhibit or misdirect the therapeutic process. The presenting problem might be distressing and urgent, yet be only one facet of a more complex situation. Furthermore, the nature of the problem situation itself might change as a result of either counseling or external events. **It may be morel useful, then, to regard goal setting as a dynamic process that remains informed by continuing developments. Priorities** may shift and new goals may emerge. Counseling or psychotherapy with terminally ill elders requires continuing awareness of the possible need to adjust goals over time, as in the following case:

Ms. B. was a spare and fussy eater who sometimes became weak and verged on metabolic imbalance because of her relative indifference to food. The social work service reported having had no contact with family members since shortly after her admission to the facility, although one staff member thought she may have had an occasional visitor.

Case Study:

Ms. B.'s terminal course became evident after an episode in which she passed out while using the bathroom. She was pale, pained, and temporarily confused upon regaining consciousness. There was blood in her stools. A diagnostic evaluation at a local hospital disclosed carcinoma of the bowels, subsequently determined to be inoperable. The institution had become the closest substitute for home and family, and so the staff members prepared themselves to see her through to the end of her life.

A psychological consultation was requested. Ms. B. had become with-drawn, responding only in monosyllables and showing almost no interest in other people or her surroundings. She had also become resistant to taking her medications. The psychologist was asked to try to revive Ms. B.'s "will to live," at least to the point where she would cooperate with treatment. The ward staff felt frustrated at not being able to do all they could to keep her going until the end.

The psychologist was fortunate in having had a previous relationship with the resident. These had not been official contacts; he and Ms. B. would just sit around and sing old-time songs together, Ms. B. carrying the tune and the psychologist providing some of the words (the songs having been sung by his parents many years before). The first phase of the current inter-action built upon the preexisting casual relationship. The psychologist and Ms. B. sang together again and recited scraps of poetry, first from memory and then from books. Ms. B.'s own buoyancy returned to a degree. She be-came more responsive to the ward staff and could be cajoled into participat-ing in her own care. The songs and poems seemed to have reminded Ms. B. of who she was and what kind of life she had lived.

This success was followed, however, by panic episodes, usually occurring at night. The staff's concern about her willingness to cooperate with treat-ment had given way to concern about her own feelings of terror. The focus of the intervention shifted to understanding the source of this terror. "Death anxiety" would have been too generalized a formulation of her feelings to be helpful. In fact, she was quite open about her concern: "I don't want to die alone, all alone." Waking up in the middle of the night and feeling that she was alone and comfortless in the dark was itself almost like dying. At this point, the intervention process was carried forward primarily by the ward staff, although the psychologist continued to visit. This intervention included moving her bed close to the nurses' station, providing a bedside light, and coming by to visit with her several times during her restless nights. Along with verbal reassurances, these were demonstrations that oth-ers cared for her and would not abandon her to her anxieties.

At a later point, therapeutic goals shifted once more. Ms. B. had become weaker and was limited to bed and chair, with a little accompanied ambu-lation twice a day. She would have been transferred to the intensive care unit, but the ward staff believed they could care for her adequately in the more familiar surroundings. One morning the charge nurse reported a new development. Ms. B. was in an unusual mood today. She was more energetic and determined than ever, but also more unrealistic—she wanted to leave the hospital. Ms. B. proved to be acutely aware of her situation, as though all her life had compressed into the present moment. The psychologist's first goal at this point was to understand Ms. B.'s current state of mind. Circumstantially at first, then with increasing focus, she explained that she could not bear to die shut away behind walls without having been part of the world again. At the same time that she reiterated her desire to leave the hospital, she also recognized the unrealistic nature of this wish.

It was New England. It was early autumn. With the blessings and cooperation of the administrator and the director of nursing, Ms. B. was given an almost day-long tour along scenic back roads as one season gave way to another. She died peacefully 2 days later.

EMIC and ETIC Perspectives on the Needs of the Dying Elder

In providing care for terminally ill elders, it is common to encounter an ever-changing configuration of needs. Counselors are in a better position to address these needs if they are alert to these changes and not rigidly committed to focusing on the initial aims. It may be useful here to borrow the ethnographer's distinction between the emic values and attitudes that are characteristic of cultural insiders and the etic values that are perceived or attributed by cultural outsiders. Counselor and client each bring their own values and attitudes to the situation. When counselor and client have much in common there may also be a commonality of goals. When they are distanced from each other by age, generation-associated life experiences, and health status, as counselors and terminally ill elders often are, this commonality becomes more unlikely. The distance may be further increased by assumptions and biases in academic instruction and clinical training that perpetuate stereotypes about both elders and dying people. It becomes important, then, for clinicians to distinguish carefully between their own goals and the client's goals.

Emic/etic discrepancies between a counselor and a terminally ill elder may, for example, produce a conflict between the values of engagement and disengagement. Gerontologists have tended to advocate an active life style for elders, quickly attacking a theory of disengagement that offered an alternative perspective (Katz, 1996). Some counselors/therapists share the gerontologists' view and accord equally high priority to the exercise of autonomy. By contrast, many elders have moved through their lives with the belief that one should not burden others or make waves. To some extent this appears to be a cohort- and gender-related attitude that is more common in women. **A psychologist might increase the discomfort of a dying elder by acting on the premise that this individual should remain highly engaged and deal assertively with situations.**

A conflict between the values of acceptance and revenge may also result from emic/etic discrepancies. In the early years of the death awareness movement, the belief that dying people do—or should—reach a "stage of acceptance" became well established in some professional circles and among the general public (Kübler-Ross, 1969). This proposition has since been criticized, not least for its lack of empirical support (Kastenbaum, 1995). **Nevertheless, many service providers continue to assume that acceptance** (seldom well defined) **is the most appropriate psychological resolution of the dying process. Many older people, however, have other values and agendas.** For example, elders who feel abused and oppressed may be motivated by the desire to assert themselves, strike back, and taste a little revenge. For some individuals, the intention to score points against a rival may be the primary motivation that keeps them going. This is but one of the many idiosyncratic motivations that can lead to conflict with psychologists or other service providers who believe that acceptance is the proper value and outcome. As with the question of engagement, counselors may use dying elders as vehicles for actualizing their own values without realizing what they are doing.

In such cases, it is possible to bridge or resolve the value differences between counselor and client—but these differences must first be recognized. **A useful guiding principle here is Avery D. Weisman's (1972) concept of an appropriate death. This is the death that a person would choose for herself or himself if given the opportunity, a death that is consistent with the individual's unique lifestyle and most cherished values.** An immediate and continuing challenge to the counselor, then, is the identification of the client's core values, which are likely to affect his or her quality of life during the dying process.

The Counselor/Therapist

Psychologists are expected to recognize the ways in which their personal characteristics may influence client and peer interactions. It is often difficult to disentangle the characteristics themselves from how they are perceived and interpreted. Consider, for example, an obvious characteristic such as age. Young counselors may approach their first interactions with a person of their own age differently than with a person three times their age. Furthermore, a counselor's expectations of how clients will interpret his or her characteristics may or may not be accurate. Some elders are at first hesitant to accept help from young service providers, wondering about their qualifications or their ability to comprehend the life situation of an older person. Others welcome the opportunity to make what they hope will be a powerful young ally to their cause; still others are so desperate for authentic human interaction that age, gender, and other characteristics are of minimal importance. **Effective counselors and therapists usually have some ability not only to assess the influence of their most salient characteristics but also to monitor their own contribution to client interactions on an ongoing basis.**

This ability to be aware of one's own contribution to the counselor-client interaction is particularly valuable in approaching terminally ill elders. Lawrence LeShan and Eda LeShan (1961), two of the first psychologists to do psychotherapy with dying people, noted the personal vulnerability of the therapist in this situation:

The psychotherapist cannot protect himself by the defense maneuver that necessity sometimes dictates to the purely medical specialist whose patients often die—the surgeon, for example, or the oncologist. This defense— brusque, armoured manner, the uninvolved relationship, the viewing of the patient's disease as of primary interest and the concentration on its technical details to the exclusion of as much else of the person as possible—may save the physician a great deal of heartache, but it is a defense which is impossible to assume for one who is in a psychotherapeutic role (p. 319).

What is the psychotherapist defending against? Usually it is both the prospect of grief—becoming involved with somebody who is likely to die soon—and the reminder of one's own mortality. **The psychologist's personal losses and experiences of grief can serve as a source of either understanding or interference. In addition, a reluctance to deal with one's own feelings about dying and death can also diminish one's ability to help another through this crisis.**

Case Study:

Mr. M. had been a hard-drinking man who eventually alienated most of his family. He was muscular, independent-minded, and functioned well "hanging" with several other male residents. With women he tended to be truculent and, at times, abusive. Despite his appearance of relatively good health, Mr. M. was never far away from cardiac and renal failure. He recovered from a life-threatening episode, but expressed his heightened anxiety through increased abuse of female residents and staff. Mr. L. had recently completed his master's degree in counseling psychology just before his 40th birthday. Mr. M. was one of his first consultations in his new position within a large geriatric facility. The psychologist reported that he and the resident had hit it off very well in their first session; he was confident he could help Mr. M. Within 2 weeks, however, it was Mr. L.'s problems that were causing the most concern. He missed appointments, became less communicative, and appeared to be going through a crisis of his own. A psychiatric consultation for the counselor revealed that Mr. L. had transferred an intense ambivalence toward his father to Mr. M. His alcoholic and abusive father had died "very badly," leaving Mr. L. with conflicted and unresolved grief. Mr. L. recognized that he had—without conscious intention—attempted to heal the relationship with his own father through the patient. Another psychologist was assigned to Mr. M.

Even a psychologist with a high degree of self-awareness may be surprised by the responses and feelings aroused in a relationship with a terminally ill elder. One's own buried griefs, childhood and adolescent fantasies, and unanswered questions about life and death may come to the fore. This reaction does not necessarily disqualify one from helping the client, but it might suggest that one discuss the situation with a respected colleague.

In addition, therapists and counselors often are dismayed by the prospect of experiencing no satisfaction in working with elderly adults. Another pioneering therapist, Sidney Levin (1964), called attention to the high incidence of depressive states among elderly patients, especially those whose death is in near prospect. "Depressed people make me depressed" is a mindset that can discourage a therapist from entering into a relationship with a person who is both aged and terminally ill. This attitude was already widespread before the concept of burnout became popular and seemed to validate the fear that interactions with a terminally ill elder would demoralize the therapist without achieving any significant benefit for the client who, in any event, had only advancing age and death ahead. **In the private office and clinic as well as the geriatric facility, elders have received much less than their share of attention from counselors and psychotherapists, particularly during the early growth years of gerontology and geriatrics. The dying elder has received the least attention of all.**

Prevailing sociocultural values constitute another barrier to establishing a therapeutic relationship with a terminally ill elder. These values take two related forms: (a) **the view of the elder as a second-class citizen and** (b) **the belief that "time is money"** (Kastenbaum, 1964). It has been known for some time that the patient's perceived status influences his or her prospects of receiving psychotherapy (Hollingshead & Redlich, 1958). Ageism has led some therapists to limit their services for elderly clients because of the fear of being seen by colleagues as working with "unimportant" people. Furthermore, psychotherapy texts have tended to recommend supportive techniques with elders, techniques often considered less prestigious or advanced. Some psychologists have therefore declined to work with "second-rate" clients using "second-rate" techniques. The time-is-money paradigm shows up in the rationalization that it is a waste of time and effort to engage in psychotherapy with a person who has only a short time to live. Quantity (duration) of life is readily substituted for quality (value) of life in a marketplace economy. From this perspective, the elderly dying person seems to be a particularly poor investment for counselors and psychotherapists.

All of these factors have contributed to the reluctance of therapists to respond to the needs of terminally ill elders. However, psychologists with a firm sense of their own identities and values and an awareness of their own feelings about personal mortality have overcome these obstacles, including the deep-rooted time-is-money paradigm. As some therapists have come to realize, the present moment is the only lived-in time that anyone experiences; when the future comes, this will be only another moment of present time. To become overly concerned about future duration of life is to lose contact with actual embodied experience. Furthermore, the time-is-money argument can easily be stood on its head. **Perhaps the limited time remaining to a terminally ill elder is precious because it is scarce. A long and unique life has come down to its final days in which all experiences and values may crystallize, and this life might come to closure as either gratifying or disappointing, depending on the state of mind and relationships at the end.**

The Client

New colleagues in psychology, psychiatry, and social work often report a personal revelation after their first few months serving in an LTC facility. At first they are overwhelmed by seeing so many frail and disabled elders under the same roof (a feeling shared by the elders as well). At this early point in their experience, residents tend to be viewed as more or less interchangeable examples of "the geriatric patient." Gradually, though, the prevailing sense of "oldness" dissipates and each resident stands out as an individual. The fact that all clients are aged makes age less relevant. To a lesser degree, the first few encounters with a dying patient are heavily weighted with their terminal status. With further experience, one does not forget the "dying part," but one relates more specifically to the meaning of the terminal experience for each individual. In many instances, counselors and therapists feel like friends and companions of people who now are entering into the final phases of their unique lives.

Psychologists can be more helpful if the generic image of the terminally ill elder is replaced by knowledge of the actual person who has had a unique life course within a unique sociohistorical context. Eliciting a client's self-narrative can itself be therapeutic, contributing to the development of the therapist–client bond and providing the opportunity for affirmation of identity and achievement. Moreover, the relationships, events, and themes that emerge from an assisted self-narrative can offer many starting points for therapeutic discussions. (Incidentally, the poignancy, power, and humor of these recollections may become part of the psychologist's own store of memories.) These self-narratives demonstrate a wide range of lifestyles and priorities. For example, in discussing personal construct therapy with elders, Linda L. Viney (1993) reports that

> [a]ll elderly people, as they come to die, will contain in their construct systems some . . . shared cultural constructs. Each has its special dominant emotions and paths of action. Yet there is also a set of metaphorical stories, that these people may have chosen to live their lives by. If so, these will be very influential in their dying. For example, elderly clients who have seen their lives as a game of cards, will still be playing to win or lose when dying. Those who have seen their lives as a series of natural cycles, each with their own meaning, will see death in the same way. Similarly, those who

*have seen their lives as a story, the meaning of which is their contribution
to life, will want to make a worthy final contribution to this history as they
approach death (p. 164).*

**From the practical standpoint, it is useful to begin the
self-narrative process before the client's ability to communicate becomes compromised by accelerating physical deterioration.** An early start also makes it possible to develop the
assisted self-narrative over the course of several meetings, during
which additional themes and events may emerge. There is now a
robust literature on elder self-narratives (e.g., Berman, 1994; Birren, 1996). Psychologists can find valuable suggestions and insights
in this literature, but one need not become a specialist in narrative
discourse to make effective use of oral biographies, which may take
various forms and have various purposes.

Co-Constructing a Life Review and Validating the Client's Life:

Since Robert N. Butler (1963) introduced the life review, it has
been an established technique in gerontology and geriatrics, and it
continues to flourish (Butler, 1995). Nevertheless, the generation
of a life review does not come easily to all elders, and most can
benefit by having an attentive and encouraging listener. The institutionalized elder who feels isolated from society and burdened
with ailments may have trouble articulating a firm sense of self
throughout the life course. Without such a sense of self, it is difficult to face the end-phase of life and the prospect of death. **Psychologists who assist dying elders in constructing or
reconstructing a coherent life review are also assisting
them in facing the end of that life** (a view in accord with Erik
Erikson's [1959] epigenetic theory of development).

Validation therapy goes beyond the establishment of a coherent
self-narrative to the affirmation of the value of the life that one has
lived and the person one has become (Agnew, 1986). The better
the psychologist knows that life, the better an opportunity he or
she will have to encourage self-validation and acceptance.

Identification of Major Sources of Fear, Guilt, and Conflict:

Clients who might otherwise be able to manage the last phase of life with resourcefulness and forbearance may continue to be tormented by an unresolved past situation. These situations, which are as varied as the lives in which they arise, will often come to the surface during the assisted self-narrative, as in the following case:

Case Study:

Ms. S. had survived the death of her twin sister, who lived in the same extended care facility, and was now herself on the danger list. She told the nursing staff that she wanted to die—and right away. However, she also expressed fear of dying and could not seem to get enough attention from physicians and nurses despite their diligence. Her attitude shifted back and forth from suicidal threats to demands to be kept alive and restored to health. Ms. S. had been a resident in the facility for more than 3 years before her sister joined her there. It was noted by staff that the twins' relationship had been tense and uncomfortable. This relationship came to the fore as Ms. S. developed her self-narrative with a social worker whom she had come to regard with affection. She returned again and again to her childhood experiences. In her view, her sister had been the family favorite; Ms. S. would do all the work and her sister would get all the credit. Several times throughout her long life, Ms. S. had made something of herself, but her sister would always manage to spoil it. The last straw was that her sister had moved into the institution in which Ms. S. had made a place for herself and, just as always, had stolen her friends and "lorded over" her. In spite of all of this, Ms. S. clearly had strong positive feelings for her sister and felt guilty about her own attitude. She was having a particularly difficult time coming to terms with what was left in her life, because her feelings were still so entangled with her sibling relationship. Relating this part of her life story to the social worker at length and with intensity did not change Ms. S.'s fundamental attitude toward her sister, but she showed less anxiety and fewer mood swings and avoided making further suicidal threats.

In addition, institutional residents may have an inadequate or incomplete understanding of their medical status and outlook. As their self-narratives develop, clients often comment on medical experiences they have had or heard about. These experiences were often conditioned by the state of medical expertise in the past and by other circumstances that do not apply to their own. Offering to have their doctor or nurse discuss these experiences with them can start a useful, anxiety-reducing intervention.

While helping elderly clients reconstruct their lives, psychologists may experience some uncomfortable moments when these clients voice "politically incorrect" attitudes. **Only seldom is it acknowledged that the present generation of elders includes many who carry forward the racist views that have plagued the United States for so many years** (Kastenbaum, 1991). One may also encounter blatant sexism and anti-Semitism, as well as a generalized xenophobia. In addition, some elders may express distrust of and antagonism to people of various national origins. It is understandable that counselors and psychotherapists might feel offended and become angered by exposure to these attitudes. **Awareness of this possibility, however, can help counselors and therapists prepare themselves to deal with such views in a mature and effective manner, despite their repugnance.**

Clients may also express confusion, disappointment, and anger about their treatment by society, another problem with sociohistorical roots. Many elders (in the community as well as in institutions) have complained about what amounts to a loss of their presumed social contract (Kastenbaum, 1993). The core lament goes as follows: "I did everything I was supposed to do. I lived by the rules. I did unto others. I worked hard. I expected respect and some comfort in my old age. Instead, everybody's running wild and I'm treated like dirt." This lament is not without foundation: The present generations of senior adults have lived through a period in which values and mutual expectations have changed substantially. It becomes more difficult to make sense of one's life and to come to terms with present-day circumstances when "the rules" seemed to have changed so drastically. The psychologist with a well-developed sense of twentieth-century social history will be better able to help the terminally ill elder deal with these altered expectations and societal relationships.

The Dying Process

Classifying a person as dying entails a major alteration in attitudes and interactions toward that person involving more apprehension and avoidant behavior and a reduction and distortion of communication (Kastenbaum, 1995). Knowing (or believing) that there is a dying person in the family, neighborhood, workplace, or ward has a powerful effect on the interaction dynamics of the group. Self-definition as a dying person may or may not accord with the judgments made by others. Some people give the impression that they are unaware of their terminal progress despite abundant evidence to the contrary; others mistake a remediable condition for one that entails certain death.

The situation is further complicated by the shifting judgments made by the people involved. Weisman (1974) uses the term middle knowledge to describe the simultaneous awareness and avoidance of dying, with subtle shifts between one position and the other. Strong need-states can induce physicians, nurses, and family members to assert views that are not well supported by the facts. For example, physicians may be so highly motivated to use their entire repetoire of interventions that they are unwilling to acknowledge "the handwriting on the wall." Furthermore, the facts themselves may be in question, and the question may be resolved on the basis of the individual's experience, motivations, and vested interests. For example, a physician with extensive background in palliative care may judge that a person is obviously dying and should receive comfort-oriented rather than cure-oriented management, whereas another physician's judgment might be that this person is not dying yet because there are some other procedures that might be tried.

Psychologists, then, will not always find it easy to determine when a client should be considered a dying person. Those who have seen expert geriatric care in action may be less ready to assume that a very ill patient is certain to die. On the other hand, elderly clients may quickly shift from relatively stable health to life-threatening illness. **This climate of ambiguity limits the psychologist's ability to establish a therapeutic plan for the dying person as such. Instead of attempting to set aside the dying person as a special type of client, psychotherapists and counselors might find it useful to cultivate a sensitivity to the currents and textures of experience when the end of life could be in near prospect. In this way, one might also reduce the likelihood that a person will be ignored until he or she is classified as dying.** For many years, it was commonplace to avoid dying patients. Although there is now somewhat more attention to the dying, this attention is not always part of the general flow of care. **An elder who might have been further isolated and ignored a few years ago upon being classified as dying might now receive special attention for that same reason; in both cases the person may have received but minimal attention before being classified as dying.** Psychologists might not want to become part of a system in which they are called upon when a person is officially classified as dying, but not during the long course of suffering and coping that may precede that situation.

The following case illustrates some of the possible elements and dynamics of working with a life-endangered elder:

Case Study:

Ms. G.'s life had changed radically after her husband died when she was 50. She had lived with a daughter but had become increasingly paranoid after the death of her cat (which may have been deliberately killed). She was admitted to a mental hospital and, upon reaching geriatric age, transferred to an extended care facility. Some years later she had become massively im-

paired. *Deaf, blind, and uncommunicative, she was restricted to bed and chair and suffered from organic brain syndrome, decubiti, arteriosclerotic heart disease, urinary tract infection, and gross tremor of the upper extremities. The psychiatric diagnosis was depression.*

When a new counseling/psychotherapy program was established in the institution, a consultation was made. Ms. G., otherwise unable to communicate, would cry out in terror during the night and shrink in fear when approached at any time of day. The responding therapist started by using touch, then added music and had the curtains opened on the patient's dark area of the ward. It turned out that Ms. G. had a little vision and a little hearing. The therapist managed to conduct an improvised form of relaxation therapy, accompanied by explanations of how this would improve her condition. The therapist acted on the assumption that Ms. G. could hear and understand at least some of what she was saying, or at least would take some comfort in being treated like a real person. Ms. G. responded with smiles and gestures, but never spoke. Whatever was happening had a welcome effect: The night terrors disappeared as well as the fear she exhibited when being approached.

Over a period of time, Ms. G.'s lungs and kidneys failed despite dedicated medical and nursing care. Her hours of wakefulness decreased. Despite her increasing proximity to death, she remained serene and responsive during her periods of alertness. The therapist (and sometimes her daughter) visited Ms. G. frequently during her last days, talking, touching, and at times, holding her. The nurses had a mixed response to the therapeutic intervention. As they saw it, Ms. G. had been close to death several times but on each occasion came back to life after contact with the therapist, which some saw as a cruel and useless extension of the patient's life. Ms. G.'s nonverbal responses near the end—including spontaneously reaching for the therapist's hand and willingly changing from mouth to nose breathing at the suggestion—indicated her awareness and participation. The nurses reported that she died with a peaceful and calm expression (Kastenbaum et al., 1981).

This case vignette illustrates several typical aspects of therapeutic interventions with terminally ill institutionalized elders: (a) **multiple physical problems;** (b) **massive communication** impairment; (c) **cognitive impairment** (of incompletely de-termined type and severity); (d) **a preexisting psychiatric state** (in this case, depression with paranoid features); **and** (e) **a shift in treatment priorities over time** (from preventing anxiety episodes to comfort during the end-phase of life). Intervention options were constricted by these conditions and by the relative lack of privacy in an open ward setting. Furthermore, the ward staff's perception that the patient was being kept alive too long by interaction with the therapist contributed to a difficult treatment milieu. Intervention during the terminal phase was, however, greatly facilitated by the prior development of a relationship with the patient. Even a therapist with remarkable primary relationship-building skills would have been unlikely to pierce Ms. G.'s com-municational isolation and depression if the therapist had first appeared on the scene when the patient was succumbing to her varied conditions.

The psychosocial literature has illuminated some aspects of the dying person's mental life and relationships but has tended to ne-glect the influence of the specific physical condition and treatment effects. Strangely, the failing body has had little place in some of the most influential writings. Physicians who have focused increased attention on the dying process are helping to correct this situation (Nuland, 1994). **Psychologists are likely to be more useful to terminally ill elders if they understand the implications of specific medical conditions and treatment than if they rely on outmoded stage theories.**

The Situation

Death as well as life is influenced by institutional rules and pat-terns. Erwin Goffman's concept of the total institution (1960) re-mains a provocative source of insight. Just as it is difficult to function as an individual within an institutional frame, so it is dif-ficult to navigate one's own way toward death. **Psychologists may find themselves caught between the obligations of functioning within institutional guidelines and providing assistance to unique individuals and their families in the**

end phase of life. Psychologists (or other human service professionals) given the mission of tending to the dying may also find themselves playing a "Dr. Death" role, an arrangement that frequently leads to a general retreat by the rest of the staff: "Dr. Death is on duty. We don't have to get involved."

A long-term education and training strategy may increase the comfort level and competence of all staff members in relating to dying residents and their families and friends. Its secondary benefits include greater understanding of and receptivity to the psychologist's interventions and suggestions. Following such a strategy requires the usual tact, caution, and skill in maneuvering through the labyrinth of vested interests and chronic conflicts between individuals and services. This can actually be the most difficult part of the process if various units (or the heads of these units) have become entrenched in their rivalry and mutual distrust; the very fact that Unit A supports a new program for the terminally ill may be sufficient reason for Unit B to oppose it.

Given a reasonably receptive institutional milieu, there are numerous potential starting points for education and training. **Perhaps the most effective technique is simply to make oneself available to other staff members when they encounter dying, death, and grief in their own lives.** Having experienced the relief of sharing their experiences with a caring person, they are more likely to make themselves available to help others. Several excellent video documentaries can help to put institutional staff members in touch with their own death-related feelings and observe the value of caring interactions during the terminal phase of life. Reading/discussion groups on topics related to dying, death, and grief can also be helpful.

A more time and labor-intensive approach involves organizing staff education/research conferences focused on improving care for the terminally ill. These conferences are sometimes known as *psychological autopsies,* especially when there are research as well as clinical objectives (Weisman & Kastenbaum, 1968). Psychologists need not, however, insist upon this term, which may be threatening or confusing to some staff members. It is often useful to include an external consultant in these proceedings, both for that person's insights and to demonstrate that the world is interested in the ways in which long lives end. Psychologists may also develop peer support groups to help staff deal with their grief after a resident's death, which also serves as an institutional acknowledgment of the fact of death and the legitimacy of its discussion.

Family involvement in the care of institutionalized elders is often complicated by distance, disability, relationship conflict, and anxiety about entering the congregate living environment. Ambivalence about visiting an institutionalized family elder often increases when that person's death seems to be in close prospect. "I should be with her—but I don't know if I can stand being there." **The need for professional counseling may be sharply reduced if the psychologist can establish an institutional milieu in which family members are genuinely valued and welcomed.** It is particularly useful to be able to call upon several staff members who are competent and comfortable with terminally ill elders and can therefore serve as quasi-models for hesitant family members.

Over-and undermedication can increase the dying person's sense of isolation and difficulties in communication. In some extended care facilities, residents are subject to chemical restraint that is nothing short of criminal abuse. Facilities with a more humane approach may nevertheless miss the mark in the management of medications. Geriatric nursing and medicine require state-of-the-art knowledge and sufficient personnel to monitor the patient's condition and make adjustments as necessary. This type of care is often difficult to come by, whether in hospital, clinic, or extended care settings. In consequence, the elder who is approaching the terminal phase of life may be suffering from infections that were preventable or remediable and from any number of drug-interaction effects. Drug side effects such as dry throat, clouded consciousness, and unsteadiness can undermine the resident's ability to comprehend and cope with his or her situation. The psychologist who enters this person's life at this time is apt to encounter difficulties in communication and relationship building that have been intensified by inadequate management of medications. **In many cases, medication-related mental and physical symptoms can interfere with attempts to help the resident deal with the dying process as such.**

Psychologists can also provide a valuable service by helping the resident to remain in familiar surroundings as long as possible and to avoid unnecessary transfers. In this regard, particular problems vary from institution to institution. It is not unusual, however, for pressure to build up to transfer a person from his or her familiar "home" in the facility to a more remote "dying place." These moves are more likely to assuage the anxieties of the staff than to benefit the dying person. In times of threat and crisis, it is natural to seek comfort in familiar places, objects, and people. Staff members sometimes assert that having a resident die "at home" would have a catastrophic effect on other residents. Experience has shown, however, that spiriting away terminally ill people and invoking the code of silence is more likely to have a depressing and frightening effect. Elders are not strangers to death and may be heartened by observing the care and respect given to their terminally ill companions. A nurse's aide, herself well along in years, encapsulated this situation in her own words:

> *When I go, I don't want to be an empty bed that nobody is supposed to talk about, like I never even had a life. The patients here feel the same way. They get shook up when somebody goes, but if they can see that you really cared for them all the way—and see the tears in your eyes—then they feel just a little better about what's waiting for them.*

The Intervention

The psychologist who encourages humane, open, and flexible practices throughout the institutional milieu will also improve care and well-being for residents entering the final phase of life. Some residents in addition, benefit from direct psychological interventions. **In many cases, the psychologist-client relationship**

may be the most important therapeutic tool. This relationship, described in passing in the previous case studies, emerges more clearly in the following example:

Case Study:

Ms. R. had suffered trauma and loss since her childhood, when both parents died as the result of a motor vehicle accident. The family's modestly affluent financial status turned to near impoverishment during the Great Depression. Several other family members and close friends died, and she had two stillborn births before her only surviving child was born. Ms. R. attempted suicide after her husband was killed in a motor vehicle accident like the one in which her parents had died. Her personal history, compiled in some detail by the social service department, suggests that she gave up one after another of her attachments and interests until her only remaining sources of emotional contact with the world were her daughter and her own enthusiasm for boxing. Ms. R. not only watched every boxing match shown on television, but demonstrated impressive boxing knowledge and analyzed various pugilists' strengths and weaknesses with skill. There were institutional rumours that she packed a mean punch herself, but she was never known to demonstrate this ability.

Her precarious adjustment was upset when Ms. R.'s daughter, diagnosed with a life-threatening illness, committed suicide by drug overdose. Ms. R. attempted suicide herself through the same method but survived. She did not have serious residual effects from the suicide attempt, but during her stay on the intensive care unit it was discovered that her cardiovascular condition was more severe than had been thought. Ms. R. could die at any time. It remained her intention, however, to take her own life once she could figure out the best way to do it. The facility was not structured or staffed for lock-and-key psychiatric observation, but the staff did not want Ms. R. to be removed from her "home," especially knowing her life-threatening cardiovascular condition.

The therapist was a foreign-born psychologist who had retired from her academic research career and decided to return to clinical practice within a geriatric setting. During the first visit, Ms. R. was lying with her face to the wall. She would not speak or even look at her visitor. This had become her characteristic behavior since recovering from the suicide attempt. The therapist made several unsuccessful attempts to establish rapport. She then surprised Ms. R. by crying out in anguish, "Ah, it's my accent, isn't it! You won't speak to me. You hate me for my accent!" Ms. R. turned to her: "No—I don't hate you for your accent. But what kind of accent is it?" The therapist went on to reveal something of her own life experiences—as devastating in their own way as the resident's. They saw each other every day (including weekends) for a number of weeks. It was clear that they had entered each other's lives. The therapist admitted that she might be acting "unprofessional" by engaging in so much mutual disclosure, which might be serving her needs as well, as the patient's. Nevertheless, it was working. Ms. R. formed a strong attachment to the therapist, and it went both ways. When the therapist became ill enough to require hospitalization herself, Ms. R. prayed for her and managed to send her a get-well card. Within about 3 months of the first visit, Ms. R. had returned to her previous mode of functioning in the institution—boxing matches included—and spoke no more of suicide. One day she expressed the urgent need to speak to the priest, with whom she had a private discussion. That night she died in her sleep.

Conclusion: Using All That We Are

Psychotherapy is challenging enough in ordinary circumstances. It is especially daunting when we enter, as strangers, into the final experiences of people who have had long, eventful, and unique lives. The therapist who came to the assistance of Ms. R. had a long, eventful, and unique life of her own, not unmarked by suffering and loss. Her approach might not have been effective if attempted by others, but this is not to say that a different therapist might not have succeeded with a different approach.

Elders in general comprise a more diversified population than younger adults, having had more time to cultivate their particular relationships, values, and lifestyles. Elders with disabilities or life-threatening illnesses remain firmly etched individuals, experiencing distress and loss of function in their own ways. Their residual strengths are also highly individual. It is not a very useful exercise, then, to outline definitive psychotherapeutic guidelines for working with terminally ill elders. The exception may be this principle: one must always ask who this client is and who one is as therapist. After experiences with several clients, one might notice that each called upon different facets of one's own personal make-up as well as of one's therapeutic repertoire. One does not forget what one already knows about counseling or psychotherapeutic technique, but one learns that what goes into a strong relationship with a terminally ill elder is nothing less than all that one can bring to life— and death.

The establishment and development of rapport provides the opportunity to move into the sphere of meaning. The therapist may be guided by a theoretical orientation in which meaning is central (e.g., logotherapy or life review therapy) or employ another route (e.g., cognitive-behavioral therapy) for the same purpose. **What is perhaps more important than the particular theoretical orientation of the therapist is the elder's own worldview: the meanings that are most cherished and the meanings that are now most threatened**. Depending upon the circumstances, the therapist may be in a position to help clients articulate and clarify their basic values. **Having these values clearly in mind again and being able to share them with another person can foster a sense of symbolic survival in clients: "What I believe in will continue after my life ends."**

One learns to be alert to the client's revelation of those values that are most jeopardized by death. People differ significantly in the nature of their death-related concerns, as James Diggory and Dorothea Rothman (1961) demonstrated in a pioneering study and as clinical experience has confirmed. Here it is useful to set aside one's own gallery of death concerns to avoid attributing them, inadvertently, to the client. For example, a young, strongly future-oriented psychologist might feel that death is a threat chiefly because it would prevent the fulfillment of personal and professional dreams. The therapist might also be preoccupied by philosophical questions regarding the nature of death and the possibility of survival. The frail, impaired, and weakening elder might not have these issues at the fore, however. Instead, his or her concerns might well be to avoid a state of complete dependency during the dying process (and/or not being a burden on the caregivers), and to ensure that funeral arrangements will be properly carried out. **Generally** (but not always), **dying clients are more concerned about the practical realities of the end-phase of life than about philosophical matters or unfulfilled personal goals. As psychologists, we will be more helpful to our clients if we work through our own feelings about mortality to an appreciable extent before showing up at their bedsides.**

"This long life ended well, and I had something to do with that" is perhaps too subjective and elusive an outcome to expect in this era of the "bottom line," but it is also an outcome that can renew one's dedication to human service.

References

Agnew, D. P. (1986). Psychotherapy of the elderly: The life validation approach in psychotherapy with elderly patients. *Journal of Geriatric Psychiatry, 26,* 87–92.

Berman, H. J. (1994). *Interpreting the aging self.* New York: Springer.

Birren, J. E. (Ed.) (1996). *Aging and biography: Explorations in adult development.* New York: Springer.

Butler, R. N. (1963). The life review: An interpretation of reminiscence in the aged. *Psychiatry, 26,* 65–76.

Butler, R. N. (1995). Life review. In G. Maddox (Ed.), *The encyclopedia of aging* (2nd ed., pp. 562–563) New York: Springer.

Diggory, J. C., & Rothman, D. Z. (1961). Values destroyed by death. *Journal of Abnormal and Social Psychology, 63,* 205–210.

Erikson, E. H. (1959). Identity and the life cycle: *Psychological issues* (Vol. 1). New York: International Universities Press.

Goffman, E. (1960). Characteristics of total institutions. In M. R. Stein, J. Vidich, & M. White (Eds.), *Identity and anxiety: Survival of the person in mass society* (pp. 449–479). Glencoe, IL: Free Press.

Hollingshead, A. B., & Redlich, F. C. (1958). *Social class and mental illness.* New York: John Wiley & Sons.

Kahana, E. (1995). Institutionalization. In G. Maddox (Ed.), *The encyclopedia of aging* (2nd ed., pp. 509–513). New York: Springer.

Kastenbaum, R. (1964). *The reluctant therapist.* In R. Kastenbaum (Ed.), New thoughts on old age (pp. 139–145). New York: Springer.

Kastenbaum, R. (1991). Racism and the older voter? Arizona's rejection of a paid holiday to honor Martin Luther King, Jr. *International Journal of Aging and Human Development, 32,* 199–209.

Kastenbaum, R. (1993). Encrusted elders: Arizona and the political spirit of postmodern aging. In T. R. Cole, W. A. Achenbaum, P. L. Jakobi, & R. Kastenbaum (Eds.), *Voices and visions of aging* (pp. 160–183). New York: Springer.

Kastenbaum, R. (1995). *Death, society, and human experience* (5th ed.). Boston: Allyn & Bacon.

Kastenbaum, R., Barber, T. X., Wilson, S. G., Ryder, B. L., & Hathaway, L, B. (1981). *Old, sick, and helpless.* Cambridge, MA: Ballinger.

Katz, S. (1996). *Disciplining old age: The formation of gerontological knowledge.* University Press of Virginia: Charlottesville, VA.

Kübler-Ross, E. (1969). *On death and dying.* New York: Macmillan.

LeShan, L., & LeShan, E. (1961). *Psychotherapy and the patient with a limited life span.* Psychiatry, *24,* 318–323.

Levin, S. (1964). Depression in the aged: The importance of external factors. In R. Kastenbaum (Ed.), *New thoughts on old age* (pp. 179–185). New York: Springer.

Nuland, S. (1994). *How we die.* New York: Alfred A. Knopf.

Saunders, C. & Kastenbaum, R. (Eds.). (1997). *Hospice care on the international scene.* New York: Springer.

U.S. Public Health Service. (1995). *An overview of nursing homes and their current residents: Data from the 1995 National Nursing Home Survey* (PHS Publication No. 97–1250). Washington, DC: U. S. Printing Office.

Viney, L. L. (1993). *Life stories.* New York: John Wiley & Sons.

Weisman, A. D. (1972). On death and denying. New York: Behavioral Publications.

Weisman, A. D. (1974) *The realization of death*. New York: Aronson.

Weisman, A. D., & Kastenbaum, R. (1968). *The psychological autopsy: A study of the terminal phase of life*. New York: Behavioral Publications.

11

Training Nursing Assistants to Care for Nursing Home Residents With Dementia

NANETTE A. KRAMER, PH.D.,
and MICHAEL C. SMITH, PH.D.

Abstract

The importance of nursing assistants in the caring of nursing home residents with dementia has been increasingly recognized in recent years. After a review of the demographics of nursing assistants, the demands of their jobs, the training requirements they must meet, and evaluation of their job performance, this chapter will present a number of training programs and instructional materials which have been developed to improve the quality of care that nursing assistants deliver. An analysis of these materials suggests several common features and themes. Most of the materials focus heavily on the psychosocial aspects of care. Some focus specifically on the psychosocial care and the behavioral management of people with dementia, while others address a broader array of psychosocial topics, including depression, adjustment problems, and death and dying. Most require a primarily didactic teaching style, although some require the incorporation of other teaching styles, such as discussion, role playing, and structured exercises. Almost all of the ideas, information, and principles of care in these materials are garnered from the work of other healthcare professions and provide only limited opportunity for the inclusion of ideas of nursing assistants. Few programs include on-the-job follow-up activities to reinforce their knowledge of the variety of approaches to nursing home residents with dementia and to help nursing assistants design, implement, and evaluate such training programs.

Introduction

In the United States, approximately 600,000 persons work as nursing assistants in nursing homes (U.S. Department of Labor, 1991), where they care for a population with an estimated 43% to 78% prevalence rate for dementia (Lair & Lefkowitz, 1990; Rovner et al., 1986; Smyer & Garfein, 1988). **Current estimates indicate that this group of workers provides 80% to 90% of all the direct, day-to-day care that nursing home residents receive** (Harper, 1986; U.S. Department of Labor, 1991), **which is five to six times as much care as is provided by licensed and registered nurses** (Administration on Aging, 1980). As the number of persons who need nursing home care swells, it is expected that by 2005 close to 1,000,000 nursing assistants will be needed in nursing homes across the country (U.S. Department of Labor, 1991).

Until recently, despite the extensive and intensive involvement of these frontline workers with nursing home residents, remarkably little information was available about their backgrounds, training for the job, actual job performance, or job satisfaction (Crown, 1994; Duffy et al., 1989; Foner, 1994a). Fortunately, there is now growing awareness of the potential impact nursing assistants can have on the quality of life (QOL) of the residents they serve (Brannon & Bodner, 1988; Burgio & Burgio, 1990). Similarly, attention is now beginning to be paid to QOL issues for the nursing assistants themselves (Bowers & Becker, 1992; Tellis-Nayak & Tellis-Nayak, 1989).

The goals of this chapter are to bring together what is already known about these workers (based on existing literature), to review efforts to help them in their work, and to suggest a variety of promising training strategies designed to enhance formal caregiving practices.

What Is Known About Nursing Home Nursing Assistants?

Available information about nursing home nursing assistants consistently suggests that the majority (90% to 95%) are women, regardless of the location or size of the institution in which they work (Chappell & Novak, 1992; Crown, 1994; Garland et al., 1988). Similarly, most studies indicate that about half of all nursing assistants are 25 to 44 years of age and approximately 30% are 45 years of age or older (Chappell & Novak, 1992; Crown, 1994). Given the heavy physical demands that this work typically entails, it is noteworthy that a sizable proportion of nursing home nursing assistants are women who are middle-aged or older.

In terms of race and ethnicity, nursing assistants who work in nursing homes are quite diverse. **Overall, it has been estimated that approximately 60% to 70% of nursing assistants are white, 25% to 30% are black, and less than 10% are members of other minority groups** (primarily Hispanic) (Crown, 1994; Quinlan, 1988). **The proportion of minorities is significantly higher than in the workforce in general (Crown, 1994) and has increased in recent years.** The more urbanized the area in which the facility is situated, the higher the concentration of aides who are of minority status or foreign born (Diamond, 1986). In rural areas and smaller towns, nursing assistants are more often white (Tellis-Nayak & Tellis-Nayak, 1989). Many foreign-born nursing assistants held jobs of higher status in their countries of origin but were unable to obtain an equivalent level of work in the United States because of differences in job requirements; thus, there may be an underlying disparity in prior job status and experience between foreign-born and American-born nursing assistants, which may be most pronounced in more urbanized settings (Tellis-Nayak & Tellis-Nayak, 1989).

About 60% of nursing home nursing assistants have completed high school and approximately 25% have not (Crown, 1994). The remaining 15% have had some college, but only a small minority (3%) are college graduates (Crown, 1994). Not surprisingly, their incomes are low, both before and after becoming employed as nursing assistants. **Typically, they "come to the nursing home weighted down with economic hardship"** (Tellis-Nayak & Tellis-Nayak, 1989, p. 310), **and they tend to receive very low wages for the nursing home work they do, often earning barely above the minimum wage** (Feldman, 1994; Marion Merrell Dow, 1992, 1993).

We were unable to find any information about demographic variables that can be used to distinguish nursing assistants who work with residents with dementia and those who do not. **Given the prevalence of dementia in nursing homes, however, almost all nursing assistants in these settings are likely to care for persons with dementia at one time or another.**

What Do Nursing Home Nursing Assistants Actually Do?

The primary function of a nursing home nursing assistant is to tend to the basic physical needs of residents who have been assigned to them, and to do so with respect and sensitivity to the patient, regardless of the task or how they themselves are treated. **Their tasks have been fittingly described as "bed and body work"** (Gubrium, 1975) **and may include partial to full assistance to residents in bathing, eating, toileting, dressing, grooming, and moving from one place to another.** Nursing assistants who work an 8-hour shift may be responsible for 8 to 12 or more residents (Foner, 1994b); the number of residents assigned to them can vary markedly with such factors as the time of day (caseloads are generally heavier later in the day and at night) and the day of the week (caseloads are usually heavier on weekends).

However, as emphasized by Foner (1994a), a mere listing of the physical tasks carried out by these workers fails to do justice to "how physically straining, emotionally wear-

ing, and dirty the work is, and how patients present problems every step of the way" (p. 32). Patient problems include a variety of physical, neurological, and psychosocial difficulties. As increasing numbers of nursing home residents are diagnosed with dementia, it is becoming clear that all staff, including nursing assistants, must possess specialized psychological and social skills in addition to physical and technical know-how.

How Are Nursing Assistants Trained to Do Their Work?

Until very recently, there were no nationwide standards for the training of nursing assistants; instead, standards and requirements varied from state to state and from facility to facility (Feldman, 1994; Institute of Medicine, 1986). Instinct and experience often served as the assistants' only guides to meeting the challenges of their work (Cervantes et al., 1995). **Since the 1987 Omnibus (OBRA 1987) went into effect in 1990, minimum education and training standards have been in place nationwide.** Nursing assistants are required to have 75 hours of training before they can be certified and begin to work. Within the 75 hours of training, a wide range of topics must be covered, including the physical and psychosocial care of residents and a minimum of 16 hours of supervised clinical experience. The topic of caring for residents with dementia constitutes only a small portion of the required training. Some states and facilities require additional time for specialized topics, but this requirement varies greatly among states and training providers (Feldman, 1994). After nursing assistants complete their training requirements and start working, they may be required to participate in continuing education programs. However, requirements for continuing education vary from state to state.

How Well Do Nursing Assistants Perform on Their Jobs?

Much of the literature on nursing assistants who work in nursing homes portrays them in largely negative terms, (i.e., as dehumanizing residents, and by being abusive and insensitive [Fontana, 1977; Kayser-Jones, 1990; Pillemer & Moore, 1989]). However, empirical research on this topic is rare. In general, little attention has been paid either to the quality of their work or to work-related factors that impinge on their effectiveness.

After reviewing some of the early research studies that examined the behavior of nursing assistants in nursing homes, especially studies done by Baltes (1988) and colleagues, Burgio and Burgio (1990) concluded that the research "supports the popular view of nursing assistants as fulfilling primarily a custodial function with the nursing home, engaging in limited interaction with their patients, and interacting with them in a manner that reinforces dependent behavior." They add that other data suggest that nursing assistants are inadequately prepared for their work, and they attribute this lack of preparation to the quality of the training the nursing assistants receive and to the unmet need for management systems to promote the application of the skills learned in training to the reality of the nursing home environment.

A high turnover rate for nursing assistants in nursing homes has also often been cited as a problem, although there is some dispute about the extent of turnover and its causes. Nationally reported annual turnover rates vary widely, from 5% (Foner, 1994a) to 75% (Waxman et al., 1984) or higher. A high turnover rate leads to many problems: information accrued by the nursing assistants regarding the specific habits and needs of specific residents is lost, residents as well as staff experience an emotional loss, and extra funds must be spent recruiting and training new workers. Some researchers who study the causes of turnover focus on characteristics of the nursing assistants themselves as predictors of turnover, whereas others attribute turnover to particular working conditions, e.g., the lack of appreciation for their work (Caudill & Patrick, 1991; Oliver & Tureman, 1988), the amount of autonomy to do their work (Streit & Brannon, 1994), and the degree of closeness they feel with the residents (Duncan & Morgan, 1994). Tellis-Nayak and Tellis-Nayak (1989) warn that the institution's failure to address the emotional needs of nursing assistants will contribute to their increased alienation.

A more recent group of ethnographic studies that focused on the performance of nursing home nursing assistants painted a somewhat brighter picture. These researchers spent extensive periods of time working and observing conditions in nursing homes. Their accounts highlight both the extremely demanding working conditions that nursing assistants face and the exceptional kindness and competence with which many of them do their work (Diamond, 1992; Foner, 1994b; Savishinsky, 1991; Shields, 1988). After working for 8 months as a volunteer with nursing assistants in a nursing home, **Foner found that most of the nursing assistants she encountered "were neither saints nor monsters"; rather, she found them to vary widely in the quality of their work. Like Burgio and Burgio** (1990)**, she suggested that many of the more problematic behaviors they exhibit stem from situational factors in their environment and training** (Foner, 1994b).

Another recent study attempted to assess the job performance of dementia care nursing assistants systematically (Oberer, 1995). Nursing assistants were repeatedly observed as they provided care to residents with a range of severity of dementia, and the nature of their responses to residents' behaviors was rated using a rigorous coding system previously developed and refined by Baltes (1988) and colleagues. **In direct contrast to descriptions of nursing assistants as uncaring and insensitive and to Baltes' findings a decade earlier, Oberer found that nursing assistants were highly sensitive to variations in capacity among their residents and that they responded spontaneously in ways that were congruent with the residents' behaviors.** More specifically, Oberer found that when residents were at less advanced stages of dementia, nursing assistants tended to encourage their independence, and when residents were more impaired by their dementia, nursing assistants were more likely to encourage them to accept assistance. Although the study was limited to only one facility, its findings lend credence to the idea that many dementia-care nursing assistants are capable as well as caring.

Finally, a recent interview study by Kramer and colleagues (1996) elicited ideas, suggestions, and guiding principles for dementia care from a sample of nursing assistants. Although the study did not assess the extent to which the nursing assistants actually put their ideas into practice, it did find that, as a group, they offered an impressive body of caregiving knowledge and advice. **Particularly striking was the finding that many of their comments reflected a sophisticated understanding of the psychological basis of dementia-induced behaviors.**

How Is the Effectiveness of Training Evaluated?

Relatively few studies have attempted to assess the effectiveness of nursing assistant training programs in increasing the participants' knowledge and improving the care they give to nursing home residents. Chartock and colleagues (1988) reported the results of a large pilot study of both professional and paraprofessional staff in four nursing homes. Staff members who participated in the study received 56 hours of classroom training (lectures, hand-outs, and group interactional exercises) on five topics: normal aging, communication, mental impairment, working with families, and team building. The study did not include a control group, and data on effectiveness were collected from only a subset of the study participants. (How this subset was selected was not reported.) Comparisons of pre- and posttraining scores on a paper-and-pencil test showed an increase in knowledge, and supervisors reported improved job performance 2 months after the training. Participants felt that the mental impairment topic was the most useful. The authors noted that the reported improvements in job performance were greater in facilities that had stronger administrative support for the program and a higher rate of staff participation.

Smyer and colleagues (1992) studied the effectiveness of two training interventions: skills training and job redesign. The skills training intervention consisted of five 1.5 hour classes for nursing assistants that focused on behavior management skills for dealing with disorientation, depression, agitation, and other problem behaviors. The curriculum was later published as a training manual,

The ABCs of Behavior Change: Skills for Working With Behavior Problems in Nursing Homes (Cohn et al., 1994), which is reviewed below. The job redesign intervention was intended to allow staff to design and implement workplace changes to improve the delivery of services to residents. Teams of 8 to 10 staff members met to formulate, plan, and carry out the changes in their facility.

The two interventions were studied separately and together along with a nonintervention control condition, forming a two-by-two design (presence-absence of skills training by presence-absence of job redesign). The study was carried out in four nursing homes, with each condition represented in one home. Three outcome measures were used in the study: staff knowledge was assessed with a multiple-choice test; the nursing assistants' perceptions of their job were assessed with a rating-scale measure; and job performance was assessed by ratings made by the nursing assistants' nursing supervisors. The outcome measures were administered before the interventions began, immediately after they ended, 3 months after, and 6 months after. The only significant effect identified was on staff knowledge; all three intervention conditions showed a modest increase in staff knowledge which was maintained over time. The job perception and job performance measures showed no change.

In discussing their results, Smyer and colleagues (1992) **proposed that the translation of an increase in knowledge into improved job performance requires strong administrative support, which may have been lacking in their study. Smyer and Wall** (1994) **expanded this point, suggesting that supervisors specifically are essential for encouraging and reinforcing the transfer of training to job performance.** They speculated that the nursing supervisors in the study by Smyer and colleagues (1992) may actually have discouraged rather than reinforced the use of the skills the nursing assistants acquired in training.

After reviewing the literature on staff training in institutions other than nursing homes (e.g., psychiatric facilities and developmental centers), Burgio and Burgio (1990) proposed a model of training for nursing assistants in nursing homes that included both skills training and staff management components. They argued that skills training was necessary but not sufficient for improving job performance and quality of patient care, and that a management system that monitors and rewards appropriate staff performance was also necessary. Initially, this model was applied to urinary incontinence. Nursing assistants were trained to use prompted-voiding procedures to manage residents' urinary incontinence. The changes in their behavior and the improvements in their residents were successfully maintained over time (Burgio et al., 1990; Burgio et al., 1994; Schelle et al., 1993).

Subsequently, this training model was applied more broadly by Burgio and colleagues (Stevens et al., 1996; Stevens et al., 1997). Nursing assistants in a nursing home received 5 hours of behavioral management skills training and additional on-the-job training, in which their interactions with residents were observed and constructive corrective feedback was provided. After the training, a formal staff management (FSM) system was instituted on some of the nursing units in the home to promote the implementation and long-term maintenance of the skills acquired during training. It included self-monitoring by the nursing assistants, monitoring by their nursing supervisors with feedback to the nursing assistants, and incentives to the nursing assistants for satisfactory performance (chances to win prizes in a lottery). Other units in the home maintained traditional supervisory practices ("conventional staff management" or CSM).

Outcome measures included direct observations of nursing assistants' interactions with residents before training, immediately after training, and every month for 12 months after. As of this writing, only partial results from the study have been reported. For two variables, giving verbal instructions to residents during care activities and making positive statements to residents, the nursing assistants in the FSM and CSM conditions showed different patterns of results. **Immediately after training, both groups of nursing assistants gave a greater number of verbal instructions and positive statements. However, these increases**

were maintained over time only in the FSM units; in the CSM unit at 19 weeks, the number of verbal instructions and positive statements was close to the initial, pre-training level. Stevens and colleagues (1997) **argued that these results bolster their contention that a staff management system is needed to maintain improvements in job performance, but they also pointed out that such a system must have institutional support** (from both labor and management), **not be overly burdensome to nursing staff, and be sustainable over time without the support of outside resources such as research staff.**

What Manuals and Videotapes Have Been Developed for Training Nursing Assistants to Carry Out Dementia Care?

One of the earliest published specialized training designed specifically for dementia care nursing assistants remains one of the most ambitious in scope, with 10 videotapes and an accompanying manual. This set of training materials, entitled *Managing and Understanding Behavior Problems in Alzheimer's Disease and Related Disorders* (Teri, 1991), offers structured, replicable training in the principles of behavior modification. Each of the videotapes in this series concentrates on one or more problems that are commonly encountered among persons with dementia, such as wandering, inappropriate sexual behaviors, anger, irritation, catastrophic reactions, language deficits, and caregiver issues. Teri, a clinical psychologist who specializes in aging, is featured on each videotape, explaining how to apply basic behavior modification techniques to ameliorate each of the targeted problems. Clinical vignettes, in which actors demonstrate the "wrong" and "right" ways to react to the problem behaviors are used to reinforce learning. Each of the tapes is designed to be used either independently or in conjunction with other tapes. Individual videotapes are 8 and 32 minutes long; the total time for all 10 videotapes is just over 3 hours. These videotapes impart an extensive amount of information that may be useful to nursing assistants in many different situations. As with any technique, however, their value may be less in settings in which the nursing assistants are overworked, underrespected, and unsupported (Hinrichsen, 1994).

Also published in 1991 was a videotape entitled, *Nurses' Aides— Making a Difference: Skills for Managing Difficult Behaviors in Dementia Victims* (31 minutes) (University of Texas Southwestern Medical Center, 1991) which was accompanied by a written guide (Chafetz et al., 1991). Like Teri's videotapes, this resource is specifically for nursing assistants. Its overriding message is that nursing assistants can learn interventions that will reduce problem behaviors among residents with dementia. Like the first set of videotapes, the interventions are founded on principles of behavior modification and thus are designed to teach staff to identify problem behaviors and to generate solutions for resolving those behaviors. However, rather than presenting information in a straightforward, lecture format, this videotape uses a mock talk-show format; actresses portray guest nursing assistants and a nurse on a panel, as well as a commentator and audience members, who are also supposed to be nursing assistants. A guest psychologist on the panel plays himself. Fictional vignettes are periodically shown to illustrate staff dealing with resident behavior problems.

The developers of this videotape chose a talk-show format to increase the likelihood that the nursing assistants would attend to the material. While the format is certainly novel, it is unclear whether it does in fact lend itself to heightened attentiveness. The manual, which is intended to guide the trainer in preparing class material, contains exercises that involve the nursing assistants directly. A number of situations are presented and the trainer is directed to lead staff members in a discussion of their feelings about working with people with behavior problems. Although the exercises encourage staff members to share their feelings, they do not appear to draw on the nursing assistants' own knowledge and skills.

A somewhat different perspective is conveyed in the sensitive and realistic training videotape with the apt title, Dress Him While He Walks: Behavior Management in Caring for Residents with Alzheimer's Disease (19 minutes) (O'Donnell, O'Donnell, &

Global Village Communications, 1993). In contrast to earlier videotapes, it shows actual nursing home residents with dementia engaged in spontaneous behaviors that are associated with their illness (wandering, angry outbursts, and delusions) and that often pose difficulty for staff. Rather than using actors, actual nursing assistants are shown, in some cases struggling in their responses to the residents. Staff members, including several nursing assistants, are interviewed about their reactions to the residents and are asked for suggestions on how to deal with the challenges they face in their work. Their responses reflect a high degree of sensitivity to the psychological needs of the patients.

The case is strongly made throughout the videotape that greater effectiveness—and humanity—is achieved by accepting residents' limitations and adapting to their reality of these limitations rather than attempting to impose unnecessary changes in their behaviors. For example, why not dress a patient while he walks if he prefers moving to staying still, rather than force him to stop walking to dress him, even though it may be the more conventional way to dress? This compelling videotape, which was developed for nurses, nursing assistants, nursing home administrators, directors of nursing volunteers and paraprofessionals, not only is highly thought provoking but also gives practical guidance on how to resolve problem behaviors effectively. It also suggests that nursing assistants may be both valuable sources of information on resident care and role models for fellow staff members.

Three training guides were published in 1994. The first was a videotape and manual entitled *Careguide for the Confused Resident* (Wylde, 1994), which was designed to teach nursing assistants (and others) how to respond to various types of confusion stemming from dementia. As in the first two videotapes discussed, training features the use of behavior modification, with lectures on how to identify triggers of problematic behavior and how to use reinforcers to shape more appropriate behavior. The lessons are divided into seven units which are intended to be taught in sequence, with each dependent on mastery of the units preceding it. Actors portray various characters, including nursing assistants struggling to work with residents and nonnursing assistants providing the answers for them.

The second manual, *The ABCs of Behavior Change: Skills for Working With Behavior Problems in Nursing Homes* (Cohn, Smyer, & Horgas, 1994), provides staff trainers with explicit lesson plans for teaching "nonlicensed staff" (including nursing assistants, dietary workers, and housekeeping staff) how to reduce or eliminate behavior problems among nursing home residents. Training topics, which are divided into five units, are directly relevant to resident care: how to communicate with nursing home residents, observe residents, guide them in developing less confused behavior, encourage less depressed behavior, and reduce agitated behavior. This program also concentrates on how to apply behavior modification techniques. The sixth and final unit of the manual discusses ways of applying training principles in the caregivers' personal lives.

The manual by Cohn and colleagues is designed for people with limited education; the material is presented in a concrete and highly structured fashion, and it is targeted to persons with fifth-grade reading ability. The manual includes homework assignments and handouts for the participants and recommends specific exercises to help them incorporate what they have learned in the classes into their actual work. As noted above, the manual grew out of a research study conducted by the authors.

Managing Behavioral Symptoms in Nursing Home Residents: A Manual for Nursing Home Staff (Taylor et al., 1994) has a wider focus, offering a range of treatment options rather than instructing trainees in just one approach. It is intended to help staff reduce their reliance on psychotropic medications, so it espouses primarily nonpharmacologic treatments such as modifying the environment, using touch, involving family members, and improving verbal and nonverbal communication skills. One particularly useful chapter provides specific management techniques for 20 of the most common behavioral symptoms seen in nursing homes. Recognizing that psychotropic medications are sometimes appropriate, the fifth and final chapter introduces basic information about common psychotropic medications, including their names, side effects, and the procedures recommended for helping people withdraw from them. The manual is intended for use by all levels of nursing staff, including nursing assistants.

The Paraprofessional in Home Health and Long-Term Care: Training Modules for Working with Older Adults (Cervantes et al., 1995) is a manual that is applicable to both institutional as well as home settings. It is divided into 11 separate training modules that cover such topics as normal aging, suicide in later life, stress, elder abuse, the effect of medications on older adults, dealing with death and dying, and understanding dementia. The authors, all of whom are social workers, recommend going through the modules in sequence but add that each module can be used independently. They estimate that a reasonable amount of time to teach each module is about 90 minutes.

While the manual was intended primarily to be used as an instructional guide by a designated trainer or leader, the authors add that nursing assistants may wish to have a copy for their own reference. **Cervantes and colleagues stand out in their emphasis on learning by doing rather than by listening to or watching others.** The manual devotes one section to principles of adult learning, in which the training leader is reminded of the problems they may encounter when using formal instructional methods to teach adults who have not been in school for years. Experiential exercises are recommended, especially practice sessions, role playing, and small group discussions. It does not offer direct guidelines, however, to help the students integrate the material into their daily work.

Caring for People with Alzheimer's Disease: A Training Manual for Direct Care Providers (Andresen, 1995) has a narrower focus: to teach people how to care for persons with dementia. However, it is aimed at a more diverse audience than many other manuals, including nurses, social workers, dietary workers, and family caregivers as well as nursing assistants. Andresen's manual is divided into seven units, each of which concentrates on a different facet of working with persons with dementia. Each unit takes approximately 50 minutes to teach to mastery. Each unit contains an extensive amount of information, and although the main thrust of the manual is didactic, each one ends with suggested learning activities that encourage active participation and sharing of ideas.

While they did not publish a training manual or videotape, Rantz and McShane (1995) reported on an unusual and interesting training program for nursing home staff working with residents with dementia. Rather than simply imparting factual information and behavior management techniques culled from outside "experts," they actively sought the ideas and suggestions of experienced staff who had direct care responsibilities with nursing home residents with dementia. Their experts included nursing assistants, nurses, recreational therapists, social workers, and occupational and speech therapists. These staff members generated many work-related suggestions and guidelines. The interventions they mention fall into four broad categories: interpreting reality, maintaining normalcy, meeting basic needs, and managing behavior disturbances. Numerous specific examples are provided for each category. **The information-rich results yielded by this approach point to the largely untapped potential of many highly experienced nursing assistants.**

Of all the training materials reviewed here, by far the most comprehensive is *The Long-Term Care Nursing Assistant Training Manual,* second edition (Anderson et al., 1996). It presents 34 modules written by 47 different contributors, all of whom have degrees in nursing. Each module contains detailed information on the roles and responsibilities nursing assistants need to master across a variety of domains. Many of the topics covered in this manual are not included in any of the other training materials reviewed thus far, such as first aid procedures and how to use restraints properly, care for residents' rooms, care for residents from other cultures, and make chart notes and other forms of documentation. While only 1 out of the 34 modules includes the term dementia in its title, the material covered in many of the other modules is clearly highly relevant to persons who work with residents who have dementia.

An additional strength of this manual is that each module ends with a test intended to help prepare students for the certification examination.

Although this manual is impressively rich in content, it lacks any teaching style other than the straightforwardly didactic; no learning exercises are proposed and no specialized teaching approaches are suggested. It appears that students are expected to simply read the text, which is dense and not broken up by illustrations. The material contained in the manual is very worthwhile, but it would be helpful to give students opportunities to discuss what they are learning and to share their reactions to it.

Another manual, which was first published in 1991 and then revised in 1996, was designed specifically to train nursing assistants (in both nursing homes and home care settings) to understand and work with persons with dementia better. Entitled *For Those Who Take Care: An Alzheimer's Disease Training Program for Nursing Assistants* (Helm & Wekstein, 1996), this manual is designed to be used as a guide for the instructor and is perhaps the most structured of all the guides reviewed thus far. Each of the eight learning sessions comes with an extensive amount of teaching materials, including lecture material that can be used verbatim. The focus in the lessons is on heightening the staff's awareness of the needs of persons with dementia. Learning is dependent on the leader. The total time needed to teach the material is estimated to be 8 hours, with lecturing as the primary method of teaching. The publishers advertise this manual as being especially useful for instructors with no experience in teaching.

Another set of training materials, *Training Manual and Video for Dementia Care Specialists* (Stehman et al., 1996), comes with two manuals (one for the instructor and one for the student) and a videotape (130 minutes). Both manuals contain very specific information that is organized into six learning modules, the first of which presents basic, factual information on dementia and the remaining five of which describe various ways of providing more positive experiences and interactions for persons with dementia. The videotape serves as a visual complement to training principles iterated in the manuals. Its emphasis is on targeting activities to levels that are appropriate to the individual with dementia and to topics of interest to them. A particularly useful idea that is mentioned is the "no-fail" activity, i.e., an activity that does not depend on skill or mastery to be enjoyable. The authors recommend that instructors be experienced in providing hands-on dementia care and in designing and implementing activity programs for patients with dementia. The intended audience includes physicians, nurses, administrators, nursing assistants, activity therapists, mental health and social work professionals, and family members.

Finally, *Speaking From Experience: Nursing Assistants Share Their Knowledge of Dementia Care* (Kramer et al., 1997) grew out of the interview study by Kramer and colleagues, which was described earlier. This manual differs from all the other published manuals reviewed so far, in that it is based exclusively on comments, ideas, and suggestions from nursing assistants themselves, and contains no material from "expert" psychologists, nurses, social workers, or other professionals. Some 25 categories of suggestions, all of which focus on the psychosocial aspects of dementia care, are presented in the manual. The presentation of each category includes a brief summary description followed by a list of quotations from the nursing assistants which exemplify the category. Following the suggestions is a section on both the stresses and the rewards of dementia care, again culled solely from the nursing assistants' comments. Photographs of the nursing assistants interacting with residents are used throughout, and an attempt is made to keep the manual as linguistically accessible as possible. The manual is intended to serve as a basis for peer-oriented (as opposed to "expert-oriented") training. It is accompanied by a trainer's guide, which offers a number of alternative ways to carry out such training. **The authors hope that a peer-oriented approach will make staff members more receptive to training, increase their motivation to implement ideas, and provide them with recognition for the difficult work they do.**

How Can Nursing Assistants Who Provide Dementia Care Be Supported in Their Work?

The provision of on-the-job support to nursing assistants to help them cope with the demands of their work can be considered a training technique with direct and ongoing applicability, for both staff and the residents they serve. While material from some of the manuals and videotapes already discussed could be adapted for staff support purposes, at least two authors have focused directly on support group approaches to working with nursing home staff.

Smith (1983) describes an ongoing problem–solving and support group program for both nurses and nursing assistants in which participants are encouraged to discuss problems they are having with particular residents and to share experiences, offer new ideas and, most importantly, support each others' feelings and reactions. Smith, a psychologist, also attends the meetings, sharing his own insights and concerns about residents and facilitating communication among the group members. A very strong effort is made to keep the comments nonjudgmental. The meetings are held every other week in the staff lounges on the nursing units and typically last 30 to 45 minutes. Although it often takes time to gather the group for the meetings, once they are started, participation and involvement are high. Smith reports that the meetings appear to contribute to a greater exchange of suggestions among staff, an increased level of psychological sophistication, stronger professional commitment, and increased feelings of validation.

Wilner (1993) also organized support groups for nursing assistants and produced a training manual and videotape entitled, *Working It Out: Support Groups for Nursing Assistants,* to describe how they were conducted. More than 200 nursing assistants participated in the groups, which were field-tested in 16 different facilities for 8 months and consisted of biweekly 1-hour sessions. The groups were led by professional leaders, either social workers or nurses with nursing home experience. Goals included reduction of staff stress and turnover, increased communication and exchange of ideas among employees at different levels of nursing, staff boosting of nursing assistants' self-esteem, improvement in nursing assistants' problem-solving abilities, and improved care for residents. Levels of stress and turnover among the participants in these support groups were compared with levels of stress and turnover among nursing assistants in 14 other nursing homes that did not receive the support group program.

A statistical analysis revealed that stress levels were not significantly reduced for the participants in the support group; Wilner attributes this to weaknesses in the measurement instrument and to the greater power of other untreated stress-inducing factors in the work environment. **On the other hand, differences in turnover rates were significant, with participants in the support groups being less likely than members of the control group to leave their jobs once the support groups had ended.** The author warns, however, that this result may have been skewed by the nonsystematic method of collecting data.

Despite the lack of strong empirical findings, Wilner's training manual contains much information that will be useful to anyone who is interested in establishing a support group, including practical considerations that are not found in any of the other training materials reviewed for this chapter (e.g., making sure everyone in the administrative "chain of command" is fully apprised of and supports the running of the group; using a meeting space with doors that close securely and an intercom that can be turned off; and asking group members open-ended, nonthreatening questions to facilitate their participation, among many other suggestions). The accompanying video (25 minutes) displays staged vignettes of typical support group meetings, with lively conversations among participating nursing assistants. The vignettes can be viewed singly or jointly. The videotape is intended both for managers, to better appreciate the rationale for and benefits of such groups, and for nursing assistants, to trigger discussion topics.

What Other Resources Offer Guidance in the Training of Dementia-Care Nursing Assistants?

Two other resources that may be useful for training are publications written specifically for nursing assistants. *The Journal of Nursing Assistants* focuses on nursing assistants' professional development and contains articles written by and for nursing assistants and home health aides. The primary goal of this journal is to enhance the nursing assistant's image and status within the healthcare environment. *The Nursing Assistant Monthly* is an outgrowth of research on nursing assistants in nursing homes. It offers nursing assistants in-service training modules on a range of QOL issues.

Conclusions and Recommendations

Awareness of the central role played by nursing assistants in providing care to nursing home residents with dementia has grown in recent years, along with recognition of the importance of training nursing assistants to prepare them for and support them in a difficult and demanding job. Accompanying this recognition has been the development of the numerous training manuals, videotapes, and programs described in this chapter.

These programs vary in a number of dimensions (Table 1), and these variations need to be considered when planning a training program to meet the needs of particular circumstances in particular facilities. These variations may also have a significant impact on the effectiveness of the training programs, although so far, we have only a little research to guide us on this question.

First, the training programs differ in their intended audience. Some are intended solely for nursing assistants and others for a wider audience of paraprofessionals or professionals, or even family members. The content of the programs also differs, with some focusing only on behavior management techniques or other psychosocial aspects of care and others including material on physical care and other issues as well. Similarly, some of the manuals and videotapes address only the care of people with dementia, whereas

Table 1

Features of Training Programs for Dementia Care Nursing Assistants

	Videotape/ Manual	For Nursing Assistant Only Y/N	Specific to Dementia Y/N	Psychological vs. Physical Focus	Didactic/ Other Teaching Style	Integration Work Setting Y/N	Expert vs. Peer-Oriented
Teri (1991)	V/M	N	Y	Psych	D	N	E
Univ. of Texas SW Med. Ctr. (1991)	V/M	Y	Y	Psych	D	N	E
O'Donnell (1993)	V	N	Y	Psych	O	N	P
Cohn (1994)	M	N	N	Psych	D/O	N	E
Taylor (1994)	M	N	N	Psych	D	N	E
Wilner (1994)	V/M	Y	N	Psych	O	Y	P

Table 1 (cont.)
Features of Training Programs for Dementia Care Nursing Assistants

	Videotape/ Manual	For Nursing Assistant Only Y/N	Specific to Dementia Y/N	Psychological vs. Physical Focus	Didactic/ Other Teaching Style	Integration Work Setting Y/N	Expert vs. Peer-Oriented
Wylde (1994)	V/M	N	Y	Psych	D	N	E
Andresen	M	N	Y	Psych	D/O	N	E
Cervantes (1995)	M	N	N	Psych	D/O	N	E
Rantz (1995)	★	N	Y	Psych	O	N	P
Anderson (1996)	M	Y	N	Physical	D	N	E
Stehman (1996)	V/M	N	Y	Psych	D/O	Y	E
Stevens (1997)	★★	Y	Y	Psych	D/O	Y	E
Kramer (1997)	M	Y	Y	Psych	O	N	P

others discuss the care of other groups as well, (e.g., nursing home residents in general or people being cared for at home).

An important way in which these programs differ is in their teaching style. Almost all of the manuals and videotapes use a primarily didactic style in which informational material is presented via readings, videotapes, or lectures and the nursing assistant is a passive recipient, expected to maintain close attention and understand and absorb the lesson. But the programs differ in how closely they follow this model, as some incorporate other teaching styles to a significant degree, including discussion, role-playing or other exercises, and on-the-job training. Only a few programs use a predominantly nondidactic teaching style, notably the support groups.

The training programs also vary in their inclusion of follow-up mechanisms to check on and/or reinforce on-the-job use of the ideas and techniques learned. Many of the programs encourage this but lack any provision for follow-up once the training period is over. The most notable exception is the program developed by Burgio and colleagues, which includes an elaborate, formal follow-up system designed to become a permanent part of the institutional routine. The support groups also deserve mention in this regard. While they do not constitute a formalized system of follow-up, they may function similarly, at least in part, because they are regular, ongoing, and permanent; are generally held on the nursing units; and include elements that encourage and reinforce improvements in the psychosocial aspects of resident care (usually with reference to specific residents), staff self-monitoring, and the setting of peer-group norms for quality care.

Almost all of the programs take their ideas, information, and principles of care from the work of various health care professions, but not from nursing assistants. Often these programs imply that nursing assistants, if left to themselves, are not capable of generating guidelines and principles of good care and thus need instruction from others; otherwise, they will provide only mediocre care, or worse. **Only a few programs take the ideas of nursing assistants as their primary source,**

thus embracing a peer-education model of training as opposed to a top-down, "expert leader" model.

Although little research has been done in this area, outcomes of the few published studies generally support the effectiveness of training in increasing nursing assistants' knowledge. There is also evidence from most of these studies that increased knowledge can result in improved job performance. Whether these improvements can be sustained over time is still unclear, however. **The work of Burgio and colleagues** (1990; Burgio et al., 1994; Stevens et al., 1997; Stevens et al., 1996) **suggests that long-term maintenance is possible only if some kind of management or support system is incorporated into the nursing homes' permanent routine and institutional structure.**

References

Administration on Aging. (1980). *Human resources in the field of aging: The nursing home industry* (USDHEW Pub. No. [OHDS] 80-20093). Washington, DC: Department of Health, Education, and Welfare.

Anderson, M., Beaver, K., & Culliton, K. (Eds.). (1996). *The long-term care nursing assistant training manual* (2nd ed.). Baltimore: Health Professions Press.

Andresen, G. (1995). *Caring for people with Alzheimer's disease: A training manual for direct care providers.* Baltimore: Health Professions Press.

Baltes, M. (1988). The etiology and maintenance of dependency in the elderly: Three phases of operant research. *Behavior Therapy, 19,* 3.

Bowers, B., & Becker, M. (1992). Nurses' aides in nursing homes: The relationship between organization and quality. *The Gerontologist, 32,* 360-366.

Brannon, D., & Bodner, J. (1988). The primary caregivers: Aides and LPNs. In M. Smyer, D. Brannon, & M. Cohn (Eds.), *Mental health consultation in nursing homes.* New York: New York University Press.

Burgio, L. D., & Burgio, K. L. (1990). Institutional staff training and management: A review of the literature and a model for geriatric, long-term care facilities. *International Journal of Aging and Human Development, 30,* 287–302.

Burgio, L. D., Engel, B., Hawkins, A., et al. (1990). A staff management system for maintaining improvements in continence with elderly nursing home residents. *Journal of Applied Behavior Analysis, 23,* 111–118.

Burgio, L. D., McCormick, K., Scheve, A., et al. (1994). The effects of changing prompted voiding schedules in the treatment of incontinence in nursing home residents. *Journal of the American Geriatrics Society, 42,* 315–320.

Caudill, M., & Patrick, M. (1991). Turnover among nursing assistants: Why they leave and why they stay. *Journal of Long Term Care Administration,* 19, 29–32.

Cervantes, E., Heid-Grubman, J., & Schuerman, C. K. (1995). *The paraprofessional in home health and long-term care: Training modules for working with older adults.* Baltimore: Health Professions Press.

Chafetz, P., Wilson, R., & West, H. (1991). *Nurse's aides—Making a difference: Skills for managing difficult behaviors in dementia victims. A viewing guide.* Dallas, TX. Southwestern Alzheimer's Disease Research Center, University of Texas Southwestern Medical Center, Dallas, TX.

Chappell, N. L., & Novak, M. (1992). The role of support in alleviating stress among nursing assistants. *The Gerontologist, 32,* 351–359.

Chartock, P., Nevins, A., Rzetelny, H., & Gilberto, P. (1988). A mental health training program in nursing homes. *The Gerontologist, 28,* 503–507.

Cohn, M. D., Smyer, M. A., & Horgas, A. L. (1994). *The ABCs of behavior change: skills for working with behavior problems in nursing homes.* State College, PA: Venture Publishing.

Crown, W. H. (1994). A national profile of home care, nursing home, and hospital aides. *Generations, 18,* 29–33.

Diamond, T. (1986). Social policy and everyday life in nursing homes: A critical ethnography. *Social Science and Medicine, 23,* 1287–1295.

Diamond, T. (1992). *Making gray gold: Narratives of nursing home care.* Chicago: University of Chicago Press.

Duffy, L. M., Hepburn, K., Christensen, R., & Brugge-Wiger, P. (1989). A research agenda in care for patients with Alzheimer's disease. *Image, 21,* 254–257.

Duncan, M. T., & Morgan, D. L. (1994). Sharing the caring: Family caregivers' views of their relationships with nursing home staff. *The Gerontologist, 34,* 235–244.

Feldman, P. H. (1994). "Dead end" work or motivating job? Prospects for frontline paraprofessional workers in LTC. *Generations, 18,* 5–10.

Foner, N. (1994a). *The caregiving dilemma: Work in an American nursing home.* Berkeley, CA: University of California Press.

Foner, N. (1994b). Nursing home aides: Saints or monsters? *The Gerontologist, 34,* 245–250.

Fontana, A. (1977). The last frontier. Beverly Hills, CA: Sage Publications.

Garland, T. N., Oyabu, N., & Gipson, G. A. (1988). Stayers and leavers: A comparison of nurse assistants employed in nursing homes. *Journal of Long-Term Care Administration, 3,* 23–29.

Gubrium, J. (1975). *Living and dying at Murray Manor.* New York: St. Martin's Press.

Harper, M. S. (1986). *Mental illness in nursing homes: Agenda for research.* Rockville, MD: National Institute of Mental Health.

Helm, B., & Wekstein, D. (1996). *For those who take care: An Alzheimer's disease training program for nursing assistants* (rev. ed.). Lexington, KY: Alzheimer's Disease Research Center, Sanders-Brown Center on Aging, University of Kentucky.

Hinrichsen, G. (1994). Audiovisual reviews: Alzheimer's disease and related disorders. *The Gerontologist, 34,* 430–432.

Institute of Medicine. (1986). *Improving the quality of care in nursing homes.* Washington, DC: National Academy Press.

Kayser-Jones, J. S. (1990). *Old, alone and neglected: Care of the aged in Scotland and the United States.* Berkeley, CA: University of California Press.

Kramer, N. A., Smith, M. C., Dabney, J., & Yang-Lewis, T. (1996, November). *Nursing assistants' conceptions of quality care for nursing home residents with dementia.* Paper presented at the Annual Meeting of the Gerontological Society of America, Washington, DC.

Kramer, N. A., Smith, M. C., Dabney, J., & Yang-Lewis, T. (1997). Speaking from experience: Nursing assistants share their knowledge of dementia care. Brooklyn, NY: Cobble Hill Health Center.

Lair, T., & Lefkowitz, K. (1990). *Mental health and functional status of residents of nursing and personal care homes* (DHHS Pub. No. 90-3470). Rockville, MD: Public Health Service.

Marion Merrell Dow. (1992). *Managed care digest: Long term care edition.* Kansas City, MO: Author.

Marion Merrell Dow. (1993). *Managed care digest: Long term care edition.* Kansas City, MO: Author.

Oberer, D. (1995). *Independence and dependence in activities of daily living: People with dementia and their caregivers.* Unpublished doctoral dissertation, Teachers College, Columbia University, New York.

O'Donnell, J. E., O'Donnell, P., & Global Village Communications. (1993). *Dress him while he walks: Behavior management in caring for residents with Alzheimer's disease* [video tape]. Chicago: Terra Nova Films.

Oliver, D., & Tureman, S. (1988). *The human factor in nursing home care.* Binghamton, NY: Haworth Press.

Pillemer, K., & Moore, D. (1989). Abuse of patients in nursing homes: Findings from a survey of staff. *The Gerontologist, 29,* 314–320.

Quinlan, A. (1988). *Chronic care workers: Crisis among paid caregivers of the elderly.* Washington, DC: Older Women's League.

Rantz, M. J., & McShane, R. E. (1995). Nursing interventions for chronically confused nursing home residents. *Geriatric Nursing, 16,* 22–27.

Rovner, B. W., Kafonek, S., & Filipp, L. (1986). Prevalence of mental illness in a community nursing home. *American Journal of Psychiatry, 143,* 1446–1449.

Savishinsky, J. (1991). *The ends of time: Life and work in a nursing home.* New York: Bergin & Garvey.

Schnelle, J. F., Newman, D., White, M., et al. (1993). Maintaining continence in nursing home residents through the application of industrial quality control. *The Gerontologist, 33,* 114–121.

Shields, R. (1988). *Uneasy endings: Daily life in an American nursing home.* Ithaca, NY: Cornell University Press.

Smith, M. (1983, November). *Problem-solving and support groups for nurses and aides in a nursing home.* Paper presented at the Annual Meeting of the Gerontological Society of America, San Francisco.

Smyer, M., Brannon, D., & Cohn, M. (1992). Improving nursing home care through training and job redesign. *The Gerontologist, 32,* 327–333.

Smyer, M., & Garfein, A. (1988). The mental health problems of nursing home residents. In M. Smyer, D. Brannon, & M. Cohn (Eds.), *Mental health consultation in nursing homes.* New York: New York University Press.

Smyer, M. A., & Wall, C. T. (1994). Design and evaluation of interventions in nursing homes. In C. B. Fisher & R. M. Lerner (Eds.), *Applied developmental psychology.* New York: McGraw-Hill.

Stehman, J. M., Strachan, G. K., Glenner, J. A., Glenner, G. G., & Neubauer, J. K. (1996). *Training manual and video for dementia care specialists.* Baltimore: Johns Hopkins University Press.

Stevens, A., Burgio, L. D., Bailey, E., et al. (1997). *Teaching and maintaining behavior management skills with nursing assistants in a nursing home.* Unpublished manuscript, Center for Aging, University of Alabama at Birmingham.

Stevens, A., Burgio, L. D., Burgio, K. L., et al. (1996, November). *Effects of a behavioral supervision model on CNA behavioral skills use.* Paper presented at the Annual Meeting of the Gerontological Society of America, Washington, DC.

Streit, A., & Brannon, D. (1994). The effect of primary nursing job design dimensions on caregiving technology and job performance in nursing homes. *Health Services Management Research, 7,* 271–278.

Taylor, J., Ray, W., & Meador, K. (1994). *Managing behavioral symptoms in nursing home residents: A manual for nursing home staff.* Nashville, TN: Vanderbilt University School of Medicine, Department of Preventive Medicine.

Tellis-Nayak, V., & Tellis-Nayak, M. (1989). Quality of care and the burden of two cultures: When the world of the nurse's aide enters the world of the nursing home. *The Gerontologist, 29, 307–313.*

Teri, L. (1991). *Managing and understanding behavior problems in Alzheimer's disease and related disorders* [videotape]. Baltimore: Health Professions Press.

U.S. Department of Labor. (1991). National industry-occupational matrix, 1990–2005. Washington, DC: Bureau of Labor Statistics.

University of Texas Southwestern Medical Center. (1991). *Nurse's aides—Making a difference: Skills for managing difficult behaviors in dementia victims.* [video tape] Dallas, TX: Author.

Waxman, H. M., Carner, E. A., & Berkenstock, G. (1984). Job turnover and job satisfaction among nursing home aides. *The Gerontologist, 24,* 503–509.

Wilner, M. A. (1993). *Working it out: Support groups for nursing assistants* [videotape and workbook]. Chicago: Terra Nova Films.

Wylde, M. A. (1994). *Careguide for the confused resident* [videotape]. Baltimore: Health Professions Press.

12

Interprofessional Health Care Teams

SUZANN M. OGLAND-HAND, PH.D.
and ANTONETTE M. ZEISS, PH.D.

Abstract

The goal of this chapter is to provide psychologists with education regarding the theory of interprofessional health care teams, and apply this theory to practice in a long term care setting. The three main objectives are to: (1) increase awareness of geriatric interprofessional health care team theory, types of teams, and a team development model and; (2) increase awareness of the functions of the professions needed for comprehensive geriatric long term care and; (3) increase awareness of direct practical issues within interprofessional health-care teams in long term care settings.

Introduction

As psychologists, we have been trained to focus not only on the symptoms our patients display but also on the "systems" from which they come and in which they currently reside. Never are the effects of social systems more obvious than when we assess and treat patients in long-term care. Residents in long-term care settings often suffer from complex and chronic problems; consequently, it is best that their treatment is provided by an interprofessional health care team. This chapter will focus on how the inter-professional health care team can have a positive effect on the lives and well-being of residents being treated in long-term care settings. The work of Zeiss and Steffen (1996), who have written on the theory and development of interdisciplinary health care teams in geriatrics and applied it in an international model (Zeiss & Steffen, 1998), will serve as the foundation for our discussion.

Interdisciplinary Health Care Teams: The Basic Unit of Geriatric Care

Zeiss and Steffen (1996) emphasize that the problems of geriatric patients are characteristically complex and chronic. These patients are characterized by their comorbidities, that is, by multiple health problems that limit their ability to function in significant ways (Manton, Cornelius & Woodberry, 1995). Geriatric residents in long-term care have been referred to as "poly-problem patients" (Borson, 1995) because of the multiple issues they present (e.g., more than one chronic medical illness; functional deficits; the need for assistance with two or more activities of daily living, such as, bathing, dressing, transferring, eating, or using the toilet; cognitive deficits; mental illness; and multiple medications). Thus, the model of patient care that can optimally manage such patients may be the interprofessional health care team (Zeiss & Steffan, 1996).

Health care teams are becoming the norm in geriatric residential settings. While only 54% of geriatric social workers in nonresidential settings are team members, more than 96% of those working in long-term care residential settings are team members (Poulin et al., 1994). Yet,

> *Saying that a group of health care providers is a "team" says very little because there are many different kinds of teams organized in different ways to perform different functions. A group that is a team shares a common workplace and set of patients, but teams differ among themselves in their membership composition, commitment to common goals, degree of collaboration in accomplishing team-related tasks, handling of leadership, and the kind of attention paid to team process (Zeiss & Steffen, 1996).*

Types of Teams:

Within geriatric literature and geriatric health care settings, frequent references are made to multidisciplinary and interdisciplinary health care teams. While the terms multidisciplinary team and *interdisciplinary* team are often used *interchangeably*, they differ in important ways. A *multidisciplinary team* is composed of practitioners from more than one discipline; this kind of team can offer a variety of services to patients. Each discipline does its own assessment of the patient, generates its own treatment plan, evaluates the patient progress, and refines the treatment plan according to the findings of each evaluation. Multidisciplinary teams are hierarchically organized. There is a designated program "chief," who is usually the highest ranking professional; unfortunately, other team members may feel tht they are responsible only for the clinical work of their discipline and need not share a sense of responsibility for program functions and team effectiveness.

The *interdisciplinary team* also consists of practitioners from more than one health care discipline. However, the disciplines work in a collaborative manner, not only to share information but also to develop a means of incorporating and assimilating data from the various disciplines involved. Team members share the responsibility of implementing a mutually developed treatment plan. Each team member must have a vast array of knowledge and skills—including skills in communication, role development, leadership, and conflict resolution—and be able to evaluate each case globally.

Team Development

The evolution of a cohesive and highly functional team has been described as involving four processes: forming, storming, norming, and performing (Tuckman, 1965; Zeiss & Steffen, 1996). **The team goes through the process of developing working relationships when a new member joins a team or when a program develops, expands, or is consolidated** (forming). Initially, team members are somewhat awkward with each other and may interact stiffly with each other. **As the team develops, conflicts about content issues are inevitable** (storming), **and the team has to develop successful methods of handling conflicts, process issues, and disagreements. When the team develops methods of addressing disagreements constructively, it can then develop working strategies, cohesiveness, and norms with which to govern itself** (norming). Finally, the team develops a high level of effectiveness; **it becomes expert at using these processes to make decisions and get work done** (*performing*). At that point, the team members experience a sense of commitment and belonging and are well focused on their task.

Interprofessional Health Care Teams: Application to Long Term Care

The interprofessional team is optimal for long-term care settings. Nonetheless, this model of care is implemented differently in different settings. Team theory does not state that there is a "correct" size or set of professions that should be represented on any team. Rather, it states that the team's membership should reflect the needs of the specific population being served and the resources available. **Furthermore, the care providers who are most important to the population being served should act in collaborative, integrative, and mutually respectful ways to provide coordinated, comprehensive care.**

Professions and Functions:

Residents in long-term care are served by a range of professions, including nursing, pharmacy, dietetics, social work, psychology, optometry, internal medicine, physical therapy, occupational therapy, speech therapy, recreational therapy, psychiatry, podiatry, and audiology. Each profession has specific training goals and a specialized and technical language. These professions also vary in the amount of training that is required to practice; this can influence the level of sophistication with which each type of practitioner approaches patient care. Therefore, the function of each profession varies in its effects on case conceptualization as well as the treatment implementation process (i.e., in deciding "what would be most helpful for a given patient in a given situation").

In order to make useful recommendations and provide more comprehensive care for a patient, psychologists in long-term care settings should (a) **be aware of the other professions** (b) **understand the functions of the other professions** (see Table 1)**, (c) know what are the professions and resources within that health care setting specifically, and** (d) **interact with other professionals in meaningful ways.**

Biomedical Model of Care:

Burgio and Scilley (1994) aptly describe the *biomedical model* of *care* in which most providers in long-term care settings have been trained, which includes extensive exposure to infection control, safety, minimum data set (see *Formal Encounters with Team Segments,* below), and care plans. In this model, the psychological needs of the residents are secondary to their medical needs and are seldom addressed directly. These authors have indicated the importance of training staff to address the psychological needs of the residents directly. The authors recommend moving toward the preferred *rehabilitation model of care* in which staff and residents have a different type of relationship, one that is geared toward maximizing the residents' ability to function. Training and team development will occur simultaneously. Without mutual understanding, interprofessional collaboration is impossible. As mutual understanding develops, the team follows the natural developmental pattern already described: forming, storming, norming, and performing.

Structure of the Long Term Care System:

The long-term care system is composed of residents, their families, and staff. The interactions among the system members can be described as a web.

Of all the members of this web, the staff forms the backbone of the organization (Daniel, Samuels & Reed, 1998). In addition to the direct care professionals described in Table 1, the staff includes the

Table 1

Functions of Geriatric Health Care Disciplines

Profession	Function
Audiology	evaluate hearing
Dietetics	evaluate nutritional status provide diet instruction for special foods and supplements
Medicine	provide physical care prescribe medication discuss Advance Directive with residents
Nursing, RN LPN NA/CNA	supervise direct care and medication distribution; distribute medication direct care
Occupational Therapy (OT)	assess environment, function, swallowing assess and increase ADL and activity function determine equipment needs instruct in energy conservation advise regarding home hazards, for discharge home
Optometry	evaluate eyesight conduct environmental assessments evaluate environmental strain, glare, inadequate light
Pharmacy	perform medication review facilitate pharmacy dispensing provide medication education monitor medication regimen
Physical Therapy (PT)	manage chronic pain (i.e., electrical stimulation, TENS, ultrasound, etc.) instruct on exercise (increase range of motion, increase strength, etc). provide orthotic/prosthetic training provide gait training

administrator or director of nursing (DON), the charge nurse, the medical director, the maintenance staff, and the housekeeping staff.

In long-term care settings, the staff is usually organized as a pyramid (Smyer, Brannon & Cohn, 1991) in which the individuals

Table 1 (cont.)
Functions of Geriatric Health Care Disciplines

Profession	Function
Podiatry	provide treatment of feet
Psychiatry	evaluate psychiatric illness prescribe psychotropic medication

Psychology	perform cognitive, affective, behavioral
	  and personality assessment provide
	psychotherapy (individual, family,
	  and group therapies)
	conduct behavioral interventions
	provide staff education regarding
	  psychological needs of residents
	clinical management strategies for
	  residents
	interactions with families
	self-care (i.e., stress management, etc.)

Recreation Therapy	perform leisure assessment coordinate meaningful and enjoyable activities

Social Work	facilitate use of community resources
	coordinate placement for discharge
	  planning
	provide family counseling; facilitate
	  family meetings for decision-making
	discuss Advance Directive with residents
	  and families
	provide outreach/marketing

Speech Pathology	evaluate and treat speech difficulties perform swallowing evaluation and treatment

at the top (director of nursing, medical director, etc.) have the most expertise and training but the least contact with residents. Staff members at the bottom of the hierarchy are responsible for most of the residential care (e.g., nurse's aides or nursing assistants) and have the least training.

The social climate of long-term care settings is largely determined by the interactions between the staff and residents (Zarit, Dolan & Leitsch, 1998). Within this context, psychologists can provide effective interventions through their participation in an interprofessional health care team.

Expect Interactions With Segments of Teams:

While it would be ideal if all the health care providers involved in resident care met routinely to share information about residents and collaborate on treatment plans, this seldom occurs. **As a psychologist in long-term care, you are part of an interprofessional health care team, but you will only have regular contact with "segments" of your team.** For example, you may receive a referral from the director of nursing to evaluate a resident directly, call a family member for additional background information, encounter the charge nurse or a nursing assistant in the hallway and ask for information about a patient, or collaborate with the occupational therapist about treatment for a specific patient. Your interactions with other professionals may not occur on a scheduled basis, but can occur nonetheless, especially when you initiate contact. When you begin a practice in a long-term care setting, the burden will be on you to initiate these contacts and to be available. As you become better established and integrated in that setting, the staff will begin to contact you more frequently regarding patient care issues.

"Formal" Encounters With Team Segments:

While routine meetings of the entire interprofessional health care team may not take place, opportunities for regular input to a segment of the team may exist, depending on the setting in which you are practicing.

Licensed facilities (i.e., skilled nursing facilities) are required by the Health Care Financing Administration (HCFA) to collect routine information about residents on admission; this information comprises the *Minimum Data Set* (MDS). Beginning in July 1998, licensed facilities began to implement the *Prospective Payment Sys-*

tem (PPS) which requires regularly scheduled reviews of MDS information about residents who receive Medicare. Typically, these reviews are scheduled 5, 14, 30, 60, and 90 days after admission. Information on residents who pay privately or use Medicaid must be reviewed 14 days and 90 days after admission. Subsequently, MDS reviews of data on each resident (regardless of payor) are required every 90 days or more frequently if there is any change in a resident's condition.

Some facilities use these treatment reviews as opportunities to gather "live input" on a regular basis from the nursing, medical, and rehabilitation staff, as well as primary caregivers. Other facilities use these meetings to review previously recorded information from the health care team and other professionals. Thus, the MDS review meetings can be opportunities for interaction with a large segment of the interprofessional health care team.

Some facilities hold *screening meetings,* during which information about individuals requesting admission is reviewed or screened. Screening meetings provide a valuable opportunity for psychologists to raise mental health issues and interact in helpful ways with other team members. Even if these meetings are not routinely scheduled, some type of admission process exists in most facilities. The facility may value the contribution of psychologists to various admission tasks, specifically (a) designing a good screening system, (b) reviewing information provided by a potential resident and family member that addresses mental health issues and broader biopsychosocial concerns, and (c) briefly interviewing new residents.

Another opportunity for psychologists to interact with a segment of the health care team is provided by *medication/behavior reviews* (Schmidt et al., 1998). According to the Omnibus Reconciliation Acts (OBRA 1987, 1989, and 1990), licensed facilities are now restricted in their use of antipsychotic medication for treating the behavioral complications of dementia. If a psychotropic drug is prescribed, psychosocial interventions must be conducted every 90 days to try to reduce the dosage and eventually discontinue the drug. This provides an opportunity for the psychologist to trial a behavioral treatment plan. Medication/behavior reviews can include the pharmacist, medical director, charge nurse, and psychologist. During the review, the resident's treatment plan is evaluated, with a particular focus on medication and behavior. The review provides a nice opportunity for psychologists to not only interact with other members of the interprofessional health care team but also to put a resident's behaviors in the psychosocial context of his or her life before admittance and the current living situation.

Finally, a regularly scheduled meeting takes place during the *shift change report*. This meeting is typically run by the charge nurse for the previous shift for the direct care staff (nursing assistants) on the present shift. By attending this meeting, the psychologist can determine the quality and amount of information that is typically passed on during staff interactions. Some psychologists also use this time to provide brief staff mini-in-services, either about a particular resident or on a particular topic.

Challenges for Team Work:

Psychologists practicing in the private sector are faced with reimbursement challenges. Those who practice in long-term care are likely to receive payment primarily from either of two sources: third-party fee-for-service payors, and/or through a pre-arranged contract with the facility, in which case they are paid with either facility-paid fees collected for services rendered, or through a retainer agreement (Lichtenberg & Hartman-Stein, 1997). Lichtenberg and Hartman-Stein (1997) provide an excellent overview on reimbursement issues.

Third-Party Payors

Many elderly payors who have private insurance also subscribe to Medicare. While each state and Medicare carrier has different guidelines regarding who can bill and for what services, Medicare (as well as other third-party payors) typically reimburses for a range of psychological services when they are provided by a fully licensed psychologist. Lichtenberg and colleagues (1998) perhaps most clearly address both the challenge of reimbursement for psychological services in long-term care facilities and the responsibility for coordination with the interprofessional team:

> *Most third-party payors require the full duration of treatment sessions to be spent in face-to-face contact with the patient and/or the patient's family, and that other important and necessary treatment-related time, such as consultation with staff, may not be third-party reimbursable. Psychologists are aware of their responsibility to spend adequate time in face-to-face treatment with each patient and to consult and coordinate with the interdisciplinary team (p. 124).*

Psychologists who work in long-term care facilities should contact the Medicare carrier, as carriers interpret reimbursement guidelines differently.

Facility Contracts

Direct negotiation of a contract with a facility—typically with the facility director or owner—is another avenue for reimbursement. These contracts can establish reimbursement through combinations of third-party fee-for-service arrangements, facility-paid fees for services rendered, retainer agreements, or some combination of the above (Lichtenberg & Hartman-Stein, 1997). They are based on the service provided and may focus on services that may not be third-party reimbursable yet are helpful for staff and residents (e.g., inservice or staff training and participation in treatment planning meetings, family support groups, etc.).

Some psychologists have not received adequate training regarding business or marketing skills (e.g., contract negotiation); however, such acumen is important and can be learned. To be successful in any marketing venture, the seller must be able to highlight the need (e.g., residents with mental health needs and staff training needs) for the buyer (e.g., the facility director or owner) and convince the buyer that the seller has the skills and abilities (i.e., training and experience in providing quality psychological services) to address the buyer's needs.

Direct Practice of Team Work: How to do This Work Well

To have successful interactions with interprofessional health care teams, the geropsychologist needs many skills beyond the scientist and practitioner training provided in most graduate programs. Interpersonal and intrapersonal skills are needed.

Maintain Posture of Inquiry, Curiosity, and Non-Defensiveness:

When interacting with other members of the interprofessional health care team, as when doing any clinical work, it is imperative to maintain a posture of inquiry, curiosity, and non-defensiveness. To work most effectively, it is important that the others see the psychologist as non-threatening and approachable. Skills used to provide good patient care can be easily used when care is provided through a treatment team. For example, when a patient with depression tells a psychologist that she is spending 22 hours a day in bed, the effective psychologist would typically not say, in an accusing manner, "Why do you do that? That doesn't make any sense at all!" Rather, the psychologist would educate the patient about symptoms of depression and help her create conditions that allow her to spend more time out of bed and engaged in pleasant activities.

The same is true when working with others on the treatment team. We begin to see that others become impassioned about issues for which we see little immediate relevance at first—the pharmacist who is concerned about a resident with a low sodium level or a "left shift"; the nurse who reports in frustration that it takes three people to help a resident to take a shower. In these situations, it may be helpful to ask about their concerns. For example:"Help me understand how a left shift affects Mr. Jones."

Through interactions with staff members from other professions, we begin to understand how our training has shaped us. We begin to realize that staff with limited training (e.g., nurse assistants or aids) may benefit from coursework or practical training in basic interviewing techniques (e.g., introducing oneself before beginning to work together; letting another staff person know what will be occurring as they work together), psychopathology (e.g., realizing that when a resident says, "I wish I were dead," it may indicate depression and that depression can be evaluated and treated), or behavior therapy (e.g., understanding that positive reinforcement can shape behavior in a more enjoyable way than negative reinforcement.

Therefore, to maximize effectiveness in long-term care settings, the psychologist should assume that each member of the treatment team is doing his or her best. Stated another way, staff persons are doing what makes sense to them given their training, background, and life experiences. **A posture of curiosity and inquiry is crucial when developing relationships and equally important in maintaining them.**

Case Study:

Mr. A, who has a progressive dementia, grabs the wrists of staff members when they try to change his Attends® geriatric diapers. During a direct observation of the nursing staff with Mr. A during an Attends change, the psychologist notes that (1) Mr. A is seated in a gerichair, (2) the staff pull the gerichair backwards into the shower room, (3) Mr. A exhibits a startled response, and (4) Mr. A then waves his hands and attempts to grab the staff persons, who are focused on the sole task of changing the wet Attends.

As a psychologist practicing in the context of an interprofessional care team, certain questions should immediately come to mind. How does the staff training of nursing assistants influence the "aggressive" behavior of Mr. A? As the psychologist, how do you respond to the referral for management of Mr. A's aggressive behavior?

After the observation and data collection are completed, the first intervention needs to be directed toward staff education. The psychologist should provide direct feedback about the following situational needs:

(1) **Making eye contact with Mr. A. and explaining the task to him** ("Mr. A, I am going to take you to the bathroom, and we are going to change your Attends.")

(2) **Describing what is happening to him during the process of providing care** ("Mr. A, I am wheeling you to the bathroom. Here's the bathroom. Now let's make you more comfortable, and get your wet Attends off. On the count of three, help me by standing up. 1–2–3–Stand. Good job. Now let me unzip your pants and pull them down. Now, I'm going to pull that wet Attend off, and put a dry one on. Now, help me pull your pants back up. I'll zip them, and then slowly let's sit you back down. There you go. Good job. Thanks for helping—and also for not grabbing my wrists.")

(3) **Positively reinforcing with genuine praise when he does something you want him to do again** ("Good job. Thanks for helping with this.")

When using this scenario, the psychologist needs to present the information in a non-defensive manner. Depending on the psychologist's relationship with staff members being trained, he or she can raise their awareness of the connections between the antecedent (pulling the chair backwards), behavior (startle response), and consequence (grabbing staff wrists) in this situation. But if these staff members feel intimidated by the psychologist and his or her presentation style, it will be difficult to persuade them to try the intervention. Ultimately, the staff may not ask the psychologist to help them with any other residents they perceive as "difficult" in the future.

Ask for Input:

By simply asking for input from other disciplines during team conferences, you can improve your rapport with other health professionals and improve your patient assessments by integrating the observations of others (Lichtenberg, 1998). Older adults in long-term care experience frequent episodes of depression and dementia. Therefore, when listening to reports from other disciplines, it is worthwhile to routinely ask other staff members specific questions about each patient: "Did you notice signs of depression?" "How well did he retain newly taught information?" (Lichtenberg, 1998).

Make Mental Health Problems Pertinent to the Tasks of Other Team Members:

Making mental health problems pertinent to the work performed by other team members is key to developing successful relationships with them (Lichtenberg, 1998). As psychologists, we are concerned about depression in a resident, but why would another staff person be? A resident's depression can make the life of a direct care staff person challenging. Perhaps the resident is grumpy and irritable during activities of daily living (ADL) care, or has constant complaints about the care the nursing assistant is providing, or is tearful, feeling hopeless, and voices repeated wishes for life to end. If the resident can control his or her depression, the rest of the treatment team will benefit. If a resident were no longer depressed, he or she would probably participate more actively and therefore be more cooperative during ADL care, complain less about the nursing assistant, and be less tearful and perhaps more hopeful about the future. Efforts that impact the practical and functional needs of a given resident will directly affect the day-to-day work of other members of the staff.

Develop a Good Working Relationship with the Director of Nursing and the Administrator:

Developing a good working relationship with the director of nursing (DON) and the facility administrator is essential for long-range effectiveness in a long-term care. Administrators and DONs typically have a very limited view of what psychologists can do to help them (Crose & Kixmiller, 1994). Let the DON know about the work you are doing, the residents you are seeing, the changes you notice about them (within the limits of confidentiality), and the effect this is having on the facility. It is clear that DONs and administrators comprise an important link to a "market" with many needs that can be served effectively by psychologists.

It is also important to clarify with the DON where and how you will receive referrals. For example, will referrals be coming from the DON, the medical director, a primary care physician, a family member, the social worker, the charge nurse, or nursing assistant? Are your referrals to be left with someone else? Do you accept referrals by word of mouth on the unit or written on a clipboard at the nursing station? This procedure should be clearly outlined by the two of you.

The theoretical work of Daniel and colleagues (Daniel, Samuels & Reed, 1998) suggests that interventions and work by psychologists for residents, families, and staff "...helps create a friendly, caring, and welcoming environment, which in turn can translate into higher admission rates, longer retention periods for staff, and more cooperative families" (p. 4). While additional empirical studies demonstrating that these relationships are needed, this hypothesis is plausible and supported by the experience of many who practice in long-term care. Discuss this hypothesis with the DON, and ask how you could help have this impact in the local setting.

Take Advantage of Multiple Sources of Information:

When providing assessment and evaluation, take advantage of the many sources of information provided by members of the interprofessional team. For example, it is important to know if the resident's records are open records, (i.e., whether the progress notes in a resident's chart the only copy that exists). In some settings, nurses keep "nursing notes" separate from the official resident record. (This is an issue of particular concern in unlicensed facilities.) For this reason, you may want to ask the DON and nursing staff specific questions about medical records in your facility:"What medical records are available?""Is there a recent history and physical on file?" "Is a record of the resident's diagnosis and how it was obtained available?" "What are the recent/current lab values?" "What medications is the resident taking?" "Why is the resident in long-term care?"

This information will give you a more comprehensive understanding of the resident, the care he or she is being provided, and other professionals' understanding of this resident's problems and concerns. It may also help you develop hypotheses for follow-up with other staff members.

Case Vignette:

Mrs. B has not been her usual self. The staff indicates that she is confused and seeing and talking with her deceased husband in her room. Prior to a face-to-face evaluation of the resident, you review her chart. Nursing notes indicate a reduction of fluid intake and a further review indicates that no lab tests have been taken for some time.

As the psychologist, how do you proceed in ruling out delirium? Your clinical interview suggests findings consistent with a delirium. You may decide to discuss your hypothesis with the physician and inform the nurse in charge or suggest that the nurse contact the physician. Given your findings, you believe that laboratory tests are necessary to rule out dehydration. You and the physician also suggest that the staff begin pushing fluids and monitor her input and output. The next day, her lab results suggest that she is dehydrated. Mrs. B is then taken to the emergency department and given IV fluids. Within a short time, she stops having visual hallucinations of her deceased husband.

As the psychologist in this case, if you had not reviewed the chart notes or lab work, you could easily have headed down the wrong diagnostic path, hypothesizing a diagnosis of depression with psychosis or dementia with psychosis, which would have led to a vastly different treatment plan than. With only clinical patient information available, these might be realistic diagnoses; but ultimately, the patient is best served by a staff that reviews chart information recorded by other professionals to inform an interview, diagnosis, and treatment process.

Be Available:

By being available at regular times, the staff (and residents) **will learn when they can expect you.** If this is not possible, let the staff know your schedule. By keeping to a schedule, you let the staff know that you are consistent, predictable, and available.

In-services: Be Clear and Realistic About Goals:

Practical experience and empirical data clearly demonstrate that the attendance of nursing assistants at a single in-service session ("next Tuesday Dr. Smith will present an in-service on behavior management") does not promote change in staff behavior. Burgio and Scilley (1994) provide evidence that a change in staff behavior (which has a direct impact on care of residents) (a) is linked with consistent in-services with specific goals (e.g., incontinence training), and (b) must be linked to their work performance.

Because time is limited for everyone, it is important to focus on what we as psychologists know will benefit the larger system. For example, providing individual treatment to a depressed resident who is described by the staff as resistive during ADL care will probably help this resident, as well as the staff working directly with this resident. However, it is a time-consuming activity. **A greater impact may be made by working with the team. For example, you can teach the administrative staff how to attend to the psychological needs of all the residents. You can design and implement effective training programs for all direct care staff to increase their sensitivity to the residents' psychological concerns.** This can affect the entire facility, including the resident-staff-family web. This is not to say that individual treatment is unimportant. Our intent is to highlight the importance of psychologists finding ways to influence larger systems in long term care as well as individual patients.

As you begin to look for ways to address systems-related issues, you may find that one-shot in-services may have some value. By providing an in-service or a free lecture on some aspect of patient care (e.g., depression in the elderly or behavioral management of problems in dementia), you may strengthen your relationship with residents, staff, and family members. You may be able to demonstrate that you are a clear communicator, available and approachable, and able to help the staff address issues to which they have had little exposure (i.e., psychological issues). You may also improve relationships among team members.

Conclusion

As psychologists, we are teachers and communication experts. We provide education about the evaluation and interpretation of behavior, demonstrate our ability to develop collegial and collaborative relationships with staff (and residents and family members), and demonstrate ways to increase productive, useful communication with staff and residents.

As psychologists, we also value an experimental approach. We realize the value of an N=1 study, and in a sense, each referral that is sent to us is an opportunity for such a study. As we demonstrate the relationship between the interventions and changes in a resident's behavior, we lay the groundwork for the rest of the staff to learn this experimental approach and apply it to similar situations that arise in the future.

Although, "by definition, no single person can make a group become an interdisciplinary team" (Zeiss & Steffen, 1996), the psychologist can foster the development of an interprofessional health care team, especially by bringing the concept to the table and trying to generate shared enthusiasm for it.

Interprofessional teams ultimately depend on and are the embodiment of a powerful principle: people support what they help create. A group can become an interdisciplinary team only if the group members decide that they want to take on the responsibilities of shared leadership and interdependence (Zeiss & Steffen, 1996).

References

Borson, S. (1995). Models in psychiatric settings. *Paper Presentation at VA Conference managing the geriatric patient with combined medical and psychiatric problems: Beyond "keep away,"* Menlo Park, CA.

Burgio, L.D., & Scilley, K. (1994). Caregiver performance in the nursing home: The use of staff training and management procedures. *Seminars in Speech and Language. 15*(4):313–322.

Crose, R., & Kixmiller, J.S. (1994). Counseling psychologists as nursing home consultants: What do administrations want? *The Counseling Psychologist, 22*(1):104–114.

Daniel, S.A., Samuels, R.M., & Reed, J. (1998). *Psychologists: Consultants for interdisciplinary care teams in long-term care facilities.* Poster presented at 106th Annual Meeting of the American Psychological Association, San Francisco, CA.

Lichtenberg, P.A. (1998). *Mental health practice in geriatric health care settings.* New York: The Haworth Press.

Lichtenberg, P.A., & Hartman-Stein, P.E. (1997). Effective geropsychology practice in nursing homes. *In: Innovations in clinical practice: A source book.* (Vol. 15, pp. 265–281). Sarasota, FL: Professional Resources Press/Professional Resource Exchange.

Lichtenberg, P.A., Smith, M., Frazer, D., Molinari, V., Rosowsky, E., Crose, R., Stillwell, N., Kramer, N., Hartman-Stein, P., Qualls, S.H., Salamon, M., Duffy, M., Parr, J., Gallagher-Thompson, D. (1998). Standards for psychological services in long-term care facilities. *The Gerontologist, 38*(1):122–127.

Manton, K.G., Cornelius, E.S., & Woodbury, M.A. (1995). Nursing home residents: A multivariate analysis of their medical, behavioral, psychosocial and service use characteristics. *Journal of Gerontology,* 50:242–251.

Poulin, J.E., Watler, C.A., & Walker, J. (1994). Interdisciplinary team membership: A survey of gerontological social workers. *Journal of Gerontological Social Work, 22*(1/2):93–107.

Schmidt, I., Claesson, C.B., Westerholm, B., Nilsson, L.G., & Svarstad, B.L. (1998). The impact of regular multidisciplinary team interventions on psychotropic prescribing in Swedish nursing homes. *Journal of the American Geriatrics Society, 46*;77–82.

Smyer, M.A., Brannon, D., & Cohn, M. (1991). Improving nursing home fare through training and job resign. *The Gerontologist, 32*:327–333.

Tuckman, B.W. (1965). Developmental sequence in small groups. *Psychological Bulletin, 64*:384–399.

Zarit, S.H., Dolan, M.M., & Leitsch, S.A. (1998). Interventions in nursing homes and other alternative living settings. In: I.H. Nordus, G.R. VandenBos, S. Berg, & P. Fromholt, Eds. *Clinical geropsychology.* Washington, DC: American Psychological Association.

Zeiss, A.M., & Steffen, A.M. (1998). Interdisciplinary health care teams in geriatrics: An international model. In: A.S Bellack & M. Hersen (Eds.), *Clinical Geropsychology of Comprehensive Clinical Psychology.* London: Pergomon Press.

Zeiss, A.M., & Steffen, A.M. (1996). Interdisciplinary health care teams: The basic unit of care. In: L.L. Carstensen, B.A. Edelstein, & L. Dornbrand, eds. *The practical handbook of clinical gerontology.* Thousand Oaks, CA: Sage Publications.

Zeiss, R.A. (1997). Interdisciplinary treatment and training issues in the acute inpatient psychiatry unit. *Journal of Interprofessional Care, 11*(3):279–286.

13

Basic Psychopharmacology in the Nursing Home

MORGAN L. LEVY, M.D.,
and HEATHER UNCAPHER, PH.D.

Abstract

PSYCHIATRIC SYMPTOMS are very common in the nursing home. When not caused by life-long psychiatric illness, these symptoms are usually the result of medical or neurological problems. This chapter is designed to help non-physicians identify patients for whom a medication might be beneficial. Common psychiatric symptoms include depression, anxiety, psychosis, agitation, apathy, euphoria, disinhibition, irritability, aberrant motor behavior, insomnia, appetite change, and cognitive impairment. Some medical conditions that frequently cause psychiatric symptoms in the nursing home include urinary tract infection, pulmonary infection, hypothyroidism, heart disease, hearing or vision impairment, skin ulcers, and constipation. Some frequent neurologic causes include Alzheimer's disease, strokes and other vascular causes of dementia, frontotemporal dementias, Parkinson's disease, and Huntington's disease. Patients in the nursing home often require both pharmacologic and non-pharmacologic treatments for psychiatric symptoms, so it is important to know which patients are likely to benefit from a pharmacologic approach.

Introduction

Psychiatric symptoms occur in 80% to 90% of nursing home residents (Rovner et al., 1986, 1990; Parmelee et al., 1989; Tariot et al., 1993). **Symptoms may include depression, anxiety, psychosis, agitation, apathy, euphoria, disinhibition, irritability, aberrant motor behavior, sleep disturbance, appetite change and cognitive impairment. These symptoms may be caused by medical illness, degenerative brain disease, or psychiatric disorders such as schizophrenia, bipolar disorder, major depression, obsessive-compulsive disorder, panic disorder, generalized anxiety disorder, somatization disorder, substance abuse, or antisocial personality disorder.** These psychiatric disorders are well described in Kaplan and Sadock's *Comprehensive Textbook of Psychiatry VI* (Kaplan & Sadock, 1995) and are further delineated for the geriatrician in Sadavoy and colleagues' *Comprehensive Review of Geriatric Psychiatry II* (Sadavoy et al., 1996). This chapter will focus on pharmacological treatments for psychiatric symptoms when they are caused by medical and neurodegenerative conditions in the nursing home setting.

This chapter is intended for psychologists so a detailed description of how to use each drug is not necessary. Rather, the authors will present a general overview of which symptom presentations might lead to a trial of a pharmacologic agent. Should a more detailed understanding of these medications be desired, the practitioner is referred to the *American Psychiatric Press Textbook of Psychopharmacology, Second Edition* (Schatsberg & Nemeroff, 1998) or *Comprehensive Review of Geriatric Psychiatry II* (Sadavoy et al., 1996). Most nonphysicians who care for geriatric residents have important questions about medications, especially when they have encountered a hard to treat psychiatric symptom in a given patient. Therefore, this chapter is organized by presenting symptoms. Under each symptom there will follow a brief description of the clinical settings in which the symptom might occur, followed by a basic discussion of medications that may be used to treat the symptom. The primary goal of this chapter is to provide some basic understanding of when psychopharmacological interventions might be helpful in a medically ill or demented nursing home resident.

Prescribing medications to older adults, especially when medical illness or dementia is present, requires special considerations. First, the maxim "start low and go slow" should generally be applied. Second, anticholinergic side effects, which may not be a problem in younger adults, may cause severe confusion or delirium in a patient with mild dementia. Many medications have this side effect and such drug-drug interactions may cause a problem. **Third, geriatric patients often have a reduced ability to maintain adequate blood pressure when standing up and many medications make this condition worse, leading to dizziness and falls. Fourth, neuroleptic medications used to treat psychosis can cause severe rigidity, akathisia, and increased risk of tardive dyskinesia in the elderly, especially in demented populations. Fifth, older patients have an increased ratio of fat to muscle, so medications that are stored in fatty tissue may take longer to reach steady states, thereby taking longer to leave the body when discontinued. Finally, renal clearance is usually decreased in the elderly; this is one reason that geriatric patients require smaller doses of most drugs.**

Depression

Major depression occurs in 12% to 16% of the nursing home population, and other depressive disorders exist in 30% to 35% of residents (Weissman et al., 1991; Parmelee et al., 1989; Rovner et al., 1986). Myocardial infarction, chronic obstructive pulmonary disease, malignancies, and endocrinological disorders (i.e., hypothyroidism) are medical conditions that are frequently associated with depression. Vascular dementia may be associated with a 25% prevalence of depression (Cummings & Sultzer, 1993), and strokes are associated with a 30% to 50% prevalence (Sharpe et al., 1990; Eastwood et al., 1989; Ebrahim et al., 1987; Robinson & Price, 1982).

Parkinson's disease may be associated with a 41% rate of depression; half of these patients have major depression and the other half have minor depression (Starkstein et al., 1990). Other neurodegenerative disorders that are associated with depression include traumatic brain injury, Huntington's disease, and Alzheimer's disease (Starkstein and Robinson, 1993).

Regardless of the cause, depression is a treatable condition. Once the underlying medical condition has been treated, residual depression may respond to a variety of antidepressants or to electroconvulsive therapy. Vegetative symptoms such as poor appetite, insomnia, decreased libido, and fatigue may be caused by a primary depression and/or an underlying medical or neurodegenerative condition. It may be more helpful to focus the assessment on symptoms such as feelings of hopelessness, guilt, worthlessness, suicidal ideation, and tearfulness because these cognitive symptoms are more likely to be caused by depression alone. However, older adults are more likely to experience weight loss, psychomotor disturbance, and hypochondriasis when depressed, rather than guilt and sadness (Caine et al., 1993) so the differential diagnosis can be difficult. Psychosocial stressors may or may not be present. Regardless of etiology, an antidepressant may be helpful if the symptoms are consistent all day, on most days, and have been present for two or more weeks.

Depression in the nursing home setting is often chronic and persistent (Parmelee et al., 1992) and can be associated with hopelessness and suicidal ideation (Uncapher et al., 1998; Uncapher et al., 1998). Even if there is no life-threatening attempt, suicidal ideation alone is a source of morbidity in these residents. Antidepressant pharmacotherapy is underused in this country and physicians are generally not up to date on the latest treatments. **Newer medications like the selective-serotonin reuptake inhibitors** (Prozac®, Zoloft®, Paxil®, Luvox®, and Celexa®) **are easy to administer and have few side effects.** It is very important to treat geriatric depression because it is associated with increased medical morbidity, mortality, service use, hospitalization, and overall health care cost (Samuels & Katz, 1995).

Antidepressant therapy generally requires two weeks before any improvement can be seen. Patients who get better in a few days are experiencing an initial placebo response. The patient's mood will generally continue to improve for the next 6 to 8 weeks. If there is no response after 4 to 6 weeks on the same medication, then a second antidepressant from a different class of agents should be tried. All antidepressants demonstrate relatively equal efficacy but vary considerably in side effect profiles. Patients who have major depression respond to an initial trial of antidepressant therapy at a rate of about 60%; however, this rate increases to about 70% to 80% if the patient is given a second trial with a different agent. If two trials of antidepressants fail, then the patient should be referred for electroconvulsive therapy (ECT) which is the safest and most effective treatment. Unfortunately, patients cannot be sent home on ECT and, therefore, medications are generally preferred. An episode of major depression usually lasts from several weeks to 6 months, but can last up to one year. Patients who have medical or neurologic illness are generally screened out of clinical trials involving these agents and we do not know how long they should be treated or how recurrent the depression is in these settings (see Table 1).

Anxiety

Anxiety is the most frequent psychiatric disturbance in the geriatric population. New onset of anxiety in late life is usually secondary to a medical or neurodegenerative condition, but many people have long-standing disorders, such as phobic disorders, panic disorder, or generalized anxiety disorder. Anxiety is a heightened state of arousal that has been triggered inappropriately. Symptoms may include fear, worry, restlessness, palpitations, sweating, trembling, shortness of breath, chest pain, dizziness, nausea, feeling of unreality, or numbness.

Cardiac, pulmonary, endocrine, or neurologic conditions may produce symptoms such as chest pain, shortness of breath, numbness, tingling, or syncope that might be confused with anxiety but may require emergent attention. **Chronic anxiety in a geriatric** resident may be due to any medical condition, but conditions frequently associated with severe anxiety include **chronic obstructive pulmonary disease, chronic pain, acute infections** (especially urinary or respiratory), **and endocrine disease.** Medications are also frequent causes of anxiety and the most common offenders include decongestants, respiratory inhalers, neuroleptics (e.g., Haldol®, Risperidone®, Zyprexa®),

Table 1
Commonly Prescribed Psychotropics in the Nursing Home

Name	SideEffects	Indications
Antidepressants		
Zoloft® (sertraline) 50–100 mgs in the AM	headache, GI distress, tremor, sexual dysfunction	depression, panic disorder, obsessive-compulsive disorder
Pamelor® (nortriptyline) 25–150 mgs at bedtime	constipation, dizziness, dry mouth, heart block, sexual dysfunction	depression, panic disorder
Wellbutrin® (bupropion) 100–200 mg twice per day	seizures, agitation, dry mouth insomnia, nausea, constipation, tremor	depression, smoking cessation
Remeron® (mirtazapine) 15–30 mgs at bedtime	sedation, antihistamine effect, weight gain	depression
Anxiolytics		
Klonopin® (clonazepam) 0.5–2 mg twice per day	sedation, dizziness, addictive, withdrawal	generalized anxiety disorder panic disorder, anxiety secondary to a general medical condition
Ativan® (lorazepam) 0.5–1 mg three or four times per day	sedation, dizziness, addictive, withdrawal problems	generalized anxiety disorder, panic disorder, anxiety

steroids,   thyroid replacement, amphetamines, or withdrawal from sedatives, hypnotics, or alcohol.

Any neurodegenerative condition may be associated with anxiety, and there has been little systematic study to determine the association of this symptom with specific disorders. **Cerebrovascular illness, Parkinson's disease and Huntington's disease are frequently associated with anxiety, but other degenera-**

Table 1 (cont.)
Commonly Prescribed Psychotropics in the Nursing Home

Name	Side Effects	Indications
Buspar® (buspirone) 5-20 mgs twice per day	dizziness, GI distress, non-addictive, 2-3 weeks until onset of action	generalized anxiety disorder, panic disorder, anxiety secondary to a general medical condition
Cognitive Enhancers		
Aricept® (donepezil) 5-10 mgs at bedtime	nausea, diarrhea, insomnia, fatigue, muscle cramps, anorexia	Alzheimer's Disease
Neuroleptics		
Haldol® (haloperidol) 0.5-10 mgs at bedtime	TD, NMS, EPS, dizziness, akathisia, somnolence	psychotic symptoms
Risperdal® (risperidone) 0.5-6 mgs at bedtime	TD, NMS, EPS, dizziness, akathisia, somnolence	psychotic symptoms
Zyprexa® (olanzapine) 2.5-15 mgs at bedtime	TD, NMS, EPS, dizziness, akathisia, somnolence	psychotic symptoms
Stimulants		
Ritalin® (methylphenidate) 5-10 mgs in the morning	stimulation, appetite loss, addictive	apathy

tive diseases, especially those that produce depression or psychosis, may also cause anxiety.

Treatment of anxiety in the nursing home is largely focused on alleviating the already mentioned conditions. If significant anxiety remains and it is primarily situational, then nonpharmacologic means of control are usually more effective, and can be considered the first line treatment. However, constant anxiety can be effectively

Table 1 (cont.)
Commonly Prescribed Psychotropics in the Nursing Home

Name	Side Effects	Indications
Sleep Aids		
Desyrel® (trazadone) 50-100 mgs at bedtime	drowsiness, dizziness, non-addictive	insomnia
Restoril® (temazapam) 7.5-30 mgs at bedtime	drowsiness, dizziness, addictive	insomnia
Ambien® (zolpidem) 5-10 mgs at bedtime	drowsiness, dizziness, non-addictive	insomnia

NMS (neuroleptic malignant syndrome) – an idiosyncratic reaction to neuroleptics that is potentially life- threatening.

TD (Tardive dyskinesia) – a permanent movement disorder caused by neuroleptic mediation.

EPS (extrapyramidal symptoms) – stiffness and rigidity caused by too high a dose of a neuroleptic medication.

treated with benzodiazepines. Longer-acting preparations such as Klonopin are preferable, but these drugs can be sedating, disinhibiting, and addictive. Buspar can be an effective nonaddictive anti-anxiety medication, but it takes several weeks to work and is not always effective. Anti-seizure medications, beta-blocking anti-hypertensives, and antidepressants with strong anti-histamine effects such as Trazadone® and Remeron are under investigation as anti-agitation agents and may also reduce anxiety in nursing home residents.

Psychosis

Hallucinations are false sensory perceptions, usually visual or auditory. Delusions are false beliefs and are commonly of the paranoid, grandiose, somatic, persecutory, and religious types. Older adults may have poor vision from cataracts or hearing impairment so it must be determined that their symptom is truly psychotic and not merely an illusion. When an older adult becomes psychotic for the first time, it is usually due to an underlying medical condition, medication, or dementing illness. In the nursing home, urinary and respiratory infections often cause delirium that can produce psychotic symptoms. Medications that may cause psychotic symptoms include anti-Parkinsonian agents, anticholinergics (Benadryl®, Cogentin®), amphetamines and steroids.

Lilliputian hallucinations sometimes occur when a geriatric person sees small animals or small cartoon-like people. These hallucinations are usually not frightening and may not be associated with any specific pathology. **Nursing home residents who report single, simple hallucinations** (seeing dead relatives, hearing voices), delusions (theft, spouse is unfaithful), **or misidentifications** (house is not their home, relatives are impostors) **may have Alzheimer's disease.** Delusions are present in 30% to 40% and hallucinations in 10% to 30% of Alzheimer's disease patients (Mendez et al., 1993; Wragg & Jeste, 1989). Vascular dementia is also associated with a high incidence of psychosis (Flynn et al., 1991; Cummings et al., 1987). Psychosis in a Parkinson's disease patient may herald the onset of dementia or may result from overmedication.

Underlying medical conditions causing psychotic symptoms need to be treated and medications require proper adjustment. Residual psychotic symptoms are likely due to a dementing illness. In Alzheimer's disease, these symptoms may fluctuate over time, but are likely to recur (Levy et al., 1996a). **Use of neuroleptic medication is more difficult in the demented population because they are more susceptible to rigidity, akathisia** (feeling that they must be in motion), **and tardive dyskinesia** (a permanent movement disorder). It is preferable to target a resident's distress level and not necessarily the degree of psychosis. Delusions and hallucinations in demented residents are often not distressful and may not require pharmacotherapy at all. When therapy is required, the newer drugs like Risperdal® and especially Zyprexa® are far superior due to their improved side effect profile. Aricept® is a new memory-enhancing medication that is specifically indicated for Alzheimer's disease but may also reduce psychotic symptoms (Kaufer et al., 1996).

Agents used to treat psychotic symptoms in the elderly may be administered in much smaller doses than are generally given to younger patients with schizophrenia. Anticholinergic medications, which are commonly given to treat side effects from neuroleptics, are relatively contraindicated because they may cause confusion in these patients. Response to antipsychotics can be seen in 1 to 7 days and the medication can often be reduced somewhat after 1 to 2 weeks. These symptoms will fluctuate over time but treatment should continue uninterrupted because these symptoms are very likely to recur (Levy, 1996a).

The Omnibus Budget Reconciliation Act of 1987 (OBRA) places restrictions on the use of neuroleptic medication in Medicaid and Medicare financed nursing facilities. A physician must document symptoms and reevaluate the need for these medications every six months. This policy has led to significant reductions in neuroleptic prescriptions without adverse effects on patients' quality of life. Neuroleptics are primarily indicated for psychosis but have been overused for nonpsychotic agitation. It can be difficult to determine if a dementia patient is psychotic when they are non-communicative, but there are several anti-agitation agents discussed later that are free of the hazardous side effects which neuroleptics possess when used in this population.

Agitation

Nursing home residents become agitated for many reasons. Nonspecific yelling, wandering, and resisting care are common behaviors in the nursing home setting. The resident may be distressed due to pain, difficulty communicating, or to a medical or psychiatric illness. Any acute agitation in a nursing home resident should result in an intense medical work-up. If the agitation is chronic, despite medical conditions having been stabilized, then the presence of a dementing illness is likely.

If the resident only becomes agitated in certain situations, such as having his or her clothes changed or receiving a bath, then pharmacologic approaches may be less helpful. **If there is an underlying level of anxiety or depression and these can be treated, then the agitation may be reduced.** Neuroleptics may be effective if there is a true psychosis, but they are often over-prescribed and can cause akathisia or rigidity. Beta-blocking anti-hypertensive agents such as Propranolol® have been shown to be safe and effective; however, physicians are frequently reluctant to use high doses of these agents in an elderly resident due to potential cardiovascular complications. Trazadone has demonstrated efficacy comparable to Haldol in treating agitation in demented subjects and is well tolerated at high doses with few side effects. (Sultzer et al., 1994). Remeron may reduce agitation through an antihistamine effect similar to Trazadone but with once per day dosing. Anti-seizure agents such as Depakote® and Tegretol® may also have a role in treating nonpsychotic agitation in residents with dementia.

Apathy

Apathy is defined as diminished motivation not attributable to decreased levels of consciousness, cognitive impairment, or emotional distress (Marin, 1990). Apathy is highly prevalent in the nursing home but has received little attention because apathetic residents are generally cooperative and do not seem distressed. One could argue that it should not be treated, but treatment could significantly improve quality of life. Apathy is traditionally viewed as a symptom of depression; it is probably a clinically distinct entity (Levy et al., 1998) with a different pathophysiology.

Numerous medical conditions cause residents to feel fatigued or tired, but residents usually retain their ability to feel happy or sad and to become motivated at appropriate times. Severely apathetic residents probably have some degree of brain injury. Frontotemporal dementia and progressive supranuclear palsy have the most severe apathy (Levy et al., 1998). It is the most frequent neuropsychiatric symptom in Alzheimer's patients. Parkinson's disease and cerebrovascular disease also cause significant apathy.

Stimulant therapy, such as low-dose Ritalin®, can effectively activate such residents. It may be given with breakfast and generally wears off by the afternoon. Aricept® has been shown to make residents less apathetic, but it will not be effective unless they have Alzheimer's disease. Parkinson's disease patients may benefit from a small increase in their Sinemet® or the addition of a direct dopamine agonist.

Euphoria, Disinhibition, and Irritability

Frontal brain injury can produce disabling apathy, but can also cause a variety of psychiatric symptoms in which the patient is more behaviorally active. It may seem counterintuitive, but apathy can coexist with euphoria, disinhibition, and irritability in these residents. However, medical conditions that affect brain function are more likely to affect frontal brain function. If a nursing home resident has significant euphoria, disinhibition, and irritability, a more thorough investigation for an underlying medical cause of their apparent delirium or dementia should then be sought.

About one-third of patients with frontotemporal dementia present with euphoria, whereas Alzheimer's patients are rarely euphoric (Levy et al., 1996b). Traumatic brain injury or cerebrovascular disease that affects the bottom part of the frontal

lobes (the orbitofrontal cortex) can produce a syndrome of so-
ciopathy, impulsivity, irritability, disinhibition, and euphoria. It is
unclear how to treat these patients; however, limited success has
been reported with serotonin reuptake inhibitors (Prozac, Zoloft,
Paxil) (Swartz et al., 1997). Euphoria in nursing home residents
who do not have a history of bipolar disorder may be treated
with lithium or an anticonvulsant. At this time, there are no
prospective trials to guide this treatment approach. The anti-agitation agents discussed previously (Desyrel, Remeron, Popra-
nolol, Depakote, Tegretol) may also be effective in reducing
irritability and disinhibition.

Aberrant Motor Behavior

**Aberrant motor behavior in the nursing home refers to
repetitive activities, such as pacing, opening and closing
drawers, repetitively dressing and undressing, winding
thread, and picking at things.** Acute onset of these behaviors
may indicate delirium or an urgent medical condition. If this behavior is more chronic, then it is likely to occur in the presence of
a dementing illness, such as Alzheimer's disease. Frontotemporal
dementias also produce repetitive behaviors, but they may be more
stereotypical with the resident being more difficult to redirect.
Serotonin agents (Prozac, Zoloft, Paxil, and Celexa) have demonstrated some ability to lessen the intensity of these behaviors
(Swartz et al., 1997).

Insomnia

Any medical or psychiatric condition is likely to interfere with
sleep. A nursing home resident without a known psychiatric illness
other than dementia who develops acute insomnia should be evaluated for medical illness. Any condition that produces anxiety,
pain, shortness of breath, or urinary frequency may cause insomnia. Alzheimer's disease may cause reduced quality of sleep; dementia "per se" does not necessarily cause insomnia. A dementia
that causes the resident to be depressed, anxious, or psychotic may
also cause insomnia.

Treatment for insomnia may be needed despite an inability to immediately treat the underlying cause. Trazadone is the best initial sleep aid. It is nonaddictive, has few side effects, and continues to be an effective sleep aid when used chronically. Restoril® is an easy and convenient sleep aid, but causes a greater level of sedation than Trazadone. Although potentially addictive, it loses its sedative effect after 3 to 4 weeks of daily use. Ambien is a new sleep aid that is potent and nonaddictive; however, it remains very expensive and may not be covered by some health care plans. Melatonin may simulate the normal daily nocturnal increase in the body's natural melatonin and may help some people sleep better. It is non–prescription, inexpensive, and largely untested as a sleep aid. Hypnotics that should be avoided in the geriatric population include Dalmane® (long half-life), Benadryl (may cause confusion), Chloral Hydrate (may cause hangover), and barbiturates (addictive).

Appetite

Nursing home residents may lose their appetite and require supplements such as Ensure® in order to stay healthy. Chronic medical illness, especially illness related directly to the gastrointestinal tract, may retard appetite. Infections are frequently a cause of acute loss of appetite. Cancer frequently causes severe weight loss, but may or may not be associated with loss of appetite. Depression is frequently associated with decreased appetite and weight loss can be substantial. Alzheimer's disease and other dementing illnesses usually do not cause appetite suppression until relatively late in the course.

The main treatment for loss of appetite is to reverse the underlying medical or psychiatric condition. Once the patient's medical management is maximized, there are medications that have weight gain as a side effect. (Remeron is an antidepressant that is associated with significant weight gain.) Stimulant medications such as Ritalin given in small doses may improve both motivation and appetite in some of these patients. The best procedure is to encourage the resident to drink supplements; if the situation worsens, an evaluation for feeding tube placement may be warranted.

Cognitive Impairment

Attention, language, memory, visuospatial skills, and executive functioning are the major domains of cognitive function. Acute impairment in any of these areas is likely due to physical illness, such as bladder or lung infection. **Gradually worsening impairment over several years is more indicative of a dementia.** One-half to three-quarters of nursing home residents are demented (Tariot et al., 1993; Rovner et al., 1986, 1990; Katz et al., 1989). Alzheimer's disease accounts for 50% to 60% of cases and vascular dementia accounts for 25% to 30% (Barnes & Raskind, 1980; Rovner et al., 1986, 1990). The only treatment that has been proven effective for cognitive impairment is cholinergic therapy for Alzheimer's disease (Rogers et al., 1996; Farlow et al., 1992).

Aricept® is a cholinergic memory enhancing agent indicated for mild to moderate Alzheimer's disease (mini-mental state examination score above 10). It is capable of retarding the downhill course of the disease by about 6 months to 1 year. It does not effect the underlying course of illness, but may allow patients to stay out of the nursing home longer. It may also improve psychiatric symptoms, such as apathy, anxiety, hallucinations, aberrant motor behavior, and disinhibition (Kaufer et al, 1996; Levy, 1998). Dopaminergic therapy for Parkinson's disease may allow a more rapid rate of thinking to occur and may or may not truly improve cognition.

Conclusion

Psychiatric symptoms are frequently presented in the nursing home. Residents often enter nursing homes because they develop psychiatric symptoms that their families cannot manage at home. These symptoms cause distress, morbidity, mortality, and an increase in health care costs. Medical and neurodegenerative conditions account for a large portion of psychiatric symptoms in this setting. Pharmacologic management can help with many aspects of these residents' care. Psychologists working in long-term care settings should have some basic knowledge of when a pharmacologic agent might be beneficial and when consultation with a psychiatrist is warranted. Integrating both pharmacologic and non-pharmacologic approaches will greatly improve the quality of life for nursing home residents.

References

Barnes R.D., & Raskind M.A. (1980). DSM-III criteria and the clinical diagnosis of dementia: a nursing home study. *Journal of Gerontology, 36,* 20–27.

Caine, F.D., Lynes, J.M., King, D.A. (1993). Reconsidering depression in the elderly. American *Journal of Geriatric Psychiatry, 1,* 4–20.

Cummings, J.L., Miller, B., Hill, M.A., et al. (1987). Neuropsychiatric aspects of multi-infarct dementia and dementia of the Alzheimer type. *Archives of Neurology, 44,* 389–393.

Cummings, J.L., & Sultzer, D.L. (1993). Depression in multi-infarct dementia. In S.E. Starkstein & R.G. Robinson (eds.), *Depression in neurologic disease.* Baltimore: Johns Hopkins University Press (pp. 165–185).

Eastwood, M.R., Rifat, S.L., Nobbs, H., et al. (1989). Mood disorder following cerebrovascular accident. *British Journal of Psychiatry, 154,* 195–200.

Ebrahim, S., & Nouri, F. (1987). Affective illness after stroke. *British Journal of Psychiatry, 151,* 52–56.

Farlow, M., Gracon, S.J., Hershey, L.A., et al. (1992). A controlled trial of tacrine in Alzheimer's disease. *Journal of the American Medical Association, 268,* 2523–2529.

Flynn, F.G., Cummings, J.L., Gornbein, J. (1991). Delusions in dementia syndromes: investigation of behavioral and neuropsychological correlates. *Journal of Neuropsychiatry and Clinical Neurosciences, 3,* 364–370.

Kaplan, H.I., & Sadock, B.J. (1995). *Comprehensive textbook of psychiatry/VI.* Baltimore: Williams & Wilkins.

Kaupher, D.I., Cummings, J.L., & Christine, D. (1996). Effect of tacrine on behavioral symptoms in Alzheimer's disease: an open-label study. *Journal of Geriatric Psychiatry and Neurology, 9,* 1–6.

Katz, I.R., Lesher, E., Kleban, M., et al. (1989). Clinical features of depression in the nursing home. *International Psychiatrics, 1,* 5–15.

Levy, M.L. (1998). Cholinergic therapy for Alzheimer's disease. *Annals of Long-Term Care, 6,* 92–96.

Levy, M.L., Cummings, J.L., Fairbanks, L.A., et al. (1996a). Longitudinal assessment of depressive, agitated, and psychotic symptoms in 181 Alzheimer's disease patients. *American Journal of Psychiatry, 153,* 1438–1443.

Levy, M.L., Cummings, J.L., Fairbanks, L.A., et al. (1998). Apathy is not depression. (In press: Journal of Neuropsychiatry and Clinical Neurosciences.)

Levy, M.L., Miller, B.L., Cummings, J.L., et al. (1996b). Alzheimer's disease and frontotemporal dementias: behavioral distinctions. *Archives of Neurology, 53,* 687–690.

Marin, R.S. (1990). Differential diagnosis and classification of apathy. *American Journal of Psychiatry, 147,* 22–30.

Mendez, M.F., Martin, R.J., Smyth, K.A., et al. (1993). Psychiatric symptoms associated with Alzheimer's disease. *Journal of Neuropsychiatry and Clinical Neurosciences, 2,* 28–33.

Parmelee, P.A., Katz, I.R., Lawton, M.P. (1992). Incidence of depression in long-term care settings. *Journal of Gerontology, 47,* M189-M196.

Parmelee, P.A., Katz, I.R., Lawton, M.P. (1989). Depression among institutionalized aged: assessment and prevalence estimation. *Journal of Gerontology, 44,* M22-M29.

Robinson, R.G., & Price, T.R. (1982). Post-stroke depressive disorders: a follow-up study of 103 patients. Stroke, *13, 635–641.*

Rogers, S.L., Friedhoff, L.T., et al. (1996). The efficacy and safety of Donepezil in patients with Alzheimer's disease: results of a US mutlicenter, randomized, double-blind, placebo-controlled trial. *Dementia, 7,* 293–303.

Rovner, B.W., Kafonek, S., Filipp, L., et al. (1986). Prevalence of mental illness in a community nursing home. *American Journal of Psychiatry, 143,* 1446–1449.

Rovner, B.W., German, P.S., Broadhead, J., et al. (1990). The prevalence and management of dementia and other psychiatric disorders in nursing homes. *International Psychogeriatrics, 2,* 13–24.

Sadavoy, J., Lazarus, L.W., Jarvik, L.F., Grossberg, G.T. (1996). Comprehensive review of geriatric psychiatry-II. Washington, DC: American Psychiatric Association Press.

Samuels, S.C., & Katz, J.R. (1995). Depression in the nursing home. *Psychiatric Annals, 25,* 419–424.

Schatzberg, A.F., & Nemeroff, C.B. (1998). American Psychiatric Drug Textbook of Psychopharmacology, Second Edition. Washington, DC: *American Psychiatric Press.*

Sharpe, M., Hawton, K., House, A., et al. (1990). Mood disorders in long-term survivors of stroke: associations with brain lesion location and volume. *Psychological Medicine, 20,* 815–828.

Starkstein, S.E., Preziosi, T.J., Bolduc, P.L., et al. (1990). Depression in Parkinson's disease. *Journal of Nervous and Mental Disease, 178,* 27–31.

Starkstein, S.E., & Robinson, R.G. (1993). *Depression in neurologic disease.* Baltimore: The Johns Hopkins University Press.

Sultzer, D.L., Gray, K.F., Gunay, I., et al. (1994). A double-blind comparison of trazadone and haloperidol for treatment of agitation in patients with dementia. *American Journal of Geriatric Psychiatry, 5,* 60–69.

Swartz, J.R., Miller, B.L., Lesser, I.M., et al. (1997). Frontotemporal dementia: treatment response to serotonin selective reuptake inhibitors. *Journal of Clinical Psychiatry, 58,* 212–216.

Tariot, P.N., Podgorske, C.A., Blazina, L., et al. (1993). Mental disorders in the nursing home: another perspective. *American Journal of Psychiatry, 150,* 1063–1069.

Uncapher, H., Gallagher-Thompson, D., Osgood, N., Bongar, B. (1998). Hopelessness and suicidal ideation in older adults. *The Gerontologist, 38,* 62–70.

Uncapher, H., Levy, M.L., Skoloda, T., et al. (1998). Suicidal thoughts in male nursing home residents. *Nursing Home Medicine, The Annals of Long-Term Care, 6*[10]:301–308.

Weissman, M.M., Bruce, M.L., Leaf, P.J., et al. (1991). Affective disorders. In Robins, L.N., & Reiger, D.A. (eds.), *Psychiatric disorders in America: the epidemiologic catchment area study.* New York: Free Press (pp. 53–80).

Wragg, R.E., & Jeste, D.V. (1989). Overview of depression and psychosis in Alzheimer's disease. *American Journal of Psychiatry, 146,* 577–587.

14

The Private/Group Practice of Psychology in Long Term Care

JOSEPH M. CASCIANI, PH.D.

Abstract

RESEARCH ON the incidence of mental and behavioral problems in LTC settings conclusively shows the presence of treatable psychological disorders and the unmet need for professional psychological care. Psychologists must address many complex issues in nursing homes, such as ageist attitudes; the interaction of physical, cognitive, and psychological abilities; and informed consent and decision making. Psychologists are expected to perform a range of professional services, and their multidimensional role will create increasing demands for their services in the LTC arena. In addition to psychotherapy and assessment, there is an ongoing need for behavior management assistance, consultation and troubleshooting, and staff training. With the national spotlight on the Medicare budget, the cost effectiveness of mental health services will come under greater scrutiny. Additional medical cost offset studies are needed to justify these programs, especially for the older adult population. A variety of patient problems may trigger referral to psychologists, who should keep several considerations in mind before initiating services. Lastly, the roles of documentation and medical necessity in justifying services and ensuring reimbursement are discussed.

Upon completion of this chapter, the reader will understand the role of diagnostics, psychotherapy, behavior management, consultation and troubleshooting, staff training, and outcomes research in LTC. The reader will also have learned the necessary steps to take when accepting new referrals, how to document and justify these services for insurance payers, and how to work with interdisciplinary treatment teams. The reader will also be aware of other issues that surface in the nursing home setting, such as case transfers and informed consent. References will guide the reader to articles on improving care in nursing homes, on aging and mental health, and on consultation.

Introduction

In 1989, following a 15-year lobbying effort by the American Psychological Association, Congress passed legislation recognizing psychologists as Medicare providers. This legislation gave beneficiaries access to extended mental health services for the first time in the history of Medicare. Preceding this, the Nursing Home Reform Act of 1987 and the Omnibus Budget Reconciliation Act (OBRA), which was signed into law the same year, put in motion significant changes in nursing home standards that enhanced residents' rights and required a greater emphasis on quality of life (QOL) and quality of care. This set the stage for introducing formal mental health programs in the nursing home setting, where psychologists and clinical social workers have become recognized members of the interdisciplinary treatment team.

This chapter addresses the application of professional psychological services in the long-term care (LTC) setting, describing some of the difficulties faced by professionals in this setting, the various types of resident problems encountered, the multidimensional role of the psychologist, and the scope of services provided. Documentation of patients' problems and of the medical necessity of treatment is vital for clinicians working in the LTC setting. Note that the terms patient and resident are used interchangeably throughout this chapter, although patient generally connotes the person receiving psychological services and resident usually refers to the person residing in the nursing home.

Incidence of Mental and Behavioral Health Problems in the Elderly

There is a consensus that the incidence of depression and related psychological disorders among the community-dwelling elderly is less than 5%. The nursing home population presents a very different picture, however. Recent studies have reported that the incidence of depression in nursing homes ranges from 30% (Rubenstein & Wieland, 1993; Randall, 1993) to 50% (Rovner & Katz, 1993). **A National Institutes of Health Consensus Development Conference report on the diagnosis and treatment of depression in late life determined that the highest rates of depression among the elderly are in nursing homes and that staff in many of these facilities are not equipped to recognize or treat patients with depression** (National Institutes of Health, 1991). **Burns and associates** (1993) **estimated that among the two thirds of nursing home residents with a mental disorder, only 4.5% receive mental health services in any 1-month period.** Rovner and Katz (1993) also reported that behavior problems were present in 64% of dementia patients and that 40% of them had additional psychiatric symptoms. These studies definitively show an unmet need for professional psychological care.

Issues in and Obstacles to the Provision of Psychological Services

Despite the awareness of the multiple stresses and losses that accompany the aging process, many individuals—from family members to professionals and paraprofessionals—believe that psychotherapy and counseling are not indicated for older adults and may be a waste of resources. These "ageist" attitudes, which are especially noticeable in nursing homes, are probably holdovers from the pre-OBRA custodial care model, in which the physical and medical needs of residents were met, but little attention was given to maintaining or restoring their functional capacities, to providing for their emotional or psychological well-being, or to addressing their need for dignity and a sense of purpose. As Gastel (1994) notes in her handbook for physicians who work with older adults, clinicians—often without realizing it—allow cultural stereotypes to influence decisions about who needs care and, in this context, who needs psychological care. The tasks before mental health professionals are to educate others about the potential benefits of providing psychological assistance to older persons and to dispel the myth that chronological age, in and of itself, limits the ability of some individuals to benefit from these services.

The psychologist in the LTC setting must also address the related question of the extent to which cognitive impairment precludes the possibility of patients benefiting from psychotherapy. The interplay of the cognitive decline that accompanies normal aging with the decline that accompanies a dementing process and the cognitive effects of a psychological disorder, such as major depression, invariably creates a diagnostic dilemma for the practicing psychologist. Beyond this, however, when does a patient's growing cognitive impairment leave him or her unable to benefit from a traditional, process-oriented therapeutic experience? For example, if a patient in the early states of dementia is experiencing mild episodes of anxiety and disorientation, should a less traditional, more supportive therapeutic approach be adopted? Some specialists believe that any level of cognitive impairment makes a patient a poor candidate for psychotherapy. At the other end of the continuum are those mental health professionals who work in a therapeutic context with patients who have moderate to advanced Alzheimer's disease (Feil, 1993). In an applied setting, however, there is some merit to both positions. **Counseling or therapy on some level is indicated to the extent that it offers the patient some relief, however brief, from the psychological symptoms he or she has been experiencing.**

Eventually, as the dementia or cognitive impairment progresses, what therapists are doing ceases to be psychotherapy and becomes another form of caregiving, one that does not require a specialist. The psychologist may play other roles in the care of these dementia patients, however, as described below.

As insurance payers have begun to examine closely the appropriate use of outside providers for mental health services, the role of in-house staff (e.g., social workers, the nursing staff, activities personnel) in meeting the routine needs of residents has become an issue. Title XVIII, Section 1819 of the Social Security Act (Department of Health and Human Services, 1997) requires that:

> a skilled nursing facility provide, directly or under arrangements with others, for the provision of medically-related social services to attain or maintain the highest practical, mental and psychosocial well-being of each resident.

Thus, for example, if a resident is experiencing difficulty adjusting to placement in a nursing home, the facility is expected to provide the necessary psychosocial care before calling a specialist for assistance. However, this course of action may depend on the type of adjustment difficulty, the presence of a coexisting psychological disorder or a prior history of emotional problems, and the in-house social worker's training with this population and ability to spend the amount of time that the patient requires. Obviously, the facility must consider many variables when making a referral to an outside specialist for these services, including the patient's need for some special intervention or approach that the nonpsychologist cannot provide. In addition, the facility should determine whether a preliminary objective assessment of cognitive and psychological function is indicated to rule out complicating factors such as dementia, impaired reality testing, or masked depression. **The elderly patient's capacity for medical decision making and ability to give informed consent also affect the provision of mental health services.** These can be thorny issues when a nursing home patient is referred for mental health services and is not designated as the responsible party, because the responsible party must give consent to bill the patient's insurance yet the patient may not want the other party (usually a family member) to know about his or her need for these professional services. The resident's consent to begin treatment is not sufficient if he or she no longer has the authority (as the responsible party) to give consent to bill the insurance carrier. Some facilities are in the habit of informing family members when any ancillary service is recommended—which appears, in the case of mental health services, to conflict with the patient's right to confidentiality. In other facilities, patients may be referred for services yet appear to lack the capacity to give informed consent regarding medical care. In these situations, even though the patient could benefit from brief counseling, education is in order for those who are uninformed about a patient's rights to treatment and to confidentiality.

The transfer of patients from one provider to another presents a final challenge to mental health providers. Transfers occur in other settings such as private practice, of course, but in a nursing home, forces beyond the control of the individual provider may be responsible for the transfer. For example, a new administrator may choose to bring to the nursing home a new group of mental health professionals with whom he or she is better acquainted. Such an administrator may need to be reminded that each patient has ultimate control over whom he or she sees to mental health care and, thus, has the right to continue seeing a therapist who has just been replaced. **Transferring patients to different mental health professionals may have many subtle ramifications, including discontinuity of care, inconsistency in treatment planning, and the disruption of established therapeutic relationships. It may also put the patient in the uncomfortable, possibly psychologically harmful position of choosing therapists. Such transfers should be avoided as much as possible; when they are unavoidable, the priority should always be to protect the patient's well-being.**

Professional Skills and Expectations for Long Term Care

Diagnostics:

As psychology becomes more established in settings in which older adults reside, the psychologist's roles is becoming increasingly multidimensional. One of the key services that psychologists distinctively provide is psychological testing. **A comprehensive assessment is the cornerstone of good clinical practice with the elderly.** A complex array of systemic changes, normal and abnormal aging processes, medications, lifestyle factors, and psychosocial conditions may affect the older adult's ability to function. In the cognitive, emotional, and behavioral arena, the presumption is that more is going on behind the scenes than is readily apparent. **The clinical interview is insufficient to detect the nature and extent of underlying problems in older persons; objective, quantifiable measures of cognitive skills are needed.** To be effective with this group, psychologists must be at ease with the practice of assessment. Extensive neuropsychological and psychological test batteries are rarely needed; however, clinicians should understand the normal aging process, the types of organic brain syndromes that affect older adults, and the interplay between functional and organic disorders.

Psychotherapy:

Psychotherapeutic techniques must be modified to be effective for older adults. In his excellent text on psychotherapeutic strategies with older adults, Knight (1986) discusses some of the factors clinicians must consider: the greater interplay between physical and psychological abilities, the real and perceived slowness of their reactions, their increased inferiority, their fragile defensive structure, and their need to be educated about psychotherapy and the therapeutic process. Knight also discusses some of the major treatment issues with older adults, including empowerment, enjoyment of life, and the process of life review. Generally speaking, a problem-focused therapeutic approach tends to be more effective for this age group than a traditional, long-term, insight-oriented approach. For the psychologist who is developing a special interest in therapy with the elderly, Knight's book offers a solid foundation.

Behavior Management:

Nonpsychologists typically do not have the background in principles of behavior and behavioral reinforcement theory that is indispensable in this setting. **Consequently, psychologists can often become leaders in developing and implementing behavior management programs.** Problems that are frequently encountered in nursing homes include verbal and physical abuse, refusal to cooperate with daily nursing care and personal care tasks, refusal to attend or participate in facility activities, agitation and wandering, suspiciousness and paranoia, inappropriate sexual behavior, and verbally disruptive behaviors. Many of these behaviors are driven by dementia and declining cognitive functions, whereas others result more from long-standing characterological disorders or acute psychological conditions. Before developing a behavior management plan, the behavior specialist should understand the following principles:

- An assessment of the resident is indicated to determine if the problem behavior is purposeful or nonpurposeful, because the type of intervention selected with depend on what is driving this behavior. The psychologist should conduct tests to better understand the identified resident's capacity for willful behavior.

- Staff input and cooperation, as well as consistency among caregivers, are critical for the success of any behavior management plan. The staff's assistance in determining the nature, frequency, possible triggers, and consequences of the behavior that has been targeted for change will facilitate the assessment of the problem.

- Staff should be taught basic behavioral principles, including how to identify and operationalize the behaviors that are targeted for change, using behavior logs to record pre- and posttreatment behaviors, and the effects of the differential reinforcement of other behaviors, as well as the use of primary or secondary reinforcers, redirection, correction, and extinction.

- All behavior management programs are fundamentally environmentally based. A behavioral change is achieved by first changing the caregivers' reactions to the resident vs. aberrant behavior and then creating an environment that controls or anticipates the triggers that set off the behavior, while differentially reinforcing other, more desirable behaviors. In other words, to change the behavior, we change the environment.

The goals of the behavior specialist are to educate the staff about the uniqueness of the resident, the triggers that set off the problematic behavior, and the rewards or reinforcers that sustain it, and to help the staff individualize caregiving to the greatest extent possible. **Thus, the emphasis in staff training is on prevention. Staff members who are aware of behavioral triggers and how the patient reacts to those triggers can anticipate problem behaviors and will be able to spend more time giving the resident quality care and less time "putting out fires."**

Consultation:

A fourth role for the psychologist in LTC settings is that of mental health consultant. As in any institutional setting, the mental health professional can have a positive impact on many aspects of care in the skilled nursing facility. The psychologist may become a role model for staff members who want to improve their skills in effective communication, problem solving, and crisis management, and may assist with employee morale and turnover issues and help develop mechanisms for improving family relations. Much of this consultation is informal and is not directly related to patient care. For example, an administrator may request the psychologist's help when he or she has to inform the rest of the staff that one of the facility's nurses has been seriously injured. Or the administrator may want the psychologist's assistance in working with a family member who has accused an aide of mistreating a resident.

In other cases, the request for help may be more formal and a more structured, consultative service may be needed. For example, if the facility is considering the development of a new unit for hospice patients, it may want guidance from the psychologist on special programs and activities that would be suited to the unique needs of these patients.

When there is ongoing friction and dissatisfaction within a particular department at the facility, the administrator may ask the psychologist to conduct a series of team-building exercises to ease the problems. Huszczo (1996) presents a number of team-building activities and suggests the following separate objectives for five team-building sessions: (a) establishing shared goals and expectations, (b) enhancing conflict resolution skills of the members, (c) improving the process of decision making and developing procedures, (d) improving the members' external relations with others, and (e) following up on plans and members' commitments. Zeiss and Steffen (1996) discuss the dilemmas of interdisciplinary treatment teams in geriatric settings. They also provide pertinent information on how to work with and enhance the effectiveness of treatment teams.

A psychologist should keep three points in mind regarding consultation in nursing homes. **First, the psychologist should be aware of his or her professional limitations, when necessary, a request for consultation should be referred to another psychologist who has training and expertise in this particular area. Second, the psychologist must always be attuned to the needs of the interdisciplinary treatment team to effectively address the residents' mental and behavioral health status.** This means that the psychologist should try to function as a member of the treatment team whenever possible, (e.g., by communicating with nursing and social services staff during each visit to the facility). Because the psychologist is usually not on staff per se and does not visit the nursing home daily, it is essential for him or her to establish a high profile as the mental health consultant. This may mean spending time at each nursing station during each visit, even when there is no reimbursement for this meeting time. Conferring with the social services staff before leaving the facility also strengthens this consultation position. **Third, the psychologist should clearly distinguish between the type of consultation services that will be provided pro bono and the types of services that are billable.** There will always be demands on our time for which we are not compensated; it is not possible to do this work without such an investment. However, we often play an important role as consultants and should be compensated accordingly.

Trainer and Educator:

Despite the incidence of emotional, behavioral, and cognitive disorders in nursing homes, most of the staff working in these facilities have little or no training in these areas. **Psychologists can offer much in the area of staff development and training, particularly regarding depression in the elderly, effective communication skills, and behavior management techniques.** The well-prepared psychologist will have a library of resources, articles, and handouts on a variety of topics relevant to aging and mental health available for in-service training. These in-service classes do not require extensive preparation and planning. **In fact, nursing home staff relish the opportunity to learn how to become better caregivers; reduce their sense of frustration, ineffectiveness, and burnout; and enhance their feeling of job satisfaction.** In his guide to finding and keeping quality nursing assistants, Pillemer (1996) presents compelling arguments for the increased use of staff training and for the positive effect such training has on employee retention.

Outcomes

The final skill set needed in LTC settings is familiarity with measuring outcomes and treatment progress. **Unfortunately for psychologists, the measurement of outcomes of mental health services has only recently received sufficient attention, largely because of managed care's emphasis on the cost-effectiveness of health care services, including mental health services.** Although fee-for-service and indemnity insurance plans may always exist, managed care organizations have increasingly become a major entity in the reimbursement structure for private practitioners. As psychologists well know, these plans will not pay for services that are deemed unnecessary or do not reduce the overall cost of health care.

The positive upside to this trend is the growing body of research evidence of the medical cost offset associated with mental health services. Cummings (1996) defines medical cost offset as "the reduction of medical/surgical utilization following the provision of mental health and chemical dependency services." **Several studies have shown the offset effect with middle-aged and younger adults** (Caudill et al., 1991; Holder & Blose, 1987; Jones & Holden, 1995; Massad, West et al., 1990; Pallak et al., 1994), **yet there is scant evidence in the literature demonstrating the same offset effect with older adults** (Strain et al., 1991; Unutzer et al., 1997). **More outcome studies are needed to show the insurance and health care industries that psychological services are not only necessary to improve patients' quality of life but that it can also result in reduced medical and hospitalization costs.** This is especially critical in the LTC arena, as Medicare and other payers are faced with fiscal restraints and seek ways to reduce unnecessary health care costs. As a profession, psychologists will increasingly be held accountable for their services and asked to show that their services are cost effective.

Appropriate Referrals in Long Term Care Settings

When a psychologist walks into a nursing home, what types of referrals can he or she expect? Although patients are referred for a wide range of problems, the psychological problems that cause the staff to make a referral seem to be of two types. **One is the *adjustment disorder/reactive depression category,* which typically develops when there is a change from independent living to placement in the facility. The other category is composed of longer-standing psychological disorders, such as panic disorder or paranoia.** Practically speaking, however, the staff may make a referral for psychological services for residents who demonstrate any of the following conditions:

- Irritability, restlessness, or resistance to daily caregiving
- Signs of depression, tearfulness, unrealistic fears, or reports of not wishing to go on
- Changes in eating or sleeping habits, particularly if physical functions are affected
- Expressed feelings of uselessness or of being abandoned by family
- Evidence of low motivation, isolation, withdrawal, or hopelessness
- A hostile or belligerent attitude or excessive demands that make caregiving difficult
- Sadness about the loss of physical functions (e.g., ambulation, incontinence) or mental ability
- Behavioral problems, such as aggressiveness, screaming, or inappropriate sexual behavior
- A history of emotional disorder or psychiatric hospitalization
- Resistance to participating in rehabilitation and signs that the patient underestimates the value of continuing rehabilitation

In addition, a resident may be referred if his or her family displays feelings of helplessness or guilt about placement or disagrees with the facility in terms of the type of caregiving that is most appropriate for the resident.

Referrals are generally made by the social services staff. The psychosocial status of the residents is the social worker's purview, and he or she is often the first person to be notified when a resident presents any problems in this area. If the social worker feels that she or he is not qualified to help the resident, a referral will be made to the mental health professional.

The social worker is also responsible for ensuring that an identified problem is noted in the resident's care plan. The care plan consists of (a) a statement of the problem in objective, measurable terms; (b) the desired goal of treatment; (c) the approximate date by which this problem is expected to be resolved; (d) the approach or intervention that will be implemented; and (e) who (or what discipline) is responsible for intervention. The care plan is drafted within 7 days of admission and reviewed quarterly thereafter. As problems are resolved, they are removed from the care plan, and new problems are added as they surface. Responsibility for the care plan remains with the various departments within the facility, and the social services department monitors the psychosocial aspects of the residents' care. **To ensure that the care plan is up to date, social worker must be kept informed about who is being referred and who is currently receiving psychological treatment. When referrals are made by other disciplines** (such as nursing) **and social services is not informed, the care plan will not be accurate; this could result in a deficiency being recorded during a state Department of Health Services chart review and affect licensure.**

A third reason for social workers to make referrals to the psychologist is the need for interaction between the social worker and psychologist and, in turn, between the social worker and the rest of the treatment team. If the social worker is not involved directly with the delivery of psychosocial services to the residents, he or she must remain at least peripherally involved in their care. Furthermore, through such referrals, the social worker can facilitate communication about the resident's psychosocial needs to the interdisciplinary team members. The psychologist keeps the social worker up to date about the resident's progress in treatment, and the social worker can convey information that is necessary for the resident's optimum psychological care to coworkers during weekly meetings (which the psychologist usually does not attend). As noted earlier, communication among the team members is vital. **The psychologist who visits the facility, sees his or her patients, and then leaves without interacting with staff is doing an injustice to the patients and neglecting an important aspect of care.**

Considerations in Processing Referrals:

In accepting a referral from a nursing home, the psychologist should take several factors into consideration before seeing the patient for services. First, the psychologist should obtain an order for mental health services from the facility's attending physician; this is often necessary because of licensing laws governing skilled nursing facilities. All services provided to residents of such facilities must be prescribed by the attending physician. At first glance, this would appear to conflict with freedom of choice laws and the right of a patient to consult a psychologist without a referral from an MD or DON. The facility's license, however, may stipulate that the doctor's order is needed to initiate psychological services, just as it is needed for physical therapy, medications, hospice care, or any other services. A physician's order is not required for reimbursement by Medicare, however.

Second, the psychologist must obtain consent to treat the resident. Essentially, the patient should be provided enough information to make an informed decision about seeking services from the psychologist. **The patient has a right to receive a description of the services to be provided** (including duration and frequency) **and to know his or her rights regarding confidentiality, the limits of these rights, the risks and benefits of treatment, and any other facts that could influence his or her decision to obtain services.** (Regarding the limits of confidentiality, the psychologist should be familiar with any state elder abuse reporting requirements.) Psychologists should rely on telephone consent only when it is absolutely necessary. Two witnesses are needed to document telephone consent, and written consent should always be obtained as soon as possible.

If the patient is not legally competent to make an informed decision about the services in question, a surrogate decision-maker should be used. Potential surrogates (listed in order of priority) are the spouse, an adult child who has the consent of other qualified adult children, the majority of the available adult children, the patient's parents, and an individual the patient identified before becoming incapacitated to act for on his or her behalf. It cannot be assumed that the patient is competent if he or she has not been judged incompetent by a court of law. In fact, many residents experience significant cognitive decline following their admission yet do not go through the costly, time-consuming process of being assigned a conservator or public guardian to make their decisions. **Thus, until or unless the patient is judged incompetent, the principle of reasonableness applies in questions of uncertainty about competence: would a group of objective, impartial observers agree that a patient possesses a meaningful capacity to make informed, competent health care decisions? If not, the provider should obtain consent from a surrogate decision-maker.**

The final factor that must be considered before providing professional services concerns financial arrangements. **The provider must obtain permission from the patient or surrogate decision-maker to bill them. They must provide the decision-maker with a list of the fees involved, insurance billing policies, and any copays or deductibles.** The policies for consent to treat also apply to consent to bill.

The Scope of Psychological Services Provided in Long Term Care Settings

Three main categories of psychological services are provided in nursing home settings (other than consultation and training): assessment, psychotherapy, and behavior management assistance. The first two categories will be touched on briefly; behavior management will be discussed in detail. Following this discussion, some of the ramifications of billing for these services will be reviewed.

Assessment:

Testing may be indicated for members of the LTC population for several reasons:

- To make a differential diagnosis; for example, to distinguish between dementia and pseudodementia or between a reactive depression and a long-standing, major depression

- To formulate strategic interventions for a problem resident, such as one who is aggressively acting out, and to provide clear and specific management approaches that take into account the patient's level of purposefulness, motivation, and capacity for self-correction

- To help answer questions about what can be realistically expected in terms of rehabilitation or transfer to another level of care, such as a return to independent living status

- To determine a patient's remaining functional capacities and potential for independent living, which may be essential for the discharge planner

- To give family members realistic information about the patient's potential for recovery or future decline

- To gain information about the resident's underlying strengths and resources that can be mobilized for his or her overall care; this will be valuable even when treatment is not indicated, such as in moderate to advanced dementia cases

- To generate baselines of function in a variety of areas and to help document change and treatment progress

In preparing reports, succinctness and practicality should be the rule. Readers of test reports are looking for caregiving assistance and tend not to be as concerned with the psychodynamic formulations and developmental history and background, which may be more appropriate for other audiences. **In addition to brief background information and behavioral observations, the report should discuss the patient's cognitive, emotional, behavioral functions, and residual strengths, as well as risk issues, diagnosis, treatment goals and objectives, and recommendations** (for both the psychologist and the facility staff).

Individual, Group, and Family Psychotherapy:

Psychological services in the nursing home typically consist of some combination of individual, group, and family psychotherapy. Finding a suitable meeting space can be a challenge in some facilities, and transporting patients to meeting rooms is time-consuming when the patient is not ambulatory. The psychologist may occasionally be given a private office, but this is the exception; therefore, the provider should be resourceful and adaptive when seeking suitable space in which to see patients. Also, it may sometimes be necessary to see a patient who is bedridden. Of course, seeing the patient without a roommate present is ideal, but it may be necessary to make a concession at times and see the resident even when the roommate is also in the room. Drawing the curtain provides some privacy, however artificial it may be.

Some referred residents will receive individual therapy after the initial assessment and treatment plan is developed. The length of each treatment session will vary, but the general rule of thumb with this population is that brief sessions (20 to 30 minutes long) and relatively few sessions overall are preferable to hourly sessions and lengthy courses of treatment. **It is most helpful to focus on specific, concrete problems that the patient is experiencing.** In some instances, hourly psychotherapy sessions are indicated, and under extreme circumstances, extended sessions of 75 to 80 minutes each are needed. Regardless of the session length or course of treatment, the provider must be prepared to justify all treatment sessions to the insurance payer.

Group therapy provides opportunities for greater social and peer interaction, feedback, support, and problem solving within the larger group (i.e., nursing home) **setting.** The logistics of group therapy can often be a problem, however, because many residents may need assistance getting to the therapy room. It is essential to enlist the staff in seeing that patients get to the correct room on time. Therapists must also clearly distinguish the psychotherapy group from activity groups, such as music or exercise groups. The latter may be useful and beneficial, but they do not qualify as psychotherapy and should not be billed as such. Specially focused psychotherapy groups may include a new resident adjustment group, a group for patients with chronic pain, and a stroke survivor's group, according to the needs of residents within the facility.

Family psychotherapy is another important adjunctive service for many residents and families of residents in the nursing home. Members of these families often face conflict in their relationships, particularly when the placement is unwanted by the resident. Disagreements or conflicts may stem from the caregiving or placement decision, or the resident and his or her family may have long-standing difficulties that are exacerbated by the placement. **Family therapy is indicated when there is a need to assist family members with the management of the resident—as long as the resident remains the focus during the treatment sessions. Family sessions may also be an appropriate time to gain background information necessary for diagnosis and treatment planning.** Family therapy may also focus on other concerns, such as reducing conflicts between the family and the resident, helping family members understand the nature of the resident's condition so that they may serve as a support for the resident, and easing communication between staff and family members to reduce conflicts over caregiving issues. However, family therapy that focuses on the effects of the resident's condition on a member of the family is not justified. Billing the patient's insurance for family therapy to treat family members' personal conflicts or marital or childrearing problems is also not appropriate.

Behavior Management Assistance:

Many, if not most, of the problem behaviors that occur in nursing homes result from diminished intellectual and cognitive functional ability, which causes patients to display problems such as agitation and restlessness, resistance to caregiving, reduced capacity for activities of daily living, and verbal and physical outbursts. In the past, these problematic behaviors were not expected to change; today, by contrast, functional assessments are conducted to identify the deficits the resident is demonstrating and the residual strengths or abilities he or she may still possess. **Because the rate of decline in functional capacity varies from one resident to another, different patients cannot be approached or treated in the same way. A functional assessment is necessary to identify the most effective interventions for each patient.** This assessment should take into account the resident's expressive and receptive communication ability, social and interpersonal skills, activity preferences, psychological status, physical impairments, capacity for self-care, and the nature of the behavior problem itself. It allows for an individualized approach to patient care, tailored to the patient's unique pattern of abilities and deficits.

Behavior management involves a number of fundamental strategies that caregivers should understand, including the following:

- The environment should be calm, because residents, especially those with dementia, have difficulty filtering out unwanted visual and auditory stimulation. The environment should also convey a feeling of safety and security. The goal is to minimize the resident's level of anxiety, which increases with uncertainty and ambiguity.

- Because of residents' difficulty in learning new information and adapting to change, the more consistency and routine in the daily schedule, room location, furniture arrangement, and assigned caregivers, the better. A structured routine also helps the resident maintain residual abilities as long as possible.

- Expectations should be realistic; psychologists should avoid the tendency to overestimate what the patient can do. Many residents easily mask the extent of dementia they are experiencing. It is easy to underestimate how severe a patient's cognitive problems are if his or her skills in grammar and syntax are intact, his or her denial mechanisms are effective, and he or she has a tendency toward confabulation (i.e., illogical, exaggerated, or unconsidered explanations of statements).

- Psychologists should provide ample opportunities for success and a sense of accomplishment to offset the sense of failure that is experienced so often. With the continuing onslaught of functional losses, acknowledging what the patient can still do is extremely helpful.

- Communication should be simple and clear and given in short, uncomplicated phrases and only after direct eye contact has been made. Avoid questions that rely on memory, and allow plenty of time to respond. When directing or instructing the patient, do so in a place that is free of external distractions, such as a television or radio.

- Distraction can be much more effective than confrontation when the patient is making unrealistic demands. Diverting a patient's attention to another topic rather than using logic and reasoning to dissuade the patient is particularly effective with patients who have moderate to advanced dementia.

- When patients become agitated, they should be removed from the situation that caused the agitation and isolated from further stimulation until they feel more settled and secure.

- Orienting the patient to time, place, person, and situation as often as necessary can be very therapeutic and will minimize outbursts. The psychologist should also reassure the individual that he or she is safe and will be taken care of. Planning activities that are geared to the patient's remaining abilities will keep his or her fear, anxiety, and frustration to a minimum.

Psychologists may prevent many flare-ups by educating the staff about the five most common triggers of problems:

1. *Catastrophic reaction.* This emotional outburst is the patient's response to demand overload. Too much stimulation, too many demands, and ambient movements that are too rapid may tax the patient beyond his or her means, often with aggressive, angry, and sometimes violent repercussions.

2. *A change in routine.* This trigger is easily overlooked by caregivers. Difficulty in adapting to change is usually behind the patient's resistance to a new seat in the dining room, a different showering procedure, or a change in any other routine to which the patient has become accustomed.

3. *The absence of outlets for physical energy and motor restlessness.* More problems tend to occur in facilities that offer residents no opportunities to expend physical energy. Of course, the need for psychotropic medication should also be considered in these situations.

4. *A perceived loss of control.* This is characteristic of nursing home residents, especially those with dementia. The resident's diminished mental and physical ability, loss of function, and growing helplessness and dependency on others all contribute to this felt loss of control. Patients easily become frustrated when their efforts to accomplish something are unsuccessful, when decisions are being made for them, or when other events occur that remind them of the persons they used to be.

5. **Impatient or insensitive caregivers.** One cannot over-
look the staff members who are faced with job pressures,
personal concerns, and countless demanding, often unco-
operative patients in a caseload. These take their toll on the
staff's patience, sensitivity, and tolerance, and should be addressed in any good behavioral management approach.

Funding and Reimbursement Issues

In LTC settings, the major insurance payer is Medicare. The federal
Medicare program is administered by the Health Care Financing
Administration (HCFA), which is a division of the Department of
Health and Human Services, and provides medical care for individuals aged 65 years and older or are disabled. The HCFA contracts with insurance companies, which are referred to as carriers
or fiscal intermediaries, to implement the Medicare program in
each of the 50 states. A single carrier may serve all Medicare beneficiaries in part of a state, in an entire state, or in several states. Although there is general uniformity among most of the Medicare
carriers, some federal guidelines may have regional interpretations
that impact psychological services in a given city or state.

Psychological services fall under Medicare Part B, which covers
professional services, including those of physicians, dentists, and ancillary health care providers. Medicare covers the first 80% of the
amount allowed for assessment services and 50% of the amount for
treatment services, after the deductible has been met. The balance,
or co-payment, may be covered by secondary insurance payers, by
Medicaid, or by private payers (including out-of-pocket payments
by the patients themselves). The amounts allowed are set by the individual carriers and vary from region to region. The fee schedule
published by the Medicare carriers contains these amounts. In
some states, Medicaid will cover the co-payment (i.e., the 20% or
50% of the allowed amount not paid by Medicare). Litigation is
pending in several states to require Medicaid programs to pay this
co-payment amount, but the states argue that the provider has already received more from Medicare than the Medicaid system
would have authorized (Johnsson, 1997). In other words, Medicaid

assumes a co-pay obligation when its allowable amounts (fee schedule) exceeds the Medicare fee schedule. There are some secondary insurance payers, sometimes referred to as Medigap policies, which pay the coinsurance amount to the provider.

It is important to find out what kind of insurance a new patient has and to determine whether psychological services are covered by his or her insurance carrier. Another vehicle for reimbursement is private pay, which is necessary when the resident has no insurance or the insurance plan does not reimburse for psychological services. **Psychologists should note that the law allowing them to participate in the Medicare program also requires them to accept assignments; that is, each psychologist must accept the fee determined by Medicare to be the entire billable amount and not bill the beneficiary for the difference between this and the psychologist's usual fee.**

Managed care plans that are on the rise in Medicare populations may present reimbursement difficulties. Typically, these plans have contracted with the Medicare carrier to provide all inpatient, outpatient, and skilled nursing services needed by the target population. The psychologist must obtain authorization for services from the managed care or health maintenance organization before initiating services.

The new Medicare provider should bear in mind that although Medicare can be considered a fairly liberal third-party payer, it has some inherent restrictions as well, just as most payers do. The following are a number of common factors that may limit reimbursement:

- **Patients receiving psychological services must have a bona fide diagnosable psychological or psychiatric disorder. Visits that are primarily social in nature cannot be billed as a psychological service, even though many residents benefit from such visits.**

- **Certain diagnoses, such as mental retardation, are excluded from the list of conditions for which a psycholo-**

gist may provide treatment. Some Medicare carriers have excluded dementia as a treatable psychological condition; other carriers will reimburse for limited treatment, when it is justified.

- There is usually a restriction on the frequency of services and on multiple services on the same day or by multiple providers. It is important to be familiar with any such restrictions imposed by the carrier.

- Some carriers have set limits (caps) on the number of services per condition or per spell of illness. Spell of illness may be an unfamiliar term for the psychologically minded professional, but it is used frequently in Medicare, especially regarding hospital stays. Although not all Medicare carriers adhere to it, 20 sessions is considered the "community standard" for length of treatment. Of course, there may be indications for fewer or more than 20 sessions, depending on patient need and medical necessity.

- The carrier's reviewers will use written documentation to determine whether extended treatment was justified or not. In some cases, the reviewers will also ask for copies of the physician's and nurses' chart entries to compare notes of the different disciplines and to look for consistency in treatment approaches.

- Psychologists may not bill Medicare for time spent in care plan meetings, treatment team meetings, staff in-services, or any similar nonpatient-related service.

- Any services required by the facility, such as preadmission assessment or annual resident review, are not covered by Medicare. Routine screening and periodic testing are neither required nor covered by Medicare.

Documentation Issues

Therapists may only be reimbursed for psychological services that are determined to be medically necessary. This determination may come with the initial submission of an insurance claim following a prepayment audit of the medical records, or during an audit that occurs well after payment for services. **For services to be considered medically necessary, the following four criteria must be met**:

1. Services must be consistent with the symptoms or diagnosis of the illness or injury under treatment.

2. Services must be necessary and consistent with generally accepted professional medical standards (e.g., not experimental or investigational).

3. Services may not be furnished primarily for the convenience of the patient, physician, or supplier.

4. Services must be furnished at the most appropriate level at which they can be provided safely and effectively for the patient.

As this definition suggests, medical necessity is an elusive, abstract concept that can be difficult to incorporate into progress notes. How does one determine whether a given series of psychological services is medically necessary? Several guidelines may be useful in applying this concept to documentation. First, medical necessity and forms of treatment should appear in the treatment goals; the success and effectiveness of the treatment could be determined by measuring the extent to which it met these goals. The expectations of the Medicare program are neither higher nor lower than those of any prudent buyer who wants assurance that he or she actually desires the service for which payment is being made.

Second, the medical record is a means of communication and a tracking mechanism that should convey the patient's condition, the diagnosis, and the rationale for and results of services rendered.

The provider should always try to ensure that other disciplines (e.g., nursing, social services, activities, dietary) **document the need for psychological services in their respective sections of the patient's medical chart.** Whenever possible, the entries should describe how the psychological symptoms are affecting the patient's medical condition. The other disciplines should also document efforts that have already been made to address the presenting problems and the outcome of those efforts. **The entire record should indicate that the condition of the patient will allow him or her to benefit from therapy.**

Third, the psychologist should treat each session as a separate billable entity and should expect to justify the medical necessity of each session. That is, each session should be able to stand alone, since the reviewers may find that some insufficiently documented sessions do not justify reimbursement yet authorize services before or even after denying reimbursement.

Medical necessity is supported when the service provider documents the condition that is being treated, the patient's response to the treatment, whether the treatment appears to be benefiting the patient, the steps taken by the provider in the form of intervention, and why these interventions were made by the provider rather than by in-house staff.

Finally, the patient's physical condition (e.g., a severe stroke) **may sometimes be considered a contraindication for psychotherapy.** The psychologist, therefore, should always be cognizant of the patient's ability to participate in the intervention and of any way in which a physical condition may impede the patient's involvement in his or her own care.

Treatment Plans:

A comprehensive treatment plan will help set the stage for the course of treatment upon which the psychologist embarks. **This treatment plan should include the following elements:** (a) **medical, family, social, and psychiatric history;** (b) **mental status examination report, observational reports, and sup-**

plemental information; (c) **a preliminary diagnosis, based on the International Classification of Diseases, 9th Revision** (ICD-9) **coding system;** (d) **treatment goals and behavioral objectives;** (e) **recommendations;** (f) **estimated length of treatment** (optional); **and** (g) **benchmarks, i.e., indicators that reflect progress toward the goal** (optional).

Treatment goals should always be operationalized (i.e., written in objective, quantifiable terms) so that the patient's progress can be readily compared with what was planned. By focusing on observable outcomes, the psychologist can document change and show how the patient is benefiting from treatment. Of course, it is not always easy to design objective treatment goals. Many conditions that are treated by mental health professionals can be very difficult to quantify, e.g., paranoia and suspiciousness. However, in this era of heightened review of health care services, the need for accountability is very real, and the provider must be able to demonstrate to outside observers, auditors, and reviewers that his or her services are making a difference. This does not minimize or eliminate the importance of subjective, interpersonal change as a result of treatment. However, operationalization is essential for documentation that is both necessary and sufficient.

While providing therapy, the psychologist is also advised to provide updates on at least a quarterly basis to include the benefits to the patient that have been achieved, as well as the patient's current status and expected future progress. This periodic treatment summary is used to keep physicians, staff, and others apprised of the effectiveness of our treatment plans, and it allows the team to integrate psychological progress into patient care.

Conclusion

Although psychological services have long been provided in LTC settings, the nursing home terrain is still new for most psychologists. As we become more accepted in these facilities and facility staff become more aware of the contributions we can make, we will become more integrated into the interdisciplinary treatment team. Our mutual efforts will be better coordinated, and ultimately, patient care will improve. Working with the older adult population can be immensely rewarding, even though it is often frustrating. The real challenge, however, lies in showing that psychological services are cost effective in LTC settings and improve residents' quality of life and quality of care.

References

Burns, B. J., Wagner, H. R., Taube, J. E., et al. (1993). Mental health service use by the elderly in nursing homes. *American Journal of Public Health, 83,* 331–337.

Caudill, M., Schnable, R., Zuttermeister, P., & Benson, H. (1991). Decreased clinic utilization by chronic pain patients after behavioral medicine intervention. *Pain, 45,* 334–335.

Cummings, N. (1996). Does managed mental health care offset costs related to medical treatment? In A. Lazarus (Ed.), *Controversies in managed mental health care* (pp. 213–227). Washington, DC: American Psychiatric Press.

Department of Health and Human Services. (1997). *Requirements for, and assuring quality of care in, skilled nursing facilities.* Social Security Act, Title XVIII, Section 1819.

Feil, N. (1993). *The validation breakthrough.* Baltimore: Health Professions Press.

Gastel, B. (1994). *Working with your older patient: A clinician's handbook.* Bethesda, MD: National Institute on Aging, National Institutes of Health.

Holder, H. D., & Blose, J. O. (1987). Changes in health care costs and utilization associated with mental health treatment. *Hospital and Community Psychiatry, 38,* 1070–1075.

Huszczo, G. E. (1996). *Tools for team excellence.* Palo Alto, CA: Davies-Black Publishing.

Johnsson, J. (1997, March 3). Medicine tells states: Time to pay fair share of Medicare co-pays. *American Medical News,* 1, 58.

Jones, N. F., & Holden, M. S. (1995). Mental health treatment and medical utilization: First pilot study in the military. *Journal of Clinical Psychology in Medical Settings, 2,* 269–274.

Knight, B. G. (1986). *Psychotherapy with the older adult.* Beverly Hills, CA: Sage Publications.

Massad, P. M., West, A. N., & Friedman, M. J. (1990). Relationship between utilization of mental health and medical services in a VA hospital. *American Journal of Psychiatry, 147,* 465–469.

National Institutes of Health. (1991). Diagnosis and treatment of depression in late life. *NIH Consensus Statement, 9*(3), 1–27.

Pallak, M. S., Cummings, N. A., & Dorken, H. (1994). Medical costs, Medicaid and managed mental health treatment: *The Hawaii study. Managed Care Quarterly, 2*(2), 64–70.

Pillemer, K. (1996). *Solving the frontline crisis in long-term care: A practical guide to finding and keeping quality nursing assistants.* Cambridge, MA: Frontline Publishing.

Randall, T. (1993). Demographers ponder the aging and the aged and await unprecedented looming elder boom. *JAMA, 269,* 2331–2332.

Rovner, B. W., & Katz, I. A. (1993). Psychiatric disorders in the nursing home: A selective review of studies related to clinical care. *International Journal of Geriatric Psychiatry, 8,* 75–87.

Rubenstein, L. C., & Wieland, D. (Eds.) (1993). *Improving care in the nursing home.* Newbury Park, NY: Sage Publications.

Strain, J., Lyons, J., Hammer, J., et al. (1991). Cost offset from a psychiatric consultation–liaison intervention with elderly hip fracture patients. *American Journal of Psychiatry, 148,* 1044–1049.

Unutzer, J., Patrick, D. L., Simon, G., et al. (1997). Depressive symptoms and the cost of health services in HMO patients aged 65 years and older. *JAMA, 277,* 1618–1623.

Zeiss, A. M., & Steffen, A. M. (1996). Interdisciplinary health care teams: The basic unit of geriatric care. In L. L. Carstensen, B. A. Edelstein, & L. Dornbrand (Eds.), *The practical handbook of clinical gerontology* (pp. 423–450). Thousand Oaks, CA: Sage Publications.

15

Ethical Issues

Jennifer Moye, Ph.D.

Abstract

THREE ETHICAL issues that often arise in long-term care facilities are consent, confidentiality, and competency; these are illustrated in this chapter with case vignettes. The ethical principles of autonomy, beneficence, fidelity, and advocacy, which also apply in this setting, will be described and compared with the ethical principles that are found in the American Psychological Association Ethics Code. The ethical issues discussed in the vignettes will be examined in light of these principles. Finally, a strategy for approaching ethical dilemmas that are likely to arise in LTC settings will be outlined. This strategy involves the identification of specific ethical issues and relevant principles and method of resolving these issues during the course of psychological assessment and treatment activities. The key learning objectives for this chapter are to identify common ethical issues confronted by psychologists in long term care, to learn the ethical principles most relevant to these ethical issues, and to develop a strategy for responding to these issues.

Introduction: What Are the Ethical Issues in Long Term Care?

Psychological practice in long term care (LTC) involves assessment and treatment activities that may conflict with ethical principles. Psychologists working in LTC need to be sensitive to such ethical issues, familiar with the types of ethical conflicts that are likely to arise in these settings, and capable of resolving such conflicts through thoughtful and ethical professional practice (Lichtenberg et al., 1998). Psychologists can be especially helpful to treatment teams by clarifying ethical issues and using evaluation and intervention methods with patients, families, teams, and systems that are designed to help resolve ethical problems.

Psychologists working in long-term care may encounter ethical dilemmas involving how consent for treatment is obtained, how confidentiality may be honored when working with team members and documenting care, and how patients competency is determined. The issues of consent, confidentiality, and competency are encountered in a wide range of therapeutic settings (Netting & Williams, 1989). The most conspicuous ethical issues seen in these settings involve death and dying, termination of treatment, abuse, and neglect. However, ethical conflicts in long-term care also involve other aspects of the older clients' care and daily life, albeit more subtly.

Many of the ethical issues that arise in LTC settings are discussed in academic and policy-making arenas: who should care for our elderly citizens? Who should pay for that care? What are the family obligations to elderly relatives? How should health care resources be allocated? How do we balance concerns about quality of life against quantity of life, especially for the individual with moderate to severe dementia? These important questions have been the subject of scholarly debate (Kapp, 1991; Post & Whitehouse, 1992). **However, the day-to-day ethical issues for psychologists in long term care are more likely to involve questions of consent, confidentiality, and competency.**

Examples of Ethical Issues in Long Term Care

One of the ethical issues psychologists typically face in the LTC setting is obtaining consent for treatment, as the following case study illustrates:

Case Vignette:

Mrs. F, an 83-year-old woman, had several cardiovascular and pulmonary conditions and evidence of lacunar infarcts on a computed tomography scan (CT), although her cognition was intact on neuropsychological testing. Mrs. F had no history of psychiatric illness, except for a brief episode of psychosis with agitation and delusions 3 years before when alprazolam, which had been prescribed for her insomnia, was discontinued during admission for an acute medical condition. The psychosis resolved once alprazolam was reinitiated and then gradually tapered. The team asked the mental health staff to evaluate Mrs. F, because she had become increasingly suspicious of staff and believed they were trying to harm her physically and even kill her. She became upset when staff approached her to assist with bathing or dressing. She was noted to be especially fearful during the night, when she often lay awake in bed; she was also noted to nap in her bed during the day. Mrs. F was evaluated jointly by the psychologist and psychiatrist, who decided that her increased suspiciousness was most likely related to a recent onset of insomnia, and that the best course of treatment was a combination of medications and psychotherapy designed to readjust her sleep-wake cycle, offer support, and modify her mistaken cognitions about the nursing staff. Mrs. F was agreeable to taking the new pills to help her sleep. She was also receptive to visiting the psychologist but did not want to schedule regular therapy sessions, insisting that she did not need mental health treatment. The psychologist was unable to obtain her consent for therapy and related billing. Furthermore, it would be difficult to justify treatment or override the need for consent, because the patient presented no imminent risk to herself or others. The psychologist believed it was possible to discuss her problems and make headway during these friendly visits, but he was uncomfortable engaging in such visits without a contractual understanding that their goal was to treat her insomnia and suspiciousness.

The second most frequently encountered ethical issue is maintaining confidentiality of treatment as illustrated by the following vignette:

Case Vignette:

Mrs. W, a 78-year-old woman who had resided in the nursing home for 3 years, was having increasing difficulty managing her diabetes. Her blood sugar levels fluctuated considerably, and the treatment team believed she was not compliant with her diet. As the team attempted to work with her on issues of compliance, she became argumentative and began to complain about other aspects of her care, stating that she had to wait too long for her call light to be answered, that her room was not adequately cleaned, and that the nursing staff rushed through morning care and did not adequately assist her with grooming. The treatment team asked the psychologist to see Mrs. W for therapy to address the issue of compliance with diet and to decrease her argumentativeness. The psychologist met with Mrs. W several times to complete an evaluation and develop a psychological treatment plan. Mrs. W admitted that she did eat foods that were not on her diet, stating that occasional sweets were one of the few remaining pleasures she had. She also reported that she had waited 15 minutes for her call light to be answered and stated that nursing staff had been impatient and acted inappropriately with her during morning care. The examples she provided of statements made by staff did seem disrespectful. She requested that the psychologist not tell the staff about her complaints about them or her eating habits and refused to discuss these issues directly with team members for fear of reprisal. When the psychologist met with the treatment team to review the evaluation, the treatment team stated that Mrs. W was "demanding" and "unreasonable." As the instigators of the referral, they requested information about her compliance and other information that was obtained during the evaluation. The psychologist believed that the situation could be improved by explaining Mrs. W's perspective to the team but was uncertain how much information from the evaluation sessions she could share with the team while still respecting the patient's confidentiality. She was not sure how to address the patient's claim that staff had made disrespectful statements.

The third most common ethical issue involves evaluating a patient's capacity to be discharged:

Case Vignette:

Mr. S, an 86-year-old widower, was admitted to the nursing home from the hospital after he fell at home and fractured his hip. Because he had no family and few friends, he received assistance through meal and home-maker services. Despite these services, the condition of his home had de-teriorated and it needed major repairs. A large number of bills had accumulated, which suggested that he was having difficulty managing his finances. In the nursing home, Mr. S made good progress in physical ther-apy; after 6 weeks he was walking steadily and was anxious to return home. The physician was concerned that Mr. S's safety would be jeopard-ized if he were discharged, noting that the patient's short-term memory was impaired. The team was reluctant to discharge him, given the absence of family or friends to provide oversight or serve as a guardian. In turn, Mr. S was becoming increasingly worried and despondent about staying in the nursing home and threatened to leave against medical advice. The team asked the psychologist to evaluate his ability to live independently at home again and to make decisions about this matter. The psychologist evaluated Mr. S's cognition and found that his memory of things he could adequately see and hear was within normal limits but also found that he had mild difficulties with executive functions. The psychologist also found Mr. S to be very concerned about going home and moderately depressed about remaining in the nursing home. The psychologist was uncertain how to relate the neuropsychological findings to the team's concerns about his capacity to live independently and felt conflicted about respecting the team's treatment plan versus the patient's desires.

These case vignettes illustrate the potential for difficult questions to arise while providing care to older adults in LTC settings. What is the responsibility to protect an older client from harm? How does a clinician proceed when the older client refuses a potentially beneficial treatment? How much information obtained from a therapy session should be released to the treatment team? Who is the client (Burstein, 1988)?

Ethical Principles and Their Relationship to the American Psychological Association Ethics Code

A number of ethical principles are frequently invoked when care is provided to the aged. Ethical principles represent ideals gleaned from the beliefs and concerns of groups of individuals for the treatment of others, but they are not necessarily linked to the religious or legal framework of any group. **The ethical principles that are especially pertinent to psychologists working in long-term care include autonomy, beneficence, fidelity and advocacy.**

In addition, psychologists have developed an ethics code that includes six principles that are relevant to professional conduct (American Psychological Association, 1992). These principles, which are outlined in Table 1, do not represent enforceable rules but rather "aspirational goals" to be used in identifying the ethical conflicts within a given situation and in guiding ethical behavior. The relationship between these principles and the four ethical principles mentioned above is discussed below.

Autonomy:

Autonomy concerns the individual's right to self-determination, (i.e., to make choices concerning his or her life [Fitting, 1984]). In the health care setting, autonomy generally infers respecting patients' right to exercise their choice among treatment options. **The emphasis on patient autonomy reflects a change in attitude toward the contractual relationship between patients and their health care providers. Formerly, physicians and health care providers were more likely to choose treatments for their patients; now, physicians are expected to share expert knowledge with patients about illnesses and treatment options and encourage the patient to decide** (Jones, 1993). Having respect for people's rights and dignity (the first principle listed in the APA Ethics Code) also means respecting the individual's fundamental right to autonomy and self-determination, as well as the privacy and confidentiality necessary to ensure that right.

Table 1
Ethical Principles in the American Psychological Association Ethics Code

Principle	Aspects of Principle
Respect for people's rights and dignity	Respect for autonomy, privacy, confidentiality; awareness of cultural and role differences
Concern for the welfare of others	Contribution towards welfare of others; sensitivity to differences in power
Competence	Recognition of limits of professional competencies; maintenance of knowledge of relevant scientific and professional information
Integrity	Honesty, fairness, respect; clarification of roles and avoidance of dual roles
Professional and scientific responsibility	Cooperation with others to meet the needs of clients; upholding professional and ethical standards
Social responsibility	Awareness of professional and scientific responsibilities to the community and society to mitigate suffering and advance human welfare

Note: Please refer to APA (1992) for full text.

Beneficence:

Beneficence concerns doing good for others, including intervening to benefit another individual in a positive manner and to prevent harm. A related principle also applied in health care settings is nonmaleficence, which means "doing no harm." These principles also imply that health care providers have an obligation to help persons who may need protection to prevent them from harming themselves or others (Fitting, 1984). Similarly, the APA Ethics Code's principle of concern for others' welfare indicates the psychologist's obligation to contribute to the welfare of all those with whom he or she interacts professionally, including patients, students, and research participants. In LTC settings, beneficence applies both to a psychologists' patients and to other residents, as well as to staff and family members (Lichtenberg, 1994).

Fidelity:

Fidelity, which concerns the obligation to be faithful and trustworthy in relationships, is especially relevant to psychologists in the context of the contractual relationships they form with patients, families, other health care providers, and health care systems. The principle of fidelity is closely related to several principles in the APA Ethics Code, including competence, integrity, and professional and scientific responsibility (Table 1). The principle of competence concerns the obligation to maintain high standards of competence, to recognize the limits of one's expertise, and to maintain knowledge of relevant scientific and professional information needed to render services. The principle of integrity concerns the obligation to be honest, fair, and respectful; to accurately describe one's qualifications, services, and fees; and to clarify one's role and avoid potentially harmful dual roles. Finally, the principle of professional and scientific responsibility cites the need for psychologists to consult with, refer to, and cooperate with other professionals to serve the best interests of their clients and to uphold professional and ethical standards of conduct for themselves and others, including the acceptance of appropriate responsibility for behavior. A psychologist may be the only representative with a mental health perspective on a multidisciplinary LTC team that is oriented to a medical model of care. In such cases, the psychologist's professional responsibility includes being an advocate for the patient in terms of mental health and appreciating the perspectives of the other disciplines (Kimmel

& Moody, 1996; Lundervold & Lewin, 1992). **The ability to maintain fidelity in relationships with clients and others in LTC settings depends upon the psychologist's competence, integrity, and sense of responsibility.**

Advocacy:

Lichtenberg and associates (1998) outlined a set of standards for psychological practice in LTC facilities, including the ethical obligation of advocacy. **Psychologists must be advocates for nursing home patients, in terms of seeking appropriate mental health services to reduce excess disability and improve their quality of life.** When mental health services are not being used or are being used inappropriately, psychologists should educate other providers to improve the delivery of care within a biopsychosocial model. The principle of advocacy is analogous to the APA Ethics Code principle of social responsibility, which refers to the obligation to go "above and beyond" intervention to benefit others, prevent harm, and strive to mitigate the causes of human suffering and advance human welfare through science and practice by avoiding the misuse of psychological work and by encouraging the development of policies that serve the interest of clients.

Three Ethical Issues in Long Term Care

Ethical issues may arise not only in the delivery of mental health services in the LTC setting but also in the delivery of medical care, with which psychologists may become involved. **In addition to concern about ethical issues that arise in clinical work, there has recently been growing concern about ethics in research activities that are conducted in LTC facilities, particularly research on adults with dementia** (Sachs, Rhymes, & Cassel, 1993; Schuster, 1996; Wichman & Sandler, 1995). Three ethical issues that arise in all three aspects of patient care are consent, confidentiality, and competency.

Consent:

The increased attention to obtaining valid informed consent for treatment has resulted in significant changes in the way health care is delivered. Current concerns include the introduction of mechanisms that can extend patient's inclusion in medical decision making, even when they are unable to participate, i.e., advanced directive and health care proxy stipulations (Jones, 1993).

Valid consent for medical or psychological treatment must reflect three elements: disclosure, voluntariness, and competency (Eth & Leong, 1992). *Disclosure* refers to the clinician providing the patient with information necessary to make a reasonable decision about treatment. This typically includes information about the diagnosis, treatment alternatives, and risks and benefits associated with various treatments, including the likelihood of its success and its effect on daily life. **Informed consent should be obtained for all aspects of treatment in long-term care, including psychotropic medications and behavioral interventions** (Lundervold & Lewin, 1992). *Voluntariness* refers to the need for the treatment decision to be made of the patient's accord, without overt or subtle coercion. The clinician can recommend courses of treatment, but the patient must choose the treatment. *Competency* refers to the patient's cognitive ability to make reasoned decisions. Recent standards for psychological services in LTC facilities describe the consent process for three competency situations (Lichtenberg et al., 1998). In the first situation, in which the individual is competent and without cognitive impairments, the psychologist is obligated to obtain the patient's informed and voluntary consent for treatment. In the second situation, in which the individual has been determined to be incompetent by a court of law, the psychologist must obtain consent from the guardian but is encouraged to maximize the patient's understanding of the treatment and its rationale. In the third situation, in which an individual has significant cognitive impairments but has not been determined incompetent in court, the psychologist is obligated to identify the legally responsible party and obtain consent from that individual and also to provide information about the treatment and its rationale to other important parties.

The doctrine of informed consent recognizes that health care decisions involve the fundamental right to determine what will happen to one's body and to know that these decisions may sustain life or hasten death. These decisions involve weighing risks and benefits in light of personal values (Karel & Gatz, 1996). It is because of the importance of evaluating treatment options in the context of individual values that the doctrine of informed consent exists. Patients should be considered the best judges of their own values and related interests (Berg et al., 1996).

Problems arise in LTC settings when patients are not offered the opportunity to provide informed consent. This sometimes occurs when patients are admitted to nursing homes without their consent. It also occurs when patients are provided medical, pharmaceutical, or mental health treatments without being provided information about their condition and alternative treatments or being given the opportunity to make a treatment choice. This often happens when the provider is convinced that the treatment is of benefit to the patient or questions the patient's competency to consent to treatment and there is no guardian. Occasionally, because of ageism, the provider may believe that the older adult need not be afforded the right to provide informed consent (Greene & Kropf, 1993). This reflects a conflict between autonomy and beneficence and represents a violation of fidelity.

Confidentiality:

Confidentiality issues are likely to arise when the psychologist shares information about a patient with other clinicians, insurers, and the patient's family. **A breach in confidentiality may result from discussions during team meetings or in the preparation of documentation. Determining whether a breach occurred involves determining how much of the detailed information that was obtained during the course of assessing and treating the patient can be conveyed to**

other parties. Underlying these conflicts are ambiguities concerning who the client is: the patient, the caregivers, the facility, or all of the above. Similarly, the goals of medical record documentation may be unclear. The ultimate goal is to help the client, but the immediate goal is less clear: are progress notes written primarily as a record of assessment and intervention (for the therapist, facility, or insurer), or to educate other care providers? Documentation can be used to suggest a different understanding of the patient, to foster empathy for the patient's perspective, and to encourage appropriate interventions by other caregivers. When used to educate other care providers, documentation becomes part of the psychologist's intervention for the patient. **Patients should be told who will have access to information about his or her case and how information arising from therapy sessions will be documented. In other words, the patient should be advised about the limits of confidentiality.**

Ethical principles that are associated with issues of confidentiality include beneficence (helping the patient by providing information to caregivers, families, and facilities to improve care), fidelity (the psychologist's obligation to honor his or her contractual relationship with the client), and autonomy, in particular, the psychologist's obligation to promote the client's autonomy by respecting privacy. Like other ethical issues, confidentiality involves a conflict between competing principles.

Competency:

Competency is necessary for informed consent. Muddled thinking about competency issues may result in ethically questionable practice. There continues to be confusion in LTC settings about the meaning of the term competency (Moye & Weik, 1996). In these settings, a "competency evaluation" usually refers to the process by which a clinician assesses a patient's ability to make decisions within a certain situation, for example, deciding to return home, to select one treatment from among several alternatives, or how to spend money. However, these are really clinical evaluations of abilities and should not be confused with the determination of legal competency (or capacity, the term now used in some states) in a court of law. In some states, physicians are permitted to make such assessments and act on them as if they were adjudicated determinations. In other states, a clinician's assessment is heavily relied upon in court adjudications. **In neither case are clinical evaluations considered equivalent to legal determinations of competency.**

In addition, clinicians may fail to recognize the need to evaluate competency and/or fail to assess it adequately by addressing situation-specific and capacity-specific concerns (Moye, 1996). **At times, clinicians erroneously assume that an individual's age or diagnosis determines global incompetency. The psychologist can challenge such assumptions by evaluating the patient's cognitive abilities and specific capacities to identify the specific areas of impairment.** Competency is a complex topic, but definitions are being clarified and assessment tools are becoming available (Department of Veterans Affairs, 1997).

Definitions of Competency

A framework reflecting the evolution of legal definitions of competency (Sabatino, 1996) is presented in Table 2. **Legal standards for incompetency formerly emphasized one criterion: a disabling condition, such as a diagnosable mental illness. Now, many states want to establish three criteria: a disabling condition, evidence that the condition causes some mental impairments, and evidence that impairment affects the individual's capacity for the activity in question.** For example, it is not sufficient to note that an individual has dementia. A diagnosis of dementia should be linked to clinically significant symptoms, such as a moderate to severe impairment in

Table 2
Framework for Clinical Evaluations for
Questions of Competency

Question	Examples
1. Is there a disabling condition?	Dementia, psychosis
2. Does the condition result in significant mental impairments?	Memory problem, delusions
3. Do the mental impairments affect the specific capacity in question?	Decisions regarding treatment, finances, residence

memory, and that mental impairment should be linked to a specific functional impairment, such as the inability to make treatment decisions.

Structuring Evaluations for Competency

Psychologists can follow a five-step approach in completing evaluations for competency questions (Department of Veterans Affairs, 1997). First, the referral question should be clarified and, where appropriate, redefined. Psychologists working in long term care who are asked to evaluate an individual's "competency" can restate the question in terms of the patient's "abilities." Second, it is necessary to plan for the evaluation by determining what sort of evaluation should be done and obtaining appropriate consent. Third, a clinical interview, cognitive testing, and functional or capacity evaluation can be completed. Fourth, the results of the evaluation should be provided to the patient, the health care team, and relevant family members. Finally, a follow-up evaluation may be recommended if appropriate.

Structuring Assessments of Decisional Capacities

In evaluating specific functions or capacities, psychologists may consider the four components of decision making, which are referred to in statutes and case law as (a) understanding, (b) appreciation, (c) reasoning, and (d) expressing a choice (Grisso & Appelbaum, 1995; Roth et al., 1977).

Understanding is the legal capacity to comprehend diagnostic and treatment-related information. This includes the ability not only to remember newly presented words and phrases but also to comprehend the meaning of these words and phrases and to demonstrate that comprehension for the physician or evaluator. *Appreciation* is the capacity to determine the significance of the treatment information with respect to one's situation, including the nature of the diagnosis and the probability that treatment will be beneficial. It involves both cognitive and affective appreciation. Whereas understanding refers to the individual's ability to comprehend basic information about conditions and treatment, appreciation refers to the individual's capacity to recognize the extent to which the information is accurate and applies to him or her. *Reasoning* involves the capacity to make decisions about treatment by comparing alternatives in light of the consequences; it includes the ability to integrate, analyze, and manipulate information and draw inferences about the impact of the alternatives on everyday life. *Expressing a choice* is the legal capacity to communicate a decision about treatment; it applies to individuals who cannot or will not express a choice or are ambivalent.

Some competency-related evaluations concern specific functional abilities, but more often questions about judgment and decision-making capacities underlie questions about function. Psychologists may find it helpful to refer to these four legal standards to organize their evaluations when decisional capacities are in question.

Strategies for Ethical Practice

Ethical conflicts in health care can be approached through strategies that explicitly acknowledge ethical issues and ethical principles (Doolittle & Herrick, 1992). Table 3 presents such a strategy for psychologists in long term care.

The first step is to identify the ethical issue and related ethical principles. For example, if a psychologist is called to intervene when a patient refuses to give consent for surgery that the treatment team recommends, the ethical issue is the need for con-

Table 3
Strategies for Ethical Practice

Step	Examples
1. Assessment of the situation	
a. What are the ethical issues?	Informed consent
b. What are the ethical principles?	Autonomy versus beneficence
2. Assessment of patient and context	
a. Individual differences	What are the goals and preferences of the patient, family, and team? What principles, values, or religious convictions underlie these?
b. Self-awareness	What are my preferences and related values? What is my role? Do I have conflicting roles and obligations?
c. Authority	Whose values have precedence? Who has the knowledge, authority, and capacity to make the decision?
3. Intervention with patient and context	Provide results of assessment of patient and context and ethical conflicts to all involved. Facilitate negotiated resolution.

sent to be informed, voluntary, and competent. Such a situation may involve a conflict between the team's desire to do good for the patient (the principle of beneficence) and the patient's right to choose (the principle of autonomy). Respecting either principle at the expense of the other may result in doing harm. Hence, the team may have to choose between their desire to do good for the patient by encouraging the patient to have the surgery and their desire to do good by respecting the patient's autonomy (Lundervold & Lewin, 1992).

The second step is to assess the goals and preferences of the patient, the treatment team, the family, the institution, and other key players by investigating the underlying principles, values, and differences in ethnicity, religion, gender, and/or socioeconomic status. The psychologist should also assess his or her own goals and preferences and be aware of the values he or she brings to the situation. Values clarification is necessary to prevent the psychologist from distorting data because of his or her own agenda (Doolittle & Herrick, 1992). **In addition, the assessment of the patient should consider the person who has the authority to make treatment decisions in the situation, and why.** If the patient is competent, he or she has the authority to make the treatment decision. If the patient's decisional capacities are unclear, the psychologist may proceed with an evaluation of these capacities to determine whether the patient may be considered competent to exercise the right to make decisions autonomously.

The third step in addressing ethical conflicts involves intervention. Intervention includes the provision of feedback to key parties about the assessment and the identified ethical issues and principles. **It is important for the psychologist to describe the ethical conflict in language that the treatment team understands.** Even though team members are probably aware of being conflicted, defining the conflict for them can be helpful. For example, the psychologist might say, "this is a difficult situation because you believe the surgery will be helpful but the patient does not want the surgery; you want to help the patient *and* you want to respect his or her right to choose." **However, the psychologist's obligation does not end with identification**

of ethical conflicts and provision of evaluation results; it also includes the negotiation of a resolution of ethical conflicts (Lichtenberg et al., 1998). In some situations, the appropriate intervention is to recommend a review by the institution's ethics board or adjudication in a court of law. In other cases, the psychologist can work with the patient and patient-care team to achieve a greater understanding through different perspectives or to maximize the patient's decision-making capacity. Providing information to the patient in a different manner (e.g., in a shortened and simplified written form, which is reviewed orally) may resolve the conflict. Alternatively, the team may need to understand the patient's capacities and acknowledge the patient's right to his or her preference, even when it conflicts with the patient-care team's preference.

Conclusion

Routine aspects of professional practice in long term care—such as obtaining informed consent, maintaining confidentiality, and determining decision-making capacities—may involve ethical dilemmas. Psychologists should be sensitive to the types of ethical issues that are common in LTC settings and understand the ethical principles that often underlie them. Psychologists should address these issues by identifying conflicts among principles; clarifying the situation, including the goals, preferences, and values of all parties (including themselves); and resolving ethical dilemmas through open negotiation.

References

American Psychological Association. (1992). Ethical principles of psychologists and code of conduct. *American Psychologist, 47,* 1597–1611.

Berg, J. W., Appelbaum, P. S., & Grisso, T. (1996). Constructing competence: Formulating standards of legal competence to make medical decisions. *Rutgers Law Review, 48,* 345–396.

Burstein, B. (1988). Involuntary aged clients: Ethical and treatment issues. Social Casework: *The Journal of Contemporary Social Work, 4,* 518–524.

Department of Veterans Affairs (1997). *Assessment of competency and capacity of the older adult: A practice guideline for psychologists* (Publication No. PB97-147904). Milwaukee, WI: National Center for Cost Containment.★

Doolittle, N. O., & Herrick, C. A. (1992). Ethics in aging: A decision-making paradigm. *Educational Gerontology, 18,* 395–408.

Eth, S., & Leong, G. B. (1992). Forensic and ethical issues. In J. E. Birren, R. B. Sloane, & G. D. Cohen (Eds.), *Handbook of mental health and aging* (2nd ed.). New York: Academic Press.

Fitting, M. D. (1984). Professional and ethical responsibilities for psychologists working with the elderly. *The Counseling Psychologist, 12,* 69–78.

Greene, R. R., & Kropf, N. P. (1993). Ethical decision making with the aged: A teaching mode. *Gerontology and Geriatrics Education, 13,* 37–52.

Grisso, T., & Appelbaum, P. S. (1995). The MacArthur treatment competency study III: Abilities of patients to consent to psychiatric and medical treatment. *Law and Human Behavior, 19,* 149–174.

Jones, R. G. (1993). Ethical and legal issues in the care of demented people. *Reviews in Clinical Gerontology, 3,* 55–68.

Kapp, M. B. (1991). Legal and ethical issues in family caregiving and the role of public policy. *Home Health Care Services* Quarterly, *12,* 5–28.

Karel, M., & Gatz, M. (1996). Factors influencing life-sustaining treatment decisions in a community sample of families. *Psychology and Aging, 11,* 226–234.

Kimmel, D. C., & Moody, H. R. (1996). Ethical issues in gerontological research and services. In J. E. Birren & K. W. Schaie (Eds.), *Handbook of the psychology of aging* (4th ed.). New York: Academic Press.

Lichtenberg, P. (1994). *A guide to psychological practice in geriatric long-term care.* New York: Haworth Press.

Lichtenberg, P., Crose, R., Frazer, D. (1998). Standards for psychological services in long-term care facilities. *The Gerontologist, 38*(1), 122–129.

Lundervold, D. A., & Lewin, L. M. (1992). *Behavior analysis and therapy in nursing homes.* Springfield, IL: Charles C. Thomas.

Moye, J. (1996). Theoretical frameworks for competency in cognitively impaired elderly adults. *Journal of Aging Studies, 10,* 27–42.

Moye, J., & Weik, P. (1996). Psychological assessments of abilities and legal determinations of competency in long-term care settings. *Psychologists in Long Term Care, 10,* 6–8.

Netting, F. E., & Williams, F. G. (1989). Ethical decision-making in case management programs for the elderly. *Health Values, 13,* 3–8.

Post, S. G., & Whitehouse, P. J. (1992). Dementia and the life-prolonging technologies used: An ethical question. *Alzheimer Disease and Associated Disorders, 6,* 3–6.

Roth, L. H., Meisel, A., & Lidz, C. A. (1977). Tests of competency to consent to treatment. *American Journal of Psychiatry, 134,* 279–284.

Sabatino, C. (1996). Competency: Refining our legal fictions. In M. Smyer, K. W. Schaie, & M. B. Kapp (Eds.), *Older adults' decision making and the law.* New York: Springer.

Sachs, G. A., Rhymes, J., & Cassel, C. K. (1993). Biomedical and behavioral research in nursing homes: Guidelines for ethical investigations. *Journal of the American Geriatrics Society, 41,* 771–777.

Schuster, E. (1996). Ethical considerations when conducting ethnographic research in a nursing home setting. *Journal of Aging Studies, 10,* 57–68.

Wichman, A., & Sandler, A. L. (1995). Research involving subjects with dementia and other cognitive impairments: Experience at NIH, and some unresolved ethical considerations. *Neurology, 45,* 1777–1778.

This publication can be obtained from the National Technical Information Service (NTIS), U.S. Department of Commerce, 5285 Port Royal Road, Springfield, VA 22161. The phone number is 703-487-4650.

The Department of Veterans' Affairs publication Assessment of Competency and Capacity of the Older Adult: A Practice Guideline can be obtained from the National Technical Information Service (NTIS), U.S. Department of Commerce, 5285 Port Royal Road, Springfield, VA 22161. The phone number is 703.487.4650; the publication number is PB97-147904.

16

Training Psychologists in Long Term Care

MICHELE J. KAREL, PH.D.,

SAMANTHA SMITH, PH.D.,

and SUZANN OGLAND-HAND, PH.D.

Abstract

THE GOAL of this chapter is to provide guidelines for psychologists who wish to establish or improve a psychology training program in a nursing home setting. The main learning objectives are to increase awareness of (a) system and reimbursement issues that influence psychology training in nursing home settings; (b) issues that arise in the training and supervision of students working with frail elders in multidisciplinary long-term care (LTC) settings; and (c) resources that are available to aid in training psychologists in nursing home settings. These objectives will be accomplished by reviewing the groundwork that should be laid in a nursing home before introducing a psychology training program, needs assessment with the trainee, the orientation of the trainee to the multidisciplinary team and the LTC environment, the orientation of the trainee to documentation requirements and informational resources, special issues in training and supervision (such as working with the treatment team and working with older and frail patients), and reimbursement issues that affect opportunities for psychology training in long-term care.

Introduction

The nursing home is a rich environment for psychology training. Students interested in geropsychology, the interface between medical and psychiatric disorders, neuropsychology, family issues, team dynamics, organizational systems, and consultation will benefit from training in LTC. These settings also present a number of challenges for psychology training, including working as a mental health professional within what is typically a medical model of care, working with frail elders whose illnesses cannot always be "cured," and providing treatment within the context of a multidisciplinary team. As psychological needs in long-term care expand, psychological services continue to be provided by individuals who lack the proper training to work with frail elders. Psychologists have a mandate to develop programs to provide such training in LTC.

This chapter offers practical suggestions for designing and implementing a psychology training program in a nursing home setting at the predoctoral extern or internship level. Lichtenberg and colleagues (1997) have written a foundational reference on standards for psychological services in LTC that may serve as a guide for supervisors and students alike.

Little research has been published on psychology training in long term care. Suggestions in this chapter are based on the authors' experiences in building psychology training programs in Department of Veterans Affairs nursing home settings, interviews with psychologists who offer training in other nursing home settings, and a review of the existing literature. For an excellent overview of geropsychology training in general, see Knight and colleagues (1995).

Groundwork: Entry Into the System

Defining the role of the psychologist and/or the psychology trainee within the LTC system is an important part of preliminary work. If a well-established psychological service exists in a nursing home, it will be easier to add a training component. Introducing a psychology service into an LTC setting entails both assessing needs in the setting and educating staff about the possible roles of the psychologist. **Many nursing homes may present an unfamiliar environment to trainees who are used to working in mental health settings and make the introduction of biopsychosocial care a challenge. Trainees will have an easier entree to the system if needs and roles are clarified beforehand.** Guidelines for initial groundwork are outlined in Table 1.

Needs Assessment for the Trainee

As in any training environment, it is helpful to assess the trainee's relevant experiences and training goals. Entry into an LTC setting can be overwhelming for trainees without prior experience with medically ill patients or patients with dementia, or without experience in medical settings, where staff may not conceptualize problems and their solutions as a psychologist would. **A thorough needs assessment can be used to help define areas on which training should focus and allow the supervisor to create a smoother transition into the training experience, thereby minimizing the effect of the trainee's competence and comfort level with different professional activities on training outcomes.** During the initial screening of students for trainee positions, it is important to make sure that the trainee's skills and those that the position will require are a good match, given the level of supervision that will be available, and that the student's training goals and expectations also match and what the training will offer (Wilber & Zarit, 1987). Table 2 contains a suggested framework for evaluating an individual's training needs.

Orientation to the Team and Environment

A trainee's work in the nursing home setting will be facilitated by a good orientation to the health care team and to the nursing home environment. The trainee will find it helpful to learn about the roles of other staff and the faculty's decision-making processes

---

Table 1

**Groundwork: Introducing Psychology Training
in the Nursing Home Setting**

---

1. **Clarify needs of the setting**
   Meet with nursing and other multidisciplinary staff to asses their behavioral and mental health concerns in working with their residents.

2. **Provide education about psychology**
   A. What the psychologist can offer
   - Neuropsychological assessment to help staff better understand a
     resident's cognitive strengths, limitations, and abilities
   - Behavioral assessment and intervention with residents and staff
     to decrease behavioral excesses
   - Individual and group psychotherapy to reduce depressive and
     anxiety disorders
   - Staff training on mental health and behavioral issues

   B. What the psychologist cannot offer
   - Prescription of psychotropic medications
   - Instant "miracle cures" for complex behavioral problems

3. **Clarify the psychology trainee's relationship with the team**
   - Indicate the psychologist's hours of availability
   - Determine whether the psychologist is viewed as a consultant or
     member of team
   - Determine how referral procedures are to be made (e.g., does the
     nursing staff identify cases of concern? Does the psychologist do
     screenings?)

---

and hierarchies (Lichtenberg, 1994; Tsukuda, 1990). What are the
different levels of nursing? What do the departments of social
work, physical therapy, recreation therapy, dietary services, pharmacy, medicine, and other services do? How do these services
work together? Being aware of turf issues can be important; for
example, is social work responsible for communicating with families? Is recreation responsible for organizing groups? What are
the organizational stresses facing the team (e.g., high turnover

Table 2

Needs Assessment for Psychology Trainees Entering the Nursing Home Settings

1. Relevant Academic Preparation

Has the trainee learned about:
- "Normal" aging?
- Psychopathology in late life?
- Dementia?
- Models of team functioning?

2. Prior Experience With Populations and Settings

Has the trainee worked with:
- Older adults?
- Frail and/or dying patients?
- Dementia patients?
- Patients in medical settings?
- Multi- or interdisciplinary teams?
- Various disciplines?

3. Prior Experience With Assessment and Intervention

Has the trainee had experience with:
- Neuropsychological testing?
- Individual, group, and/or family psychotherapy?
- Various models of .0psychotherapy?
- Consultant work?
- Providing staff training?

4. Prior Experience With Supervision

Has the trainee benefited from audio or videotaped psychotherapy supervision in the past?

5. Special Interests

What skills does the trainee most hope to gain: assessment, psychotherapy, or consultation/training skills?

or short staffing)? **Awareness of these issues will help the trainee foster collaborative working relationships with other staff. Working with a multidisciplinary team will give the trainee a clearer sense of his or her worldview as a psychologist and an appreciation of the different ways in**

which each profession is trained to focus on and interpret data (Lundervold & Lewin, 1992; Qualls & Czirr, 1988).

It is important to clarify expectations about communication. Does the trainee need to check in with the head nurse? May the trainee interview staff members when necessary? How are referrals to the psychology trainee made: through the team meeting, the head nurse, the physician, or other staff persons? Does the trainee need permission to interview residents? If so, from whom? Through what channels should psychological recommendations be communicated: a team meeting, a chart note, a head nurse, and/or individual staff members?

There may be creative ways to introduce a trainee to the way a nursing home works. With staff support, a trainee may "shadow" an aide for a day, spend time simply observing what goes on (e.g., patient behaviors, how different staff and patients interact, what situations escalate, what situations resolve by themselves, how staff interact with each other). Trainees may accompany the recreation staff on an outing; being able to view resident interactions outside of the institutional setting can build empathy for people who reside in the institution. **Psychologists frequently enter the nursing home to conduct tests or provide psychotherapy for residents without having the opportunity to get a sense of how the whole system works. A trainee will do a better job in a consulting role if he or she can see what staff members experience on a day-to-day basis.**

Orientation to Information and Documentation

It is helpful to offer trainees a concrete orientation to available resources and documentation requirements in the nursing home. This orientation should include an introduction to such documentation concerns as the medical records, the ethical and clinical aspects of documenting progress notes, and treatment planning; and information and resources regarding the practice of psychology in the nursing home as well as medical illnesses, pharmacology, common abbreviations, psychological assessment tools, and state and federal regulations relevant to psychology practice.

Documentation:

Attention to the documentation of psychological services in the nursing home is an important part of training. Standards for documentation vary somewhat from setting to setting but will be influenced by institutional and state regulations and by ethical considerations.

The Medical Record

The psychologist should make sure that new trainees know where information can be found in the medical record. For example, are there initial nursing assessment forms? Medication lists? Problem lists? Treatment plans? Physician's orders? Old charts? Where is information to be filed? What are the standards for electronic records?

Progress Notes

Notes must document the patient's progress towards meeting treatment goals. Since confidentiality is an ethical concern when psychological interventions are documented in documenting psychology intervention in a multidisciplinary system, it is important to encourage trainees to discuss the limits of confidentiality with their patients. **Trainees must learn to appreciate the potential conflict between respecting the patient's confidentiality and communicating relevant treatment issues to care providers.**

Furthermore, trainees should be encouraged to write notes that are simple, free of jargon, and to the point and that emphasize potential practical implications for ongoing optimal nursing care for the patient. **It is extremely important to sensitize trainees to the potentially negative impact of documentation that appears to be judgmental or critical of other staff's work.** For example, it is common in therapy for patients to complain about their care. **Trainees should maintain empathy with the resident, but stated concerns should not always be accepted at face value and the trainees' notes should communicate issues in ways that facilitate good working relationships with**

other professional caregivers; blaming or statements that are critical of staff should be avoided. It is very helpful for trainees to have examples of reports or notes to use as models, such as an initial assessment interview, a neuropsychology report, an individual psychotherapy progress note, and a group psychotherapy progress note.

Treatment Planning

It is important to help trainees develop clear goals and objectives for their work and understand how their work fits into the multidisciplinary treatment plan. Settings differ in the nature and extent of multidisciplinary collaboration in treatment planning, as well as in requirements for documentation. Trainees need to become familiar with institutional requirements for treatment planning and documentation to ensure that problems areas and interventions involving psychology are represented accurately. In the authors' experience, patients are often misdiagnosed with dementia, schizophrenia, or other psychiatric disorders. A psychology trainee can become increasingly empowered to offer alternative perspectives of patient behaviors and formulating behavioral treatment plans. **Trainees will learn to re-evaluate the psychology treatment plan on the basis of a continued assessment of progress toward treatment goals.**

Information / Bibliographic Resources:

Suggested resources in this section are taken from the authors' own experience and from Knight and colleagues (1995), which provides a good overview of resources and training materials for clinical geropsychologists. The suggestions offered below are not intended to be comprehensive but to serve as a starting point.

Geropsychology and Psychology Practice in the
Nursing Home Setting

The numbers of resources about clinical geropsychology and psychology practice in the nursing home is increasing. Appendix A includes a selection of references for geropsychology practice.

Medical and Psychiatric Illness

Most LTC residents have medical, neurological, and/or psychiatric comorbidities. For trainees without much experience in medical settings, the list of diagnoses and potential implications for behavioral assessment and intervention can be overwhelming. Appendix B includes sources of information on common medical and psychiatric conditions that occur in late life.

Geropsychological/Neuropsychological Assessment

Many resources are available on assessment; a few are listed in Appendix C. It is important that age-appropriate norms for any tests being used are made available to trainees.

Pharmacology

Although psychology trainees need not become experts on pharmacology, they should have access to references about common medications and their potential side effects or interactions. It is particularly helpful to have a reference on psychopharmacology (Appendix D). In addition, trainees should be encouraged to ask pharmacy, nursing, or medical staff about the purpose of certain medications.

Medical Abbreviations

Trainees who are new to medical records will feel as if they are reading a foreign language, especially because of the abbreviations that are frequently used for common medical conditions and procedures. Over time, it may be possible to develop a list of the most commonly used abbreviations into a "dictionary" for trainees. For example, HTN=hypertension, CHF=congestive heart failure, CA=cancer, and so on. A helpful reference that can be purchased directly from the publisher is listed in Appendix E.

State and Federal Regulations and Local Systems

Trainees need to be oriented to regulations that govern psychology services in LTC facilities in their area, including standards and related requirements for documentation for services to be reimbursed. Trainees will also benefit from an orientation to insurance issues and Medicaid and Medicare reimbursement issues in the private sector, as well as eligibility policies within the Veterans Affairs health care system (for those training in this system). Trainees who may become involved in discharge planning with patients should have access to information on local community resources. See the appendix for selected references.

Training and Supervision

Psychology training in the nursing home may focus as much, if not more, on the trainee's relationship with the system as on his or her relationship with the individual patient. Supervision will include attention to the trainee's reactions to the challenges of working with the team, special issues associated with working with older and frail patients and with designing and evaluating interventions. The form of supervision will likely depend on the trainee's prior experience and his or her comfort with close guidance as opposed to relative autonomy. As the balance between these may shift over time, so shall the form of supervision.

Format of Supervision:

Trainees may benefit greatly from watching a supervisor conduct a few interviews (or testing or therapy sessions) **before working with or being observed by the supervisor and, in turn, working independently.** If at all possible, audiotapes or videotapes should be made of the trainee conducting interviews or therapy sessions with patients (Duffy, 1992; Wilber & Zarit, 1987), especially if the trainee has not had the benefit of this type of supervision in the past, and also because issues about the communication style that was used with older, frail patients may not be identified by the trainee's report alone

Group supervision (in addition to individual supervision) **of a set of trainees may be extremely helpful to both trainees and supervisors** (Wilber & Zarit, 1987), as it allows the individuals in the group to give one another support, learn from one another's experiences, and brainstorm about possible interventions for patients with complex behaviors in complicated LTC systems. Possible formats for additional training experiences include case conferences and grand rounds (Duffy, 1992).

Working With the Team:

One of the greatest challenges to psychology trainees in the nursing home setting is learning how to work with a wide range of staff persons who bring different perspectives to the understanding of patient behaviors. Nursing home staff are characterized by diversity in professional, educational, and ethnic/cultural background (Smyer et al., 1988). This diversity leads to various levels of appreciation for the complex factors that influence resident behaviors. Staff may underestimate the role of environmental factors or neurological/psychiatric disorders in determining patient behavior and, at times, attribute difficult behaviors to a resident's personality or "manipulative intentions." At times, trainees may have trouble finding their voice within the treatment system and mechanisms for offering alternative perspectives on problems. **Trainees must also learn how to incorporate the perspectives of other disciplines into their own way of perceiving patients, being especially careful not to underestimate medical, functional, and medication factors that may influence a patient's behavior** (Lewinsohn et al., 1984).

Recurrent questions to be answered during training include the following: Who is the client? What responsibility does the trainee have to the resident? To the family? To the treatment team (Duffy, 1992; Wilber & Zarit, 1987)? During supervision, trainees should also be evaluated for their ability to explore turf issues and the feelings of distrust, anger, or dissatisfaction which can result when the roles and responsibilities of team members are ambiguous (Qualls & Czirr, 1988; Tsukuda, 1990). **Training, therefore, focuses to some extent on helping the trainee negotiate relationships with the multidisciplinary team, find his or her voice within the system, and discuss his or her emotional**

reactions to working with the team insofar as the trainee wishes or as these reactions influence his or her clinical and consultative work. Frequently, the workings of the team must be understood from the perspective of the broader system, taking into account institutional politics, stressors, or morale issues that may be influencing communication among team members and their various styles of working with residents. Supervision can encourage the trainee to maintain a respectful, empathic, and assertive stance with the team and patients alike.

Working With Older and Frail Patients:

The kind of supervision used to evaluate the trainee's ability to conduct individual assessments or therapy will obviously depend on the interaction of style and theoretical orientations of the supervisor and trainee, the patient's issues, and the nursing home system. However, learning to work with older patients has several common challenges: confronting ageist beliefs, adapting psychotherapy to the needs of this population, setting realistic goals for psychological intervention, appreciating transference and countertransference issues, and considering the ethical dimensions of care.

Confronting Ageist Beliefs

For trainees with little exposure to working with older adults outside of the nursing home setting, perceptions of what it means to be "old" may be skewed by the training experience. Discussions of "normal aging" as opposed to disease processes may be appropriate (Wilber & Zarit, 1987). Providing trainees the opportunity to interact with healthy elderly people will help them learn how to distinguish psychopathology in late life from ageist stereotypes (Hubbard, 1984; Peake & Philpot, 1991). **Ideally, psychology training in the nursing home setting should be complemented by geropsychology training that offers exposure to a wider range of older adults in outpatient and community settings.**

Adaptations of Psychotherapy for Frail Elders

Psychotherapy with older adults in LTC may not take the form of the "50-minute hour" with which trainees may be accustomed. **Learning to adapt assessment and psychotherapy techniques to the potential sensory deficits, attentional limitations or fatigue, cognitive deficits, or communication difficulties of the older person will be part of the training process. Furthermore, cohort, educational, and cross-cultural issues that may influence an older person's style of self-expression and ease with verbal communication need to be recognized and discussed during trainee supervision** (Knight, 1996; Wilber & Zarit, 1987). Similar adaptations of group and family therapies to the abilities of the patients and changing late-life family dynamics will also be part of the training. In addition, psychological assessment and intervention in the nursing home must take into account space limitations and other environmental challenges; working at the bedside and coping with a shortage of private meeting spaces and noisy surroundings are frequently new experiences for trainees (Lewinsohn et al., 1984). Learning to be comfortable with flexibility is also an important part of psychology training in LTC.

Setting Realistic Goals for Psychological Intervention

An unfortunate consequence of improved reimbursement for psychological services in long-term care has been financial abuse, including the submission of claims for psychological services for residents who are unable to benefit from such services. **An important part of supervision includes helping trainees to determine when psychological intervention is possible and potentially beneficial and when it is not.** Learning to recognize treatable syndromes and offer appropriate and effective interventions is the key to training in this setting. **It is important to help trainees set realistic goals for psychological intervention, which may mean taking note of small changes that improve the patient's quality of life rather than trying to** offer a "cure" (Hubbard, 1984; Lewinsohn et al., 1984; Peake & Philpot, 1991; Wilber & Zarit, 1987).

Transference and Countertransference

Trainees may have a range of reactions to working with people living in a nursing home. **This typically frail, frequently cognitive-impaired, and often terminally ill population can arouse feelings of anxiety, helplessness, and despair among trainees** (Peake & Philpot, 1991). Depending on the trainee's age and personal life, these feelings may include fears about one's own mortality or the aging, disability, and death of one's parents (Hubbard, 1984). People who work with frail elders often develop a desire to "save" the person, do everything one can to help, or become a substitute for a social network; such reactions can place an unrealistic emotional burden on the trainee and may foster dependency in the elder (Lewinsohn et al., 1984; Wilber & Zarit, 1987). Alternatively, trainees may be reluctant to become engaged with the resident, fearing that they will feel helpless or angry in the face of the resident's predicament. The trainees' work may also be influenced by concerns about their own age and inexperience relative to that of their patients (Duffy, 1992; Hubbard, 1984; Peake & Philpot, 1991; Wilber & Zarit, 1987), difficulties with terminating psychotherapy relationships, and reactions to "inappropriate" behaviors by their patients. **Good supervision will provide a venue for trainees to discuss how these emotional reactions may be affecting their work with older patients.**

Transference issues that arise in psychotherapy with older adults may also be confusing for trainees. **An older person's relationship with a therapist can take on many meanings, which are not always defined by the age or gender of the therapist.** Given the older person's complex life history, the therapist may come to represent a child, a grandchild, a parent, another authority figure, or a sexual or romantic object (Knight, 1996). As Peake and Philpot (1991) suggest, it is important to ask, "What role is the therapist being recruited to play?" Sometimes those roles may feel uncomfortable or confusing for a younger trainee who expects a certain type of relationship with an older person. **In the authors' experiences, many older adults are very comfortable with a reality-based psychologist-client relationship, and most are not nearly as concerned about age differences as trainees are.**

Ethical Dimensions of Care

Training and supervision of psychologists in the nursing home should also focus on the many ethical dilemmas that arise in this setting, including the need to respect the autonomy of the older person; to secure informed consent for treatment; and to address questions of decision-making capacity, confidentiality, and risk assessment. (See Moye chapter in this volume.) Trainees may struggle with the many "gray" areas that arise in clinical situations and may be guided through a process of resolving ethical dilemmas. Frequently, answers are not obvious and can be subjective and value-laden. Helping trainees identify the values that they bring to their work and the values of patients, families, and other care providers will facilitate the development of informed, ethical interventions.

Designing and Evaluating Interventions:

Although trainees should be aware of and use empirically documented interventions, relatively little is known about the efficacy of many interventions that are used in nursing homes. **Trainees should be encouraged to develop creative therapeutic strategies in their work in these settings.** For example, in the authors' experience, trainees have brought admirable energy and enthusiasm to the development of new psychotherapy groups. **As scientist-practitioners, trainees should be encouraged to document the outcomes of their interventions by selecting appropriate pre- and postintervention measures.** At this point in the development of the field, psychologists in long-term care can benefit from sharing successes and failures by reviewing case studies, and trainees may be encouraged to write particularly challenging or interesting cases. Controlled research is another possible method of evaluating treatment outcomes. If research opportunities are available, trainees must be introduced to the ethical dimensions of conducting research in LTC settings.

The Didactic Component of Training

Whether or not a formal didactic component is part of psychology training in a nursing home setting will, obviously, depend on the resources of the site and the time availability of supervisors. **If possible, the training program should include a seminar, especially if there are multiple trainees at a site.** The authors have found it helpful to present didactic information during the early months of the seminar, then have trainees present topics of particular interest to them. Possible presentation formats include case presentations as part of the seminar or having the seminar function as a "journal club," with group members sharing information on the latest research literature. Several helpful resources for planning the didactic component of a seminar include outlines of useful topics to cover (e.g., Gallagher-Thompson & Thompson, 1995; Lewinsohn et al., 1984).

Reimbursement for Psychology Training in Nursing Home Settings

Before discussing funding and reimbursement, it is important to emphasize that psychologists are not likely to be involved in training primarily for monetary rewards. Motivations include the opportunity to contribute to the training of future geropsychologists, to increase the sensitization of future psychologists to aging issues, to gain exposure to current science and practice issues, to improve patient care, and to improve job satisfaction through the energy and enthusiasm gained by training students.

Financial and reimbursement issues depend on three factors: (a) **the site of practice and training,** (b) **the educational level of the student, and** (c) **the patient's insurance.** These issues will be discussed in the context of practice within the Department of Veterans Affairs and within the private sector.

The Federal Setting—Veterans Affairs:

The Department of Veterans Affairs has been an important setting for geropsychology training at the internship and postdoctoral level (Cooley, 1995). Those practicing and providing training in a Department of Veterans Affairs setting will face issues that are different from those in the private sector. **Within the Veterans Administration setting, training opportunities** (for psychology externs, interns, or postdoctoral fellows) **typically depend on the relationships among the psychology service, the director of training, the medical director, various service chiefs** (extended care, nursing, and psychiatry)**, and the staff of other hospitals within the health care system and network.** As the Department of Veterans Affairs health care system continues to be restructured and begins to address issues of financial accountability, training programs in this system may eventually face financial viability challenges similar to those in the private sector. However, for the present time, reimbursement for psychology training in this federal setting is less problematic.

The Private Sector:

Psychologists who practice and provide training in the private sector, by contrast, are faced with challenges that involve billing, reimbursement, and covering costs. Training practicum students, psychology externs, and other students who receive no stipend is straightforward. These students provide psychological interventions and gain expertise within the context of learning, free-of-charge to the patient, under the license of the supervisor. Neither the student nor the supervisor is reimbursed for his or her time. Malpractice insurance must be covered by the student, the university, or the supervisor's insurance (Qualls et al., 1995). The supervisor may or may not have a contract arrangement with a nursing home, but he or she is not eligible to bill Medicare or insurance carriers for services provided by students. Preinternship training incurs no "direct" costs for the supervisor exist (except insurance, in some cases). The basis of "indirect" costs is two-fold: (a) time to select, train, and supervise students; and (b) time, cost, and effort to attain and maintain competence in geropsychology in order to be able to provide adequate training to others and keep up with rapid developments in the field.

Training psychology interns and postdoctoral fellows in a private sector setting is more challenging. Typically, interns and fellows receive a stipend from the institution at which they are training. These stipends, while low from the student's perspective, comprise an added expense for the institution. The student on stipend may be evaluated from a cost perspective; i.e., is the student covering his or her costs, making money for the institution, or costing the institution money? **Because it is becoming more and more difficult to cover costs, successful training programs require commitment to training at a variety of levels within the institution: the psychology staff must provide supervision with minimal monetary compensation for their time, and the executive staff and board of directors must support training both philosophically and financially.**

Many elderly persons have Medicare as their primary insurance. Each state and Medicare carrier has different guidelines regarding who can bill Medicare and for what services. **Medicare does not reimburse for mental health services unless the provider of those services has been approved by Medicare** (typically, a fully licensed psychologist or social worker). **Although the typical psychology intern or postdoctoral fellow has a masters degree** (and therefore has qualifications equivalent to those of the individual with a masters in social work)**, neither is eligible to bill Medicare for reimbursement for providing assessment or psychotherapy services because neither is fully licensed.** It is important to be knowledgeable about regulations for reimbursement in one's state, as they will affect the financial viability of any training program.

Psychology interns and postdoctoral fellows may co-lead group therapy in nursing home settings with fully licensed psychologists who can bill Medicare. Such co-leading can provide both excellent training and a rewarding professional experience for the licensed psychologist. **In addition, some facilities, institutions, and individual providers have negotiated contracts with HMOs that allow trainees to provide individual therapy and assessment under the supervision of a licensed psychologist.** Finally, some psychologists (and/or psychology students) have obtained private grants to partially offset the costs involved in training. In these situations, the student provides mental health services free-of-charge to the patient but receives some remuneration for his or her time.

Conclusion

Psychology training in LTC settings carries both challenges and rewards. Planning a training program entails a fair degree of commitment to serving the present and future mental health needs of the most vulnerable older adults by ensuring that psychologists have the skills necessary to work with this growing, underserved population. Although many financial and systemic barriers to providing such training exist, creative strategies will allow psychologists to continue to provide training in nursing home settings. This article provides practical guidelines for psychology training and supervision in long term care, as well as suggested resources for trainees and supervisors.

Appendix
Suggested Bibliography / References for Trainees

A. Geropsychology and Psychology Practice in the Nursing Home

Birren, J. E., Sloane, R. B., & Cohen G. D. (Eds.). (1992). *Handbook of mental health and aging* (2nd ed.). San Diego, CA: Academic Press.

Carstenson, L. L., Edelstein, B. A., & Dornbrand, L. (Eds.). (1996). *The practical handbook of clinical gerontology.* Thousand Oaks, CA: Sage Publications.

Hartz, G. W., & Splain, D. M. (1997). *Psychological intervention in long-term care: An advanced guide.* Binghamton, NY: Haworth Press.

Hersen, M., & Van Hasselt, V. B. (1996). *Psychological treatment of older adults: An introductory text.* New York: Plenum Publishing.

Hussian, R. A., & Davis, R. L. (1985). *Responsive care: Interventions with elderly persons.* Champaign, IL: Research Press.

Kane, R. K., & Caplan, A. L. (Eds.). (1990). *Everyday ethics: Resolving dilemmas in nursing home life.* New York: Springer Publishing.

Knight, B. G. (1996). *Psychotherapy with older adults* (2nd ed.). Thousand Oaks, CA: Sage Publications.

Lichtenberg, P. A. (1994). *A guide to psychological practice in geriatric long-term care.* New York: Haworth Press.

Qualls, S. H., & Czirr, R. (1988). Geriatric health teams: Classifying models of professional and team functioning. *The Gerontologist, 28,* 372–376.

Smyer, M., Cohn, M., & Brannon, D. (1988). *Mental health consultation in nursing homes.* New York: New York University Press.

Zarit, S. H., & Knight, B. G. (Eds.) (1996). *A guide to psychotherapy and aging: Effective clinical interventions in a life-stage context.* Washington, DC: American Psychological Association.

B. Medical and Psychiatric Illness

Abrams, W. B., Beers, M. H., & Berkow, R. (Eds.). (1995). *The Merck manual of geriatrics* (2nd ed.). Whitehouse Station, NJ: Merck.

Beers, M. H., & Urice, S. K. (1992). *Aging in good health: A complete, essential medical guide for older men and women and their families.* New York: Simon & Schuster.

Appendix (cont.)
Suggested Bibliography / References for Trainees

Busse, E. W., & Blazer, D. G. (Eds.). (1996). *Textbook of geriatric psychiatry* (2nd ed.). Washington, DC: American Psychiatric Press.

Cassel, C. K., Riesenberg, D. E., Sorenson, L. B., & Walsh, J. R. (Eds.). (1990). *Geriatric medicine* (2nd ed.). New York: Springer-Verlag.

Cummings, J. L., & Benson, D. F. (1992). *Dementia: A clinical approach* (2nd ed.). Boston: Butterworths-Heinemann.

Sadavoy, J., Lazarus, L. W., Jarvik, L. F., & Grossberg, G. T. (Eds.). (1996). *Comprehensive review of geriatric psychiatry* (2nd ed.). Washington, DC: American Psychiatric Press.

Williams, M. E. (1995). *The American Geriatrics Society's complete guide to aging and health.* New York: Harmony Books.

C. Gero/Neuropsychological Assessment

Albert, M. A., & Moss, M. B. (1988). *Geriatric neuropsychology.* New York: Guilford Press.

LaRue, A. (1992). *Aging and neuropsychological assessment.* New York: Plenum Press.

U.S. Department of Veterans Affairs, National Center for Cost Containment. (1996). Geropsychological assessment resource guide. Milwaukee, WI: Author. (Copies available from National Technical Information Service, U.S. Department of Commerce, 5285 Port Royal Road, Springfield, VA 22161, (703) 487–4650.) *This is an excellent resource for psychological assessment tools appropriate for use with older adults, with information on reliability, validity, references, and how to obtain tests.*

Storandt, M., & VandenBos, G.R. (1994). *Neuropsychological assessment of dementia and depression in older adults: A clinician's guide.* Washington, DC: American Psychological Association.

D. Pharmacology

DiGregorio, G. J., Barbieri, E. J., Kennedy, M. C., & Ferko, A. P., et al. (1993). *Handbook of commonly prescribed geriatric drugs.* Westchester, PA: Medical Surveillance.

Silverman, H. M. (Ed.). (1996). *The pill book.* New York: Bantam.

Smith, P. F., & Darlington, C. L. (1996). Clinical psychopharmacology: A primer.

Appendix (cont.)
Suggested Bibliography / References for Trainees

E.   Medical Abbreviations

Davis, N. M. (1997). *Medical abbreviations: 12,000 conveniences at the expense of communications and safety.* Huntington Valley, PA: Neill M. Davis Associates.

F.   State and Federal Regulations

Hartman-Stein, R. (1997). *Innovative behavioral healthcare for older adults: A guidebook for changing times.* San Francisco: Jossey-Bass.

Lombardo, N. E., Fogel, B. S., Robinson, G. K., & Weiss, H. P. (1995). Achieving mental health of nursing home residents: Overcoming barriers to mental health care. *Journal of Mental Health and Aging, 1,* 165–211.

Robinson, G. K., Haggard, L., & Rohrer, C. F. (1990). *Nursing home reform and its implications for mental health care.* Washington, DC: Mental Health Policy Resource Center.

References

Cooley, S. (1995). Geropsychology services and training in the U.S. Department of Veterans Affairs. In B. G. Knight, L. Teri, P. Wohlford, & J. Santos (Eds.), *Mental health services for older adults: Implications for training and practice in geropsychology* (pp. 11–20). Washington, DC: American Psychological Association.

Duffy, M. (1992). A multimethod model for practicum and clinical supervision in nursing homes. *Counselor Education and Supervision, 32,* 61–69.

Gallagher-Thompson, D., & Thompson, L. W. (1995). Issues in geropsychology training at the internship level. In B. G. Knight, L. Teri, P. Wohlford, & J. Santos (Eds.), *Mental health services for older adults: Implications for training and practice in geropsychology* (pp. 129–142). Washington, DC: American Psychological Association.

Hubbard, R. W. (1984). Clinical issues in the supervision of geriatric mental health trainees. *Educational Gerontology, 10,* 317–323.

Knight, B. G. (1996). *Psychotherapy with older adults* (2nd ed.). Thousand Oaks, CA: Sage Publications.

Knight, B. G., Teri, L., Wohlford, P., & Santos, J. (Eds.) (1995). *Mental health services for older adults: Implications for training and practice in geropsychology.* Washington, DC: American Psychological Association.

Lewinsohn, P. M., Teri, L., & Hautzinger, M. (1984). Training clinical psychologists for work with older adults: A working model. *Professional Psychology: Research and Practice, 15,* 187–202.

Lichtenberg, P. A. (1994). *A guide to psychological practice in geriatric long-term care.* New York: Haworth Press.

Lichtenberg, P. A., Smith, M., Frazer, D., et al. (1998). Standards for psychological services in long term care facilities. *The Gerontologist, 38,* 122–127.

Lundervold, D. A., & Lewin, L. M. (1992). *Behavior analysis and therapy in nursing homes.* Springfield, IL: Charles C. Thomas.

Peake, T. H. & Philpot, C. (1991). Psychotherapy with older adults: Hopes and fears. Special settings, stages and mind sets. *Clinical Supervisor, 9,* 185–202.

Qualls, S. H., & Czirr, R. (1988). Geriatric health teams: Classifying models of professional and team functioning. *The Gerontologist, 28,* 372–376.

Qualls, S. H., Duffy, M., & Crose, R. (1995). Clinical supervision and practicum placements in graduate training. In B. G. Knight, L. Teri, P. Wohlford, & J. Santos (Eds.), *Mental health services for older adults: Implications for training and practice in geropsychology* (pp. 119–128). Washington, DC: American Psychological Association.

Smyer, M., Cohn, M., & Brannon, D. (1988). *Mental health consultation in nursing homes.* New York: New York University Press.

Tsukuda, R. A. (1990). *Interdisciplinary collaboration: Teamwork in geriatrics.* In C. K. Cassel, D. E. Riesenberg, L. B. Sorensen, & J. R. Walsh (Eds.), Geriatric Medicine (2nd ed., pp. 668–678). New York: Springer-Verlag.

Wilber, K. H., & Zarit, S. H. (1987). Practicum training in gerontological counseling. *Educational Gerontology, 13,* 15–32.

17

The Impact of Culture and Gender on Mental Health

ROYDA CROSE, PH.D.

Abstract

ISSUES OF culture and gender in long term care (LTC) have not yet been sufficiently addressed in the research literature or in clinical description. However, the psychologist must be able to recognize and respect the distinctive aspects of adjusting to living in institutionalized care for older men and women and for ethnic minorities. This chapter outlines some of the gender and cultural issues reflected in patient and staff struggles for control, relationships, and responses to stress in long term care. Case examples are provided to illustrate some special gender and cultural concerns, and references to the research literature of gender and cultural differences in the general population are provided.

Objectives: After reading this chapter, the learner will:

1. Be able to recognize the cultural and engendered environment of long-term care facilities.
2. Be aware of gender and cultural differences in coping with control, relationships, and stress for patients and staff in long term care.
3. Recognize some special concerns and issues of women, men, and ethnic minorities in long term care.
4. Be sensitive to his or her own countertransference issues when working with patients in long term care.

Introduction

Most information and research on older adults, especially those in long term care, tends to view the process of aging and illness as generic and universal. Although some concern for individual differences has been expressed for diagnostic and treatment protocols, little attention has been paid to gender, culture, race, class, and other issues that reflect the ever widening diversity of the aging population. **Varying lifetime experiences, educational levels, family structures, religious views, and other individual characteristics make older people a much more complex group than children, adolescents, or even younger adults.**

The elders of today remember two world wars, the Great Depression, and a time when women and minorities were denied the right to vote and equal protection under the law, employment, education, and housing. The older women and minorities who currently live in nursing homes grew up at a time of unquestioned white male rule and have experienced discrimination throughout most of their lives. Many arrived in this country as immigrants or were born to immigrant parents for whom English was a second or third language. These unique life experiences have shaped their worldviews, beliefs, and behaviors. **Younger health care workers, including psychologists, need to recognize and respect**

the historical and cultural context in which these remarkable elders have managed to develop the resilience, pride, and coping skills that enabled them to survive into old age. Too many health care workers see only the old, frail bodies of their patients and not the individuals within who have their own long histories of pain, triumph, problems, and successes.

Psychologists are too often called in to the LTC setting to correct "manipulative" or "disruptive" behaviors which are viewed only within the context of institutional efficiency for assembly line care. These problems are identified by a young, overworked, underpaid, and psychologically unsophisticated staff which is expected to run their medically-oriented facility with efficiency and economy and to keep their patients quiet and compliant, if not happy. The meaning of these behaviors and the possibility that they may serve some beneficial purpose for the patients are rarely considered in the rush to diagnose and change the behaviors.

It is essential for the psychologist to investigate and highlight the context in which these behaviors occur by uncovering the historical, cultural, and gender influences that may have led to the problems being exhibited. Such individual information has often been lost over time; with high staff turnover rates, few caregivers know much about their LTC patients (especially those with no family to provide ongoing information) other than what is in their medical charts. **Historical and contextual information may often allow "problem behaviors" to be reframed as adaptive coping mechanisms that make sense for particular patients.**

Of course, gender and cultural influences also affect the perspectives and behaviors of other residents, staff, and family members, and the psychologist must consider all these issues in determining the best treatment plan for an individual patient. Unfortunately, the research literature and clinical descriptions have not sufficiently addressed the topics of gender and culture in LTC, particularly in regards to psychological and mental health issues.

This chapter discusses the literature on gender and cultural influences in lifespan development and other contexts, and this knowledge is then applied to case studies based on the author's personal experience as a consultant to LTC facilities. The case examples presented are composites, and any identifying details have been changed to protect confidentiality.

The Environment of the Long Term Care Facility

When you enter a nursing home, you are typically entering a world of white, lower- to upper-middle-class women in which residents, staff, and families must interact under stressful and psychologically challenging dynamics. **At least two thirds of nursing home residents and almost all nursing home staff persons** (including volunteers and students-in-training) **are female** (see Savishinsky, 1991, for a description of modern nursing homes). **Most of the family caregivers directly involved in decision making for residents are women** (daughters, daughters-in-law, nieces, sisters, granddaughters, etc.). **Few residents and only a small proportion of staff are people of color or members of other ethnic minorities** (although more ethnic minorities tend to work on staff in large metropolitan areas than in smaller community facilities). As a result, most LTC facilities are homes and workplaces for white women who have few alternative options for care or for employment. Whereas the residents may view the LTC facility as a place where they will spend the last days of their lives, many of the staff consider their jobs merely temporary, expecting to hold them only until they can gain more skills or obtain more education in order to find better ones. The resignation, discontent, and hopelessness of many residents and the high turnover rates for the nursing home staff are testimony to these conditions.

Of course, there are exceptions to these generalizations. About one third of all nursing home residents and most nursing home physicians, owners, and corporate executives are male. Increasing numbers of ethnic minorities are entering long term care, and some facilities located in the inner cities or in minority neighborhoods or communities have large numbers of African-American and/or Hispanic residents and staff. A few residents have freely chosen to move into LTC facilities and are happy to be there because they may be cleaner, safer, and more comfortable than places in which they previously lived. Some are only there for rehabilitation after surgery or a stay in the hospital and will return home when they are well enough to do so. In addition, some staff love their work and intend to stay for a long time. **However, most of the people within the nursing home or LTC environment are trying to make the best of a difficult situation they did not freely choose for themselves, one in which they have little independence or control. Finding ways to maintain or gain control in work and/or life, establishing reciprocal and meaningful relationships, and learning to cope with the significant stress that institutional care produces are the issues that most often require psychological consultation. The psychologist should be knowledgeable about the gender and cultural considerations that affect each of these issues.**

Control Issues

Older people grew up in a time when there were clearly defined gender roles. Men were the providers and worked outside the home; women were the nurturers and caretakers within the home (see Gutmann, 1987). Even women who worked outside their homes still did almost all of the housework and provided child care for their families. Men often did physical labor or ran small businesses in which they had control of their bodies and their lives. **For both men and women, an institutional environment in which others take care of all their needs may represent a significant and distressing loss of control.**

In a time when women had little power in society, their homes were the source of control for them. They made decisions regarding meals, schedules, laundry, and housecleaning. For them to live in a place where they can perform none of these activities and where others make all of these decisions is very difficult. **Food,**

laundry, and other domestic concerns thus become the focus of discontent for many women patients in long-term care. Men, who are used to having food prepared by someone else and to being served their meals, are less apt to complain about the food or housekeeping. But for women, losing control over these functions means losing power in their lives. Many despair that they can no longer take care of themselves or others in these meaningful ways, some constantly complain about the quality or taste of the food, and some even develop eating disorders that are usually thought to afflict primarily younger women in this society. Family caregivers (usually women) may feel guilty about relinquishing control of their loved one to professional health care workers, and these feelings may be expressed as demanding and complaining behaviors toward the nurses and nurse's aides. **Understanding these losses and the resulting problems as struggles for control can help the staff depersonalize such complaints and work more effectively with residents and families. The psychologist is often asked to intervene in struggles for control over basic activities of daily living, such as eating, bathing, grooming, and toileting.**

Food and Eating Issues:

When, what, and with whom we eat are important to us throughout life. In an environment where almost all other controls are taken away and when one is frail and weak, food becomes one of the few mechanisms for asserting control.

Case Study:

Ms. M, a 90-year-old patient, had stopped eating anything but the candy and cookies that she received from family and friends. Her weight dropped to 85 pounds and she seemed very fragile. She stayed curled in a fetal position in her bed most of the day. She had been chronically depressed for most of her adult life and had consulted many physicians, including psychiatrists, who could find no medical reasons for her complaints of constant stomach pain. Her psychiatrist had instructed the staff to get her out of bed, dressed, and into the congregate dining room to eat her meals. He believed that socialization was important for relief from her depression. Ms. M did not agree and insisted on taking her meals in her room. The more the staff pressured her to go to the dining room, the less she ate and the more time she spent in bed. She lost her appetite for any food but the sweets that came to her from outside the nursing home.

Staff members were quite worried about but also very irritated by Ms. M's stubborn refusal to eat and became locked in a no-win struggle with her for control. They were also caught in the middle between the orders and expectations of the male physician and the patient's resistance to his recommendations. In uncovering this woman's history, the psychologist discovered that Ms. M had been a rather pampered wife and a socialite in her community. She did not want to socialize with the other residents. She much preferred special treatment from the staff. Her refusal to eat provided her with more attention from staff than she would have obtained had she been compliant. It was one of the few ways she had to relieve the isolation and loneliness that she often felt, and it also served to explain her stomach pains. In this case, the psychologist consulted with the psychiatrist and the staff to negotiate a plan for Ms. M to get out of bed and get dressed but to be served her meals in her room as she desired. With that concession, the patient was then agreeable to work with the psychologist in psychotherapy for treatment of her depression.

A similar behavior struggled for control but with a different meaning was exhibited by a male resident.

Case Study:

Mr. C made no bones about hating his life in the nursing home. He did not appreciate the staff always telling him what to do, what to eat, and how he should feel about things. One of the things he missed most was his beer. He had no family or friends to get beer for him and he had no way to get it for himself. Staff members did not see this as important and discounted his requests. Some of them disapproved on moral grounds, others felt that it was not good for his health, and those who might have helped him did not want to be blamed by the others. He finally went on a food strike in protest and declared that he would not eat until he could have beer to drink.

The psychologist consulted with the physician and learned that there were no health reasons that the patient should be denied his request. Upon the psychologist's suggestion, the physician wrote an order for one beer a day, which the staff was then obligated to obtain and keep in the refrigerator for him. Mr. C began to eat his food and felt that he had won a major victory in gaining some control over his life. The staff members were also satisfied because they were following the doctor's order.

Control of food, housekeeping, bathing, and grooming are also influenced by cultural factors. The menus in most LTC institutions are designed around middle-class caucasian preferences. This leaves ethnic minorities dissatisfied and sometimes at risk because they do not eat enough to meet their dietary needs. For example, most meals in institutions and in home-delivered meal programs for the homebound contain dairy products. No allowances are made for the prevalence of lactose intolerance among many African Americans or for the religious restrictions of Orthodox Jews. If the dairy products are not eaten, then those patients' nutritional needs are not being met, no matter how carefully the culturally insensitive dietary staff has planned and regulated the meals.

Bathing and Grooming Issues:

Many older people grew up in a time when bathing every day, or even more than once a week, was considered wasteful and detrimental to health. They may find an insistence on bathing on a more frequent schedule distressful and even demeaning, particularly if staff members suggest that they are unclean unless they do so. Some religions have strict rules about hairstyles, cosmetics, and dress. For example, some Pentecostal groups require women to wear long sleeves, dresses, and hose, avoid jewelry or make-up, and never cut their hair. Muslim beliefs also focus on covering women's bodies with special clothing. Some Orthodox Jewish women wear wigs to cover their heads. As long as women from such groups have family to advise about or attend to these special needs, they may be able to continue to follow these religious teachings; however, if these patients suffer from a communication disorder such as a stroke or dementia and family are not available, they may not be able to explain these special needs. Many will show distress if these rules of dress and grooming are not followed by the staff who dress and care for them.

Case Vignette:

Ms. R was an orthodox Jew who emigrated from eastern Europe. As her dementia worsened, she used English less and less and spoke mostly in Polish. The staff could not understand what she wanted most of the time. However, she was usually cooperative and pleasant, except when they tried to arrange her long, silvery hair into attractive styles. She would push them away and become visibly upset. Ms. R's son lived nearby but rarely visited her and took very little interest in her day-to-day care. As Ms. R's ability to communicate deteriorated, she became more oppositional to personal care, and the staff asked the psychologist for an evaluation and recommendations.

Since the son offered very little help in this evaluation, the psychologist called Ms. R's sister, who lived in another state, to get the family history and more information about the patient. The sister mentioned that Ms. R had always worn a wig to cover her head as part of her religious beliefs. With this piece of information, staff members were then able to help her maintain her dignity in grooming, even when she could no longer speak for herself. When a wig was not feasible, a scarf usually sufficed to comfort her and reduce her resistance to care. Even though the staff thought that her beautiful hair was much more attractive, Ms. R much preferred keeping her hair covered with a wig or scarf.

Men do not typically have the same control issues regarding food, dress, and grooming, but they may be more stressed by administrative issues, like building maintenance and design, the perceived inefficiency of staff, or the idle-

ness of other residents. They may complain about the meaningless small talk of the women and the fact that there is nothing for them to do. The following case exemplifies a man's efforts for control by critiquing administrative policies.

Case Vignette:

Mr. B was a 95-year-old retired engineer with a degenerative spinal disorder who had recently been diagnosed with prostate cancer. His primary complaints were that others in the nursing home were too content and were not addressing the institutional issues that were apparent to him. He wrote long letters to the administrators about the need for visitors to sign in to avoid invading his privacy. He also made formal complaints about the furniture arrangements in the dining room, the unsightly vending machines, and the behavior of the community cat. Less educated staff viewed him as a thorn in their sides, and the administrator ignored his letters and threw them in the wastebasket.

This man had been active in the community and felt a strong obligation to make the world a better place. Although his world had been reduced to the nursing home, he continued to advocate for change by identifying problems and making recommendations to the people in charge. Finally, a new administrator took his letters seriously and began to schedule time each month to sit down with this very frail elderly man to ask for his input. This was just the right thing to do for Mr. B's mental well being. Even though the administrator seldom acted on his suggestions, Mr. B felt that he was involved and was satisfied that he had been heard.

Men also seem to have more difficulty accepting personal care from staff and may respond to physical and emotional care in inappropriate ways. Men are more apt to make sexual overtures to female staff members who provide personal care such as bathing, dressing, or emotional support. These older men have typically had little experience in receiving such personal attention from anyone with whom they were not involved in a romantic, sexually intimate relationship. It may come as a surprise to unsuspecting staff when a male patient becomes aggressive or when he becomes resistant to personal care, because they do not realize the sexual connotations that these procedures bring up for him.

Case Vignette:

Mr. V, a lifelong businessman, had been placed in an LTC facility when he began to suffer from increased confusion and depression and his wife was no longer able to care for him in their home. He adjusted to the new environment fairly well, with his wife visiting every day and taking care of most of his needs. When it was time for him to be bathed, however, he resisted the staff's assistance to the point of becoming combative.

In investigating the history of this man, the psychologist discovered that he had always kept a very strict time schedule. He habitually consulted his appointment book for his daily activities. Staff members were able to use this information to their advantage by giving Mr. V a little appointment book in which they listed his daily activities in the nursing home, including his meals and his bathing schedule. When he resisted going with them into the shower room, they asked him to check his book to verify that it was on his schedule. This seemed to reassure him that bathing was a necessary activity, and he became much more cooperative.

Relational Issues

Gender differences in identity development and relationships have been described by feminist scholars, psychologists, and gerontologists (Crose, 1997; Crose et al., 1992; Gilligan, 1982; Miller, 1976; Neugarten & Gutmann, 1964). In their challenge to traditional views of human development, **Jordan and colleagues** (1991) **called for a recognition that women develop identity as a "self-in-relation" to others rather than following the "autonomous self" model that traditional psychology typically views as normal.** They argue that women learn to be more interdependent than men, but the normal behaviors of women are too often diagnosed as pathological because of gender bias in mainstream psychology (see Crose, 1991, for further discussion). **Women's relational skills lead them to take caregiving roles in society; because of sex discrimination, however, these roles are not valued as highly as the roles typically played by men.** The hierarchical structure of LTC facilities and the caregiving nature of the environment make nursing homes fertile ground for study of such dynamics.

Staff and Patient Relationships:

Jean Baker Miller's (1976) account of the relegation of women to work that is considered subordinate in our society describes not only the former experience of many women residents but also the current experience of nurses and nurse's aides in long term care.

> . . . subordinates are assigned generally less-valued tasks. It is interesting to note that these tasks usually involve providing bodily needs and comforts. Subordinates are expected to make pleasant, orderly, or clean those parts of the body or things to do with the body that are perceived as unpleasant, uncontrollable, or dirty. (p. 22)

Nurse's aides and practical nurses are on the frontline of care and are subordinate to everyone else in the LTC system. They have to deal with resistant, combative, aggressive, and sometimes discriminatory behaviors of residents, and they are also the first to be blamed by residents, family members, and supervisors when things do not go well. Yet they have the least say about who is admitted, what residents' treatment plans will be, and what actions will be taken in their care. **These work demands, as well as their own personal problems, such as low incomes and family concerns, often place them under high-stress conditions that may diminish their effectiveness as caregivers to their patients** (Crose & Kixmiller, 1994). **If these low-level staff follow a "self-in-relation" model for identity and validation, they are more likely to develop relationships with residents and coworkers that affect their own emotional well-being. This effect, however, may be both positive and negative.**

Job satisfaction for LTC staff often centers around relationships with their patients, in which they tend to project personal meaning to their patients' actions rather than maintain a professional distance, as is done by those in higher positions. As a result, resident behaviors may be interpreted as personal affronts by these caregivers, who then feel abused and manipulated by their patients. **The relationship between caregiver and patient may develop into a fight for control in such a hierarchical system, in which the direct care staff have little control over their work and the residents have even less over their lives.**

Isolation in Long Term Care:

Although the patients and staff who live and work in LTC facilities are mostly white and female, they are far from being a homogeneous group. Both patients and caregivers differ widely in education, family structures, religious beliefs, and life experiences. There is probably no other setting in which people with such wide-ranging differences are forced to coexist in such close quarters. Even without introducing gender and ethnicity as major issues, relationship problems are common for the women who live and work in LTC facilities.

Men are less apt to have such relational problems because they are used to being more isolated and their identity development is centered around autonomy and self-sufficiency. They do not join in the group activities or chat with staff or other residents as much as women. **Because of sex role stereotypes, staff may not question reclusiveness in men as much as they would in women.** An activity director once revealed, "I don't expect men to be as interested in the activities as women are, so I don't push them to participate." For this staff member, women who did not want to participate would be considered withdrawn and depressed, but similar men were just acting normally.

Minorities are also often more isolated in LTC facilities as a result of a long history of racial discrimination in this society. These older adults have learned to be cautious in a white culture and to be careful about revealing themselves for fear of be-

386   PROFESSIONAL PSYCHOLOGY IN LONG TERM CARE

ing seriously hurt (Padgett, 1995). **Even though the facility may have nondiscriminatory policies, older whites** (as well as some younger staff persons and family members) **who have grown up in a racist culture may use language and behaviors that are discriminatory toward other residents as well as toward minority staff members and visitors.** Such racial issues in long-term care have not been studied and are rarely discussed, but psychologists should be on the alert for such cultural influences on the mental health of both staff and residents. Some researchers have described several minority groups as having closer family ties than whites, whereas others have disputed or questioned these findings. The following case demonstrates some of the issues of isolation and family relationships that may arise in long term care:

Case Vignette:

Ms. D was the only African-American patient in the nursing home. Although most of the residents and all of the staff were kind to her, she just didn't feel at ease. Some of the other residents made it clear that they did not want to sit with her at mealtime, and one had even made several racially biased comments. Her family was upset that she had to be there, and they knew that she was feeling lonely and isolated, so they visited as often as they could and called upon other relatives, friends, and members of her church to visit as well. The staff began to complain that they could not schedule her personal care or housekeeping because of her having so many visitors all day long.

The typical nursing home resident has few visitors, which makes staff and other residents their primary social network. When family and friends visit LTC patients regularly, routines have to be adjusted and staff members may complain about such disruptions in their routine duties. Some may even view such support as tiring and unhealthy for the patient. **Although outside attention and support may delay or prevent the integration of patients into the LTC social environment, it may be necessary for the well being of patients from minority ethnic or racial**

groups. Indeed, most residents would benefit from more visitation from people outside the facility, even though this would interfere with the demands of institutional care. One administrator confessed that sometimes her job would be much easier if "all my residents were orphans." As LTC facilities become more culturally and ethnically diverse, staff routines will have to accommodate the differing relationship needs of their patients.

Complex family, staff, and patient relationships have an important bearing on psychological issues in long term care. Relational conflicts or misunderstandings abound among patients, staff, and family caregivers, and among members of each of these groups. Gender differences in relationships and the need for ethnic affiliation and protection against ethnic discrimination complicate these problems. Sexual issues add even more complexity to the relational mix.

Sexual Issues:

Consensual sexual relationships are difficult for LTC patients because of illness and lack of privacy. Even masturbating in private is often problematic, as doors are usually required to be unlocked and staff may be in the habit of entering without knocking and waiting for an invitation. Patients who desire heterosexual relationships sometimes face opposition from the staff and/or family, so the psychologist may need to serve as an advocate for their rights. Gay and lesbian issues in nursing homes are so controversial that they have not begun to be recognized, must less discussed, in the literature or in clinical work.

Sexual desire on the part of one individual (usually a male) for another patient who is confused or unwilling may take the form of sexual harassment or even, in some cases, sexual assault. This occurs most often with demented patients who have lost inhibitions and social controls. **Active intervention has to be taken to prevent sexual assault, but the more subtle forms of sexual harassment may be ignored by staff members who do not understand the stress it causes for the victim.** Sometimes such behavior may even be viewed by staff as "cute" or "romantic" rather than harassing.

Case Vignette:

Ms. L had become increasingly anxious and distressed after her husband's death. It had been almost a year since he died, but she was unable to sleep and was more fatigued, confused, and distressed than she had been earlier in her grief process. During a clinical interview with the psychologist, she revealed that she did not feel safe and was often unable to go to sleep; once asleep, she would have disturbing dreams. She complained about a disoriented, rather threatening-looking man who would sometimes come in her room during the day and try to get into bed with her while she was resting. She would yell at him and he would leave, but she was increasingly worried that he might come in at night while she was asleep and she wouldn't be able to scare him away.

The staff saw this man as harmless and felt that he was just confused about where his own room was, so they did not take Ms. L's concerns seriously. They joked and assured her that he was harmless and that he just had a crush on her because she was so attractive. The psychological assessment pointed out to them that this attraction was taking a toll on Ms. L's health. When staff arranged for her to move to a different wing of the facility, she began to feel safer and was finally able to sleep through the night without worrying about being accosted. Although the apparently confused assailant may not have intended to sexually harass this new widow, his behaviors were threatening her well-being in much the same way that overt sexual harassment might in another situation.

Countertransference Issues:

Genevay and Katz (1990) offer a description of countertransference in relationships with older patients. **Younger clinicians may be more susceptible to countertransference with older geriatric clients than in other therapeutic relationships.** Staff members may view their clients as lovable old people or, alternatively, as shrewd manipulators, depending on their own past experiences with older relatives and their own hopes and fears about aging. Without training in geropsychology that explores such personal dynamics, health care professionals may fall prey to countertransference problems.

Case Vignette:

Dr. S was a young psychologist who was seeking ways to build her practice in the climate of managed care. She had recently signed on with a group that provides psychological services to nursing home residents. Although she did not have specialized training in geropsychology, the company assured her that she could do the job and provided her with a manual and psychological tests and protocols geared to the elderly population. She had always been very compassionate toward older people, and for the most part she enjoyed her work. However, one of her older male clients had recently become more and more sexually suggestive in his remarks to her, and once, when she was leaving his room, he grabbed her and kissed her on the mouth. She couldn't get over the fact that this man reminded her of her Great Uncle Marcus, who used to do the same thing when she was a little girl. She had felt very uncomfortable then, and she had the same feelings about the nursing home resident's inappropriate behavior.

Such inexperience with aging, gender, and countertransference issues may interfere with the treatment of LTC patients. **Sexual issues emerge between health care professionals and older patients just as they do with younger clients.** Given the prevalence of sexual abuse of young girls by older men, countertransference issues for female caregivers in LTC settings may involve childhood experiences of sexual abuse, assault, or molestation by an older person. Psychologists who are untrained or inexperienced in geriatrics may be surprised by or even ignore such dynamics in their relationships with older people, as well as in the relationships of the LTC staff with their patients.

Many times psychologists are most susceptible to countertransference with clients who are the kind of individuals that they imagine they might become as older persons, as in the following case:

Case Vignette:

Ms. A was an intelligent 85-year-old retired professional who had recently been widowed and had suffered a stroke, which left her very impaired. Her cognitive abilities were normal, but she had significant expressive aphasia and was in poor physical condition. She was liberal in her attitudes and did not fit into the various support groups composed of homemakers and conservative religious women. She much preferred younger and more sophisticated discussion groups, but could not find transportation or other support systems to enable her to participate in such programs.

She was depressed but not as hopeless as her psychologist, Dr. B, became in trying to help her. After a few sessions, Ms. A told Dr. B that she was discounting her abilities just as others had been doing. Dr. B sought peer supervision and was confronted with her own depression about aging and disability. She learned that she was projecting her own fears onto the situation while the patient still had hope for improvement.

With this realization, Dr. B became able to listen to Ms. A's needs rather than feel defeated by her own fears. She helped Ms. A. plan to relocate to a retirement center that provided many of the cultural and socialization opportunities that she needed. Such a move improved the patient's quality of life during the 2 years that she lived after that experience. If Dr. B had not become aware of her own countertransference issues, she would have failed to help this patient.

Gender and Cultural Influences on Stress

Women's relational perspectives also lead them to take on more stress because they identify with the stress of others as well as their own. Gender differences in handling stress have been documented by several researchers (Barnett et al., 1987; Crose, 1997). Men learn to respond to stress by being tough, denying it, or acting out in aggressive, sometimes violent ways. Women learn to recognize stress, not only in themselves but also in those they care for, and to take on the stress of significant others in their environments. **In LTC settings, where both men and women patients are usually ill and their defenses against stress are weak, a stressful environment can pose a significant threat to mental well-being or even trigger catastrophic responses.**

Lack of privacy is one of the biggest stressors in LTC facilities. Most nursing homes have shared rooms; with the staggering costs of long term care, few people could afford the luxury of a private room, even if they were readily available. Roommate assignments often become the source of much conflict and distress.

Case Vignette:

Ms. R, a politically and religiously liberal woman who had had a successful career, was an avid reader, and had no children or other surviving family was arbitrarily placed in a room with Ms. P, a fundamentally religious woman who had little education, had lived on a farm all her life, had many children, grandchildren, and great-grandchildren, and loved to watch soap operas on television all day long. It was difficult for the more reclusive Ms. R to sit and read while Ms. P had the television on or was visiting with some of her many daily visitors. Negotiating living arrangements in the best interest of both residents was next to impossible. In addition, staff were under regulations to keep all residents involved in scheduled activities (such as bingo, discussion groups, and sing-a-longs) that did not appeal to either of these women. Yet staff members were persistent in encouraging residents to join in the activities and viewed those who did not comply as withdrawn, depressed, or resistant. Thus, these two women were neither suited for the activities outside their room nor able to have the privacy they needed to engage in their specialized interests within their room.

While these two women were of the same race, their cultural needs were very different. What was good for the mental health of one might be stress producing for the other. In such cases, a systems intervention might be necessary to correct the roommate pairing before beginning any individual treatment for depression, acting-out behaviors, or conflict resolution.

Privacy and control were also major concerns of the following resident:

Case Vignette:

Miss K was an 85-year-old, white female who did not want to be called by her first name and insisted on the title of Miss rather than Ms. or Mrs. because she was "old-fashioned" and "an old maid." She had become disoriented and had fallen in her apartment in the retirement village. She was transferred to the health care center, and the staff requested a psychological evaluation. She tolerated questions from the psychologist, Dr. J, for about 15 minutes before informing her that she did not want to continue and that she had no need of such services in the future. Dr. J respected her wishes and left, but noticed that on each subsequent occasion when she visited the facility, Miss K would position herself so that she could observe the psychologist's interactions with other residents. After a couple of months, she called Dr. J and informed her that she was now back in her apartment and had reconsidered. She wanted to cooperate with an evaluation, but she did not want the staff to know that she had conceded to such psychological assessment. Dr. J agreed to meet with her on her terms. Miss K consented to having a copy of the psychological report sent to her physician; she kept a copy as well in the event that she decided to share the information with the staff at a later date. She did not agree with a recommendation for treatment of her anxiety disorder, but she did consent to allowing a graduate student to visit her weekly to help with the student's training and education in psychology.

Several years later, Miss K became a permanent resident of the nursing home connected to the retirement village where she had lived. She was alert and well-adjusted, and she always greeted Dr. J as a friend and confidante whenever she saw her in the facility.

Communication skills are also related to stress in long-term care. Command of a common language is extremely important to function within any group. **Communication problems are affected by gender and cultural differences, especially when health conditions, such as stroke or dementia, impair a person's ability to communicate his or her needs, desires, and pain.** Women are more apt to seek help and to ask for assistance than men, yet men may be feeling as much pain and despair as women, if not more. The high rate of suicide among older white males indicates their failure to communicate. Many of the older men who commit suicide had just consulted with their physicians, yet they gave no indication of their intention to take their own lives (see McIntosh et al. 1994, for a discussion of elder suicide). Therefore, health care professionals must be sensitive to men's tendency to discount or deny their need for help. The following case exemplifies such a reaction to personal care:

Case Study:

Mr. P was a big, strong farmer who was widowed and was becoming increasingly demented. The nurse's aides were having trouble caring for him because he would either fight them off when they tried to help him to the toilet or he would go limp when they were assisting him and they could not hold up his weight. A couple of the staff had suffered minor back injuries as a result. Except for these outbursts of negative behavior, Mr. P was a model patient.

When the psychologist went to evaluate this man, he found him in bed in a quiet, darkened room with music playing softly on the radio. He was calm and cooperative as long as the psychologist talked to him softly and slowly. He could understand simple questions and could respond appropriately and provide some history of his life. After a while, he indicated that he needed to go to the bathroom, so the psychologist summoned the nurse's aides for assistance.

Two well-meaning and very pleasant staff members burst into the room, chattering away with each other, flipped on the lights, and greeted Mr. P with a loud, cheery, "How are you doing? Let's get you up and going!" On their entry, they invaded his quiet environment with the hustle and bustle from outside the room. They approached his bed abruptly and immediately started tugging on him to get up. He was shaken from the slow-paced thought processes of which he felt in control, to be bombarded with light, noise, and small talk, and at the same time he was being pushed and pulled in efforts to get him out of bed.

He began to push against the nurse's aides. They persisted, and after they got him up and on his way to the toilet, he gave up resisting and went limp. The psychologist observed the nurse's aides literally having to drag him the few remaining steps into the adjoining bathroom.

The psychologist observed that Mr. P used aggressiveness when he felt controlled by others; when he eventually had to succumb to their control, he just gave up altogether. The psychologist met with the staff assigned to Mr. P's care and explained this, which enabled the caregivers to put themselves in Mr. P's world so that they could understand his catastrophic reaction to their well-intentioned treatment of him.

Language barriers are also stressful for patients and staff in long term care. For many older patients, English is not their first language. Even though they may have lived in this country for most of their adult lives, their brains are programmed from formative years to communicate in a foreign language. This becomes very apparent in various brain disorders in which the older person reverts to use of the first language and may even forget English altogether. The staff have to spend more time determining the needs of these impaired communicators and may have to intuit what they are saying by focusing on facial expressions and body language and seeking help from family members or bilingual dictionaries.

Some Additional Case Examples

Staff members often suffer from even more stress than patients; however, referrals to the psychologist will typically be based on behavioral management problems with residents. In the following cases a variety of control, relationship, and stress issues are affected by gender and culture, which made them challenging for the consulting psychologists.

Two referrals from a physician at a local nursing facility requesting behavioral management recommendations for residents who were resisting care turned out to have quite different solutions.

Case Vignette:

From the perspective of the referring physician, Ms. E and Ms. M were presenting similar problems, "resistance to care," and the staff wanted a behavioral management plan to get them to comply. Both women were white, financially well-off, and in their late eighties. Ms. E had been widowed twice. She had no children and was dependent on a niece and nephew for her family support; they visited her on occasion and had taken her to their homes for holiday celebrations. She had engaged in a successful career as a surgical nurse for most of her life and had always been very independent and eccentric, according to family members. They reported, however, that she had become increasingly disoriented, belligerent, and verbally aggressive and cruel to family and staff in the past year. Before that time, she had always been socially aloof but appropriate and proper in her behavior. They had stopped taking her to their homes and no longer knew how to relate to her when they visited her in the nursing home.

Case Vignette:

Ms. E was small and frail but often combative (biting, scratching, and fighting) when staff approached her for personal care. The staff agreed that her behavior was unpredictable but that she seemed to respond better when a male nurse was present or when staff members went to her room in pairs. She refused to cooperate whenever the psychologist attempted to do an assessment; she either barked repetitive orders for the psychologist to cover her feet, adjust her pillows, or make her comfortable in some way, or she was asleep when he arrived and couldn't be aroused so that he could conduct a clinical interview. Based on her personal and medical history, he determined that she was experiencing delusional, psychotic reactions as her dementing condition grew progressively worse, but that she was also struggling for the control of her life that she had always valued.

Case Vignette:

Ms. M, by contrast, was obese, slow-moving, and slow-thinking but pleas-

ant and cooperative when the psychologist approached her for an interview and assessment. Although she had some difficulty with memory, she was functioning very well and showed only minor depressive symptoms. She had been a housewife all her life and had remarried after being a widow for about 10 years. Her second husband lived close by in a set of adjoining apartments but did not visit her very often. Her daughter (who had power of attorney and received no help from her two brothers in their mother's care) could not imagine why the staff had asked for an assessment and was unaware of any problems. The daughter visited several times a week and felt that her mother's relationship with her second husband had deteriorated since her mother had been admitted to the nursing home.

Staff gave conflicting stories about the resident's resistance to care. Most seemed to have little or no trouble with her and shared in the daughter's curiosity about the reason for the referral. A review of her medical records showed that she was incontinent of bladder and sometimes of bowel, and the only staff notes about resistance seemed to involve the occasions when she needed to be cleaned up after these episodes of incontinence. It was also noted that only two staff members had noted such resistance. In talking to the resident further, it was determined that she did not like to be hurried or chided by staff and became defensive and irritated when staff were less than understanding about her incontinence. Conclusions on this case were that the problem involved the impatience and irritation of individual staff members with Ms. M's slowness and incontinence rather than the behavior of the resident.

These cases exemplify the complex issues that surround psychological consultation in nursing homes. The first case was more a straightforward, typical situation involving a prior psychological dysfunction (detachment, eccentricity, etc.) that had become full-blown in old age with increasing dementia. The staff and family all had the same perspective on the problem and essentially were doing the best they could with a difficult situation. The physician experimented with different medications and dosages for the patient, and the staff were analyzing the best ways to approach her care. There was not much that a psychologist could offer other than validation and support for the staff in dealing with a difficult situation.

The second case, however, had more cultural and gender over-tones. The staff and family did not agree that there was a problem. Stress on the staff because of having to clean up an obese, slow-moving, incontinent patient and the patient's embarrassment at having to be cleaned up and scolded for her "accidents" were the surface of the problem. Underlying issues of caregiving responsibilities between different staff members, the daughter, and the absent husband and sons were also threatening this patient's psychological well-being. In this case, the patient was not exhibiting as much distress as staff and family caregivers, and the psychologist's recommendations were to address the staff and family issues rather than change the behavior of the resident.

An example of countertransference by family and professional health care workers was apparent in the following legal situation, which called for a psychological evaluation.

Case Study:

Mr. and Ms. S had run off and married against the wishes of their children and the advice of their friends. They were both in their eighties and were showing symptoms of dementia, but when they met at the senior center, he swept her off her feet. They lived together for a couple of years before Mr. S had a heart attack and had to be placed in a local nursing home. Several years later, as Ms S's dementia became worse, her daughter moved her to a nursing home 100 miles away nearer to her home, where she could look out for her mother. Mr. S's children filed a legal action to have Ms. S returned to the nursing home her husband lived in. Ms. S's daughter, by contrast, was trying to get an annulment of the marriage because her mother, in her impaired state, could not remember the man that she had married. In addition, Ms. S had acquired quite a bit of money from her first marriage, and Mr. S was essentially destitute, so the decision of the court affected not only family caregiving but also financial responsibility for Mr. S's health care costs. The female lawyer for Mr. S's family and the staff from his nursing home described the union very romantically and argued for the rights of older people to live their lives as they pleased. Ms. S's male lawyer and the staff at her nursing home viewed this as exploitation of a demented woman by Mr. S's family and had little concern about Mr. S's well-being. Dr. W was asked to advise the court on the best interest of both patients in this case.

By the time Dr. W was called in, neither person really remembered the relationship that was either idealized or demonized by the others involved. Ms. S talked about the visits from her daughter and grandchildren and didn't mention Mr. S or even remember him when she was shown his picture. Mr. S was delusional and believed that Ms. S visited him by crawling through the window of his room whenever he called for her. It was the female staff and lawyer who were viewing this situation from a positive, romantic perspective and were determined to keep this cute little couple together. It was the male lawyer who was suspicious of the intentions of Mr. S's son and viewed this union as a plot to gain access to Ms. S's money. Dr. W's objective psychological report to the court pointed out that the fight about how the relationship was consummated was unimportant at this time. The best interest of the two people in their current mental states was for them to be close to the family members who were responsible for their care. Ms. S's family made a cash settlement with Mr. S's son and the marriage was annulled.

Conclusion

Geropsychologists in LTC work primarily with very old, frail white women who have survived a time when women had little control of their lives and suffered much discrimination. Whereas some of these older women have had the advantage of a good education, many were not able to even finish high school. Although some have supportive family and friends, many are placed in the nursing homes because they have dysfunctional families or they never had children and have survived the other members of their family. Some have been well cared for, but many others have suffered emotional, physical, and sexual abuse throughout their lives. The majority of staff are overworked, underpaid white females who often face many stressful family problems that affect their relationships with their patients. Residents who are male and/or members of minority groups may be more isolated or have needs and responses to their environment that are different than those of white women. These gender and cultural influences are important in understanding the stress, the need for control, and the relationship dynamics that exist in institutional long term care.

Psychologists must also be very aware of their own countertransference dynamics when working with this geriatric population. Younger therapists' own fears of aging, of illness and death enter into their therapeutic relationships with institutionalized older patients. Psychologists who work in long term care must weed out their own sexist, racist, and ageist attitudes through training and supervision in gerontology and in their study of the psychology of women and gender and multicultural psychology. Understanding the dynamics of complex control, stress, and relational issues in long term care requires a perspective that incorporates lifespan development, gender, and culture as well as the standard psychological knowledge base that is necessary the diagnosis and treatment of LTC patients.

References

Barnett, R. C., Biener, L., & Baruch, G. K. (Eds.). (1987). *Gender and stress: The groundbreaking investigation of how stress is caused and experienced – differently – in the lives of women and men.* New York: Free Press.

Crose, R. (1991). *What's special about counseling older women? Canadian Journal of Counseling, 25,* 617–623.

Crose, R. (1997). *Why women live longer than men . . . and what men can learn from them.* San Francisco: Jossey-Bass.

Crose, R., & Kixmiller, J. (1994). Counseling psychologists as nursing home consultants: What do administrators want? *The Counseling Psychologist, 22,* 104–114

Crose, R., Nicholas, D., Gobble, D., & Frank, B. (1992). Gender and wellness: A multidimensional systems model for counseling. *Journal of Counseling and Development, 71,* 149–156.

Genevay, B., & Katz, R. S. (Eds.). (1990). *Countertransference and older clients.* Newbury Park, CA: Sage Publications.

Gilligan, C. (1982). In a different voice: *Psychological theory and women's development*. Cambridge, MA: Harvard University Press.

Gutmann, D. L. (1987). *Reclaimed powers: Toward a new psychology of men and women in late life*. New York: Basic Books.

Jordan, J. V., Kaplan, A. G., Miller, J. B., Stiver, I. P., & Surrey, J. L. (1991). Women's growth in connection: *Writings from the Stone Center*. New York: Guilford Press.

McIntosh, J. L., Santos, J. F., Hubbard, R. W., & Overholser, J. C. (1994). *Elder suicide: Research, theory, and treatment*. Washington, DC: American Psychological Association.

Miller, J. B. (1976). *Toward a new psychology of women*. Boston: Beacon Press.

Neugarten, B. L., & Gutmann, D. L. (1964). Age-sex roles and personality in middle age: A thematic apperception study. In B. L. Neugarten & Associates (Eds.), *Personality in middle and late life*. New York: Atherton.

Padgett, D. K. (Ed.). (1995). *Handbook on ethnicity, aging, and mental health*. Westport, CT: Greenwood Press.

Savishinsky, J. S. (1991). *The ends of time: Life and work in a nursing home*. New York: Bergin & Garvey.

18

Clinical Research in Long Term Care:
What the Future Holds

CAMERON J. CAMP, PH.D.

Abstract

FUTURE CLINICAL research in long-term care (LTC) will focus on intervention, and will address problems associated with caring for persons with dementia. This is due to the fact that a number of factors that promote longevity have produced a population that is older, more physically frail, and more cognitively impaired at entry into nursing homes than in the past. The challenge to psychologists is to create interventions that can be accommodated in such settings and still effective for improving the quality of life for both LTC residents and the staff who serve them. This chapter presents a brief overview of management problems involving persons with dementia. It also discusses a model designed by Kitwood for conceptualizing factors that influence the expression of dementia, including the personality, biography, physical health, neurological impairments, and social psychology of the individual. This model emphasizes the focus of psychological interventions on the sociopsychological aspects of dementia; examples of such interventions are provided. Also presented is an outline of Lichtenberg's discussion of factors that needed to work effectively in LTC settings, including administrative support, a collaborative relationship with staff, expertise in behavioral technology and current practices in geriatric psychiatry, and appropriately structured staff meetings. Examples of LTC research topics are presented, including program evaluation, staff retention and retraining, and the marketing of interventions and technology as a means of disseminating effective research strategies.

Introduction

Current and emerging demographic trends indicate that dementia care, especially for the frail elderly, will continue to be a central concern in long-term care (LTC). This chapter describes dementia in terms of research efforts in long-term care and discusses a model for conceptualizing dementia–related research. Since research in long-term care is likely to have an applied psychogeronotological focus, this chapter will describe models for conducting such research (primarily intervention research) at several levels—that of the individual resident, groups of residents or staff persons serving residents within a unit, unit and/or facility-wide studies, and multi-site research. Such research should not be seen as compartmentalized, however. Instead, the interventions developed at any level can be applied at any level of hierarchy. For instance, a case study can lead to interventions for a large number of residents across multiple sites, or a change in a facility's management philosophy can produce new patterns of interaction between a staff member and a resident. Examples of research at each level are provided.

The Long Term Care Population

More than 1.5 million persons reside in nursing homes in the United States (Strahan, 1997). Within 20 years, 3.6 million older adults will be in need of a nursing home bed (NAOA Fact Sheet, 1997). The typical nursing home resident is a woman in her mid-80s who has problems with activities of daily living, some cognitive impairment (generally dementia), and a host of physical illnesses requiring multiple medications (Lair & Lefkowitz, 1990). Adults more than 85 years of age comprise the fastest-growing segment of the population (Papalia, Camp, & Feldman, 1996). The rapid development of alternative means of caring for older adults, such as assisted living facilities and home health care, is likely to ensure that less impaired older adults stay out of long term care until their condition substantially deteriorates. **Such trends will result in large numbers of nursing home residents having even higher levels of impairment than are currently seen.**

These data imply that psychologists who conduct research in long term care must consider the effects of dementia and related cognitive impairments, as well as physical disabilities, pharmaceutical issues, and care delivery systems that are based on a medical model, and competition for access to research participants. Like patients seen by psychologists in hospital settings, LTC residents may have a variety of individuals competing for their time, ranging from a family member who doesn't want to give up visiting time to a physical therapist to a nurse's aide who must toilet or bathe the resident on a schedule. Gathering data under these conditions requires flexibility and patience. Data will be missing from most sets of outcome measures, and the laboratory concept of control is hard to maintain. For example, an observational data collecting session may be disrupted by a sudden fire drill. Persistence and a sense of humor are crucial. Change often takes place slowly in LTC. However, this is literally where the older adults you serve live, and therefore you have the rest of their lives to work with them—a sometimes frightening, sometimes encouraging truth.

An Overview of Dementia

Definition of Dememtia:

Dementia refers to a gradual and progressive deterioration of cognitive ability. Memory impairment is a hallmark of dementia, especially the loss of memory for newly presented information. Dementia also involves such deficits as language disturbances; impaired motor functions; failure to recognize or identify objects; and disturbances in the ability to plan, organize, or reason abstractly. For defining features of specific types of dementia, the reader is referred to the *Diagnostic and Statistical Manual of Mental Disorders*, fourth edition (American Psychiatric Association, 1994).

Managing Problems in Persons with Dementia:

Because dementia is generally progressive, most services for adults with dementia have assumed that the best approach to care is to maintain the current functional level and provide a nonchallenging, comfortable environment. This has led to the establishment of special care units in nursing homes. These units are usually designed for persons in the early stages of dementia for whom activities of daily living (ADLs) and self-care are not problematic. The idea is to create, as much as possible, the atmosphere of a group home or boarding house. A similar philosophy is behind the rapid expansion of assisted living facilities for older adults. Under the best of circumstances, a medical model of care is replaced by a psychosocial support system. But this approach can be quickly abandoned as the infusion of more impaired residents rises and/or the aging-in-place process creates a resident population that is unable to maintain independence and self-care.

An innovative approach to managing problems associated with Alzheimer's Disease (AD) **is based on the philosophy of reducing disability by reducing the demands of the task environment.** The emphasis is on recapturing lost or abandoned abilities, reducing disabilities, or restructuring activities so that they can be accomplished successfully in spite of deficits attributable to dementia. **Interventions that accommodate or compensate for losses in cognitive abilities should have a substantial impact on the ability of older adults to maintain their independence.** This approach is elaborated in the model described below.

A Dialectical Model for Research in Long Term Care

Kitwood (1996) proposes a dialectical framework for understanding interventions for dementia, one that is useful for clinical gerontological research in general and in long term care in particular. Kitwood first describes the "standard paradigm" for understanding and treating dementia as follows:

$$X \longrightarrow \text{neuropathic change} \longrightarrow \text{dementia}$$

X can represent any genetic factor and/or other conditions necessary to precipitate a progressive neuropathic change, which in turn produces progressively worsening dementia. The biomedical model of research focuses its interventions on X; thus, drug research is designed to slow, modify, or eliminate the causes of neuropathic change. Similarly, genetic researchers hope to identify and perhaps one day eliminate genetic factors that can precipitate neuropathic damage that results in dementia.

Kitwood discusses three significant problems with this model. First, although correlations between measures of dementia and indices of the extent of neuropathology may reach statistical significance, they are often quite weak. Second, some individuals show rapid degeneration in short periods of time, far faster than could be attributed to the rate of nervous tissue degeneration. Third, dementia can stabilize for long periods of time; the patient may even "rement," i.e., display partial recovery of function. Kitwood views these as problems resulting from difficulties in relating aspects of mind and brain.

Kitwood proposed this alternative model:

$$D = P + B + H + NI + SP$$

Dementia (D) in any particular individual is manifested through the combined effects of five key factors. Three of these, personality (P), biography or personal life history (B), and neurological impairment (NI), are relatively outside the control of psychologists and fixed. Although they vary across individuals and account for variability in how people react to their conditions, adhere to medication regiments, etc., these dimensions are not the targets of psychological intervention. Physical health (H), (e.g., whether the person has a healthy diet, high blood pressure, etc.), certainly plays a key role in the manifestation of dementia and affects the ability to maintain competence and interact with the social and physical environment. However, intervention-based psychological research in dementia is at most only peripherally involved with physical health.

The fifth factor, social psychology (SP), surrounds the individual and critically influences the way in which dementia is manifested to and interpreted by society. **Although Kitwood states that everything should be done to promote the highest level of physical health in persons with dementia, the social psychology of dementia should be the focus of intervention for psychologists working with people with this disorder.**

Kitwood notes that many patterns of interaction between the person with dementia and caregivers can amount to a malignant social psychology. Such patterns include disempowerment, infantilizaiton, intimidation, outpacing, and objectification, to name but a few. However, Kitwood also gives examples of elements of social psychology that contribute to the well-being of the individual. These include providing a safe and stable setting where powerful emotions can be expressed (holding); accepting the reality of the experience of the person with dementia (validation); enabling persons with dementia to do what they otherwise could not (facilitation); creating situations in which the person with dementia and their caregivers can do something they both truly enjoy (celebration); and stimulation of the senses (stimulation).

Kitwood describes the interaction of these factors in the overall model as follows:

> In a very general way, then, the symptomatic presentation of dementia in any individual arises from a complex interaction

between all five factors, while the progression of the illness depends primarily on the interplay between NI and SP, and this interplay . . . may properly be characterized as dialectical (p. 274).

For example, a person with mixed Alzheimer's and vascular dementia may suffer a sudden stroke (change in NI). As a result, previous levels of facilitation will no longer be effective in enabling the person to maintain earlier levels of independence. Without a corresponding shift in level of facilitation (change in SP), dementia will progress rapidly. In another example, a husband with dementia may suddenly lose his wife's support because of her death (change in SP); whereas NI may remain the same, manifestations of dementia will rapidly progress if the level of facilitation formerly provided by his wife is not forthcoming.

Implications of the Model for Clinical Research

Kitwood's model suggests that any attempt to determine the relationships among the factors that contribute to dementia and the ways in which dementia is manifested will be a fruitful area of research. With regard to personality, for example, Strauss and his colleagues (Chatterjee et al., 1992; Strauss, 1995; Strauss & Pasupathi, 1994; Strauss, Pasupathi, & Chatterjee, 1993; Strauss et al., in press) have shown that the NEO-PI personality inventory scales are sensitive to personality changes related to the onset of AD as well as to changes that occur during course of AD.

The influence of an individual's biography on behavior is exemplified in the case of an older gentleman with dementia who had worked in construction and who was continually approaching an exit doorway and attempting to leave a locked unit. Yellow tape from a construction site stating "Do Not Enter: Construction Zone" was placed on the doorway, and the man stopped approaching the door.

Although neurological impairments cannot be reversed through psychological intervention, it is important to understand their neuropsychological manifestations. In par-

ticular, it is helpful to encourage patients to use abilities that are spared or less impaired over the course of dementia as the basis for improving their sociopsychological environment in LTC. For example, Squire (1992, 1994) has described a number of techniques, (such as classical conditioning and priming), skills, and habits that might serve as the basis for interventions for persons with dementia (Camp & Foss, 1997; Camp & McKitrick, 1992; Camp et al., 1993, 1996).

Camp and colleagues (1997) took a similar approach in creating an intergenerational program in which individuals with dementia living on a special care unit served as teachers and mentors for preschool children, using Montessori teaching materials and lessons to teach. Residents who participated in the program demonstrated high levels of competence in this role. **Whereas disengagement from the sociopsychological environment was common on the unit, as evidenced by observational data, it was not seen when the residents were fulfilling their roles as teachers and mentors to children.**

These examples illustrate two important points. First, while we may not be able to change the "fixed" factors of Kitwood's model, such as the biography or personality, we can and must take them into account when designing psychosocial interventions. Second, successful applied research must be based on theory.

The Focus on Applied Research

Clinical research in a LTC facility will usually be applied research. **This does not mean that applied research is a weak stepsister of "pure" or "basic" research. Effective applied research in LTC demands a healthy respect for theory, since successful interventions generally have a sound theoretical basis.** The challenge to clinical researchers is to recognize the manifestation of theoretical constructs in natural settings. For example, it is one thing to know that older adults with dementia suffer from severe short-term memory deficits but quite another to recognize such a deficit as the basis for a behavior that is described as "pestering the nursing staff." To paraphrase a statement made by Paul Meehl, it is very possible to see that a problem exists without knowing how to fix it. **Once the underlying cause of a problem is recognized, clinicians must take this knowledge and use it to design an effective intervention that serves the needs and protects the dignity of both staff and residents.**

Environmental cueing is generally an effective method of modifying or facilitating behavior in persons with dementia, especially in helping them recognize components of their environment (Camp & Foss, 1997; Camp et al., 1996). In addition, the ability to read, at least simple words and phrases, remains intact far into the course of dementia. For example, we have shown that persons with advanced dementia who can no longer recognize themselves in a mirror can still read their names, even when they are presented on name tags as part of their reflection in a mirror (Bologna & Camp, 1995, 1997).

Signs, labels, or other written materials created for persons with dementia must take into account changes in vision that accompany both aging and dementia. For example, it has been demonstrated that individuals with AD experience a substantial loss of both high spatial frequencies and contrast sensitivity (Gilmore, in press; Gilmore & Levy, 1991; Gilmore & Whitehouse, 1995; Gilmore, Turner, & Mendez, 1991). In practice, this means that printed letters must be thick and there must be a high contrast between the letter and its background.

The following intervention was developed in part from research conducted at our facility:

Case Study:

A dementia unit resident reportedly entered another person's room, became anxious, and became involved in an altercation with the room's occupant. After being taken to the nurses' station, she refused to take oral medication for anxiety. In addition, she spoke only Russian. I was called when the problem arose because of my involvement in a series of projects at Menorah

Park that were designed to enable the staff to communicate more effectively with Russian-speaking LTC residents (Burant & Camp, 1996; Camp, Burant, & Graham, 1996; Mattern & Camp, in press; Sterns & Camp, 1998). On the way to the unit, I enlisted the help of a bilingual resident, who accompanied me to the unit (giving the gentleman doing the interpretation the chance to assist me was an intervention in itself, but that is another case study). Once at the nurses' station, we found the resident calm but still refusing to take her medication. I asked the woman a series of questions through my interpreter to determine how this situation arose. In designing an intervention, it was important to attempt to see the world through her eyes. When she was asked why she did not want to take the medication, she responded that she did not feel sick, was as healthy as a horse, and didn't need it. When asked why she was at the nurses' station, she replied that she did not know. She also stated, after questioning, that she did not remember being in anyone else's room, being upset, or getting into an altercation; that she would never go into someone else's room; and that she did not know where her own room was located.

I then asked the staff what she had been doing in the other person's room. They replied that she had been puttering around, trying to fix things up. When the room's occupant saw her belongings being handled by the Russian woman, an argument ensued, with each party speaking loudly in her own language. The problem, as defined by nursing staff, was that the Russian-speaking resident had become agitated, refused to take oral medication for agitation, and as a result might have to be restrained while the medication was administered by injection. After pointing out that the resident seemed to have calmed down and did not appear in need of the medication at that time, I suggested that a long-term solution should be sought to prevent her entry into other residents' rooms. At this point, a reasonable hypothesis was emerging: the Russian-speaking resident had confused someone else's room for her own. Further questioning of the staff revealed that the resident ventured into the rooms of four other residents on a regular basis. The next step was to design an intervention.

Following the principle of environmental cueing, we wished to determine whether labeling could facilitate this resident's ability to recognize her room. Initially, I wrote some words in Russian, using the Cyrillic alphabet, and it was determined that she could read them easily. I then wrote her name, which she also identified correctly. Research staff members then created signs in Cyrillic that contained the names of the persons residing in the five rooms in question (her room and the four others she entered frequently). The names of the residents whose rooms she was consistently entering were printed on a background of one color, while the Russian-speaking resident's name was printed on a background of a different color. This was done after determining that she could identify and name the different background colors. Contrasting background colors, which allow relatively effortless or unconscious learning of different categories, are used extensively in Montessori educational methods for children, and these methods have served to guide our construction of materials, processes, and activities as the basis of interventions for persons with dementia (Camp & Mattern, in press; Camp et al., 1993; Vance et al., 1996). These names were placed by the entryway of the target rooms, with each name placed in the same general area of the entryway. Staff were instructed to encourage the resident to look for her name when she was about to enter her room. This enabled her to use the relatively preserved abilities of procedural memory and spatial location memory to learn a new behavior.

As mentioned previously, these and other abilities that are relatively preserved in persons with dementia may serve as the basis for a variety of interventions (Camp & Foss, 1997; Camp et al., 1993, 1996). In this case, the intervention produced the desired effect: staff reported that the resident no longer entered the rooms of other residents. This intervention was driven by a specific problem that was identified by the staff. Recognizing the underlying causes and dynamics of the problem, identifying preserved abilities that could be used for an intervention, and obtaining staff cooperation in implementing the intervention were all critical to the success of the intervention. It took time to secure staff cooperation; suggestions for preparing the LTC environment to be receptive to research are presented in the next section.

Conducting Applied Research in Long Term Care

Lichtenberg (1994) describes how psychologists can improve psychosocial treatment for older adults in LTC by developing consultation services. Researchers may often find themselves in the role of consultant when gathering data for an intervention in an LTC setting. Even if the researcher and the LTC facility where data are gathered have a less formal relationship, Lichtenberg's points are important and generally relevant. He notes that four features are critical for consultants to be effective and for their suggested interventions to be implemented: (a) nontoken administrative support; (b) a collaborative relationship with facility personnel; (c) expertise in behavioral therapy and familiarity with general geriatric psychiatry; and (d) regular staff meetings that focus on improving psychosocial care. It is worthwhile to examine each of these features in turn.

Nontoken Administrative Support

A clinical researcher/consultant working in an applied gerontological setting should be prepared to be the first professional representing the discipline of psychology to be seen by caregivers or staff. They may not know what to make of the clinical researcher and may look to persons in authority to determine whether or not to invest their time and attention in listening to this stranger. **Words of introduction, the presence or absence of supervisors at initial meetings with staff, and the respect supervisors show the researcher's opinion will have a critical effect on the way in which the researcher's words are received by caregivers and staff.** Administrators will decide which personnel get to spend time with a consultant, as well as influence topics of discussion, questions, and, most critically, what happens after the researcher leaves.

Attempting to design interventions without strong administrative support is not productive in the long run. If the researcher tries to implement an intervention, there will be little or no follow-through. If staff members are asked to implement an intervention under such circumstances, it will be done inappropriately, if at all. It is critical for the researcher not to blame the victim. In such cases, time spent by the staff to implement prescribed interventions is time taken away from activities that are valued more by administration. To be effective within a system, the researcher must first either find administrators who share his or her values and support staff who wish to implement psychosocial interventions or educate/persuade the existing administrators and staff to do so.

Collaborative Relationship With Staff

Although it may appear attractive to set up monthly or quarterly staff meetings that involve a didactic presentation of information, this approach to staff training does not create collaborative relationships. For one thing, it removes the consultant from the position of partner and resource to a position of manager in the eyes of line staff. Such meetings become just one more mandatory in-service that will result in the staff having to work harder to catch up with their duties afterward. It also makes it easy for staff to just listen and leave, without engaging in dialogue or addressing the issues most pressing to them.

In setting up a collaborative relationship, it helps to understand what the work is like for the line staff. What are their duties? What are the characteristics of the population they serve? What kinds of problems do they typically encounter? What are the most stressful situations they face, and how do they cope with them? What are the most and least satisfying aspects of their jobs? In the same vein, it is important to get to know the duties, routines, and responsibilities of personnel from the various disciplines within a system. Lichtenberg (1994) discusses models for developing interdisciplinary teams in organizations that care for older adults. To create such teams and facilitate their effective operation, the applied researcher must know what practitioners of each of the participating disciplines face in their jobs. **Only when staff members believe that the consultant understands the**

"realities" of their jobs will they begin to trust his or her recommendations.

Consultant Expertise

Applied research in real-world settings requires two types of expertise. The first is a firm grounding in behavioral therapy. Regardless of one's initial training, behavioral therapy is incredibly useful when working with impaired older adults, especially for creating systemic interventions, such as changing the way the staff reacts to the behavioral problems of residents. Many of the basic principles of conditioning and reinforcement are foreign to line staff, who are nonetheless interested in finding ways to improve their working conditions. **Teaching the staff ways of effectively managing the behavior of patients is a key step toward securing staff cooperation for implementing future interventions.**

Staff training also allows the applied researcher to restructure the beliefs of personnel within the system. For example, when designing interventions for persons with AD and related disorders, it is useful to start with the assumption that behavior is not random. Although psychologists and behavioral scientists generally assume this, caregivers and some institutional staff often do not; this systemic problem may be the greatest difficulty facing the applied researcher. Persons who take care of individuals with dementia may assume that inappropriate, problematic, and/or "unexplainable" behavior is a manifestation of the disease process. The logic used is circular: "Why is the person acting that way? Because they have dementia. How do you know they have dementia? Because they are acting that way." Behavior of persons with AD may thus be viewed as unpredictable, irrational, and largely uncontrollable except through chemical or physical means.

The second area of expertise required by the applied researcher is general geriatric psychiatry. Most frail elders will be cared for in settings that are heavily, if not exclusively, influenced by a medical model. **To communicate with staff of various disciplines and to be taken seriously, the researcher must**

become conversant with diagnostic categories, geriatric pharmacology, admission and discharge procedures, prototypically utilized therapies and prostheses, etc. Only then can the applied researcher effectively interface with the system, emphasize the unique contributions that he or she can offer, find interventions that will actually be used within the existing system or, if necessary, attempt to change the system.

Regular Staff Meetings

Staff meetings should focus on psychosocial care and interventions. This can be done on a variety of levels. **At the level of the individual client or patient, time in staff meetings can be used to find solutions to individual behavioral problems.** In some cases, just bringing the staff together to communicate can lead to a solution for the problem. One inventive staff member may have already found a way to reduce or eliminate a problem behavior and can share the technique with the rest of the staff (e.g., "I always put on a tape of his favorite music when I help him use the toilet, and it seems to calm him down"). New interventions (as well as ways to document their implementation and outcome) can also be formulated in staff meetings, as occurred in the following case:

Case Vignette:

A resident was hoarding food that he took from a refrigerator that was used by staff. Hidden within a drawer or closet in the resident's room, the food would often spoil, and the staff worried that the resident might become ill from eating some of the spoiled food. The staff was asked why the resident hoarded food. After some thought, an aide remarked that the resident said something about shopping for his food when he was confronted about being near the refrigerator. The intervention involved placing canned goods in a refrigerator on which the resident's name was written in large letters and placing a sign on the refrigerator telling the resident to take only his food. Thus, instead of attempting to inhibit his behavior, the intervention channeled and controlled it in a socially appropriate way. The resident quickly learned to identify his own food, and because the food was in cans, it would not be eaten or spoil. In addition, the cans could be recycled through the refrigerator. Staff were freed from having to closely monitor or confront the resident, and the resident's affect toward staff became more positive.

In addition, staff meetings should use the time to set goals and priorities, as well as to introduce or sustain appropriate attitudes and values. For example, at one staff meeting in an LTC facility, nursing assistants were asked to describe what they found most satisfying about their jobs. The most frequent response was one-on-one contact with residents in social situations. However, the nursing assistants also stated that their schedules for providing care provided little time for this, and they worried that time spent socializing with residents might not be approved by administrative staff. In response, the unit coordinator and the activities director began a policy of scheduling a particular time slot each week during which one staff member on the shift could interact one-on-one with a particular resident or a small group of residents of the staff member's choosing. This slot was rotated through the line staff so that each person could have this opportunity.

This staff-targeted intervention did several things. First, it validated the responses of the line staff; this ensured that they would be more likely to provide information in the future when queried. Second, it provided evidence that the administration not only valued their opinion but also valued psychosocial care. **Thus, through communication and flexibility, an intervention was implemented within the existing parameters of this system. To be effective, the interventions recommended by applied researchers must take these parameters into account.**

Examples of Research in Long Term Care

Another example of a staff-targeted intervention is provided by the following case (Burant & Camp, 1996):

Case Study:

A nursing home resident who was blind, had advanced Alzheimer's disease, and spoke only Russian was unable to feed herself and became agitated and combative when the staff tried to feed her. It was hypothesized that staff's inability to speak Russian contributed to her aggressive behavior. To test this hypothesis, a Russian-speaking staff member from another department was recruited to feed her at breakfast. When he fed her, she conversed calmly with him, sang an occasional song, and ate most of the food that was offered. The question then became one of how to teach this ability to line staff.

The first step in designing an intervention was to define the boundary conditions of the problem. We did not wish to create an intervention that would significantly increase the work load of line staff. The intervention had to provide Russian language at the time and place it was needed without encumbering the staff members' hands (so that hands could be free for feeding, giving medications, etc.). The intervention needed to be easy to implement with a minimum of training, appealing to staff, and capable of being used by a variety of staff members for a variety of residents. It had to be relatively inexpensive, portable (so that it could be used in different settings), flexible (adaptable to changing needs), and efficient (containing only language essential for staff members to do their jobs). Finally, of course, it had to work.

An intervention was devised that involved a thick posterboard on which cards were placed. These cards contained phonetic spellings of Russian phrases printed in a large type that could be read from far away. Staff members were trained briefly before each meal on the pronunciation of Russian phrases on the board, and the poster was placed behind the woman during meals. Staff could read the words as they fed her the menu item. They also asked if food or beverages tasted good, used courtesy phrases ("please" and "thank you"), and told her "hello" and "good-bye." The resident's aggressive behaviors decreased markedly, and positive interactions between the staff and the resident increased substantially, as did the resident's food intake.

Since that initial case study, the same intervention has been implemented in most of the units of the original facility and within a second facility. In addition, we are in the process of creating prototypes in other languages (e.g., Japanese and Spanish). Furthermore, we have created tabletop versions of the intervention for use by residents. For facilities with Russian-speaking residents, the intervention consists of Russian phrases printed in Cyrillic and the English of the phrases written phonetically and printed in Cyrillic. Using this intervention, Russian-speaking residents can request "fish, not chicken, please" at a meal by reading from the tabletop version of the intervention and be understood by staff. Plans are underway to market the intervention as a means of extending its impact to a large number of institutions.

Marketing Interventions:

The marketing of interventions and technologies developed by applied research is a growing cottage industry. For example, researchers at the Hebrew Home for the Aged in Riverdale, New York, developed a method that uses pen lights and bar code technology to allow LTC staff to efficiently document the types of services they provide to residents and the length of time they spend providing those services. They also designed a computer-based system for downloading data from the bar codes and generating reports.

Lund and colleagues (1995) created a series of videotapes for persons with dementia that was designed to hold their attention for 20 to 50 minutes, thus giving caregivers a brief respite. Different targeted subgroups of persons with dementia (e.g., women, men, African Americans, and Hispanics) and different topics (remembering, Christmas, etc.) are represented in different videotapes. The intervention is designed "as part of an overall package of services" (p. 687) and not as a replacement for caregiver or professional care.

These marketable interventions illustrate two important points about applied research. **First, effective interventions for the frail elderly require a systems perspective and a focus on the sociopsychological aspects of the caregiving system** (as in Kitwood's model for dementia). **Second, most professional service delivery systems for older adults see the purchase of finished products as a more efficient way of treating problems than reading journal articles and then attempting to recreate interventions gleaned from such sources.**

Other Examples

There is a variety of other ways in which clinical research can improve the quality of long term care. Many involve determining the effects of interventions imposed by management or outside agencies. For example, researchers may be asked to determine the effects of shifting from a medical model to a psychosocial or customer relations model of management in an LTC facility. Expertise in program evaluation should prove extremely useful in this regard. Good management involves creating policies and programs that are based on and can be modified by an accurate assessment of the effects of policies and programs.

Another area that may call for an expanded presence of clinical researchers in long term care may be the assessment of the effects of newly developed pharmacological agents for treatment of symptoms of dementia. This is an extremely competitive and fast-moving industry, with many agents in various stages of development. Generally, AD is used as a prototype disorder for the development of an anti-dementia agent, and clinical trial investigators usually select for their patient population community-dwelling, relatively healthy adults with AD who are 60 to 75 years of age. Results of studies using such samples may not generalize well to LTC residents, who have a very different demographic profile. Outcome measures used in drug trials may also not be relevant to LTC staff, who may be more interested in whether a drug affects the amount of time they need to care for a resident rather than the change on a mental status score.

Nursing homes traditionally have a high staff turnover in those positions that involve the greatest amount of direct contact between staff and residents. Researchers can address the need to recruit and retain staff. For example, Burgio (1991; Burgio &

Stevens, in press) describes the use of behavioral therapy—including modeling, contingency management procedures, feedback, participatory management, and maintenance of skills—as a means of staff training and management. **Such procedures can significantly improve the quality of care, job satisfaction, and retention rates of staff.** There is an obvious need for similar research projects throughout the LTC industry, and clinical researchers are in an excellent position to conduct such research within and across facilities.

Conclusions

There are a number of ways in which clinicians can conduct meaningful research within LTC facilities. To do so successfully requires an appreciation of the special characteristics of the resident population, the LTC environment, and the dynamics of dementia. LTC settings also present unique opportunities for clinicians with creativity and an entrepreneurial spirit, and a great deal of applied research is waiting to be done. Clinicians in this setting will find their work challenging, rewarding, and deeply appreciated.

References

American Psychiatric Association. (1994). *Diagnostic and statistical manual of mental disorders* (4th ed.). Washington, DC: Author.

Bologna, S. M., & Camp, C. J. (1995). Self-recognition in AD: Evidence of an explicit/implicit dissociation. *Clinical Gerontologist, 15,* 51–54.

Bologna, S. M., & Camp, C. J. (1997). Covert versus overt self-recognition in late stage Alzheimer's disease. *Journal of the International Neuropsychological Society, 3,* 195–198.

Burant, C. J., & Camp, C. J. (1996). Language boards: Enabling direct care staff to speak foreign languages. *Clinical Gerontologist, 16,* 83–85.

Burgio, L. D. (1991). Behavioral staff training and management in geriatric long-term care facilities. In P. A. Wisocki (Ed.), *Handbook of clinical behavioral therapy with the elderly client* (pp. 423–438). New York: Plenum Press.

Burgio, L. D., & Stevens, A.B. (in press). Behavioral interventions in the nursing home: Motivating staff to apply a therapeutic model of care. In R. Schulz, M. P. Lawton, & G. Maddox, (Eds.) *Annual review of gerontology and geriatrics* (Vol. 18). New York: Springer.

Camp, C. J., Burant, C. J., & Graham, G. C. (1996). The InterpreCare System: Overcoming language barriers in long-term care. *The Gerontologist, 36,* 821–823.

Camp, C. J., & Foss, J.W. (1997). Designing ecologically valid memory interventions for persons with dementia. In D. G. Payne & F. G. Conrad (Eds.), *Intersections in basic and applied memory research* (pp. 311–325). Mahwah, NJ: Lawrence Erlbaum & Assoc.

Camp, C. J., Foss, J. W., O'Hanlon, A. M., & Stevens, A.B. (1996). Memory interventions for persons with dementia. *Applied Cognitive Psychology, 10,* 193–210.

Camp, C. J., Foss, J. W., Stevens, A. B., et al. (1993). Memory training in normal and demented populations: The E-I-E-I-O model. *Experimental Aging Research, 19,* 277–290.

Camp, C. J., & Mattern, J. M. (in press). Innovations in managing Alzheimer's disease. In D. E. Biegel & A. Blum (Eds.), *Innovations in practice and service delivery across the lifespan.* New York: Oxford University Press.

Camp, C. J., & McKitrick, L. A. (1992). Memory interventions in DAT populations: Methodological and theoretical issues. In R. L. West & J. D. Sinnott (Eds.), *Everyday memory and aging: Current research and methodology.* New York: Springer-Verlag.

Camp, C. J., Judge, K. S., Bye, C. A.(1997). An intergenerational program for persons with dementia using Montessori methods. *The Gerontologist, 37,* 688–692.

Chatterjee, A., Strauss, M. E., Smyth, K. A., & Whitehouse, P. W. (1992). *Personality changes in Alzheimer's disease. Archives of Neurology, 49,* 486–491.

Gilmore, G. C. (in press). Perception. In J. Birren (Ed.), *Encyclopedia of gerontology.* San Diego, CA: Academic Press.

Gilmore, G. C., & Levy, J. (1991). Spatial contrast sensitivity in Alzheimer's Disease: A comparison of two methods. *Optometry and Vision Science, 68,* 790–794.

Gilmore, G. C., Turner, J., & Mendez, M. (1991). Contrast sensitivity and Alzheimer disease: A comparison of two methods. *Optometry and Vision Science, 68,* 790–794.

Gilmore, G. C., & Whitehouse, P. (1995). Contrast sensitivity in Alzheimer's disease: A one year longitudinal analysis. *Optometry and Vision Science, 72,* 83–91.

Kitwood, T. (1996). A dialectical framework for dementia. In R. T. Woods (Ed.), *Handbook of the clinical psychology of aging* (pp. 267–282). Chichester, UK: John Wiley.

Lair, T., & Lefkowitz, D. (1990). *Mental health and functional status in nursing homes and personal care homes* (DHHS pub. no. PHS 90-3470). Rockville, MD: Department of Health and Human Services, Agency for Health Care Policy and Research.

Lichtenberg, P. (1994). *A guide to psychological practice in geriatric long-term care.* New York: Haworth Press.

Lund, D. A., Hill, R. D., Caserta, M. S., & Wright, S. D. (1995). Video respite: An innovative resource for family, professional caregivers, and persons with dementia. *The Gerontologist, 35,* 683–687.

Mattern, J. M., & Camp, C. J. (in press). Increasing the use of foreign language phrases by direct care staff in a nursing home setting. *Clinical Gerontologist.*

NAOA fact sheet: Facts on long-term care (1997). *Gerontology News, 24,* 7–8.

Papalia, D. E., Camp, C. J., & Feldman, R. D. (1996). *Adult development and aging.* New York: McGraw-Hill.

Squire, L. R. (1992). Memory and the hippocampus: A synthesis from findings with rats, monkeys, and humans. *Psychological Review, 99,* 195–231.

Squire, L. R. (1994). Declarative and nondeclarative memory: Multiple brain system supporting learning and memory. In D. L. Schacter & E. Tulving (Eds.), *Memory systems,* 1994 (pp. 203–232). Cambridge, MA: MIT Press.

Sterns, H. L., & Camp, C. J. (1998). Applied gerontology. *Applied Psychology: An International Review, 47, 175–198.*

Strahan, G. W. (1997). *An overview of nursing homes and their current residents: Data from the 1995 National Nursing Home Survey.* Hyattsville, MD: National Center for Health Statistics.

Strauss, M. E. (1995). Ontogeny of depression in Alzheimer's disease. In M. Gergener, S. Kanowski, & J. Brocklehurst (Eds.), *Aging, health and healing* (pp. 441–456). New York: Springer.

Strauss, M. E., & Pasupathi, M. (1994). Primary caregivers' descriptions of Alzheimer patients' personality traits: *Temporal reliability and sensitivity to change. Alzheimer Disease and Related Disorders, 8,* 166–176.

Strauss, M. E., Pasupathi, M., & Chatterjee, A. (1993). Concordance between observers in descriptions of personality change in Alzheimer's disease. *Psychology and Aging, 8,* 475–480.

Strauss, M. E., Pasupathi, M., Stuckey, J. C., & Moore, A. (in press). Accuracy of retrospective descriptions of personality during the course of Alzheimer's disease. *Journal of Clinical Geropsychology.*

Vance, D., Camp, C., Kabacoff, M., & Greenwalt, L. (1996, winter). Montessori methods: Innovative interventions for adults with Alzheimer's Disease. *Montessori Life,* 10–11.

19

Public Policy and the Delivery of Mental Health Care to Older Adults

MARGARET P. NORRIS, PH.D.

Abstract

KNOWLEDGE OF public policy issues is pivotal to the careers of psychologists working in long-term care settings because federal and state governments, as well as private insurers, enact policies that define the boundaries of practice and establish reimbursement rates. These policies, which are established by organizations other than professional psychology associations, determine such critical issues as who can provide services, which diagnoses are considered treatable, whether neuropsychological assessments warrant reimbursement, and what fees will be allowed. This chapter reviews policies that regulate the financing and delivery of mental health services for patients in long-term care. Standards of care are established by OBRA policies, many of which directly impact mental health care. Financing and reimbursement issues are reviewed to instruct mental health providers in the mechanisms and policies of Medicare, Medicaid, and the private insurance industry. Future directions in long term care are also reviewed, including the trend toward younger patients; more frequent use of home and community-based care services; alternative inpatient settings, such as assisted living facilities; and the outlook for mental health services as an increasing share of the costs of long term care is being absorbed by the private sector.

Introduction

Despite the trepidation felt by the public and health care providers following the inroads made by managed care, geropsychologists are increasingly optimistic because public policies have been redirected toward the expansion of mental health services for older adults. With the predicted expansion of the elderly population and decline in the number of available caregivers, a growing number of older adults will seek health care—including mental health care—in long-term care settings (see *Future Trends in Long-term Care*, below). With an increased demand for services and the current trend in policy making, we have advanced from an era in which the financial survival of psychologists working in long-term care settings was tenuous at best. Independent practice that relied on work in long-term care settings was not feasible because psychological services were minimally reimbursed, if at all, by primary insurance organizations. In addition administrators of long-term care settings had little incentive to provide psychological services, or were unaware of their value and, thus, did not hire psychologists often. Psychological services in long-term care settings are now mandated by law, and primary health insurers are reimbursing psychologists for their professional services. Thus, we have indeed come a long way; yet, further advancements are awaited. Keeping apprised of the policies that regulate mental health services in long-term care settings and contemporary trends in geropsychology is the psychologist's first step toward providing a valued service that may become either the cornerstone or at least a small segment of his or her professional practice.

The demand for mental health services in institutional long-term care settings is extensive. Mental disorders are far more prevalent in skilled nursing facilities, where roughly 45% to 70% of residents are affected (Georgoulakis, 1998; Wykle & Musil, 1993), which is substantially greater than the estimated 8% of community-dwelling older adults who are in need of mental health services. These figures suggest that nursing homes have become de facto inpatient mental health facilities. The high incidence of mental disorders among nursing home residents is due to the need for 24-hour care for patients with moderate to severe dementia, as well as the strong relationship between poor physical health and depression. In response to the high rate of mental illness among nursing home patients, in 1987 the federal government mandated the provision of mental health services in nursing homes. As reviewed below, this law and others have greatly impacted the delivery of mental health services in long-term care settings.

Public Policy: Regulating Standards of Care

Prior to the passage of legislation such as OBRA and the Patient Self-Determination Act (see below), nursing homes were often stereotyped as warehouses for decline and ultimately death. Individual needs were minimally addressed, and mental health problems were especially neglected, except when restraints were used to abate symptoms, an effort that was arguably for the benefit of staff members who were responsible for too many patients. Long-term care patients now have significantly more rights, dignity, and decision-making power than ever before.

The Omnibus Reconciliation Acts (OBRAs)

Regulation of long term care was established primarily through the Omnibus Reconciliation Acts (OBRAs) of 1986, 1987, 1989, and 1990. Perhaps the most comprehensive reforms came as a result of OBRA 1987, much of which impacted the mental health needs of community-dwelling and nursing-home residents. **Reforms instated by OBRA 1987 included a higher cap on the amount paid by Medicare for outpatient mental health care** (the cap was repealed in 1989)**, a mandate that mental health services be made available for nursing home residents increased in-service training on mental health issues, restricted use of chemical agents and physical**

restraints, and use of standardized methods to document cognitive, behavioral, and psychiatric functioning of all residents.

The major changes mandated by OBRA 1987 appear to have improved nursing home care significantly. Interviews with nursing home administrators, staff, residents, regulators, advocacy groups, and professional organizations suggest that improvements have been widespread (Marek, Rantz, Fagin, & Krejci, 1996). In particular, the majority of those interviewed believed that the implementation of OBRA 1987 regulations significantly reduced the use of restraints, gave greater attention to residents rights, and promoted the use of standardized record-keeping procedures which improved continuity and quality of care (Marek et al., 1996).

For mental health providers, one of the most relevant and important reforms mandated by OBRA 1987 addressed the misuse and overuse of psychotropic medications by nursing home residents. The law mandated that nursing home patients taking antipsychotics or anxiolytics have a specific diagnosis indicating the need for each drug and be assessed to identify indications for their continued use, as well as any side effects of the medication. The law appears to have had the intended effect. The percent of patients taking antipsychotic, anxiolytic, and sedative–hypnotic medications declined, the dosages were reduced, and polypharmacy with psychotropic medications also declined (Lantz, Giambanco, & Buchalter, 1996). **The more recent upward trend in the prescription of antidepressant medications may reflect greater awareness of the prevalence of depression in nursing home residents as well as the availability of new antidepressant medications.** Overall, OBRA 1987 seems to have been helpful in reducing the misuse of medications, while allowing for their appropriate use by many patients whose quality of life can be improved by minimizing disturbing psychiatric symptoms. Unfortunately, little research has been done to examine the extent to which chemical treatment has been replaced with psychological and behavioral therapy in nursing homes.

The Patient Self-Determination Act

The Patient Self-Determination Act of 1990, enacted to foster greater patient autonomy in making medical decisions, is particularly relevant to long-term care patients. Enacted in response to the case of Nancy Cruzan—a young woman whose life was prolonged by artificial means after she was left in a persistent vegetative state following a motor vehicle accident—the Patient Self-Determination Act requires health care professionals to facilitate each patient's participation in the medical decision-making process, particularly when it involves deciding whether life-sustaining efforts should be attempted if an individual becomes severely ill and incapacitated. Individuals may execute legal documents, living wills, to specify which medical procedures (e.g., mechanical ventilation, resuscitation, dialysis, artificial feeding, and antibiotics) may be used to sustain their lives. The durable power of attorney identifies an individual who has the legal right to make medical decisions for the patient in the event that the patient is incapacitated. Mental health providers often play a central role in the life-sustaining decision-making process. They may provide emotional support when individuals are making these decisions, when families must make decisions because the patient did not state or document his or her wishes, or when there is a question about a patient's mental competence make these decisions.

Financing Long Term Care

Public policies and laws also have a great impact on the methods of financing mental health services in long-term care. After World War II, a strong lobby for a national health insurance program faced much opposition, including, ironically, opposition from the American Medical Association (Burke, 1997). A compromise in this dispute resulted in the provision of health insurance for only the most needy. In 1965, Medicare, the health insurance program for older Americans, and Medicaid, the insurance program for the poor, were enacted. Thus, the 15% of Americans who do not have health insurance today (Block, 1997) are primarily young and middle-aged workers who do not receive health insurance benefits from an employer. In contrast, almost all older Americans have health insurance through Medicare, a component of the Social Security Retirement program.

Medicare insurance is divided into two components. *Medicare Part A* covers hospitalization and is financed through current Social Security payroll taxes; thus, the recipient does not pay a premium for Part A. *Medicare Part B* pays some of the costs for outpatient health care, including mental health care. It is voluntary and is financed through monthly premiums paid by the beneficiary. Many older adults covered by Medicare also have either Medigap or Medicaid. *Medigap* is private insurance that supplements many of the costs not covered by Medicare. It is also optional, and the beneficiary pays a monthly premium for it. *Medicaid* is the public insurance program for poor and disabled persons and does not require a premium.

Who Pays for Long Term Care?

Long-term care costs are paid primarily by four sources: Medicaid, which pays the largest proportion of costs (44%); **individuals and their families, who pay approximately 33%; Medicare, which pays 16% of acute care costs in long-term care facilities; and private long-term care insurance, which pays for only 6% of these costs** (Cohen, 1998; National Academy on Aging, 1997). Approximately $100 billion is spent annually on long-term care (Cohen, 1998). With medical advances extending life expectancy, these costs are expected to more than double within 25 years

Medicaid policies have favored institutional care. Of the approximately $40 billion Medicaid has spent annually on long term care, 90% has been for institutional care and the remaining 10% for home and community-based services (National Academy on Aging, 1997). Ironically, Medicare, the health insurance policy for older adults, does not pay for long-term nursing home care. Although it is the largest provider of home health care services for older adults, it provides only limited coverage for short-term or post–acute institutional care. Consequently, many older patients are transferred from hospitals to skilled nursing facilities for short-term (i.e., maximum of 100 days) rehabilitative care. When longer stays are necessary, the patient is responsible for the additional costs, unless he or she receives Medicaid.

The out-of-pocket expenses for long-term care place a substantial financial burden on many families and often result in older patients spending all their assets on medical care. When this occurs, the person qualifies for Medicaid. This system has resulted in the common practice of "spending-down." In order to qualify for Medicaid, older adults may give their assets to their adult children as "gifts." Unfortunately, spending down can result in conflicts within families when adult children exercise more control over their parents' finances than the parents feel is appropriate. Psychologists may be called upon to address these family issues in psychotherapy with long-term care clients.

Who Should Pay?

The question of who is responsible for paying for the cost of long-term care is the basis of sociopolitical debate. While the population is "greying," the federal budget for health care is also changing color, albeit in the direction of red. Public sentiment appears to support the idea that some older adults cannot, perhaps should not, rely on the government to provide full medical care. Two-thirds of older adults do not support the notion that the government should be responsible for paying for the long-term care of all elderly citizens (Cohen & Kumar, 1997). Furthermore, the public is not optimistic that such support will be available; three-fourths of older adults believe that they will have to pay for their own long-term care (Cohen & Kumar, 1997). There are reasons for this zeitgeist. Older Americans are financially better off than ever before. In 1960, the earnings of an alarming 30% of elders fell below the poverty level, compared with approximately 12% today (Cohen, 1998). In addition, there is greater political support for programs that assist only financially needy older adults rather than all older adults.

The health insurance system in the United States is a passionately debated topic. The principal argument against a national health insurance system is the fear of an overwhelming cost to the federal government and, ultimately, the taxpayer. However, this argument loses credibility when the cost of the current US system is compared with that of other developed nations. Sixteen percent of the US gross national product (GNP) is spent on medical care, which is substantially higher than for other industrialized nations: 10% in Canada, 6% in Great Britain, 8% in Austria, 7% in Japan, and 7.7% of the combined European Union GNP (Georgoulakis, 1998). These figures suggest that our current health care system is very expensive and demands greater financial reform.

Financing Mental Health Care For Older Adults

Prior to 1989, ambulatory mental health care for older Americans barely existed because Medicare had a $250 annual cap on payment for outpatient mental health care. This cap was abolished by OBRA 1989, and Medicare B currently pays 50% of the cost of outpatient mental health care. Furthermore, Medicare did not recognize psychologists as providers of mental health care until 1990. Despite these considerable advances, mental health providers are still forced to lobby against the 50% copayment, which seems discriminatory when it is compared with the 20% copayment for other types of outpatient health care. Only 2.5% of Medicare reimbursements are for mental health care, which indicates that even with the increase in outpatient coverage, the cost of mental health care still comprises a minuscule part of health care for older Americans (Finkel, 1993). Three sources may pay the remaining 50% of outpatient mental health care costs. As mandated by OBRA 1990, all Medigap policies must pay the 50% copayment (with some exclusions for some older adults with insurance policies initiated prior to 1990): Medicaid pays the copayment for qualified patients, or the patient pays if he or she has neither Medigap nor Medicaid. It is important to bear in mind that these outpatient costs include psychotherapy for community-dwelling older adults and patients residing in long-term care settings.

Reimbursement Policies

Historically, reimbursement rates for medical care were determined solely by the amount billed by providers. This fee-based system was referred to as Customary, Prevailing, and Reasonable (CPR). In the wake of rising physician fees and the enormous increase in Medicare expenditures during the 1970s and 1980s, reforms were adopted to contain costs. Congress initiated the Resource-Based Relative Value Scale (RBRVS), which determines the fees paid to health care providers. The fee is based on the relative value of the resources needed to provide particular medical services, including providers' work (e.g., time and complexity of work), practice expense, and malpractice expense. Further adjustments are made for other variables, such as geographical modifiers. The RBRVS system, which undergoes continual refinement, has become the basis for the universal fee schedule adopted by the insurance industry. The Health Care Financing Administration (HCFA) began using the RBRVS fee schedule in 1992. Many providers argue that the RBRVS fees paid to psychologists, social workers, and psychiatrists are restrictive and result in poor incentives for providing mental health services to elderly patients. In fact, the low level of reimbursement was identified by psychologists as one of the most common barriers to expanding geropsychology services (Barrick, Karuza, & Dundon, 1995).

Costs and standards for mental health service also vary geographically as a result of Medicaid policies. Medicaid is a federal-state matching program in which the federal government sets minimum standards for eligibility and benefits, but each state has a great deal of latitude in setting specific policies. Thus, there are large geographical differences in the way each addresses funding mechanisms, expenditures, financial eligibility, reimbursement rates, the nature of services, and so forth.

Medicare and private Medigap policies have innumerable policies and restrictions that regulate reimbursement for mental health services. **Because these policies are constantly in flux and**

vary by state and insurance carrier, examples of the more uniform policies will be briefly described.

Psychological services are reimbursed by Medicare only when they are provided by clinical psychologists or clinical social workers. Clinical social workers are restricted from providing psychotherapy in long-term care settings; this policy is currently being appealed. Medicare policy makers are debating the merits of following private insurance industry by adding less expensive, masters-level mental health practitioners to their provider lists.

Some Medigap policies and Medicaid programs will not pay for psychotherapy if the patient has a diagnosis of dementia. Psychologists have, of course, vehemently argued against this restriction because psychotherapy is effective for dementia patients in many instances. For example, mildly impaired patients can benefit from supportive therapies that help them adjust to recognized deterioration, patients in later stages of dementia with behavioral problems may benefit from behavioral therapies, and families of patients with dementia may find that psychotherapy helps them make healthier adjustments and more sound decisions (Zarit & Teri, 1991).

Psychologists are required to consult with a Medicare patient's primary or attending physician "within a reasonable amount of time" after the patient consents to the consultation. The consultation is not required if the patient was referred by a physician, and the consultation may simply consist of notification that the psychologist is providing services to the patient (although a more extensive consultation may be clinically appropriate).

Finally, poorly defined restriction of therapy is inherent in the ubiquitous "medical necessity" requirement. Almost all insurance companies, including Medicare and Medicaid, will not pay for therapy that is not deemed "medically necessary." In some instances, this distinction is rather clear; for example, group therapies that provide cognitive stimulation, socialization, and recreation are usually not reimbursable, but those with therapy goals that address emotional distress and maladaptive behavior may be reimbursable. Claims that are denied because the medical necessity has not been established are often the reason for filing appeals with insurance companies. Disagreements over the appropriateness of psychotherapy will continue until this exclusionary term is better defined by the insurance industry and mental health practitioners.

Medicare and Managed Care

Managed care is a new model of health care that links the financing and delivery of long term care. Medicare has lagged far behind Medicaid and the private sector in embracing managed care. From the inception of Medicare, the medical profession has opposed prepaid health care programs. The promotion of managed care to contain costs was first attempted in 1972 through Social Security amendments that authorized Medicare to contract with HMOs for capitated payments (i.e., fixed, prepaid payment rates). Stiff restrictions prevented much growth during this early period. During the mid-1970s, HCFA sponsored several demonstration projects to test prepaid plans for the elderly. The perceived success of these projects and the rapid growth in Medicare expenditures sparked renewed interest in HMOs as a cost savings mechanism for Medicare. In 1982 (during the Reagan administration), Congress passed the Tax Equity and Fiscal Responsibility Act, which encouraged HMO enrollment for Medicare beneficiaries. The number of risk plans contracting with Medicare rose from 96 to 171; however, 13 years later, only 10% of Medicare beneficiaries were enrolled in HMOs (Oberlander, 1997). More than 50% of these enrolled beneficiaries were from only two states: California and Florida.

The predicted insolvency of the Medicare Hospital Trust Fund gave rise to additional reforms in Medicare financing, which were established by the Balanced Budget Act of 1997 (Ettinger, 1998). These reforms promoted greater flexibility and incentives for Medicare beneficiaries to enroll in various types of managed care programs, such as health maintenance organizations (HMOs), preferred provider organizations (PPOs), or Provider Sponsored Organizations (PSOs). The PSO, which is the most recent of the managed care models, is a group of providers that contracts directly with Medicare, thus eliminating the middle man. They return much control over health care delivery to the health care providers, but in a more competitive environment than that of the traditional CPR or fee-for-service system, in which providers had a great deal of autonomy in setting costs.

The Pros and Cons of Medicare Managed Care Policies

Managed care organizations are responsible for providing and managing multiple levels of health care as well as assuming the financial risk for doing so at a predetermined rate. The assumed advantages of such organizations are lower costs and coordination of care. They also have certain disadvantages and limitations. **A primary distinction between the traditional fee-for-service systems and managed health care systems is the degree of choice patients have in selecting health care providers.** Under managed care, patients pay a higher portion of their health care costs if they see a physician, psychologist, or other provider who is not on their insurance company's list of health care providers. This limited access to providers significantly restricts access to mental health care.

Many older patients receive mental health services at the suggestion and assistance of their physicians. In managed care programs, however, this practice can be limited by "gatekeeping," when physicians withhold such referrals to comply with the insurance company's effort to curtail the cost of specialized care. Insufficient referring also occurs when physicians under-value specialties such as psychology or when they are overly confident in their own abilities to treat mental health problems.

Is Managed Care the Best Option for Older Adults?

A number of challenges must still be addressed in future models of managed care for elderly patients. First, the quality of medical care is often at odds with the cost savings. Second, patients and health care providers have not been fully satisfied with these programs because of restrictions imposed by program managers (Block, 1997). Third, "skimming" for the healthiest patients is still practiced, even by programs that target frail adults with substantial health problems and disabilities (Cohen, 1998). If lower-risk patients are systematically selected by these programs, their ultimate goal is compromised. Fourth, the financial savings hoped for from these programs have been disappointing. Medicare reimburses managed care at a capitated rate of 95% of the average fee-for-service costs; however, the medical costs for Medicare HMO enrollees were estimated to be 11% less than for Medicare beneficiaries who were not on HMO plans (Oberlander, 1997). Thus, Medicare has lost, not saved, money by contracting with managed care organizations. **The reason appears to lie in the biased selection of managed care enrollees: managed care enrollees tend to be in better health than their Medicare counterparts** (Oberlander, 1997).

Future Trends in Long Term Care

Several factors point to an increased use of long-term care facilities: the number of elderly will rise from 32 million in 1990 to 70 million in 2040, medical advances are extending life expectancy, baby boomers will begin to retire in approximately 15 years, and smaller family sizes will mean fewer caregivers. This growth in the demand for long-term care will also be accompanied by changes in two far-reaching anticipated effects. First, a larger portion of long-term care recipients will not be elderly. Currently, only about two-thirds of US nursing home residents are elderly (National Academy on Aging, 1997); the remainder are young and middle-aged adults with chronic illnesses and disabilities who require long-term assistance with daily care. As the survival rate increases for persons with traumatic injuries (such as motor vehicle accidents) and severe illnesses (such as AIDS), the proportion of nonelderly residents in institutional settings will continue to increase. This change will introduce a demand for psychologists that is directly opposite to the current need for specialization in geropsychology. As the survival rate of young and middle-aged patients with severe illnesses continues, geropsychologists in long-term care will need to maintain their skills in working with nonelderly patients. For example, in contrast to common problems seen in frail elderly long-term patients, younger patients may mostly struggle with such issues as boredom, sexuality, and despair over spending much of their adult life in an institution.

Second, a dramatic increase in the use of home and community-based services by the elderly will continue. In fact, home and community-based health care is the fastest growing component of long term care in the United States (National Academy on Aging, 1997). These services include adult day care centers, rehabilitative treatment centers, nursing services, and various therapies, including psychotherapy and psychodiagnostic assessment. Home health care is greatly preferred by most elders, not only for reasons of personal comfort, but also because long term care is more costly than home health care. The average monthly cost of nursing home care in 1995 was approximately $3,200, which is substantially more expensive than the average $370 out-of-pocket expenses for home health care (Cohen, 1998). It is important to note that these figures reflect not only lower costs for care in the home but also the better health status of community- dwelling older adults. Some researchers and policy makers argue that home and community-based care do not replace or delay nursing home care; while they may improve the quality of life, they may ultimately increase the overall cost of care (Kane, Kane, Ladd, & Veazie, 1998).

With these anticipated changes, long-term care services are expanding beyond the traditional nursing home. Skilled nursing care centers are integrating a continuum of settings to meet the various levels of care required by individuals with diverse and changing health care needs. An increasing number of nursing homes offer more comprehensive services within one facility, including assisted living units, adult day care centers, rehabilitation outpatient services, and subacute care units.

The assisted living facility presents new challenges because it is a new type of long-term care setting. The residents of these facilities are relatively healthy and require unskilled assistance rather than nursing care. Now more than a $10 billion industry, it is expected to continue to grow as many older adults seek the combination of a private homelike setting and supportive services (Cohen, 1998). Other benefits may include delaying nursing home placement and reduced costs relative to nursing home care. Unfortunately, public and private insurance policies rarely pay for assisted living care; thus, the market has been restricted to older adults who can afford large out-of-pocket expenses. In addition to the lack of funding, the assisted living industry is under limited regulation, which has resulted in much variability in standards of care. Without greater regulation, assisted living facilities could become throwbacks to pre-OBRA days. Mental health care in particular is often neglected in assisted living residents.

Who Will Pay?

Another significant change in long-term care is a shift in the sources that are responsible for paying long-term costs. Reducing expenditures is a major priority because Medicare is one of the most sharply growing federal budget items, rising by 10% annually (Oberlander, 1997). Cost savings may be procured from various sources, including federal and state governments, the insurance industry, health care providers, and beneficiaries. States are being given more latitude in administering Medicaid resources, but with fewer dollars. Medicare is trying to develop strategies to curtail the rapidly growing costs of home health care. Federal and state policy makers are also looking for ways in which a greater share of long-term care costs can be absorbed by the private sector. These efforts may include changes that impact mental health care delivery negatively, such as limiting programs to indigent populations, lowering expenditures for patients receiving both Medicare and Medicaid benefits (many of whom are nursing home residents), and decreasing coverage for services that are regarded as ancillary, such as psychotherapy and psychological evaluations. Private funding sources—such as long-term care insurance, medical savings accounts, and employee health benefits—may also grow if the government promotes their appeal through strong regulations and tax incentives. The outlook for mental health care under these new private systems may not bode well unless professional health care organizations take a proactive position to ensure that the mental health needs of older patients are not ignored.

As consumers absorb greater financial responsibility for long-term care, the demand for high quality of care will inevitably increase. Medicare may recognize the need to better monitor the quality of health care that is provided by managed care organizations. Managed care organizations are inexperienced with frail elderly enrollees; therefore, encouraging or mandating the hiring of more geriatric specialists by HMOs and similar plans is of critical importance. As older patients pay more, greater flexibility in the use of benefits will be expected, i.e., the patient and health care provider will expect to be allowed to decide if care should be provided in the home or an inpatient facility, what type and amount of long-term care is appropriate, and whether psychological services will be included.

Conclusions

Psychologists must work under the restrictions of policies established by federal and state laws as well as the insurance industry. It is vital to understand the policies that are mandated by these systems. However, these policies are not our only guiding structure. We must also operate under the ethical codes of our profession (American Psychological Association, 1992) and those recently established by experts in geropsychology (Lichtenberg et al., 1998). Furthermore, psychologists must attend to the needs of the immediate environments in which we practice. Older adults receiving long-term care do not receive psychological services in isolation. **The geropsychologist will provide better care if the patient's family, primary care physician, and staff in the long-term facility become an integral part of the therapeutic process.**

Psychologists are poised to make greater inroads in the delivery of health care in diverse long-term care settings. As the character of long term care changes, psychologists in these facilities will need to serve a more heterogeneous population, which may include a wider age range, more acute rehabilitation needs, AIDS-related disabilities, and so forth. At the same time, elderly patients who have several concurrent medical problems complicated by psychological disturbance will require expertise in traditional clinical geropsychology. In addition, psychological consultation should be provided in new settings including assisted living facilities, adult day care centers, rehabilitation facilities, and retirement communities. Meeting these diverse mental health needs will call for doctoral training and professional workshops to increase providers' understanding of the numerous clinical issues that are unique to long-term care patients.

The public policies of the last two decades have indeed made mental health care available to more older adults than in the past. More older adults have mental health benefits, with higher limits on annual and lifetime payments. The mental health needs of institutionalized, long-term care patients have received greater recognition, and more humane treatments are available. The public outcry against prohibitive and intrusive practices from private industry has been effective in achieving more balanced policies. And yet, there are still serious gaps in care for older adults with emotional, cognitive, or behavioral problems. The funding systems for long-term nursing care are in a precarious state, at best. Proposed reforms suggest solutions for older persons who have personal financial resources and generous retirement benefits but neglect the needs of lower income elders. With continued vigilance and debate, a wider array of mental health care may become available to all older adults, regardless of extraneous factors such as income, institutional status, diagnoses, and insurance carrier.

References

American Psychological Association. (1992). Ethical principles of psychologists and code of conduct. *American Psychologist, 47,* 1597–1611.

Barrick, C., Karuza, J., & Dundon, M. (1995). Older adults, reimbursement, and referrals: Implications for psychologists after Medicare reimbursement changes and before health care reform. *Professional Psychology, Research, and Practice., 26,* 598–601.

Block, L. E. (1997). Evolution, growth, and status of managed care in the United States. *Public Health Reviews, 25,* 193–244.

Burke, M. J. (1997). Clinicoeconomics in geropsychiatry. *Psychiatry Clinics in North America, 20,* 219–240.

Cohen, M. A. (1998). Emerging trends in the finance and delivery of long-term care: Public and private opportunities and challenges. *The Gerontologist, 38,* 80–89.

Cohen, M. & Kumar, N. (1997). The changing face of long-term care insurance in 1994: Profiles and innovations in a dynamic market. *Inquiry, 34,* 50–61.

Ettinger, W. H. (1998). The Balanced Budget Act of 1997: Implications for the practice of geriatric medicine. *Journal of the American Geriatrics Society, 46,* 530–533.

Finkel, S. I. (1993). Mental health and aging: A decade of progress. In M. A. Smyer (Ed.), *Mental health and aging* (pp. 45–58). New York: Springer.

Georgoulakis, J. M. (1998). Integrating physical and mental health services: What the United States can learn from Canada. In P. E. Hartman-Stein (Ed.), *Innovative behavioral healthcare for older adults* (pp. 41–56). San Francisco: Jossey-Bass.

Kane, R. L., Kane, R. A., Ladd, R. C., & Veazie, W. N. (1998). Variation in state spending for long-term care: Factors associated with more balanced systems. *Journal of Health Politics, Policy, and Law, 23,* 363–390.

Lantz, M. S., Giambanco, V. & Buchalter, E. N. (1996). A ten-year review of the effect of OBRA-87 on psychotropic prescribing practices in an academic nursing home. *Psychiatric Services, 47,* 951–955.

Lichtenberg, P. A., Smith, M., Frazer, D., Molinari, V., Rosowsky, E., Crose, R., Stillwell, N., Kramer, N., Hartman-Stein, P., Qualls, S., Salamon, M., Duffy, M., Parr, J., Gallagher-Thompson, D. (1998). Standards for psychological services in long-term care facilities. *The Gerontologist, 38,* 122–127.

Marek, K. D., Rantz, M. J., Fagin, C. M., Krejci, J. W. (1996). OBRA '87: Has it resulted in better quality of care? *Journal of Gerontological Nursing, 22,* 28–36.

National Academy on Aging (1997, September). Facts on long-term care. *Gerontology News,* 7–8.

Oberlander, J. B. (1997). Managed care and Medicare reform. *Journal of Health Politics, Policy, and Law, 22,* 595–631.

Wykle, M. L., & Musil, C. M. (1993). Mental health of older persons: Social and cultural factors. In M. A. Smyer (Ed.), *Mental health and aging,* (pp. 3–17). New York: Springer.

Zarit, S. H., & Teri, L. (1991). Interventions and services for family caregivers. *Annual Review of Gerontology and Geriatrics, 11,* 287–310.

APPENDIX

Standards for Psychological Services in Long Term Care Facilities

PETER A. LICHTENBERG, PH.D., ABPP[1]

MICHAEL C. SMITH, PH.D.,[2]

DEBORAH FRAZER, PH.D.,[3]

VICTOR MOLINARI, PH.D.,[4]

ERLENE ROSOWSKY, PSYD.,[5]

ROYDA CROSE, PH.D.,[6]

NICK STILLWELL, PH.D.,[7]

NANETTE A. KRAMER, PH.D.,[8]

PAULA HARTMAN-STEIN, PH.D.,[9]

SARA HONN QUALLS, PH.D.,[10]

MICHAEL SALAMON, PH.D.,[11]

MICHAEL DUFFY, PH.D.,[12]

JOYCE PARR, PH.D.,[13]

and DOLORES GALLAGHER-THOMPSON, PH.D.[14]

1 Address correspondence to Peter A. Lichtenberg, Rehabilitation Institute of Michigan, 261 Mack Boulevard., Detroit, MI 48201, E-mail, lichtenberg@iog.wayne, edu
2 Peninsula Hospital, Far Rockaway, NY.
3 Genesis Healthcare, Philadelphia, PA.
4 Veterans Administration Medical Center, Houston, TX.
5 Private practice, Boston, MA.
6 Ball State University, Muncie, IN.
7 Private practice, New York, NY.
8 Columbia University, New York, NY.
9 Center for Healthy Aging, Akron, OH.
10 University of Colorado, Colorado Springs.
11 Adult Developmental Center, Woodmere, NY.
12 Texas A&M University, College Station.
13 University of South Florida, Tampa.
14 Veterans Administration Medical Center, Palo Alto, CA.

I N November 1995, members of the national network, Psychologists in Long-Term Care (PLTC), began to discuss the idea of crafting standards for psychological services in long-term care facilities. For a number of years prior to the 1995 meeting, PLTC members were actively involved in delivering continuing education programs in clinical geropsychology. These programs were always well attended, particularly by experienced private practice clinicians who, due to changes in the health care market, were expanding their practices into the nursing home to care for older adults. These seasoned clinicians were typically bewildered by the many complex issues they were confronted within geriatric care, including a variety of assessment, treatment, and staff consultation concerns. PLTC members determined, therefore, that both clinicians and long-term care facility administrators needed standards that laid out the process of psychological service delivery in long-term care settings.

There were three distinct phases to the development of these standards. In phase one (November 1995 through August 1996), the PLTC workgroup completed an initial draft of the standards. Through the network's newsletter and the American Psychological Association (APA) Division 20 (Adult Development and Aging) E-mail network, comments were solicited from both the PLTC and Division 20 memberships through October 1996. In November 1996, a second draft of the standards was completed. Comments were again solicited from the aforementioned psychology groups, and in addition, the second draft of the standards was sent out to several organizations with interest in this topic. These included the American Association of Homes and Services for the Aging, the State Medicare Directors work group, the Mental Health and Aging interest group of The Gerontological Society of America, the Nursing Home Reform Coalition, the American Association of Retired Persons Public Policy Institute, the Alzheimer's Association, and several divisions within the APA. Comments on the third draft were accepted through March 1997, when the final draft of the standards was completed.

Introduction

Older adults make up a diverse group. For many people, later life is a time of good physical health, personal growth, and heightened life satisfaction. Among community-dwelling older adults, the rates of depression and many other mental disorders are lower than for younger adults. The experience of older adults in long-term care facilities is quite different. Residents of long-term care facilities have very high rates of depression, dementia, and other mental disorders. Long-term care residents often have a combination of serious medical and psychological disorders, which reflect the interdependence of biological, psychological, and social factors in aging.

The growth of interdisciplinary health teams in long-term care reflects the emphasis on a biopsychosocial model of clinical work with residents. In the long-term care population, comorbidity of multiple physical diseases and cognitive and affective disorders is common.

The psychologist's role on the interdisciplinary team is to detect and treat cognitive, affective, and behavioral disturbance using psychological diagnostic and therapeutic tools. These tools may include cognitive, affective, behavioral, and personality assessments; individual, family, and group therapies; behavioral interventions; and staff education regarding the psychological needs of and clinical management strategies for residents in long-term care facilities.

Historically, psychological services for older adults were severely limited. In the first three decades of Medicare (until 1987), outpatient mental health services were capped at an annual rate of $250 per beneficiary. Reimbursement changes since then have encouraged a substantial increase in the number of psychologists practicing in long-term care settings. Toward the end of the 1980s, the cap was gradually raised, and it was removed altogether in July 1990. Some limiting factors in reimbursement continue because the required copayment remains at 50%, compared to the 20% copayment for medical services.

Mental health service opportunities in long-term care were greatly expanded with the passage of the Omnibus Reconciliation

Act (OBRA 1989), which permitted licensed psychologists and social workers to serve as independent mental health providers under Medicare. In addition, OBRA 1987, 1989, and 1990 regulations included the Nursing Home Reform Act, which stressed the value of psychological services in the long-term care setting and the need to attempt psychosocial interventions before using chemical or physical restraints.

The expansion of geriatric mental health opportunities has greatly increased the demand for services at a time when the supply of well-trained practitioners is low. It will be a number of years before clinical training programs adequately incorporate the knowledge base and practice concepts of clinical geropsychology. During this transitional period, we urge practitioners to seek out continuing education opportunities in mental health and aging. In addition, we encourage experienced geropsychologists to share their expertise with new providers and consumers of mental health services for the aging. In this spirit, Psychologists in Long-Term Care proposes the following standards of practice. We hope that they will be used by practicing psychologists as general principles of assessment and treatment for residents of long-term care facilities and by other long term care professionals as a guide toward understanding the role of psychologists.

Standards for Psychological Services in Long Term Care Facilities

1. Providers

A. Psychologists who are graduates of doctoral programs in psychology and are licensed in their respective states of practice.

B. There are three categories of psychologists who practice in long term care:

1. Psychologists who are trained, experienced and competent in geropsychology service provision (see Appendix, Note 1).

2. Psychologists who have formal training in geropsychology but are not yet experienced; these psychologists are super-

vised by experienced and competent geropsychologists (see category 1 above).

3. Psychologists who are actively obtaining continuing education in geropsychology and are supervised by experienced and competent geropsychologists (see category 1 above).

II. Referral for Psychological Services

A. Residents of long-term care facilities who are appropriate for psychological services exhibit behavioral, cognitive, or emotional disturbance. Examples of behaviors that may trigger referral include cognitive decline, excessive crying, withdrawal from social contact or other signs of depression, personality changes (e.g., excessively demanding behavior), aggressive or combative behavior, inappropriate sexual behavior, or psychotic behavior. Psychologists encourage the referral source to be as specific as possible about the presenting problem. Standing or "prn" orders for psychological services are discouraged.

B. In addition to direct assessment and treatment of patients referred for psychological services, psychologists may also provide staff consultation and advisement, staff training and education, family consultation and advisement, design and implementation of preventive screening and other institutional programs, environmental assessment, behavioral analysis and design of behavior management programs, and other services.

Psychologists are aware that many of these latter services may not be third-party reimbursable.

III. Assessment

A. In order to provide cost-effective and high quality treatment, psychologists assess the cognitive, emotional, and behavioral functioning of their patients. Assessment procedures may include the following components:

1. Assessment of mental status through clinical interviews, mental status questionnaires, and information obtained from family, staff, or other informants.

2. Psychological testing, including assessments of personality, emotional functioning, and psychopathology, using mea sures or instruments that are consistent with current stan dard professional practice (see Appendix, Note 2).

3. Neurobehavioral testing, which serves to determine cogni tive strengths and weaknesses, memory capacities, and spe cific neuropsychological impairments. Such testing may include assessments of attentional, language, memory, visu ospatial, and abstract reasoning skills. Testing time may be brief. Reasons for neurobehavioral testing may include (a) resolving diagnostic ambiguities (e.g., whether dementia or depression or both are present), (b) assessing sudden cogni tive declines or changes (e.g., whether delirium is present); (c) profiling cognitive strengths and weaknesses (e.g., for treatment planning), (d) determining the level of care needed for a patient, (e) planning a program of rehabilita tion, and (f) determining competency.

4. Functional assessments, which address a range of behaviors relevant to overall daily functioning, including self-care skills and everyday living skills. Functional assessments of ten augment personality, mental status, and neurobehav ioral assessments.

5. Behavioral observation and analysis, which includes the systematic observation and recording of behavior and stim ulus–response and response–reinforcement contingencies, in order to design behavioral interventions that will in crease the frequency of positive behaviors and decrease the frequency of negative behaviors.

B. Psychologists are aware of their responsibilities, as integral members of interdisciplinary teams, to work with their med ical and pharmaceutical colleagues to develop and implement integrated plans of service delivery. Psychologists encourage appropriate medical and physical examinations, including lab oratory tests and radiological studies, to rule out reversible causes of functional impairment, such as medically treatable illnesses.

IV. Treatment

A. Treatment plan

1. Each patient has an individualized treatment plan that is based on the specific findings of a psychological assess ment and that addresses the referral question.

2. The treatment plan includes a diagnosis and specific therapeutic modalities to achieve short-term and long-term goals.

3. When treatment frequency deviates from standard prac tice, it must be justified in the treatment plan.

4. Changes in clinical status are reflected by changes in the treatment plan.

B. Treatment process

1. Treatments are chosen that best address each patient's di agnosis and presenting symptoms.

2. Treatment modalities may include, separately or in con junction, individual psychotherapy, behavior therapy and behavior modification, group psychotherapy, and family psychotherapy.

3. Treatments are empirically informed and reflect current standards of geropsychological practice.

4. Psychologists are aware that most third-party reimburse ment requires the full duration of treatment sessions to be spent in face-to-face contact with the patient and/or the patient's family, and that other important and necessary treatment-related time, such as consultation with staff, may not be third-party reimbursable.

5. Psychologists are aware of their responsibility to spend ad equate time in face-to-face treatment with each patient and to consult and coordinate with the interdisciplinary team. Psychologists do not attempt to treat an excessive or inordinate number of patients in a single day.

6. Treatment continues when emotional, cognitive, or behav ioral progress toward a goal can be demonstrated. When no such progress can be demonstrated, but the patient appears

to benefit from a social visit, appropriate recommendations for friendly visitors, activities, etc., are made.

7. When treatment is ended, termination is conducted in an orderly manner; the patient is prepared and given appro priate notice, and issues involving termination are ad dressed.

C. Outcomes

1. Patient progress toward stated goals is regularly monitored and documented to determine if treatment is effective and whether it should be continued, modified, or terminated. Such monitoring is done at least every 3 months.

2. Treatment outcome can be measured in multiple domains, including affective, cognitive, or behavioral domains.

3. Positive treatment outcome can include stabilization of mental and behavioral disorder where decline would be expected in the absence of treatment. However, when treatment for such a patient is long-term, attempts are made to decrease the frequency of service. If the patient re sponds with a worsening of symptoms, then treatment can be reinitiated.

D. Documentation

1. Psychologists provide timely and clear documentation of each patient's diagnosis, treatment plan, progress, and out come in accordance with current ethical and legal standards.

V. Ethical Issues (see Appendix, Note 3)

A. Informed consent

1. Informed consent decisions are based on the legal compe tency of the patient to make informed decisions regarding health care, the patient's knowledge of the long-term care setting, the cognitive ability of the patient, the availability of family members, and the acuity of the psychological condition requiring treatment.

a. For a competent person without significant cognitive impairment, before any psychological services are ren dered, the psychologist provides to the patient a clear statement of the condition warranting psychological services, what services are to be rendered, and the possible consequences of accepting or refusing services.

  b. For a patient who is declared legally incompetent, the psychologist provides to the guardian a clear statement of the condition warranting psychological services, what services are to be rendered, and the possible consequences of accepting or refusing services. Although informed consent must be given by the guardian, the psychologist also attempts to help the patient understand the rationale for treatment (within the limits of the patient's cognitive abilities).

  c. For a patient with significant cognitive impairment who is deemed to be without the capacity to understand the rationale for treatment but who has not been declared legally incompetent, the psychologist identifies the responsible party and provides the rationale for treatment to that party. Although, technically, the patient still legally retains the right of decision making, ethically, the clinician must contact caregivers to help with decision making. The psychologist also attempts to help the patient understand the rationale for treatment.

  d. Consent for services is not required if the patient is considered dangerous to self or others (as defined by applicable state law).

2. Psychologists who are part of a staff institutional team, privileged by the institution to provide services, and covered by a general institutional consent do not need to get separate informed consent before implementing treatment. Consulting psychologists who are not part of the staff institutional treatment team must get separate informed consent as described in Section A, Part 1, before services are provided.

B. Confidentiality

1. Patients in long-term care facilities have the same rights to confidentiality regarding psychological services as all other

patients, and information about this right to confidentiality, as well as its limits, is offered to patients, guardians, or responsible parties as part of the informed consent process prior to service delivery.

2. Psychologists are aware of limits to confidentiality and make every effort to reconcile these limits with the rights of their patients.

   a. Although competent patients, guardians, or responsible parties have rights concerning what information is given to the staff in a long-term care facility, these rights do not extend to information that is deemed critical to protecting the resident from harming self or others.

   b. Confidentiality standards must be consistent with the reporting/charting regulations within which the facility must operate. If a conflict arises, the psychologist strives to work with the facility to achieve maximum consistency.

   c. Confidentiality standards should allow for the demands of the psychologist's role as an active member of an institutional treatment team that shares pertinent information with other health professionals.

C. Privacy

1. Psychologists try to ensure that psychological services are provided in the most private manner possible.

2. Psychologists often need to be creative in meeting the privacy standard. Some long-term care facilities provide private consulting rooms for psychologists but many do not. When no consulting room is available or the patient is bedridden, services may be provided at the patient's bed side. If the patient is in a nonprivate room, the psychologist may request that the roommate leave until the session is over and then close the door. If the roommate is also bedridden or refuses to leave the room, the session may be conducted (with the roommate's consent) by drawing the curtain around the bed to provide some privacy. Nursing

staff are notified so that they know where the patient can be found and so that they do not interrupt the session.

3. Psychologists are aware of facility/state/federal regulations regarding treatment privacy.

4. Patients are consulted regarding their comfort with privacy arrangements prior to a treatment session, and every effort is made to accommodate their wishes.

D. Conflict of interest

1. Psychologists self-refer only if a need for psychological services is identified and members of the interdisciplinary treatment team are made aware of the need for services.

2. Psychologists are aware that at times the interests of the facility and the patient may not coincide and make every effort to resolve the conflict in the best interests of the patient.

3. Psychologists try to ensure that patients receive proper continuity of care. If psychological services are interrupted due to payment issues, institutional barriers, or other non clinical reasons, the psychologist follows accepted profess-ional standards regarding proper therapeutic closure and transfer of care via referral.

4. Psychologists are aware of the rules and regulations governing third-party reimbursement and follow them when billing for reimbursable services, but patient care decisions are guided by the best interests of the patient and are not dominated by reimbursement considerations. When psychologists believe that reimbursement regulations require revision, they attempt to secure appropriate changes from state/federal agencies and private insurers.

E. Advocacy

1. Psychologists advocate for the appropriate use of mental health services to reduce excess disability and improve quality of life.

2. When mental health services are not being used or are being used inappropriately, psychologists strive to educate other care providers to improve the delivery of care in

order to be consistent with a biopsychosocial approach to the assessment and treatment of older adults.

Conclusions

PLTC's membership and the authors of these standards are widely known for their decades of work in long-term care. All of the authors were involved in delivering psychological practice in long-term care well before Medicare payments became available to psychologists. In 1990, Peter Lichtenberg, the first author credited on these standards and this article, was the first person to write a book for psychologists on how to practice in geriatric long term care[1] (1994 [Binghamton, NY: Haworth Press]). These authors thus not only possess the experience and familiarity with long term care necessary to develop these standards, but will also use them to disseminate these standards and to educate others in their proper usage.

During the summer of 1997, PLTC created a task force headed by Erlene Rosowsky to develop a strategic plan for the dissemination of these standards. It is anticipated that the standards will be aimed at three major audiences: psychologists, long-term care facility administrators, and insurers and regulatory personnel (i.e., Medicare carriers, state Medicare Medical Directors, and representatives of the Health Care Financing Administration [HCFA]). It is crucial that psychologists practicing in long-term care settings become aware of these standards and that they attempt to conform to the practices described therein. Long-term care facility administrators are becoming more familiar with the services that psychologists can provide and will benefit from using these standards to help ensure quality service provision. Finally, administrators of insurance and regulatory agencies need to become aware of the progress that psychologists themselves have made in defining their own practice. It is hoped that these standards will help insurance claim reviewers and regulatory boards make logical and balanced decisions about what is and what is not acceptable geropsychological practice.

1. Lichtenberg, P. (1994). A guide to psychological practice in geriatric long-term care. Binghamton, NY: Haworth Press.

Notes

1. For further discussion of these issues, see the Draft Report of the APA Interdivisional Task Force on Qualifications for Practice in Clinical and Applied Geropsychology, 1996, Section II (Clinical Geropsychology) of Division 12 (Clinical Psychology) and Division 20 (Adult Development and Aging), which may be obtained through the corresponding author. Category 1 includes psychologists who have either a generalist or a specialist level of training in clinical geropsychology, as these levels are defined in the Draft Report.

2. See, for example, U.S. Department of Veterans Affairs Geropsychology Assessment Resource Guide, 1996 Revision. This guide may be obtained for a fee through the National Technical Information Service, U.S. Department of Commerce, 5285 Port Royal Road, Springfield, VA 22161. Request publication #PB96-144365.

3. In addition to the standards presented here, psychologists follow the APA Ethics Code (American Psychological Association. [1992]. Ethical principles of psychologists and code of conduct. Washington, DC: Author; also published in American Psychologist, 47, 1597-1611).

QUESTIONS

How to earn CE using this book

The primary mission of a Hatherleigh CE Book is to provide mental health professionals with a review of authoritative, practical information that illuminates the common and challenging clinical issues they encounter in their daily work and to include with that information an exam that enables them to earn relicensure credit.

The chapters in Professional Psychology in Long Term Care *were written for inclusion on the basis of their fundamental importance to the growing field of geropsychology. The material provides mental health professionals with detailed knowledge they can use to improve the care of patients in long-term care settings.*

The chapters can be used to earn continuing education credits via the CE Appendix. To earn CE credits using this book, simply call Hatherleigh to order a quiz response form using the toll free number, 1-800-367-2550. Hatherleigh representatives will inform you of the options available to you as a participant in one of our CE programs.

The Hatherleigh Company, Ltd. is approved by the American Psychological Association to offer continuing education for psychologists. Hatherleigh maintains responsibility for the content of this book.

The Hatherleigh Company, Ltd. is accredited by the Accreditation Council for Continuing Medical Education (ACCME) to sponsor continuing medical education for physicians. The Hatherleigh Company, Ltd. designates Professional Psychology in Long Term Care *for no more than 30 credit hours in Category I of the Physician's Recognition Award of the American Medical Association. This CME Activity was planned and produced in accordance with the ACCME Essentials.*

The Hatherleigh Company, Ltd. is approved as a provider of continuing education for nurses by the New York State Nurses Association which is accredited by the American Nurses Credentialing Center's Commission on Accreditation.

Professional Psychology in Long Term Care *is pre-approved by the National Board of Certified Counselors (NBCC), the Commission on Rehabilitation Counselor Certification (CRCC), the Certified Disability Management Specialists Commission (CDMSC) to offer continuing education for NCCs, CRCs, CDMSCs, and CCMs. Hatherleigh adheres to the continuing education guidelines of all aforementioned groups.*

CHAPTER 1
Assessment of Psychopathology
page 1

1. **Special considerations in assessing older adults do *not* include:**
   A. Development of rapport.
   B. Appropriate use of touch.
   C. Use of written information.
   D. A paternalistic manner of test administration.

2. **Reviewing the nature of the referral question:**
   A. Is not necessary in LTC settings.
   B. Has as its main purpose to assist with billing.
   C. Is central in guiding the subsequent assessment.
   D. Does not help in understanding the goal of assessment.

3. **Measures of affect and personality in LTC settings:**
   A. Are not necessary with frail older adults.
   B. Can be appropriately used with many nursing home residents.
   C. Can be interpreted validly without reference to research with older adults.
   D. Are rarely helpful because it is impossible to disentangle cognitive impairment from depression and pre-morbid personality traits.

CHAPTER 2
Neuropsychological Assessment in Geriatric Facilities
page 29

4. **The most common cause of dementia is:**
   A. Alzheimer's disease.
   B. Multiple strokes.

C. Alcohol abuse.

D. Nutritional deficits.

5. **Vascular dementia is associated with:**
   A. Gradual and progressive cognitive decline.
   B. Abrupt onset of neurological symptoms and a stepwise progression.
   C. Location of lacunas.
   D. Lack of psychotic symptomatology.

6. **The findings on brief neuropsychological batteries suggest that:**
   A. They are ineffective in assessing cognitive problems in LTC settings.
   B. Cognitive assessment can be completed in a timely, cost-effective fashion without sacrificing diagnostic accuracy.
   C. They are rarely valid with frail older residents.
   D. They need not have age-appropriate norms to be effective.

CHAPTER 3

Conducting a Medical and Psychiatric Assessment

page 51

7. **Pseudodementia refers to:**
   A. Cognitive impairment associated with depression in the elderly.
   B. Dementia due to non-specific causes.
   C. Malingering.
   D. Delirium.

8. **Delirium is a disturbance characterized by:**
   A. Changes in consciousness that develop over a short period of time and tend to fluctuate.
   B. Negative psychotic symptoms (i.e., social withdrawal).
   C. Chronic memory impairment.
   D. Acute situational distress.

9. **Sakauye and Camp's (1992) guiding principles for delivering psychiatric services in LTC settings do *not* include the following:**
    A. Learning still occurs
    B. Make the patient human
    C. Assume no behavior is random
    D. Depression and psychosis are rare

CHAPTER 4
Individual Therapy
page 73

10. **What ingredient is most important in successful psychotherapy?**
    A. Technical skills
    B. Therapeutic relationship
    C. Competence in behavior analysis
    D. Social skills training

11. **Which of the following statements about privacy and psychotherapy in LTC settings is correct?**
    A. Privacy must be absolute.
    B. Psychologists should not conduct therapy at bedside.
    C. Flexibility is the guiding principle.
    D. Use of "natural environment" settings are distinctly disadvantageous.

12. **Psychotherapy may be the treatment of choice for each of the following, *except*:**
    A. Late-life anxiety.
    B. Depression.
    C. Unfinished life review.
    D. Severe confusion.

CHAPTER 5

Working With Families in Nursing Homes

page 91

13. In which of the following systems do psychologists work with families in long-term care settings?
A. Political/Legal
B. Economic
C. Cultural
D. All of the above

14. Sources of difficulties for families in nursing homes do *not* include:
A. Systematic confusion.
B. Residents' needs for family support.
C. Incongruent role expectations.
D. Long-standing family conflict.

15. Specific family problems that might generate a psychological referral do *not* typically include:
A. Decision-making dilemmas.
B. Families' abandonment of resident.
C. Families' critcizing staff.
D. Caregiver depression.

CHAPTER 6

Group Psychotherapy in the Nursing Home

page 113

16. Common themes with the nursing home population include:
A. Adjusting to institutional life.
B. Coping with loss.
C. Interpersonal conflicts.
D. All of the above

17. **A type of group *not* typically encountered in LTC settings is the:**
    A. Support group.
    B. Psychoeducational group.
    C. Vocational rehabilitation group.
    D. Reminiscence group.

18. **Institution-related challenges of running therapy groups include all of the following, *except*:**
    A. Size of the facility.
    B. Administrative support.
    C. Finding a space for the group.
    D. Assistance from staff.

CHAPTER 7

Enhancing Quality of Life

page 133

19. **Strategies to enhance quality of life in LTC settings include all of the following, *except*:**
    A. Cheerful and compassionate staff.
    B. Doing everything for the patient.
    C. Pleasant activities.
    D. Family involvement.

20. **Autonomy issues ranked important in Cohn and Sugar (1991) study do *not* include:**
    A. Private place to be alone.
    B. Telephone access.
    C. Choosing one's television program.
    D. Availability of transportation.

21. **Goals of the best LTC programs include:**
    A. Maximizing residents' day-to-day functioning.
    B. Providing recreational and therapeutic activities.

C. Preventing or treating psychological and behavioral prob
   lems.
D. All of the above

CHAPTER 8
Interventions for Older Adults With Personality Disorders
page 161

22. **The intervention model of assessment is based on answering all of the following questions,** *except:*
    A. Where is the distress?
    B. Where is the setting?
    C. Where is the resistance?
    D. Where is the opportunity for positive change with the least resistance?

23. **Therapy for LTC patients with PD includes all of the following premises,** *except:*
    A. Staff is unconcerned about maintaining a smooth and efficient routine.
    B. The background for all therapy is the meaning to the individual of being in a nursing home.
    C. Any change in any part of the system will effect changes in other parts of the system.
    D. Identification of both the PD and the level of intervention can provide a useful template for guiding a specific treatment strategy.

24. **PD clusters include all of the below,** *except:*
    A. Eccentric.
    B. Dramatic.
    C. Masochistic.
    D. Anxious.

CHAPTER 9
Behavioral Interventions for Patients With Dementia
page 179

25. Topigraphical assessment:
   A. Focuses on the observable appearance of behavior.
   B. Identifies target behaviors.
   C. Describes intensity and frequency of behaviors.
   D. Is sufficient by itself for treatment planning.

26. Behavioral interventions can reduce all of the following, *except*:
   A. Aggression.
   B. Underlying personality characteristics.
   C. Wandering.
   D. Disruptive vocalizations.

27. Subtypes of wanderers as described by Hussian (1987) include all of the following, *except*:
   A. Exit seekers.
   B. Modelers.
   C. Self-stimulators.
   D. Risk-takers.

CHAPTER 10
Counseling the Elderly Dying Patient
page 201

28. A psychologist working with dying patients should assume:
   A. All terminally ill patients should accept their impending death.
   B. All dying patients want to remain engaged.
   C. All dying patients should talk with a psychologist.

D. An appropriate death is one that a person would choose if given the opportunity.

29. The "typical" older institutionalized patient has all of the following, *except*:
   A. Multiple physical problems.
   B. Massive communication impairment.
   C. Preexisting psychiatric condition.
   D. Clear minded status.

30. The most important therapeutic tool for psychologists working with the terminally ill is:
   A. Knowledge of the invariant stages of dying.
   B. Therapist–patient relationship.
   C. Pain-management techniques.
   D. Hypnosis.

CHAPTER 11

Training Nursing Assistants to Care for Nursing Home Residents With Dementia

page 227

31. Most nursing home assistant are:
   A. White males.
   B. White females.
   C. African-American females.
   D. Hispanic females.

32. Most nursing home assistants help residents with:
   A. Activities of daily living.
   B. Financial planning.
   C. Legal matters.
   D. Family counseling.

33. Improvements in nursing assistant performance require all of the recommendations, *except*:
   A. Strong administrative support.

B. Supervisor encouragement.

C. Skills classes.

D. Unsupervised bibliotherapy.

CHAPTER 12
Interprofessional Health Care Teams
page 257

34. **The unique aspect of an interdisciplinary health care team is:**
    A. Members work together to develop a conceptual model which assimilates data from all disciplines.
    B. Members mutually develop a treatment plan.
    C. Members share responsibilities for implementation of a treatment plan.
    D. All of the above

35. **Team development does *not* involve the process of:**
    A. Forming.
    B. Storming.
    C. Negating.
    D. Performing.

36. **Promoting successful teamwork requires the psychologist to:**
    A. Play the "expert".
    B. Confront administrators with the facility's shortcomings.
    C. Utilize only normative psychological testing data.
    D. Maintain posture of curiosity and non-defensiveness.

CHAPTER 13
Basic Psychopharmacology in the Nursing Home
page 279

37. **What is the occurrence of psychiatric symptoms in nursing home residents?**

A. 20% to 30%

B. 40% to 50%

C. 60% to 70%

D. 80% to 90%

38. **Medical conditions frequently associated with severe anxiety in geriatric patients include:**

A. Chronic obstructive pulmonary disease.

B. Endocrine disease.

C. Chronic pain.

D. All of the above

39. **Which of the following is correct when considering pharmacologic interventions in older adults?**

A. Anticholinergic side effects are generally not a problem for older adults.

B. Renal clearance is increased in the elderly.

C. It is best to "start low and go slow" when prescribing medications.

D. There are no special considerations in prescribing medications to older adults.

CHAPTER 14

The Private/Group Practice of Psychology in Long Term Care

page 299

40. **Transfer of patients to other mental health professionals:**

A. Is rarely a problem.

B. Can result in discontinuity of care.

C. Should be avoided to protect the therapist's income.

D. Does not disrupt the therapeutic relationship.

41. **Which statement is true regarding comprehensive assessment?**

A. A clinical interview is sufficient to detect underlying emotional problems.

B. Quantifiable measures of cognitive functioning are needed.

C. Extensive neuropsychological batteries are always needed.

D. Assessment is simpler with older adults than younger adults.

42. **For services to be considered medically necessary:**
    A. They must be consistent with the diagnosis.
    B. They can be experimental.
    C. They may be furnished primarily for the convenience of the provider.
    D. They need not be shown to be safe or effective when used appropriately.

CHAPTER 15

Ethical Issues

page 329

43. **Day-to-day ethical issues for psychologists in LTC settings are likely to involve questions regarding all of the following, *except*:**
    A. Consent.
    B. Child custody.
    C. Confidentiality.
    D. Competency.

44. **Ethical principles that are especially pertinent to psychologists working in LTC settings include all of the following, *except*:**
    A. Autonomy.
    B. Beneficence.
    C. Fidelity.
    D. Misrepresentation.

45. **Which of the following statements is correct regarding competency:**
   A. Clinicians sometimes assume that an individual's age determines global incompetence.
   B. Competency is unnecessary for informed consent.
   C. Legal determinations of competency is equivalent to clini cal evaluations.
   D. Competency can be easily determined through a screening evaluation.

CHAPTER 16
Training Psychologists in Long Term Care
page 349

46. **In the initial screening of students for training position, it is *not* important to:**
   A. Match the gender and/or culture of supervisor and super visee.
   B. Assure a good match between the trainee's skill and those that the position will require.
   C. Make a good match between a student's training goals and what the training will offer.
   D. None of the above

47. **Reimbursement for psychology training in nursing home settings depends on the:**
   A. Site of practice and training.
   B. Educational level of the student.
   C. Patient's insurance.
   D. All of the above

48. **One of the most important over-arching learning experiences and challenges for trainees is:**
   A. Interdisciplinary teamwork.
   B. Gestalt therapy.
   C. Participation in social activities.
   D. Family observation

CHAPTER 17

The Impact of Culture and Gender on Mental Health
page 373

49. **Older adults are more complex than:**
    A. Children.
    B. Adolescents.
    C. Younger adults.
    D. All of the above

50. **At the least, what percentage of nursing home residents and nursing home staff are women?**
    A. 66%
    B. 10%
    C. 20%
    D. 50%

51. **What types of relational issues are important in nursing homes?**
    A. Staff/patient relations
    B. Isolation
    C. Therapeutic countertransference
    D. All of the above

CHAPTER 18

Clinical Research in Long Term Care: What the Future Holds
page 401

52. **What philosophy can best maintain an older adult's independence in managing problems associated with dementia?**
    A. Laissez-faire philosophy
    B. Disengagement theory

C. Activity theory

D. Reduce disability by reducing the demands of the environment

53. What is the role of theory in applied research?

A. Unimportant

B. Too "ivory-tower"

C. Successful applied interventions are guided by theory

D. There are no theories to guide research

54. Which is *not* a critical feature for effective applied research?

A. Nontoken administrative support

B. A collaborative relationship with staff

C. Expertise in behavioral therapy and geriatric psychiatry

D. "Hands-off" consultant role

CHAPTER 19

Public Policy and the Delivery of Mental Health Care to Older Adults

page 425

55. All of the following are anticipated trends in LTC, *except*:

A. Increase in young adult patients with chronic disabilities.

B. Increase in use of community-based health care services.

C. Decrease in the elderly population

D. Demand for practitioners who possess skills in working both with the elderly and the nonelderly population.

56. All of the following are reforms instated by OBRA 1987, *except:*

A. Corrected misuse and overuse of psychotropic medications given by nursing home staff.

B. Appropriate prescribing of antidepressants to improve the quality of life for patients with psychiatric symptoms.

C. The replacement of chemical treatment with psychological and behavioral therapy.

D. A higher cap on teh amount paid by Medicare for outpatient mental health care.

57. What is a possible advantage of managed care policies for the elderly:
A. Lower cost and coordination for healthier older patients.
B. Unlimited access to providers.
C. Generous referrals to mental health services by physicians.
D. Unbiased selection of healthy or less healthy patients.

INDEX

Numbers in italics refer to tables or figures.

INDEX OF NAMES

09- 593